Renmin Chinese Law Review

RENMIN CHINESE LAW REVIEW: SELECTED PAPERS OF *THE JURIST* (法学家)

Series Editor: *Liming Wang, Editor in Chief,* The Jurist *and Professor of Law, Renmin University of China Law School*

Legal scholarship in China has grown dramatically in recent years. This work has become particularly important as China dramatically expands its economic and political influence in the world. *Renmin Chinese Law Review* aims, as a series, to publish the best work on the Chinese legal system, written by top legal scholars researching and working throughout China. Each volume in the series will present the best contributions to *Renmin Chinese Law Review* (*The Jurist*) from the preceding year. The volumes in this series intend to bring this important body of research to a wider readership including academics, students, and law practitioners.

For a full list of Edward Elgar published titles, including the titles in this series, visit our website at www.e-elgar.com.

Renmin Chinese Law Review

Selected Papers of *The Jurist* (法学家), Volume 12

Edited by

Liming Wang

Editor in Chief, The Jurist *(法学家) and Professor of Law, Renmin University of China Law School, China*

中国人民大学法学院
RENMIN UNIVERSITY OF CHINA LAW SCHOOL

A JOINT PUBLICATION OF *THE JURIST* (法学家) AND EDWARD ELGAR PUBLISHING

Edward Elgar PUBLISHING

Cheltenham, UK • Northampton, MA, USA

Published by

Edward Elgar Publishing Limited
The Lypiatts
15 Lansdown Road
Cheltenham
Glos GL50 2JA
UK

Edward Elgar Publishing, Inc.
William Pratt House
9 Dewey Court
Northampton
Massachusetts 01060
USA

Authorised representative in the EU for GPSR queries only: Easy Access System Europe – Mustamäe tee 50, 10621 Tallinn, Estonia, gpsr.requests@easproject.com

A catalogue record for this book is available from the British Library

Library of Congress Control Number: 2026934062

This book is available electronically in the **Elgar**online
Law subject collection
https://doi.org/10.4337/9781035383207

MIX
Paper | Supporting responsible forestry
FSC® C014540

ISBN 978 1 0353 8319 1 (cased)
ISBN 978 1 0353 8320 7 (eBook)
ISBN 978 1 0353 8321 4 (ePub)

Printed and bound in the UK by Short Run Press Ltd, Exeter EX2 7LW

Contents

List of contributors

Chen Kun,[1] Professor, Nanjing University Law School.

Geng Jianing, Associate Professor, China University of Political Science and Law Criminal Justice School.

Li Yi, Postdoctoral Researcher, School of International Law, Peking University.

Lou Chanhou, Postdoctoral Fellow, University of Macao.

Ma Zhiyong, Research Associate, Shandong University School of Law.

Shi Hongpeng, Associate Professor, Fudan University Law School.

Xiao Peng, Postdoctoral Researcher, Beijing Institute of Technology Law School.

Xiong Hao, Associate Professor, Fudan University Law School.

Zhang Mujun, Assistant Professor, School of Law, Tsinghua University.

Zhang Songlun, Associate Professor, Institute of Land Law, Guangdong University of Foreign Studies.

Zhang Xuefu, Ph.D. Candidate, China University of Political Science and Law.

Zhu Xiaoyan, Research Assistant, Jilin University School of Law.

---

1 The authors' name are presented in the Chinese convention: that is, family name (Chen) before the given name (Kun).

1. The concept of regulatory taking and the property rights protection system

Li Yi

According to Article 13, Clause 3 of the Constitution, typical expropriation exhibits the following characteristics: First, it is predicated upon the necessity of public interest. Second, it must have a legal basis. Third, it results in a transformation of property ownership.[1] Fourth, compensation must be provided.

However, at both the legislative level[2] and the administrative level,[3] there is currently a significant occurrence of partial restrictions being imposed on

1 In 2004, Wang Zhaoguo, who was the Vice Chairman of the Standing Committee of the National People's Congress at the time, explicitly stated in his explanation regarding the "Draft Amendment to the Constitution of the People's Republic of China" that "expropriation primarily involves the transfer of ownership." See the "Bulletin of the Standing Committee of the National People's Congress of the People's Republic of China" (2018 Special Issue), page 71.

2 For instance, Article 6 of the "Law on Desertification Prevention and Control" stipulates: "Units and individuals using land have the obligation to prevent land desertification. Units and individuals using land that has already undergone desertification have the obligation to control the desertified land." Article 32, paragraph 2, of the "Regulations on Nature Reserves" states: "Projects constructed in the peripheral protective zones of nature reserves shall not harm the environmental quality within the nature reserve. If damage has already occurred, it shall be remedied within a specified time." Article 35 of the "Regulations on the Protection of Historical and Cultural Cities, Towns, and Villages" provides: "External repair and decoration, addition of facilities, or alterations to the structure or use of historical buildings shall be approved by the urban or county people's government's urban and rural planning authority in conjunction with the local cultural relics authority, and relevant procedures shall be completed in accordance with the relevant laws and regulations."

3 For example, in 2001, the Dalian Municipal Government issued a "Notice on the Closure of Certain Sauna Bath Facilities" to mitigate water supply shortages. The notice mandated the closure of all sauna bath establishments in the city's six districts and development zones, excluding star-rated hotels, foreign-related

citizens' property rights without transforming their property ownership. In these scenarios, citizens' property rights are diminished to varying degrees. However, they do not constitute the typical "expropriation" as defined in the Constitution. If the restrictions imposed on property rights by public authorities exceed the minimum threshold that citizens' property rights must tolerate, what norm should be invoked to provide remedies for property owners? Many scholars contend that the concept of "expropriation" in Article 13, Clause 3 of the Constitution should be interpreted expansively to include these situations within the existing constitutional framework of expropriation compensation. This means that compensation should be provided according to the requirements of expropriation norms whenever there are consequences of diminished property value.[4] This approach is indeed inspired by the concept of "regulatory

---

hotels, and public baths, effective from the notice's publication date. Failure to comply would lead to forced closure by the municipal government. In 2002, the Nanning Municipal Government issued "Opinions on Reducing the Total Number of Motorcycles in Nanning, Halting Motorcycle Registration, and Operation" to preserve transportation and urban environments, resulting in the suspension of motorcycle registration and operation. In 2005, Zhuhai City issued the "Zhuhai Special Economic Zone Road Traffic Safety Management Regulations" (revised in 2011) to enhance road traffic safety. It prohibited the registration and operation of non-motorized vehicles with power drive devices such as human-powered tricycles, electric bicycles, and pedal-assist bicycles. In 2008, the Beijing Municipal Government issued a "Notice on Temporary Traffic Management Measures for Motor Vehicles in Beijing During the 2008 Beijing Olympic Games and Paralympic Games," imposing restrictions on motor vehicle movement based on odd–even license plate numbers. During the 2014 APEC Summit in Beijing, the odd–even license plate restriction policy was introduced as a temporary traffic control measure. Subsequently, it was gradually normalized, with cities like Jinan, Lanzhou, Chongqing, and Zhengzhou implementing it for environmental protection reasons. In 2017, the Dali Municipal People's Government issued a "Notice on the Special Rectification of Catering and Guesthouse Services in the Core Area of the Erhai Lake Basin Water Ecological Protection Zone," mandating the suspension of operations for all catering and guesthouse operators in the core area of the Erhai Lake Basin Water Ecological Protection Zone for rectification.

[4] For instance, Zhou Xingmei argues that "the scope of public interest expropriation should not be limited to the deprivation of property ownership, permanent deprivation of usufruct rights, such as land and other natural resource usage rights, and other rights with property value. It should also encompass losses resulting from excessive restrictions on property rights and the collateral effects of administrative actions that affect citizens." [Zhou Xingmei, "On the Definition of the Concept of Public Interest Expropriation in China," (2009) 2 *Henan Social Sciences*, 80]. Similarly, Fang Shaokun expands the scope of expropriation targets in his paper, advocating for "further expanding the range of expropriation targets to include

taking" in US law.[5] Consequently, manyattempts have been made to establish a "regulatory taking" system in China, essentially advocating for the substantiation of "regulatory taking".[6] However, if the concept of "regulatory taking" is

---

land contract and management rights, homestead usage rights, and compensating for other property and debt burdens on collective land and villagers' residences." [Fang Shaokun, "Legislative Improvement of the Land Expropriation System – An Analysis of the Draft Amendment to the Land Administration Law," (2019) 4 *Law Journal* 1].

5 The academic community generally translates "regulatory taking" as "管制性征收", but this article suggests that "规制性征收" ("regulatory taking") is a more appropriate translation. According to the Mahon case, which gave rise to the concept of "regulatory taking," only when a "regulation" goes too far can it be considered a "regulatory taking" [See *Pennsylvania Coal Co. v. Mahon*, 260 U. 393 (1922), 415]. In the context of regulatory theory, "regulation" as "规制" has already been widely accepted in China's academic circles. In the field of administrative law, with the rise of administrative regulation and regulatory governance, translating "regulation" as "规制" aligns better with the development direction of modern administrative law. On one hand, it better emphasizes the legal nature of modern administrative law. Compared to the strong control and mandatory implications of regulation, "规制" is more neutral and moderate. It highlights an adjustment function and takes the existence of legal norms as a prerequisite for adjustment [See Barack Obama, "What Is Regulation," translated by Li Qin, Administrative Law Review (Volume 25), Law Press 2020, 120–130]. On the other hand, it better expresses the duality of current administrative management. Compared to the limitations and controls implied by regulation, "规制" has both negative and positive aspects. It involves both restraint and guidance and can encompass both active and passive administrative regulation, which is characteristic of modern administrative management [See Jiang Bixin, "On Fundamental Theoretical Issues of Administrative Regulation," (2012) 12 *Law Journa*l 17]. Based on this, if "regulation" is taken as the core for translating "regulatory taking," it is clear that "规制性征收" ("regulatory taking") better conveys the notion of expropriation arising from excessive interference with property rights by administrative regulation in the context of regulatory governance.

6 For example, Xu Yingchun held that "The absence of a regulatory expropriation system in China has resulted in insufficient attention to the numerous issues surrounding regulatory expropriation in practice. These problems remain unaddressed, allowing contradictions to emerge and escalate. Consequently, China urgently needs to establish a corresponding regulatory expropriation system" [Xu Yingchun, "On the US Regulatory Taking System and Its Implications for China," (2019) 4 *Rule of Law Studies* 138–139]. Guo Hui proposed that "The Chinese Constitution should introduce the concept of 'regulatory expropriation' or 'quasi-expropriation' to broaden the narrow concept of expropriation. This expanded concept of expropriation should encompass the compulsory acquisition of private property rights and property rights restrictions that exceed social obligations"

introduced in China, expanding the application of the constitutional norm of "expropriation" and incorporating numerous regulatory actions into the constitutional compensation framework to compensate for infringed property rights, does this truly align with the requirements of constitutional property rights protection? In other words, can it genuinely provide adequate protection for constitutional property rights? Based on this premise, this chapter intends to conduct a thoughtful examination of "regulatory taking," explore the potential crises that its substantiation might entail, and attempt to propose solutions.

1. INTRODUCTION OF THE CONCEPT OF REGULATORY TAKING

The concept of "regulatory taking" emerged in the context of expanding police powers, with the aim of compensating for property losses caused by excessive governmental regulation through the broadening of expropriation norms. It offers a novel approach to safeguarding property rights. Following this line of thought, the administrative management phenomenon widely described by scholars in China as "regulatory taking" can also be incorporated into the constitutional compensation system for expropriation. Moreover, Article 13 of the Constitution seems to provide a normative foundation for the introduction of this system. Therefore, the establishment of a "regulatory taking" system to achieve empirical implementation of such expropriation appears to be an inevitable trend.

1.1 Path of the Concept of Regulatory Taking Entering the Academic Community in China

However, within the academic community, there has been a significant amount of discussion surrounding this concept, with the most prominent and concentrated research in the following three areas of administrative management.

First, research on expropriation related to land regulation. Some scholars have analyzed the widespread occurrence of land regulation in China, arguing that the limitations on land use stipulated by the Land Management Law, protective measures for scenic areas and ecological preservation zones, prohibitions on the use of environmentally harmful land, and so forth, should all

---

[Guo Hui, "Social Obligations of Property Rights and Regulatory Expropriation," (2019) 2 *Hebei Academic Journal* 218]. Wang Ding also advocated for the establishment of a quasi-expropriation system in China, which, as the author stated, is roughly synonymous with the US legal concept of regulatory taking [Wang Ding, "On the Construction Path of the Quasi-Expropriation System," (2021) 2 *Administrative Law Research* 67–69].

be regarded as a form of regulatory taking. Consequently, in accordance with the compensation standards mandated by the Constitution, extensive property rights that have been infringed upon due to regulation should be compensated.[7] Furthermore, some scholars have proposed that when local governments acquire land through the demolition of unauthorized constructions instead of following the provisions of the "Regulations on the Expropriation and Compensation of Buildings on State-owned Land," it effectively constitutes an act of regulatory taking. In such circumstances, in order to safeguard citizens' private property rights, compensation should be provided.[8]

Second, research on expropriation related to natural resource regulation. For instance, some scholars advocate considering China's ongoing development of national parks as a form of regulatory taking, aimed at compensating for restricted rights to excessively used natural resources.[9] Based on this premise, numerous scholars have extensively studied the ecological compensation mechanisms for national parks, asserting that compensation constitutes the foundation supporting the national park system. As a result, the establishment of national parks has also been encompassed within the scope of expropriation.[10]

Third, research on expropriation related to transportation regulation. Some scholars have conducted an analysis of the specific practices of legalizing ride-hailing services. They contend that the legalization of ride-hailing services essentially stems from the government's relaxation of regulations on traditional taxis. As a consequence of ride-hailing services becoming legalized, the property rights of existing taxi operating license holders have been diminished. This has disrupted the reasonable investment expectations of previous taxi investors based on their right to fair competition. This constitutes a form of regulatory taking of the existing taxi operating licenses, necessitating

7 See Zhang Peng and Gao Bo, "Quasi-Expropriation of Land and Compensation: A Perspective on Land Development Rights," (2015) 2 *Journal of Nanjing Agricultural University (Social Sciences Edition)* 64–71. The term "quasi-expropriation" employed by the authors in this article is essentially synonymous with "regulatory taking."

8 See Wei Jian, "Protection of Urban Property Rights: Liability Rules, Property Rules, and Regulatory Taking,"(2012) 3 *Journal of Law*, 36–42.

9 See Pan Jia, "Regulatory Taking or Protection of Servitude: Institutional Choices in National Park Legislation," (2021) 2 *Administrative Law Research* 76–84.

10 See Zhang Ruiping and Zeng Yu, "Realizing the National Park Ecological Compensation Mechanism – From the Perspective of Stakeholder Balance," (2021) 9 *Guangxi Social Sciences* 118–123.

compensation for the losses incurred by the original taxi operating license holders.[11]

However, regardless of the approach taken, the interpretation solutions currently proposed by scholars for the empirical substantiation of "regulatory taking" all point to Article 13, Paragraph 3 of the Constitution of China. The key lies in an expansive reinterpretation of the concept of "expropriation" within the Constitution, broadening it to encompass not only the conventional expropriation actions involving the deprivation of property ownership in the traditional sense, but also actions that impose restrictions solely on property usage rights or other entitlements. This approach aims to incorporate "regulatory taking" into the constitutional framework for expropriation compensation, ultimately achieving a more effective protection of property rights.[12] In fact, some scholars, on the basis of such approach, proposed to the Standing Committee of the National People's Congress to expand the interpretation of the terms "expropriation" and "requisition" within Article 13, Paragraph 3 of the Constitution of China.[13] By doing so, they aim to encompass the notion of

---

[11] See Liu Liantai, "The Legalization of Ride-Hailing as Regulatory Taking of Taxi License," (2017) 6 *Journal of Legal and Economic Research* 70.

[12] For example, some scholars have pointed out that by expansively interpreting the terms "expropriation" and "requisition" in Article 13, Clause 3 of China's Constitution, the concept of "regulatory taking" can be incorporated into China's constitutional system of expropriation compensation. See Liu Liantai, "Establishing the Coordinates of 'Regulatory Taking'," (2014) 3 *Rule of Law Studies* 43.

[13] In fact, this practice of expanding the concept of "regulatory taking" based on the concepts of "expropriation" and "requisition" is also an expression of the expansion of the concept of "expropriation." According to the explanations provided by constitutional scholars regarding the 2004 constitutional amendments and the distinctions made by scholars such as Professor Liang Huixing between "expropriation" and "requisition," it is known that "expropriation" primarily refers to the "transfer of ownership," while "requisition" points to the "transfer of the right of use" under "emergency conditions" (see Note 1; Liang Huixing, "Suggested Draft of China's Property Rights Law: Articles, Explanations, Reasons, and Reference Legislative Examples," Social Science Literature Press 2000, 194). However, in recent years, represented by Professor Liu Liantai and Professor Fang Shaokun, there has been a tendency to combine "expropriation" and "requisition" into the concept of "regulatory taking", as seen in Liu Liantai's work "Normative Interpretation of Expropriation in Constitutional Texts – With a Focus on Article 13, Clause 3 of the Chinese Constitution" (China University of Political Science and Law Press 2014) 123–124, and Fang Shaokun and Wang Hongping's "Research on Public Interest Expropriation Law" (Renmin University of China Press 2011) 119. It is precisely in this context that an expansion based

"regulatory taking" from the American legal context into the regulatory scope of expropriation clauses in China.[14]

1.2 Motivation for the Introduction of the Concept of Regulatory Taking into the Chinese Academic Community

The fundamental reason why "regulatory taking" has captured significant attention from many scholars is that it appears to offer a reasonable approach to addressing the regulatory gaps in remedying certain actions that restrict property rights. These issues are widely present in China's judicial and enforcement practices, yet they do not fit the conventional definition of "expropriation" under the current Constitution. Moreover, it is challenging to identify other clauses that provide a comprehensive interpretation for such cases. "Regulatory taking," in turn, allows the application of expropriation norms to situations where excessive government regulation results in an excessive burden on property rights. This provides a systemic justification for imposing compensation obligations on actions that may not qualify as expropriation but impose an undue burden on property rights holders. Following this line of thought, it seems that the numerous cases of undue burdens on property rights caused by legislation and administrative regulation in China's practice could potentially receive appropriate remedies. As suggested by some scholars, the introduction of "regulatory taking" is rooted in the practical needs of China. The scenario where expropriation effects arise due to government regulations is not uncommon in Chinese law. Even if these land use regulations have legitimacy, there may be instances where "some individuals bear burdens that should have been borne by the public according to principles of fairness and justice." Should the government provide compensation? … If private property is acknowledged to be legally protected and the primacy of private property in serving individual interests is emphasized, compensation should be granted. However, the issue lies in the fact that there is no concept of regulatory taking in Chinese law. Yet, this does not imply that the concept of regulatory taking cannot be constructed within the framework of Chinese law.[15]

---

on the concepts of "expropriation" and "requisition" is needed to encompass all situations indicated by "regulatory taking", whether they involve restrictions on ownership or restrictions on the right of use, within the scope of Article 13, Clause 3 of the Constitution.

[14] See Xiao Zesheng, "The Boundary between Property Rights' Social Obligations and Expropriation," (Zhejiang University Press 2011) 345.

[15] Certainly, similar discussions can be found in works such as Jin Jian and Zhang Xianguo, "Criteria for Determining Quasi-Expropriation of Property Rights," (2014) 2 *Comparative Law Research* 26–45; Peng Tao, "A Brief History

The above discussion indicates that the introduction of the concept of "regulatory taking" is driven by the necessity to prevent the detrimental consequences of citizen property rights being harmed due to excessive government regulation without compensation. In practice, whether through legislative measures or administrative actions, restrictions placed on property rights under the guise of "regulation" often lack compensation, resulting in an implicit infringement upon citizens' property rights.[16] Given that government regulations driven by public management and public service needs are inevitable, in order to strike a balance between fulfilling governmental functions and safeguarding citizens' private property rights, the introduction of the concept of "regulatory taking" becomes essential. From a legislative standpoint, it is necessary to establish the concept of "regulatory taking" and its compensation framework to achieve this balance.[17] Based on the discussion presented earlier, it is evident that the introduction of the concept of "regulatory taking" into the academic circles in China seems to be firmly grounded in significant practical reasons. This introduction emerges as an inventive institutional innovation designed to effectively address specific Chinese issues. Moreover, as indicated by the discussion in the "approach" section, current research has already proposed seemingly "perfect" expansion interpretation approaches.

Whether examined from the standpoint of the "methodology" or the "application," the empirical implementation of "regulatory taking" appears to be "fully prepared, only awaiting the right conditions." However, the empirical implementation of "regulatory taking" may raise two concerns. On one hand, due to the inherent flexibility of the concept of regulatory taking, it might lead to the constitutionalization of many property rights restriction actions that are not fundamentally expropriatory in nature, under the guise of "regulatory taking." We refer to this as the generalized concern of regulatory taking. On the other hand, if we focus on the "expropriation" concept itself, "regulatory taking" could face challenges in qualifying as a form of "expropriation," as it might not adequately constitute a rational "expropriation" concept. We label this as the concern for the nature of regulatory taking. In addressing the generalized concern related to regulatory taking, given that "regulatory taking" has not been empirically established in Chinese law, it necessitates a reasoned argument grounded in observations of the American experience. As for the

---

of the US Regulatory Taking Legal System and Its Implications," (2015) 3 *Journal of Northwest University (Philosophy and Social Sciences Edition)* 100–107; Xu Yingchun, "On the US Regulatory Taking System and Its Implications for China," (2019) 4 *Rule of Law Studies* 138–139.

16 See Zhang Huilin, "On Excessive Ownership Restrictions in China and Legislative Improvements," (2013) 3 *Law Forum* 120.

17 *Supra* note 16, 123–124.

concern for the nature of regulatory taking, a definitive conclusion must be reached through meticulous conceptual analysis.

2. CONCERNS ABOUT THE CONCEPT OF REGULATORY TAKING

The potential problem that could arise directly from the empirical implementation of "regulatory taking" is the broadening of the concept of "expropriation," which has already become conspicuous in the long-standing judicial practice in the United States. The reason for being cautious about this broadening of "expropriation" is that it may lead to a reduction in the level of protection for property rights.

When viewed from the perspective of the regulatory frameworks for property rights in different countries and the value connotation for property rights, the protection of property rights should adhere to a structural order, prioritizing continuity protection over value protection. The generalization of "expropriation" could potentially undermine the safeguarding of continuity protection of property rights, making value protection the primary or even sole measure of safeguarding property rights. Consequently, numerous unconstitutional restrictions on property rights may be legitimized through compensation, posing a risk of hollowing out the core content and intrinsic value of property rights.

2.1 Consistent Analytical Framework: Which Takes Priority – Continuity Protection or Value Safeguarding for Property Rights?

In general, there are two ways to protect property rights: one is continuity protection (also referred to as primary protection), and the other is value protection (also referred to as secondary protection).[18] The concept of continuity protection focuses on maintaining the existing legal status of property rights, preventing any alteration in the legal status of property rights due to state expropriation or restrictive actions. On the other hand, value protection emphasizes the preservation of the economic value underlying property rights, preventing a decrease in the value of property rights due to state expropriation or restrictions. The effects of these two forms of protection are not parallel but rather involve a difference in priority, with continuity protection taking precedence over value protection. When viewed from the perspective of the

[18] Compare Mangoldt/Klein/Starck, *Grundgesetz Kommentar*, 7th ed., Munich: C. H. Beck, 2018, para. 457–460.

structural arrangements and provisions of property rights in various countries' constitutions, the priority of safeguarding the continuity of property rights is the prerequisite for property rights to truly exist without being emptied by governmental authority.

From the normative structure of property rights provisions in constitutions worldwide, the inviolability of property rights is often positioned at the forefront of the structure,[19] given that the various values and functions associated with property rights are all contingent on the continued existence of this right. In strict terms, continuity protection is the exclusive measure to ensure the integrity of the content of property rights. It safeguards a range of rights with self-determination significance, including the right to occupy, use, and dispose of property, which are inherent to property rights. It is only through continuity protection that citizens' property rights can be truly realized. Otherwise, the various rights, such as possession, use, and transfer, associated with property rights would all evaporate. They would also be unable to exercise further control over their lives based on the property rights they already possess. Compared to the inviolability clause of property rights, property rights' compensation clauses are often positioned at the bottom layer of the normative structure of property rights. This is due to the inherent relativity of property rights, which necessitates that property rights should permit the intrusion of state authority in exceptional circumstances. Consequently, when such state authority imposes a substantial burden on property rights (typified by expropriation) in specific situations, the protection of property rights should shift from continuity protection to value protection, thereby achieving a balance between safeguarding property rights and the exercise of state authority. It can be seen that value protection is merely a remedy employed when the continuity protection is practically unattainable. Specifically, within the normative structure of Article 13 of China's Constitution, the first and second clauses inherently encompass the fundamental requirement of safeguarding the continuity of property rights. The third clause pertains to exceptional circumstances where the emergence of expropriation necessitates a shift from the continuity protection to value protection. In the context of safeguarding property rights within the constitutional framework, the priority of continuity protection is closely linked to the inherent values in property rights outlined in the Constitution, which aim to promote human development and self-realization. Property rights within the constitutional context concern the moral values closely associated with individual subjects, namely, the foundational significance of property rights for individual dignity and personal development. This

19 See Lin Laifan, "Constitutional Protection of Private Property Rights," (1999) 3 *Journal of Law* 14.

emphasis is based on the ethical importance of property rights, not on the wealth or economically related interests that lie behind property. The moral value closely associated with property rights as outlined in the Constitution cannot be realized through monetary compensation. It is only through the continuous existence of property rights that the integrity of this value can be ensured.

The "Hamburg Flood Protection" Case, ruled by the Federal Constitutional Court of Germany in 1968, highlighted that property rights are a fundamental entitlement inherently connected to safeguarding individual freedom. Within the broader framework of fundamental rights, its role is to secure the economic liberty of property owners, allowing them to autonomously pursue their lives.[20] In the tradition of property rights protection in the United States, following Locke's theory of property rights, property rights have a deep pre-political tradition. They are defined as rights that precede political rights. The government's purpose, of course, is to safeguard the continuation of property rights rather than eliminate them.[21] From the perspective of systemic interpretation, property rights in the Constitution of China similarly encompass such a personal value. Article 33, Clause 3 of China's Constitution confirms the state's respect for and protection of human rights. As the governing provision in the chapter on fundamental rights, the value expressed in this clause, which is "respecting and protecting human rights," should naturally extend to all the fundamental rights throughout the entire Constitution. As a vital fundamental right, the protection of property rights and the property system it encompasses should consistently uphold the fundamental value of respecting and safeguarding human rights. The "continuity-value" binary framework for property rights protection will serve as the consistent analytical framework throughout this article. If the subsequent description of "regulatory taking" and its resulting "expropriation generalization" can be regarded as an objective review of the American experience, then the evaluation of "expropriation generalization" unavoidably engages in a debate concerning the hierarchy of values in property rights protection. Based on the subsequent discussion, it becomes evident that the differences in the prioritization of the two safeguarding logics would lead to opposite qualitative conclusions regarding "expropriation generalization." Similar situations will also arise in the discussion of the "hidden concerns of nature" section. The foundation behind these two distinct protection value orientations is different concepts of expropriation.

---

20 BVerfGE 24, 367 (389).

21 See Carol M. Rose, "Mahon Reconstructed: Why the Takings Issue is Still a Muddle," (1984) 4 *Southern California Law Review* 594.

Different concepts of expropriation may not have a definite ranking of superiority or inferiority. However, if the value predominance of property rights protection logic indeed exists, it implies that not all expropriation concepts align with rationality. In other words, only expropriation concepts that align with the predominant logic can meet the genuine requirements of contemporary property rights protection. Therefore, the "continuity-value" binary framework for safeguarding property rights serves not only as a basis for evaluating the phenomenon of "expropriation generalization" but also as an exploration of the theoretical foundation for rational expropriation concepts.

2.2 The "Expropriation Generalization" Phenomenon Caused by Regulatory Taking in US Law

"Regulatory taking" originated from the 1922 case of "Mahon." However, this case only established the possibility of incorporating government regulations into the norms of "expropriation" for adjustment, but it did not establish a solid legal foundation for "regulatory taking." In this case, the court issued a dual critique of the Kohler Act. On one hand, it was deemed insufficient to constitute a general public interest.[22] On the other hand, it imposed an unduly burdensome and unfair load on mining right holders.[23] The court ultimately determined that the government's regulations based on the Kohler Act were invalid. However, it did not analyze the invalid constitutional basis in this case: this invalidity could be attributed to either the regulation itself imposing an unfair burden on property rights holders, thereby violating substantive due process. It could also result from the regulation effectively leading to expropriation without providing just compensation.[24] In other words, the "Mahon case" established the concept of "regulatory taking." However, it did not address the following question: if a regulation that imposes an excessive burden on an individual's property rights itself violates substantive due process, should that regulation be invalidated? Or can this regulation still be considered as "expropriation," and by providing compensation, can it survive temporarily or permanently?[25] The essence of the above question lies in how the court should appropriately manage the relationship between expropriation and substantive due process within the context of "regulatory taking." Unfortunately, the court almost abandoned the requirements of substantive due process in

22 See *Pennsylvania Coal Co. v. Mahon*, 260 US 393 (1922), 413–415.

23 ibid., 22.

24 See Richard L. Settle, "Regulatory Taking Doctrine in Washington: Now You See It, Now You Don't," (1989) 3 *University of Puget Sound Law Review* 348.

25 *Supra* note 24, 351.

its scrutiny of "regulatory taking" after the "Mahong case."[26] "Consequently, this has led to the unlimited expansion of 'expropriation' norms: through a very lenient scrutiny of public use, the majority of government regulatory actions can be incorporated into the framework of 'regulatory taking,' thus naturally entering the discussion of whether compensation should be granted." Therefore, many scholars argue that the long-term judicial practice of "regulatory taking" by the courts has not contributed to the refinement of the theory of "regulatory taking" but has merely been continuously expanding the scope of "expropriation."[27] "Regulatory taking" can incorporate regulations, ordinances, orders, or measures issued by federal, state, and local governments. Relevant areas may include land management, zoning, environmental protection, urban road planning, and a range of other fields. In this process, regulations that prohibit certain types of businesses from operating in specific locations or city housing regulations that require tenants to vacate substandard housing can all be included within the scope of "regulatory taking."[28] The above situations are generally considered exercises of "police powers." If the owners of the relevant property rights file a lawsuit, claiming that these regulations impose an excessive burden on them, the courts generally review the validity of the regulations within the confines of the Fifth Amendment to the Constitution. The standard for their judgment is whether fair compensation has been provided.[29]

From this, it can be understood that the concept of "regulatory taking" itself may not be as perfect as Chinese scholars have envisioned. While it can provide a valuable framework for addressing property rights restrictions resulting from non-typical expropriations due to the expansion of government power in a welfare state context, it must also be acknowledged that the concept's weak

---

26 See Norman Karlin, "Substantive Due Process: A Doctrine for Regulatory Control," (1983) 3 *Southwestern University Law Review* 479.

27 See John A. Humbach, "A Unifying Theory for the Just-Compensation Cases: Takings, Regulation, and Public Use," (1982) 2 *Rutgers Law Review* 244. The author points out that regulatory expropriation based on police power is, in itself, a hodgepodge, and due to a long-standing lack of theoretical foundation, its doctrinal system has progressed slowly. See footnote 21, p. 562. The author notes that what the courts are doing is merely making arbitrary expropriation judgments rather than exploring and shaping a principled methodological foundation. Susan Rose-Ackerman, "Against Ad Hocery: A Comment on Michelman," (1988) 88 *Columbia Law Review* 1711. The author highlights that the courts are only continuously expanding the concept of expropriation to make it more inclusive, without attempting to seek a principled approach.

28 See C. Kevin Kelso, "Substantive Due Process as a Limit on Police Power Regulatory Takings," (1983) 1 *Willamette Law Review* 1–2.

29 *Supra* note 28, 2.

legal foundation has indeed caused confusion and ambiguity in both theory and practice. To some extent, it has contributed to the broadening of the scope of "expropriation" in US judicial practice.

2.3 Is "Expropriation Generalization" a Danger?

The generalization of "expropriation" has emerged alongside numerous non-typical expropriation practices in order to ensure that property rights can seek remedies under expropriation norms when subjected to excessive government regulations. At first glance, the practice of extensive "expropriation" expansion may appear to safeguard citizens' property rights. Without such expansion of "expropriation," there seems to be a lack of regulatory basis for property rights that have suffered adverse consequences due to excessive government regulations to seek compensation remedies in reality.

It would be unjust if citizens' property rights are subject to excessive government regulations without the possibility of compensation. However, it is precisely at this point that a logical rupture occurs in property rights protection. It neglects the steps of continuity protection for property rights and directly delves into the realm of value protection, making compensation the sole criterion for justifying property rights restrictions, thus diminishing the level of property rights protection. In simpler terms, property rights that could have been safeguarded through continuity protection may, due to insufficient consideration of whether government constraints are necessary, skip continuity protection and directly move to a stage where property rights restrictions are legitimized through compensation. Why does the broadening of the concept of "property requisition" lead to "compensation" as a means and method for legitimizing property rights restrictions?

On one hand, this is related to the inherent connotation of "public interest" within the concept of "property requisition." "Public interest" is a significant component of the "property requisition" concept. When we use the term "property requisition," it often implies that the related actions already meet the requirements of public interest. In theory, there exists a logical paradox in the phrase "illegal expropriation and requisition of property": if expropriation and requisition are understood as legitimate government actions, then illegal expropriation and requisition no longer qualify as expropriation and requisition.[30] When all actions restricting property rights are included within the scope of "expropriation," it leads us to a presumption that these restrictions are

[30] See Liu Liantai, Normative Interpretation of Expropriation in Constitutional Texts – With a Focus on Article 13, Clause 3 of the Chinese Constitution (China University of Political Science and Law Press 2014) 122.

inherently just and constitutional. It is precisely based on this presumption that we tend to overlook the question of whether these restrictions should have been imposed in the first place and instead focus on whether compensation should be provided for the restrictions that have already been imposed. On the other hand, it is also related to the continuous expansion of government power in the context of a welfare state, which has led to a loosening of the "public interest" standard. When government authority increasingly intervenes in the property rights of citizens to better facilitate property distribution and contribute to the collective welfare of the people, the standard of "public interest" becomes increasingly difficult to adopt in a strict defining manner. Otherwise, it may lead to legal rigidity and hinder implementation. As the standard of "public interest" becomes more flexible,[31] it becomes easier to pass the scrutiny of the "public interest" in the context of "expropriation."

As a result, the level of attention given to "public interest" continues to decline, shifting the focus to the legal consequences of "expropriation" – the issue of "compensation." From both a theoretical and practical standpoint, the concept of using "compensation" as a significant basis for legitimizing property rights restrictions is not uncommon in China. Taking the normalization of vehicle restrictions as an example, during the deliberation of the "Revised Draft of the Law on the Prevention and Control of Atmospheric Pollution" by the Standing Committee of the National People's Congress, some committee members explicitly proposed that if local governments were to be authorized with the power to restrict the use of motor vehicles, it would be necessary for the government to specify compensation measures.[32] The implicit message here is that vehicle restrictions can be justified as long as compensation is provided. In the first national case challenging the "motorcycle ban," the plaintiff argued that the "motorcycle ban" unilaterally altered the administrative permit obtained by the plaintiff through vehicle registration, which had allowed motorcycle riders to travel on urban roads. This alteration partially revoked the administrative permit for motorcycle drivers without corresponding compensation, rendering the "motorcycle ban" illegal.[33]

---

31 See Huang Zhong, "Cluster Development and Land Expropriation," (2020) 5 *Legal Studies* 83.

32 See the National People's Congress, "Cannot Easily Allow the Normalization of Odd–Even License Plate Restrictions," available on the Chinese National People's Congress website at http://www.npc.gov.cn/zgrdw/npc/cwhhy/12jcwh/2014-12/28/content_1891786.htm. Accessed on March 30, 2022.

33 See Hong Kefei, "First National Case Questioning 'Motorcycle Ban' Begins Trial in Changsha," published in China Youth Daily at http://zqb.cyol.com/content/2004-10/28/content_975320.htm. Accessed on July 22, 2022.

In a discussion by scholars on whether the legalization of ride-sharing services constitutes regulatory exaction on taxi operators, they primarily emphasized the examination of the financial losses incurred by taxi license holders due to the legalization of ride-sharing services. They also raised the question of how to provide reasonable compensation, without delving into the issue of whether ride-sharing services themselves should be legalized.[34] During this process, the continuity protection of property rights is nearly eliminated, while only value protection remains. This, undoubtedly, hinders the achievement of the objective of property rights protection. It could lead to a scenario where many property rights, initially possessing lasting value, can solely access a fraction of their beneficial value through value protection, posing challenges to preserving their integrity. In fact, in the long-standing practice of "regulatory taking" in the United States, scholars have long been keenly aware of the issue of inadequate protection of property rights resulting from the broadening of the concept of "expropriation."

During the scrutiny of "regulatory taking," the courts have almost abandoned the requirements of substantive due process. This means that, in practice, the courts have effectively differentiated between property rights and other civil liberties. While the courts continue to vigorously protect the latter from legislative encroachment through the requirements of substantive due process, they have been somewhat neglectful in the case of property rights. Essentially, they have left the door wide open for legislative intrusion into the realm of property rights.[35]

As Professor Alexander has pointed out, US courts tend to protect property rights through "expropriation" clauses. Compared to other civil liberties, the connection between property rights and substantive due process remains relatively weak, allowing government power to enter the private domain of property rights as long as it meets the loose scrutiny standards of "reasonableness." Therefore, property rights do not seem to possess the same "foundational" status as required by substantive due process.[36]

3. CONCEPT OF RATIONAL EXPROPRIATION

From a comparative law perspective, the reason why the previous discussion referred to the potential "generalization of expropriation" resulting from "regulatory taking" as a hidden concern is that "regulatory taking" has not been concretely codified in China's Constitution and laws. The notion of the

---

34 *Supra* note 11, 70–78.

35 *Supra* note 26, 479–480.

36 See Gregory S. Alexander, "Property as a Fundamental Constitutional Right – The German Example," (2003) 3 *Cornell Law Review* 734–736.

"generalization of expropriation" is merely a reasonable concern based on the American experience, and no one can assert with certainty whether the phenomenon of "regulatory taking" will necessarily reappear after its introduction into China's current regulatory framework. Nevertheless, from the perspective of a comprehensive empirical decision-making logic, treating the "generalization of expropriation" as a "possible risk" or "hidden concern" and incorporating it into the central elements of (empirical) strategic decision-making is quite necessary.

However, this also implies that solely relying on generalization arguments is far from sufficient to definitively answer the question of whether or not "regulatory taking" can be empirically implemented. The only way to truly address this issue is to return to the concept of "regulatory taking" itself and, through a nature-compliance argument, clarify the essential nature of "regulatory taking." As previously discussed, since a concept and nature-compliance argument is to be conducted, the primary task is to identify a good "expropriation" concept, namely, a "concept of rational expropriation" that aligns with the core values of contemporary property rights protection. The "continuity-value" binary framework for property rights protection should also be employed.

3.1 The Broad Concept of "Expropriation" with Ambiguous Boundaries

During the era of expropriation rulings led by the Federal Constitutional Court of Germany, a broad concept of "expropriation" emerged as a result of judges' expansive interpretation of the term within the Constitution. In terms of functionality, this broad concept of "expropriation" is essentially equivalent to "regulatory taking" as they both aim to address the compensation issue for property rights burdened excessively due to government regulations.

Even during the Imperial Court period, the concept of "expropriation" exhibited an expanding tendency: any excessive restriction of property rights by law should be considered expropriation. When the Basic Law came into effect, the Federal Constitutional Court continued the Imperial Court's line of thinking by expanding the concept of "expropriation" as a means of safeguarding property rights. In 1952, the Federal Constitutional Court developed the "special sacrifice theory" (Sonderopfertheorie). According to this theory, expropriation is not a general and equally effective limitation on property rights. Instead, it is a legally permitted coercive intervention by the state in property rights, which should be considered expropriation if the consequences of this intervention on individuals and groups related to property rights are unjust and unequal compared to other parties. In 1957, the Federal Administrative Court introduced the "severity theory" (Schweretheorie). According to this theory, the core of distinguishing expropriation from non-expropriation lies in the "severity of infringement and its scope of impact." Within the broad concept of "expropriation," the boundary between expropriation and non-expropriation is distinguished based on the degree of restriction, essentially determined by the judges. Just as Carl Schmitt criticized the unrestricted expansion of the expropriation concept by the courts during the Weimar Constitution era: under the trend of expanding the concept of "expropriation," the courts could always find a reason to categorize any exercise of public authority that disadvantaged people's property as "expropriation" without the need to demonstrate what constitutes "expropriation." This practice, with the help of judicial power, circumvented the constraints formed by legislators and did not represent the ideals of a rule of law state.[37] The neglect of the qualitative issue of "expropriation" under the broad concept of expropriation also exists in "regulatory taking." Since the inception of "regulatory taking," federal and state-level courts in the United States have engaged in extensive argumentation and practice. During this period, various standards such as the "physical invasion standard,"[38] the "total economic deprivation standard,"[39] and the "multi-factor balancing test" emerged.[40] These standards sparked considerable debate, leading to the generation of even more standards. However, despite these efforts, judges continued to exercise their discretion in practical adjudication, ultimately failing to establish a principled resolution. Disputes related to expropriation remain chaotic, primarily because the fundamental question of what constitutes "expropriation" in US law has not been definitively answered.[41]

3.2 The Narrow Concept of "Expropriation" in Line with Priority for Continuity Protection

In 1981, the Federal Constitutional Court of Germany abandoned the broad concept of "expropriation" advocated by the Federal Supreme Court and the Federal Administrative Court in the "Nassau Gravel Mining Decision" (Nassauskiesungsbeschluss). Instead, it established the separation theory (Trennungstheorie). According to this theory, the definition and boundaries

---

[37] Compare Carl Schmitt, "Die Auflösung des Enteignungsbegriffs," in Carl Schmitt, Verfassungsrechtliche Aufsätze aus den Jahren 1924–1954, Berlin: Duncker & Humblot, 1973, p. 112.

[38] This standard was established in the case of *Loretto v. Teleprompter Manhattan CATV Corp.*, 458 U.S. 419 (1982).

[39] This standard was established in the case of *Lucas v. South Carolina Coastal Council*, 505 U.S. 1003 (1992).

[40] This standard was established in the case of *Penn Central Transportation Co. v. New York City*, 438 U.S. 104 (1978).

[41] Supra note 21, 561–562.

of property rights are strictly distinguished from expropriation, with no possibility of conversion between the two.[42] What is meant by "expropriation" in this narrow sense refers exclusively to actions that deprive property rights as defined in Article 14, Paragraph 1 of the Basic Law.[43] This narrow concept of "expropriation" has been upheld by the Federal Constitutional Court to this day, with recent trends even moving toward a more classical and narrower concept of "expropriation."

In 2001, the Federal Constitutional Court, in a judgment concerning the redistribution of building land, introduced the element of property creation (Gu'terbeschaffung)[44] as a distinguishing factor for expropriation.[45] To date, the Federal Constitutional Court has reached a relatively consistent conclusion regarding the definition of expropriation: it refers to actions that, for the purpose of accomplishing specific public tasks, either through legislation (legislative acts) or in accordance with the law (administrative acts), deliberately and wholly or partially deprive specific property rights. Moreover, this action must be in the form of creating property rights, all done to promote public interest or the interests of other beneficiaries.

From a property rights protection perspective, the transition from the broad concept of expropriation to the narrow concept also aimed to shift the focus from compensation priority to continuity priority. Under the Federal Supreme Court's broad expropriation concept, compensation had effectively become the primary avenue for property rights relief and protection. Any adverse

42 Compare BVerfGE 58, 300.

43 *Supra* note 42, 323.

44 In German law, the classical notion of expropriation also encompasses the element of "Gu'terbeschaffung," which Professor Chen Xinmin translates as "property creation." In his perspective, classical expropriation necessitates the presence of a public project to fulfill the requirements of the public interest. In this process, through the exercise of state sovereignty, property rights are transferred from citizens to a specific public project. Essentially, this resembles the establishment of a new property right for the state [See Chen Xinmin, "Fundamental Theories of German Public Law (Revised Edition, Volume 1)," (Law Press 2010) 468]. However, based on the original German meaning of "Gu'terbeschaffung," it primarily emphasizes the procurement or acquisition of property. The author adopts Professor Chen Xinmin's translation mainly because the term "expropriation" inherently implies the compulsory acquisition of property and compensation. This process can be likely described as the government's compulsory procurement procedure. Nevertheless, the key emphasis by the Federal Constitutional Court through this concept is that, following the government's compulsory acquisition of citizens' property and provision of compensation, property rights are transferred to a specific public project.

45 Compare BVerfGE 104, 1(10).

consequences resulting from government intervention and property rights restrictions were compensated for, with little consideration given to whether the infringement itself should be reversed.[46] The Federal Constitutional Court was dissatisfied with this indiscriminate reliance on compensation as a means to safeguard citizens' property rights. It asserted that compensation must have a legal foundation. Citizens could only initiate compensation lawsuits when relevant expropriation laws existed, specifying the method and scope of compensation. If such laws did not address compensation, they were deemed unconstitutional, rendering the expropriation actions conducted under them unconstitutional as well. In such cases, where a legal basis for compensation was absent, citizens could only initiate lawsuits in administrative courts to overturn the expropriation actions, rather than filing compensation lawsuits. Thus, citizens did not have the option to choose between revocation and compensation.[47] Through this approach, the Federal Constitutional Court underscored the priority of property rights continuity protection.

3.3 Does "Regulatory Taking" Conform to the "Concept of Rational Expropriation"?

In both the judicial practices of the United States and the adoption and integration of "regulatory taking" by Chinese scholars, the nature of "regulatory taking" has remained in a state of ambiguity. No one recognizes it as traditional "expropriation" in the conventional sense, but if it isn't "expropriation," then what is it? This question has not been explored or answered. It is precisely this ambiguity that has led to the neglect of the qualitative nature of "regulatory taking" itself.

When examining the practice of "regulatory taking" in US law, it consistently moves between the concepts of "police power" and "expropriation." The same act of restricting property rights may be classified as "police power" in one situation and as "expropriation" in another. Regarding how "regulatory taking" should be characterized, more attention has been given to quantitative issues. The criteria used to determine "regulatory taking" do not actually classify it; instead, they differentiate the extent of government "regulation" based on various standards. These standards primarily serve the purpose of distinguishing between "police power" and "expropriation," rather than providing a categorical definition for "regulatory taking" itself.

---

[46] See Li Jianliang, "Compensation for Losses," in Weng Yuesheng (Ed.), "Administrative Law (Volume II)," (China Legal System Publishing House 2009) 1732–1733; [German] Hartmut Maurer, "General Administrative Law," translated by Gao Jiawei, (Law Press 2000) 671–672.

[47] *Supra* note 42, 323.

The disregard for characterizing "regulatory taking" aligns with the issue of characterizing "expropriation" under the broad concept of expropriation. Within the broad concept of expropriation, the characterization of "expropriation" often focuses on different situations arising from individual cases, effectively rendering the concept of "expropriation" more theoretical than practical.

From the perspective of safeguarding the continuity and value of property rights, "expropriation" must inherently embody the value of prioritizing the continuity of property rights. An act of "expropriation" that violates the primacy of property rights continuity cannot be defined as "expropriation" because such an act contravenes the foundational principles of the expropriation system. This system stipulates that governmental intervention in property rights should only occur in exceptional circumstances and with the utmost respect for the integrity of property rights. To uphold this value, "expropriation" should be limited to a narrow scope. Expanding the concept of "expropriation" only blurs the boundaries and categories between expropriation and non-expropriation, resulting in an unrestricted expansion of property rights value protection and an unlimited reduction of property rights continuity protection.

Whether viewed from the perspective of legal order stability, the need for clarity within the "expropriation" category, or the ultimate goal of property rights protection, the conditions and scope of "expropriation" should be clearly defined based on the constitutional realities of each country. The inherent ambiguity of "regulatory taking" and its consequences for dissolving the framework for safeguarding property rights' continuity and value inevitably render it an irrational concept of expropriation.

4. THE NECESSARY FRAMEWORK FOR PROPERTY RIGHTS PROTECTION

Within the binary framework of safeguarding property rights' "continuity and value," the empirical application of "regulatory taking" not only has the potential to trigger the practical risk of "expropriation expansion" but also fails to meet the substantive requirements of China's current Constitution, which prioritizes the continuity of citizens' property rights. In other words, "regulatory taking" cannot be fundamentally considered a form of "rational expropriation." It could even be argued that if the "concept of rational expropriation" is regarded as the exclusive normative reference for "expropriation," then, in essence, "regulatory taking" does not constitute a form of "expropriation." This might be why some scholars label it as "quasi-expropriation."

However, as evident from the previous discussion, the practical effectiveness of "regulatory taking" provides sufficient motivation for empirical application. Considering the reasons stated above, at least in the current stage where there is no definitive conclusion, it is imperative to maintain a cautious and vigilant stance toward this trend. The specific approach entails adhering to the narrow concept of "expropriation" established by China's existing Constitution and utilizing it as the foundation for establishing a constitutional system for safeguarding property rights.

4.1 Upholding the Narrow Concept of "Expropriation" in China's Constitution

If a historical and semantic interpretation of the concept of "expropriation" in Article 13, Clause 3 of China's Constitution were to be provided, the concept of "expropriation" in China's Constitution could be attributed with a narrow connotation.

Firstly, expropriation is confined to actions involving the deprivation of property rights, with a specific emphasis on the transfer of private property ownership to public ownership. As early as 2000, Professor Liang Huixing provided a clear explanation of the concept of "expropriation" in his draft proposal for the Chinese Property Rights Law. He contended that "expropriation" solely pertained to the government unilaterally acquiring ownership or other property rights through coercive measures.[48] Before the constitutional amendment in 2004, China's Constitution did not encompass the concept of "expropriation" but solely referred to "requisition." The inclusion of "expropriation" in the Constitution, as elucidated by the framers of the Constitution, aimed to accommodate the various situations of "expropriation" and "requisition" that arose within the context of a market economy. In alignment with Professor Liang Huixing's interpretation of "expropriation," the framers of the Constitution also underscored that "expropriation" is distinguished by the transfer of ownership.[49] Secondly, only "administrative expropriation" exists, with no "legal expropriation." Article 14 of the German Basic Law (Grundgesetz) stipulates two forms of expropriation: administrative expropriation and legal expropriation. Within the expropriation system established by the Basic Law, expropriation can be carried out through administrative measures by government authorities, or it can be directly implemented through legislation. However, if a strict semantic interpretation of Article 13, Clause 3 of China's Constitution is applied, it becomes evident that this provision only emphasizes the possibility of expropriation being carried out "in accordance with the law," without explicitly allowing for the possibility of expropriation "through legal provisions." Consequently, many scholars argue that China's

48 *Supra* note 30, 194.
49 *Supra* note 1, 71–72.

Constitution should also recognize "legal expropriation" to better protect the private property of citizens.[50]

In fact, the concept of "legal expropriation" has been a contentious issue in Germany since the Weimar era.[51] Despite the formal establishment of "legal expropriation" in the German Basic Law, the Federal Constitutional Court has always maintained a cautious stance toward it. This is because citizens can seek adequate remedies through administrative litigation procedures and constitutional appeals when it comes to the legality of "administrative expropriation." However, if citizens question the constitutionality of "legal expropriation," it can only be examined through a constitutional review process. Due to the difficulty of challenging the legitimacy of "legal expropriation," if it were widely applied, it would effectively open the door for legislators to arbitrarily deprive citizens of their property rights based on compensation conditions. Therefore, "legal expropriation" in Germany is considered an exceptional circumstance. In essence, "expropriation" should still be an act carried out by administrative authorities based on their administrative functions.[52]

Based on the previous discussion, the connotation of "expropriation" in China's Constitution can be defined as follows: "Expropriation" refers to the state's administrative actions aimed at depriving citizens of all property rights with economic value and providing compensation in return. "Expropriation" must primarily feature the "deprivation of rights" and should be limited exclusively to administrative actions, excluding legislative actions.

4.2 Constructing a Constitutional Property Rights Protection System Based on the Narrow Concept of "Expropriation"

From a formal legal perspective, the narrow concept of "expropriation" undoubtedly contributes to establishing a clear legal conceptual framework. In this framework, it becomes the legislator's responsibility to precisely define which situations constitute expropriation and which do not. Conversely, if the concept of expropriation were allowed to expand or become generalized, the courts could potentially find suitable grounds to classify any exercise of governmental power that infringes on citizens' property rights (whether legislative or administrative) as expropriation. Adherence to the narrow concept of

50 See Fang Shaokun and Wang Hongping, "Examining China's Expropriation Legislation Choice from the Perspective of Expropriation Types in American and German Law – With a Focus on Defining the Concept of 'Public Interest Expropriation'," (2010) 1 *Tsinghua Law Journal* 93.

51 *Supra* note 44, 473.

52 See [German] Hartmut Maurer: "General Administrative Law," translated by Gao Jiawei (Law Press 2000) 689.

"expropriation" confines judicial discretion within reasonable boundaries in practice. This ensures formal consistency and predictability in distinguishing and defining expropriation from non-expropriation concerning property rights. Thus, it prevents the same restriction on property rights from being classified as expropriation in one scenario and as a limitation on property rights content in another.

From a substantive legal perspective, the narrow concept of "expropriation" can best achieve the goal of safeguarding citizens' property rights. Concerning the effectiveness of property rights protection, two major approaches are considered: continuity protection and value protection. Only by giving thorough consideration to the circumstances of individual cases can a fair and reasonable judgment be made on the choice between continuity protection and value protection, so as to strike a balance between citizens' property rights and the public interest.

However, under the broad concept of "expropriation," value protection effectively becomes the primary, and often the only, approach to property rights protection. Governmental intervention in citizens' property rights is simplified to two possibilities: first, if this intervention constitutes "expropriation," value protection applies, and fair compensation is provided; second, if this intervention does not constitute "expropriation" and pertains to the boundaries of property rights, neither value protection nor continuity protection applies, and the limitation on property rights is considered legitimate.

Nonetheless, this singular value protection model fundamentally contradicts the goal of safeguarding citizens' property rights. The Federal Constitutional Court of Germany, using the narrow concept of "expropriation" as a benchmark, distinguishes between "expropriation" and "property rights' content and limitations" as two separate levels, depriving the possibility of transformation between them. In this context, the Federal Constitutional Court categorizes various situations involving governmental intervention in property rights, expropriation, and compensation as follows: first, legitimate expropriation of property rights should receive fair compensation; second, illegitimate expropriation of property rights should not receive compensation and should be revoked;[53] third, limitations on property rights that are legitimate and do not exceed a certain limit fall within the realm of property rights' social obliga-

[53] Specifically, if the court, in the course of adjudicating an expropriation case, finds that the law to be applied violates Article 14 of the Basic Law, it must not provide compensation to the parties but rather raise the issue of the constitutionality of that law for review by the Federal Constitutional Court. If the property rights holder believes that the restriction imposed on their property rights by government authority is illegal, they should initiate administrative litigation to request the annulment of this restriction rather than seeking compensation. See Li

tions and do not require compensation; fourth, limitations on property rights that are legitimate but exceed a certain limit still fall within the realm of property rights' social obligations but should receive compensation. It is evident that the narrow concept of "expropriation" allows for a comprehensive approach that combines property rights' continuity protection and value protection, with priority given to continuity protection. This comprehensive property rights protection system prevents the actual infringement of citizens' property rights under the guise of "compensation" within a single value protection model, making it better suited to the needs of safeguarding citizens' property rights. Drawing inspiration from the doctrinal system of property rights protection in the Federal Constitutional Court of Germany and considering both formal and substantive legal requirements, the fundamental framework of property rights protection should be based on the narrow "expropriation" concept outlined in Article 13 of the Constitution.

First, starting from the characteristics of the restricting actions, judgments should be made regarding the specific types of property rights restrictions in practice. If this restrictive action constitutes the "deprivation" of property rights, it should be categorized as expropriation.[54] If this restrictive action does not manifest as a form of "deprivation" of rights, then it should be considered a restriction on property rights content rather than expropriation.

Next, if this restrictive action exhibits characteristics of expropriation, judgments regarding the constitutionality of this specific property rights restriction should be made based on the constitutional standards for expropriation. There are three possible scenarios.

In the first scenario, if the act of expropriation itself is unjust or unnecessary (e.g., it doesn't serve a legitimate public interest or lacks a legal basis), continuity protection should apply. This involves revoking the action that restricts property rights to maintain the integrity of citizens' property rights, and citizens are not entitled to compensation based on expropriation.

In the second scenario, if the restrictive action is deemed necessary (this determination requires an assessment based on both the form and substance of expropriation), then continuity protection can shift towards value protection. The integrity of citizens' property rights cannot be maintained, and they

---

Jianliang, "Compensation for Losses," in Weng Yuesheng (Ed.), "Administrative Law (Volume II)," (China Legal System Publishing House 2009) 1737.

54 To narrow down the scope of "expropriation," it is essential to make judgments based on formal characteristics. According to the explanations of constitutional amendments and discussions by relevant scholars concerning the concept of "expropriation," within the context of the Chinese Constitution, whether it constitutes a "deprivation" of property rights is indeed a significant formal characteristic of "expropriation."

can only receive compensation based on expropriation. However, if there are constitutional issues with the compensation for expropriation (e.g., it doesn't adhere to the principles of fairness and reasonableness), the legitimization of the restrictive action should be achieved through making the compensation fair and reasonable.

In the third scenario, if the restrictive action is deemed necessary, and the compensation provided for this restriction is legitimate, then this restriction can continue in the name of constitutional expropriation.

Finally, for those restrictive actions that do not fall under expropriation, they should be automatically categorized as limitations on property rights content not subject to expropriation. The constitutional review of their constitutionality may also present three possible scenarios.

In the first scenario, if the establishment of this limitation on property rights is inherently unnecessary (e.g., the action lacks a legal basis, does not adhere to the principle of proportionality, or violates the principle of protection of legitimate expectations), then this limitation should be revoked, and the integrity of citizens' property rights should be preserved.

In the second scenario, if the establishment of this limitation on property rights is necessary (i.e., the content boundary is in line with the principle of proportionality and the principle of protection of legitimate expectations), but citizens bear an excessively heavy burden in specific circumstances, compensation should be provided to balance the excessive burden they bear, bringing it in line with the originally proportionate burden they should bear.

In the third scenario, if the establishment of this limitation on property rights is necessary, and citizens do not bear a burden in specific circumstances that exceeds what they should naturally bear due to the social nature of their property rights, then this provision regarding the limitation on property rights is constitutional and should be upheld.

5. CONCLUSION

Based on the priority order of property rights continuity protection and value protection, the widespread application of "regulatory taking" may struggle to avoid the consequences of a generalized concept of "expropriation." This could potentially reverse the hierarchy of continuity protection and value protection, leading to a reduction in the level of property rights protection.

Within the binary framework of continuity protection and value protection, a rational concept of expropriation should be narrow and should rely on the characteristics of the act of "expropriation" itself for clear definition. "Regulatory taking" does not concern itself with the qualitative aspects of expropriation. Its quantitative considerations of expropriation lead to a blurred boundary between expropriation and non-expropriation, making it difficult to establish a rational concept of expropriation.

If the approach to property rights protection under "regulatory taking" is to be abandoned, the priority for constitutionalizing restrictions of non-expropriatory property rights, which exist in a large number of cases in reality, should be the justifiability of the restriction itself. If the reasons for the restriction itself lack constitutional legitimacy, then the path of property rights continuity protection should be adopted. This involves revoking the restrictive action to preserve the integrity of property rights. Only when the establishment of this restrictive action itself is legitimate should the issue of the extent of the restriction be considered, at which point property rights value protection becomes relevant.

2. Clarification and determination of the concept of legal interpretation

Chen Kun

1. INTRODUCTION

There has been controversy in academic circles about the concept and nature of legal interpretation. For example, some scholars argue that 'all legal texts ... need to be interpreted',[1] 'without interpretation, there can be no application of the law and no judgment';[2] some other scholars hold that interpretation that occurs only in 'automatic subsumption ... is impossible',[3] or only refers to problems in communication that cannot be determined by conventions or stipulations.[4] With the continuous deepening of research, some external theoretical resources have been introduced into the discussion of issues related to legal interpretation. However, the introduction of these external theoretical resources has brought more confusion instead of settling the existing controversies. For example, based on the theory of direct reference, Nicos Stavropoulos believes that legal interpretation is to explore the true meaning of legal terms;[5] and based on communication theory, Larry Alexander believes that legal interpretation is to probe into legislative intent.[6] Some of these divergences of opinion are rhetorical, deriving from the use of terms such as 'interpretation' and 'legal interpretation' in different senses, while others are substantive, deriving

[1] Karl Larenz, Methodology of Law (Huang Jiazhen tr, Commercial Press 2020) 265.

[2] Liang Huixing, Methods of Judgement (3rd ed., Law Press 2017) 75.

[3] See Rolf Wank, Interpretation of Law (Jiang Yi and Ji Hongming tr, Peking University Press 2020) 24.

[4] See Andrei Marmor, Interpretation and Legal Theory (Cheng Chaoyang tr, China University of Political Science and Law Press 2012) 23, 26, 39.

[5] See Nicos Stavropoulos, Objectivity in Law (Clarendon Press 1996) 15–34.

[6] See Larry Alexander, 'Originalism, the Why and the What' (2013) 82 (2) Fordham Law Review 539–544.

from mistaken views of some empirical or normative questions, or from the improper application of some external theories.

To eliminate the obstacles caused by these divergences, this chapter attempts to define the concept of legal interpretation and clarify its nature. This work is also partly rhetorical and partly substantive. Rhetorically, this essay will endeavor to show why one specific understanding of 'interpretation', or 'legal interpretation' is appropriate and competing understandings are not. In terms of substance, this chapter will try to eliminate some misconceptions or applications of empirical, normative, or theoretical issues. Clarification and determination of the concept of legal interpretation not only helps to think about the necessity, legitimacy, and objectivity of legal interpretation under a clear conceptual framework, but also helps to reveal how to discuss the principles, positions, and methods of legal interpretation. In practice, because 'what counts as interpretation determines what is undisputedly counted as judicial cause',[7] clarification and determination of the concept of legal interpretation will help to define the boundaries of judges' activities and promote the development of the rule of law in our country.

2. STATUS QUO, CONSENSUS AND PROBLEMS

2.1 Existing Types of Definition: Distinction Based on a General Idea

For what is legal interpretation, there are so many definitions in academic circles that it is difficult to list them all. However, starting from the general idea of definition, it can be roughly divided into the following three categories: The first category is from the general sense of 'interpretation', which defines 'legal interpretation' as 'interpretation of legal text'. For example, Zhang Zhiming believes that 'legal interpretation is the understanding and explanation of the meaning of legal texts',[8] Aharon Barak argues that 'legal interpretation is a rational activity that gives meaning to legal texts.[9] The second category is from the process of legal application, defining 'legal interpretation' as a link of legal application, or a method to solve some legal difficulties. For example, Shu Yihong believes that 'adjudicative interpretation can be defined as in the con-

[7] Tom Campbell, 'Grounding Theories of Legal Interpretation' in Jeffrey Goldsworthy & Tom Campbell (eds), Legal Interpretation in Democratic States (Ashgate 2002) 29.

[8] Zhang Zhiming, Hermeneutics of Law (China Renmin University Press 2015) 11.

[9] Aharon Barak, Purposive Interpretation in Law (Princeton University Press 2005) 3.

text of specific legal issues, in order to demonstrate the rationality of legal reasoning conclusions, the adjudicator's inferring process of the major and minor premises of legal reasoning through the collection, organization of arguments, and the use of specific methods',[10] while Scott Soames emphasizes that 'legal interpretation is an authoritative answer to the question of what the law is when it is applied to a specific case'.[11] The third category is from the theory of linguistics (philosophy of language), which defines 'legal interpretation' as an activity that reveals some specific meaning of legal texts. For example, from the perspective of communication theory, some scholars define 'legal interpretation' as the revelation of the intended meaning of the legislator,[12] and from realism of meaning, some scholars hold that 'legal interpretation' is an inquiry into the essence of the things referred to by relevant general legal terms.[13]

The distinction of the above three different types is only a sorting based on the needs of the following investigation and is not a logical division in a strict sense. They are neither complete nor exclusive. The reason why this chapter starts from them to sum up the different definition schemes in academic circles is just that they together trigger some problems worth discussing.

2.2 Consensus: 'Legal Text' and 'Meaning'

In the above three types of definitions of legal interpretation, there are always two key words, namely 'legal text' and 'meaning'. Although people put forward different definitions of what is meant by 'legal interpretation', they all agree that legal interpretation is an activity related to the meaning of legal texts. This consensus is the starting point for us to think further about the concept of legal interpretation. While it is neutral to specific debates (for example, whether interpretation should discover or create meaning, whether it should follow the original meaning or keep pace with the times), it does pose the most basic limitation on what activities can be counted as legal interpretation.

---

10 Yu Yihong, An Experimental Course of Legal Hermeneutics: Principles of Judgment Interpretation and Experimental Operation (Peking University Press, 2008) 13.

11 Scott Soames, Toward a Theory of Legal Interpretation (Princeton University Press 2014) 299.

12 See Stanley Fish, 'There is no Textualist Position' (2005) 42 (2) San Diego Law Review 629–650; Larry Alexander and Saikrishna Prakash, 'Is That English You're Speaking? Why Intention Free Interpretation is an Impossibility' (2004) 41 (3) San Diego Law Review 967–980; Stephen Knapp and Walter B. Michaels, 'Not a Matter of Interpretation' (2005) 42 (2) San Diego Law Review 651–668.

13 See Michael Moore, 'A Natural Law Theory of Interpretation' (1985) 58 (1–2) Southern California Law Review 291–301.

The direct goal of legal interpretation is to clarify the meaning of legal texts. Perhaps in the view of some scholars, there are other goals of legal interpretation, such as the realization of fairness in individual cases, but these are indirect goals. The inherent prescription of a practical activity is provided by its direct objectives rather than by its indirect objectives, which may be achieved through many different activities. In addition, the success of a practice should also be evaluated by the achievement of its direct objectives rather than its indirect objectives. Legal interpretation helps to achieve fairness in individual cases, but its realization does not depend solely on legal interpretation.

Starting from the direct goal of legal interpretation, any kind of activity is legal interpretation only when it is related to both 'legal text' and 'meaning'. On the one hand, any activity is legal interpretation only if it can be reasonably understood by examining legal texts. For example, some inquiries into the intentions of legislators are legal interpretation because they can be understood as inquiries into the speaker's meaning of legal texts; some inquiries into the nature of things are legal interpretation because they can be understood to explore the true meaning of a term in the legal texts. On the other hand, any kind of activity is a legal interpretation activity only when it can be reasonably understood as the meaning of inquiry. Legal interpretation focuses on the meaning of legal texts, not on their force, legitimacy, or whether they should be applicable in certain cases. This is not to say that all activities to inquire into these latter questions are not legal interpretation, but only that they are legal interpretation only if they are at the same time inquiries into meaning or are part of inquiries into meaning. For example, the activity of eliminating conflicts between two clauses generally does not belong to legal interpretation, but if this activity also determines the meaning of a certain clause by examining whether it conflicts with other clauses, it can be said to be legal interpretation.

2.3 Issues for Further Consideration

The existing definitions have achieved some consensus but have left more disputes. The disputes mentioned here do not refer to which kind of thought is reasonable but refer to the internal disputes of each thought. It is these controversies that raise questions that require further consideration.

In the first definition of 'interpretation' in the general sense, the controversy mainly revolves around how to understand 'the relationship between understanding and interpretation'. To understand this controversy, we first need to have an initial definition of 'understanding' and 'interpretation'. Generally speaking, understanding is a mental state. To understand a declarative sentence is to know what kind of fact it describes, and to understand an imperative sentence is to know what kind of command, suggestion, or request it makes. Interpretation is an activity aimed at achieving understanding. Since it is so, do all understandings involve this activity? The question is partly rhetorical and depends on whether the given interpretation includes only those conscious activities or also those unconscious processes of understanding. The problem is also partly substantive. On the one hand, although interpretation involves all processes of understanding if it includes those unconscious processes of comprehending meaning, not all scholars who argue that 'all understanding involves interpretation' count all processes of comprehending meaning as interpretation. For example, what Donald Davidson called 'radical interpretation' and what Hans-Georg Gadamer called 'the identity of understanding and interpretation' can support the above view.[14] On the other hand, there are scholars who understand interpretation as conscious activity, and further argue that it occurs only when language conventions do not provide clear meaning.[15] Even if it is appropriate to understand interpretation as conscious activity, it is also possible to ask: is interpretation needed whenever language conventions fail to provide clear meaning? And is interpretation required only if language conventions fail to provide a clear meaning? These issues can only be discussed effectively within a clear conceptual framework. These questions will be considered in the third section of this chapter.

In the second definition of the above, the dispute mainly revolves around what role legal interpretation plays in the process of legal application. In the view of some scholars, every legal application requires legal interpretation because interpretation gives legal meaning to legal texts,[16] or because interpretation bridges the logical gap between rules and facts;[17] but in the view of other scholars, legal interpretation is only required in hard cases. The latter view can be subdivided into two types: one is that legal interpretation solves all legal mysteries,[18] and the other is that legal interpretation only solves the mysteries related to the meaning of legal texts.[19] The fourth section of this chapter attempts to resolve this controversy.

The third approach todefinition starts from a certain linguistic philosophy theory and defines legal interpretation as an activity exploring certain meanings of legal texts. This line of thinking seems reasonable at first glance. Since

---

14 See Owen Fiss, 'Objectivity and Interpretation' (1982) 34 (4) Stanford Law Review 739.

15 *Supra* note 4, 39.

16 *Supra* note 9, 6–7.

17 See Drucilla Cornell, The Philosophy of the Limit (Routledge 1992) 102.

18 Yu Yihong, An Experimental Course of Legal Hermeneutics: Principles of Judgment Interpretation and Experimental Operation (Peking University Press 2008) 11–14.

19 See Timothy A. O. Endicott, Ambiguity in Law (Cheng Chaoyang tr, Peking University Press 2010) 66–71.

legal interpretation is the activity exploring the meaning of legal texts, and meaning is the core concern of the philosophy of language, then the philosophy of language should be able to provide insights for further understanding of legal interpretation. But the controversies in this line of thinking lie in the question of: in the face of different meaning theories, which one should be used as the basis to define legal interpretation? The fifth section of this chapter tries to point out that no matter what kind of meaning theory should be used as the basis for defining legal interpretation, the above thought is wrong from the beginning. This is fundamentally because legal interpretation is a normative activity. The concept of legal interpretation does not inherently refer to any meaning type. What kind of meaning should be explored is a question that should be answered during interpretation.

3. LEGAL INTERPRETATION AS A CONSCIOUS ACTIVITY

3.1 Proper Concept of 'Interpretation'

On the issue of the relationship between understanding and interpretation, much confusion has arisen because of the confusion of terms and misunderstandings of some philosophical theories. To eliminate the confusion, it is necessary to clarify what the different philosophical claims are saying, and this requires first finding out in what sense they use 'understanding' and 'interpretation'. As mentioned, understanding is a mental state. For example, suppose that in a classroom teacher A orders student B to 'close the door'. B turns his head and finds that the front door of the classroom is not closed, so he walks over and closes the door. This shows that B understood A's order. Understanding a command is knowing how to execute it. The reason why B can understand this command is that B and A are in the same language community, share some language conventions, and know what 'door' is and what counts as 'close'. Suppose B turns his head and finds that the front door and the back door of the classroom are both open, and he does not know which door A is referring to. At this time, B may ask A to get a more specific order, such as 'please close the front door'. But when it is inconvenient to ask A, B needs to figure out which door A refers to. This speculation may involve A's personality, preferences, goals, etc. No matter how you think about it, it's a conscious reasoning process. We need, then, to distinguish between two different kinds of understanding; one kind of understanding is almost instantaneous without a conscious reasoning process, and the other is the understanding that is achieved by a conscious reasoning process. These two kinds of understanding can be called spontaneous understanding and conscious understanding respectively. The fact that some understandings are spontaneous does not mean that no thought processes are involved, only that these thought processes are made automatically by the cognitive system[20] thus making the relevant text 'obvious' to us. This shows that there is no question in our mind about the meaning of the texts. If interpretation is understood to include this thought process, then all understandings involve interpretation. But if interpretation refers only to activities of explicit meaning to achieve conscious understanding, then the process of spontaneous understanding does not seem to involve interpretation. In this sense, Timothy Endicott has said that 'we don't explain the stop sign'.[21] So what kind of definition of 'interpretation' is appropriate? My answer is the latter.

First, the latter definition is more in line with language conventions. According to Richard E. Palmer, the most common use of 'interpretation' in the history of doctrine is 'to make something foreign and strange into familiar and intelligible by stating, explaining or translating'.[22] The most typical feature of 'foreign' and 'strange' is the inability to achieve spontaneous understanding. Language conventions are not only directly reflected in how people use a word, but also in the presupposition of word usage when discussing related issues. In legal hermeneutics, people's discussions of related issues presuppose this definition of interpretation. For example, the various methods of legal interpretation that people discuss, such as textual interpretation, systematic interpretation, historical interpretation, purpose interpretation, etc., all revolve around how to determine the meaning of legal texts when spontaneous understanding cannot be achieved or there are multiple possible understandings. Another example is 'authoritative interpretation' which people often say refers to the authoritative explanation of the meaning of legal texts by the specialized organs of the state within the scope of their statutory functions and powers, and this explanation is only necessary when the meaning of legal texts is not clear.

Second, this definition helps clarify the conceptual framework. Since the distinction between spontaneous understanding and conscious understanding (or the process of spontaneous thought and the activity of conscious reasoning) is objective, if interpretation is understood to include both, it is necessary to distinguish them in another way. For example, Liu Ping divides interpretation into 'descriptive interpretation' and 'discretionary interpretation'.[23] But it

---

20 Some cognitive linguists view spontaneous understanding as a decoding process, see Dan Sperber and Deirdre Wilson, 'Relevance: Communication and Cognition' (Jiang Yan tr, China Social Sciences Press 2008) 4–11.

21 *Supra* note 19, 17.

22 Richard E. Palmer, Hermeneutics: Interpretation Theory in Schleiermacher, Dilthey, Heidegger and Gadamer (Northwestern University Press, 1969) 13–14.

23 See Liu Ping, Legal Interpretation: A New Mechanism for Good Law and Good Governance (Shanghai People's Publishing, 2015) 38–39.

seems obvious to me that to speak of spontaneous understanding as 'descriptive interpretation' and conscious interpretation as 'discretionary interpretation' unnecessarily adds to the complexity of the conceptual framework. In fact, the difference between the spontaneous thinking process and conscious reasoning activity not only exists objectively but also manifests itself in many aspects. Integrating them under the same concept is not conducive to clarity of thought and may result in contradictions. For example, on the one hand, Barack believes that interpretation involves all understanding processes and, on the other hand, he believes that interpretation is a rational activity.[24] This evidently doesn't make sense since only conscious activities can be 'rationalized'.

Finally, this definition facilitates the exploration of the question of interpretation. In the field of law, the reason why people pay attention to interpretation is to provide appropriate methodological guidance for legal interpretation activities, and methodological guidance is only meaningful for those conscious activities. For the process of spontaneous thinking, we can only describe its process and reveal various factors affecting it, but cannot talk about how this process 'should' proceed.

3.2 Misunderstandings of the Theories of Davidson and Gadamer

Since interpretation is a conscious activity, the process of spontaneous understanding does not involve interpretation. But not everyone agrees. Some scholars disagree with the above point of view simply because they use the concept of 'interpretation' in different senses. That's off the table. But other scholars disagree because they misunderstand Davidson's 'radical interpretation' or Gadamer's 'identity of understanding and interpretation', and thus believe that interpretation refers not only to the activity of explicit meaning to achieve conscious understanding, but also to all processes of understanding.

Davidson pointed out that the problem of interpretation is not only for a different language but also for the same language. In the same language, some assumptions taken for granted are often ignored, which highlights the importance of 'radical interpretation'. Because 'radical interpretation' does not presuppose any knowledge of the meaning of the language used by the speaker, but only of the speaker's hold-true attitudes and environmental conditions. Only by recognizing how 'radical interpretation' is possible can we build a theory of meaning with truth as its basic concept.[25] Clearly, Davidson does not mean that any understanding requires a radical interpretation, but that any

24 *Supra* note 9, 3–13.

25 See Donald Davidson, Inquiries into Truth and Interpretation (Clarendon Press, 1984) 125–139.

understanding involves a theory of meaning established by examining radical interpretation.

If what Davidson offers is mostly a theory of meaning, what Gadamer offers is primarily an epistemology of how spontaneous understanding is possible. Gadamer has said: 'The task of hermeneutics is not at all to develop a procedure of understanding, but to clarify the conditions under which understanding takes place. … These conditions are so devoid of a methodological character that we can apply them optionally, which must in fact be given.'[26] It is in this sense that Gadamer talks about foresight, horizons, and fusions of horizons. Therefore, when Gadamer speaks of the identity of understanding and interpretation, he does not mean that any understanding requires conscious interpretive activities, but that no understanding can be separated from the interpretative framework determined by the 'historical experience of the community to which the interpreter belongs'.

3.3 Interpretation and Language Conventions

If interpretation does not occur in all processes of understanding, under what circumstances does it appear? In Andrei Marmor's view, we need to 'account for the distinction between those aspects of communication that are rule-determined and those that are not';[27] interpretation as a conscious activity involves 'those aspects of communication that are not determined by semantic rules or conventions'.[28] Marmor means that interpretation occurs and only occurs when language conventions do not provide a clear meaning, that is (1) if language conventions do not provide a clear meaning, then interpretation is required; (2) if language conventions can provide a clear meaning, no interpretation is needed. The following attempts to illustrate that, although interpretation usually occurs in situations where language conventions do not provide a clear meaning, they are not so closely related.

First, there are times when conscious interpretive activities are not required, even if language conventions do not provide explicit meaning. Take the close door command as an example. As mentioned above, suppose A orders B to 'close the door', and B turns his head and finds that the front door and the back door are both open. At this time, he may not know which door A is referring to. But B may not be puzzled, because he knows that A has a habit of entering the classroom and closing the front door. At this point, B's spontaneous comprehension is achieved, although language conventions do not provide a definite

[26] Hans-Georg Gadamer, Truth and Method (Hong Handing tr, Shanghai Translation Publishing 2004) 379.
[27] *Supra* note 4, 23.
[28] *Supra* note 4, 26.

meaning. This spontaneous understanding does not rely on language conventions, but on specific background knowledge shared by both communicators. This background knowledge forms part of what is often referred to as 'context'. Spontaneous understanding is achieved jointly by language conventions and context. Context includes not only the linguistic context, but also other situations such as communication time, places, participants, scenes, etc., as well as general or individual background knowledge.[29] In fact, the core problem of pragmatic theories is to describe how listeners use context to understand each attributive sentence they encounter. Although there are still disagreements about how to understand this phenomenon, there is no doubt that context can be used to compensate for the inadequacy of language conventions to achieve spontaneous understanding.

Second, in some cases, even if language conventions can provide definite meanings, conscious interpretation activities are still required because what language conventions provide is only the conventional meaning of expressions. Although the question of what kind of meaning is to be explored in interpretation is still controversial, it is obvious that it cannot meet the needs of most interpretation practices if we only stick to the conventional meaning. For example, in the field of everyday communication, interpretation mainly involves exploring the meaning that the speaker intends to express, rather than the conventional meaning of the texts.[30] In the field of literary criticism and the arts, interpretation involves not only the conventional meaning, the meaning intended by the speaker, but possibly even the reader's aesthetic experience.[31] In the field of law, interpretation also involves different meanings. As Rolf Wank said, legal interpretation begins with the meaning of the text, but it is still questionable which sense of the text is intended: 'semantics in everyday language or semantics in law, actual semantics or possible semantics, general legal semantics or special legal semantics, interpreter's meaning understanding or established semantics, the semantics when generated or when applicable'.[32] Thus, sometimes, although there is a definite conventional meaning, if there are reasons to believe that the conventional meaning is not consistent with the speaker's intended meaning or other reasonable meanings, interpretation may still be required.

---

[29] General background knowledge is encyclopedic knowledge, or common sense. To further understand the discussion of context, see Stephen C. Levinson, Pragmatics (Cambridge University Press, 1983) 23.

[30] See H. P. Grice, 'Utterer's Meaning, Sentence Meaning, and Word Meaning' (1968) 4 (3) Foundations of Language 225–242.

[31] See Joseph Raz, 'Interpretation without Intention' (1993) 18 (2) Tel Aviv University Law Review 407.

[32] *Supra* note 3, 69.

From the above discussion, although interpretation often occurs when language conventions cannot provide clear meanings, the failure of language conventions to provide clear meanings is neither a necessary condition nor a sufficient condition for interpretation. Fundamentally speaking, interpretation is not related to language conventions, but related to spontaneous understanding. Interpretation occurs when there are problems with spontaneous understanding. There are two situations: the language conventions cannot provide a clear meaning, so the spontaneous understanding cannot be achieved; there are reasons to believe that the meaning provided by language conventions is not a proper, correct, or optimal understanding of the text. It is worth noting that, although in the second case interpretation occurs because it is reasonable to believe that the meaning provided by the language conventions is not an adequate, correct, or optimal understanding of the text, this does not mean that it must give way to other understandings.

4. LEGAL INTERPRETATION AS A PROBLEM-SOLVING ACTIVITY

Different from daily communication and literary criticism, the legal interpretation is ultimately to apply the law to the individual case in order to draw a reasonable or correct judgment. Therefore, to deeply understand the legal interpretation, it is not only necessary to understand the interpretation in the general sense but also to think about what activities in the application process of the law can be reasonably called interpretation.

4.1 The Process of Law Application

Let us use a simple example to examine the process of law application and the problems that may arise. Suppose a town has issued a regulation that ‘cars are prohibited from entering the park’ (regulation 1).[33] Now let’s look at how this rule applies in different situations.[34]

---

[33] Hart discussed the ‘open structure’ of the law with the example of ‘banning vehicles from the park’. For the convenience of the following discussion, the ‘vehicle’ is replaced here with the more commonly used ‘automobile’ in Chinese.

[34] The six cases listed below are not all possible cases where the law applies; they are only necessary for the discussion in this chapter. For example, as we will see below, there are lexical ambiguities in addition to syntactic ambiguities mentioned in case 3.

Case 1: Alice drives the truck A into the park.

This is the simplest case: according to regulation 1, A should be prohibited from entering the park. This applicable process can be described in the form of first-order predicate logic as follows:

(1) For every x, if x is a car, then x is prohibited from entering the park.
(2) A is a car.
(3) A is prohibited from entering the park.

Among them, (1) is the major premise for expressing the content of regulation 1, (2) is the minor premise for expressing the facts of the case at hand, and (3) is the conclusion. This simple application process is often called the legal syllogism. This application process can proceed smoothly because it is easy to judge whether A is a car. According to our language habits and common sense of life, trucks are obviously cars. But that judgment is not easy in all cases. For example, in the following case.

Case 2: Budd drives the electric tricycle B into the park.

In this case, the application of the regulation may be puzzling, because the language habits and common sense of life do not tell us whether the electric tricycle is a car. Since it is doubtful whether the car includes electric tricycles, it is doubtful that the small premise 'B is a car' is true, which makes the applicant unable to draw the conclusion that 'b is prohibited from entering the park'.

In the process of applying law, such problems are common, such as whether a man who knows and buys fakes is a 'consumer',[35] whether a tomato is a 'fruit',[36] and whether hydrochloric acid is a 'weapon'.[37] In the process of law application, not only the minor premise but also the major premise may have problems, for example, in the following case 3.

---

[35] There are different answers to this question in judicial practice. In 2019, for two cases with highly similar circumstances, the Qingdao Intermediate People's Court and the Beijing Third Intermediate People's Court made different judgments. The Qingdao Intermediate People's Court found that the act of buying fake goods is a consumer behavior, while the Beijing Third Intermediate People's Court found that the person who bought fake goods is not a consumer. See the Civil Judgment of the Intermediate People's Court of Qingdao, Shandong Province (2019) No. 263, Lu 02, and the Civil judgment of the Third Intermediate People's Court of Beijing. Beijing (2019) No. 6950, Jing 03.

[36] See Nix v. Hedden, 149 US 304 (1893).

[37] See Arthur Kaufmann and Winfold Hasmer, Introduction to Contemporary Legal Philosophy and Legal Theory (Zheng Yongliu tr, Law Press 2002) 183–184.

Case 3: The regulation in the management regulation is not 'cars are prohibited from entering the park', but 'large animals or cars are prohibited from entering the park'. Clare drives a little car C into the park.

In this case, it is necessary to determine the application area of the word 'large', that is, whether the regulation means 'prohibit (large animals) or (cars)' or 'prohibit large (animals or cars)'. In judicial practice, such difficult problems are common too. For example, Article 244 (I) of Chinese criminal law stipulates:

> Where an employer, in violation of the laws and regulations on labor administration, hires minors under the age of 16 to conduct extremely intensive physical labor, work at heights or work underground or work under an explosive, flammable, radioactive or poisonous environment, if the circumstance is serious, the persons who are held to be directly responsible shall be sentenced to fixed-term imprisonment of not more than three years or limited incarceration, and shall also be fined …

According to the regulation, the crime of employing child workers to engage in serious labor covers three circumstances: (1) employing child labor to engage in super intensity physical labor; (2) employing child labor to engage in heights and underground work; (3) employing child labor to work in explosive, flammable, radioactive, toxic, and other dangerous environments. It is unclear whether the condition of 'serious circumstances' applies only to the third or all three cases mentioned above.

Case 4: Regulation 1 is still 'cars are prohibited from entering the park', but another management regulation of the town stipulates that 'no place shall obstruct the entry of police vehicles' (regulation 2). Deford drives the police car D into the park.

In this case, since D is a car, it can be concluded that D is prohibited from entering the park under regulation 1. However, D is also a police vehicle, and according to regulation 2, D is allowed to enter the park. Obviously, these two conclusions cannot be held together. To determine which conclusion is true, we first need to resolve the conflicts between the rules.

Case 5: The regulations still state that 'cars are prohibited from entering the park'. There was a fire in the park. Elan drives the fire engine E into the park.

In this case, it may be difficult to apply the rules as to whether E is to be barred from the park. But this is not because the person applying the regulation does not know whether E is a car (according to our linguistic habits and common sense of life, the fire engine is obviously a car), but because the person applying the regulation feels that although E is a car, it is still reasonable to allow it in.

There are usually two different interpretations of this. One understanding is that there is an implicit regulation in the legal order allowing fire engines to enter the park, and that this implicit regulation is more effective than the plain stipulation 1. In this way, case 5 can be classified as case 4. Another understanding is that any plain regulation in the statute is not absolute, or is said to carry an implied exception, that is 'unless …'. If a strict application of the express regulation would result in grossly unreasonable or unjust consequences, the 'unless …' part will work.

Case 6: The regulation in the management regulation is still 'no cars from entering the park'. Frank drives a modified bike with a power plant, F, and tries to enter the park.

In this case, although F is not a car, it is reasonable to 'treat' it as a car and prohibit it from entering. If in case 5 the regulation presents an 'over-inclusive' problem by including objects that should not have been included, then in case 6 the regulation presents an 'under-inclusive' problem, that is, objects that should be included are not included. Over-coverage and under-coverage may be collectively described as inadequate coverage.

Of the six cases listed above, only in case 1 is the regulation applied smoothly, and cases 2 to 6 encounter different kinds of problems. In case 1, the conclusion can be drawn by combining the major and minor premises. However, in cases 2 to 6, the major and minor premises must be clarified. We can refer to the applicable activities in case 1 as conventional applications, and to the activities in cases 2 to 6 that specify the major and minor premises as problem-solving activities in unconventional applications. The question now is whether all kinds of problem-solving activities in unconventional applications are legal interpretations.

4.2 Legal Interpretation Aims at Clarifying the Meaning of the Law

First, there is no dispute that the above problem-solving activities in cases 2 and 3 are interpretations. Cases 2 and 3 both deal with the question of the meaning of legal texts. In case 2, to determine whether an electric tricycle is a car, it is first necessary to make clear what is the 'car' mentioned in the regulation. Neil MacCormick has called determining whether an electric tricycle is a car a *'classification problem, identification problem or qualitative problem'*.[38] If only in terms of the judgment activity itself, MacCormick's above statement is correct, but the activity designed to solve the difficulty of judgment is not 'classification', 'identification' or 'qualitative', but providing the basis for these. This basis is a statement of the meaning of a general term. Case 3 is an example of a syntactic ambiguity, which first needs to be removed when stipulating that a syntactic ambiguity exists. Linguistics refers to this process as disambiguation. Disambiguation, as a conscious activity, aims to clarify the meaning of expressions, so it is also an interpretive activity. In legal texts, there is not only syntactic ambiguity, but also lexical ambiguity. For example, Article 122 of the General Principles of the Civil Law, adopted in 1986, provides that '[i]f a product's unqualified quality causes property or personal damage to others, the manufacturer or seller of the product shall bear civil liability according to law …'. The 'civil liability' may be 'fault liability' or 'no-fault liability'.

Although both case 2 and 3 are interpretations, they play different roles in legal reasoning. The doubt-solving activity in case 2 determines the minor premise in the legal syllogism, while the troubleshooting activity in case 3 determines the major premise. It is precisely because the problem-solving activities of interpretation can determine both minor premises and major premises that some scholars define legal interpretation as 'the process in which the adjudicator collects, organizes arguments, and deduces the major premises and minor premises of legal reasoning by using specific methods in order to demonstrate the rationality of legal reasoning conclusions under the scenario of specific legal problems.'[39] The problem with this definition is that not all activities that derive major and minor premises are interpretations. For example, few would consider the troubleshooting activity in case 4 to be an interpretation, but it is an activity that deduces the major premises.

In dispute are case 5 and 6. There are obvious differences between cases 5 and 6, and cases 2 and 3. The difficulties in cases 2 and 3 result from unclear legal regulations, while the difficulties in cases 5 and 6 do not. In cases 5 and 6, the rule is clear, and the question is whether it should be applied. Specifically, in case 5, the question is whether to add an implicit exception to the rule. In case 6, the question arises as to whether the regulation should be applied by analogy to the facts of cases not covered by it. None of these questions are about the meaning of the rules. If the person who applies the rule eventually decides to add an implied exception or apply it by analogy, it cannot be said that the meaning of the rule has been clarified, but only that the rule itself has

---

[38] See Neil MacCormick, Rhetoric and the Rule of Law: A Theory of Legal Reasoning (Cheng Chaoyang tr, Peking University Press 2014) 58.

[39] *Supra* note 10, 13.

been modified. That is, in case 5, the regulation is amended to 'No motor vehicles are allowed to enter the park, except fire engines.' In case 6, the regulation was amended to 'No cars or bicycles with power mounts are allowed to enter the park.' It is in this sense that the problem-solving activities in cases 5 and 6 are often referred to as 'Richterliche Rechtsfortbildung'. However, there are still some scholars who refer to the activities covered improperly in situations 5 and 6 as legal interpretation.[40] This view is in effect a claim that Richterliche Rechtsfortbildung is a form of legal interpretation. This broad interpretation of the law is not appropriate.

In another article, I discuss three important aspects that distinguish the continuation of law from the interpretation of law: (1) The continuation of law needs to bear additional argumentation responsibility; (2) The continuation of law requires special institutional restrictions; (3) The continuation of law needs special methodological norms.[41] Starting from these three aspects, if Richterliche Rechtsfortbildung is regarded as a kind of legal interpretation, it will reduce the necessity, legitimacy, and objectivity of legal interpretation.

4.3 Does Routine Application Also Require Legal Interpretation?

There are three common arguments in support of the claim that 'conventional application also requires legal interpretation': (1) H. L. A. Hart's 'rules do not apply to themselves',[42] or Arthur Kaufman's description of the logical gap between norms and facts;[43] (2) There is always the possibility of multiple understandings of the meaning of a legal text; (3) The meaning or legal content of a legal text is given by the process of interpretation. I have criticized the first two reasons elsewhere,[44] so I only discuss the third reason here.

---

40 *Supra* note 2, 117. The book talks about broad approaches to legal interpretation, including 'narrow approaches to legal interpretation', 'loophole supplemental approaches', and 'value supplemental approaches to uncertain concepts'; *Supra* note 23, 46. The book expounds 'the complexity of social phenomena that cannot be exhausted by legal norms ... There are loopholes and deficiencies, and there needs to be a mechanism to make up for them after the fact. In practice, the best mechanism to make up for them is legal interpretation'.

41 See Chen Kun, 'Standard between Legal Interpretation and Richterliche Rechtsfortbildung' (2021) 43 (4) Chinese Journal of Law 22–25.

42 H. L. A. Hart, Essays in Jurisprudence and Philosophy (Clarendon Press, 1983) 106.

43 *Supra* note 37, 184.

44 See Chen Kun, 'Reiterating the Principle of Clarity of Legal Interpretation' (2013) 30 (1) Studies in Law and Business 87–88.

For Barak, interpretation is the rational activity that gives meaning to a legal text.[45] This activity is divided into two parts: one is to identify several possible linguistic meanings of legal texts, and the other is to identify one of these linguistic meanings as legal meaning.[46] If Barak is right about the process of applying the law, then even the plainest legal text needs to be explained, because without interpretation it has no legal meaning. The so-called 'straightforwardness' only means that it has only one possible linguistic meaning, and we still need to identify this linguistic meaning as the legal meaning.

There are two different understandings of the statement of 'giving meaning to the legal text' in the above reasons. One understanding is that a legal text does not have legal meaning until the interpretation is complete. Another interpretation holds that this statement is metaphorical; that is, before interpretation, the legal text already has legal significance, and the process of interpretation only reveals it. In my opinion, whatever understanding is taken, this reason is untenable.

The first understanding says that the legal text does not have legal meaning until the completion of the interpretation. In fact, it says that the rules in the legal text are created by the interpreter rather than the legislator through the act of interpretation. This is not only different from people's conventional views on law, but also makes law lose its role in regulating justice. As Karl Larenz points out in his criticism of Gadamer's neglect of the function of rules as standards: 'legal workers ask about the "normative binding force of the understood meaning" precisely because he rightly regards norms as a standard by which "cases" can be measured. The question is how the standard can possibly weigh a case if it itself must be determined in an "applicable" process to determine its final content.'[47] Moreover, if the rule is created in the act of interpretation, then the legal text will have a different meaning in each course of application. 'A standard requires itself to apply to all such cases. If the content of the standard must be understood differently according to each moment, that is, according to each specific environment, the standard will not become the standard ... The idea of same standard as one of the basic elements of justice will become a pure fantasy.'[48]

The second understanding is that the interpretation process is only to reveal or confirm the legal significance of the legal text. When the legal text is clear,

---

45 *Supra* note 9, 6–7.

46 Lawrence Solum takes a similar view, except that he calls the first part 'interpretation' and the second 'construction'. See Lawrence B. Solum, 'The Interpretation-Construction Distinction' (2010) 27 (1) Constitutional Commentary 95–118. Lawrence Solum's claims are detailed in section 5.

47 *Supra* note 1, 274–275.

48 *Supra* note 1, 275

people directly understand the legal meaning and do not need an additional disclosure and confirmation activity. For example, in case 1, it is absurd to say that the person applying the regulation first finds that the linguistic meaning of the provision 'no cars entering the park' is 'no cars entering the park', and then confirms that its legal meaning is 'no cars entering the park'. The person who applies the rule directly understands the meaning of the rule and applies it to the case.[49] When the legal text is unclear, people do not first give several possible linguistic meanings and then choose one of them. In Barak's view, language encompasses a range of different possibilities, but it is not infinite or without boundaries.[50] Thus, we can first give several possible meaning options and then determine one of them as the legal meaning. If only the conventional meaning of the text is considered, then Barak's statement is correct. But interpretation is not necessarily limited by conventional meaning, at least sometimes by the meaning that the speaker wants to express, and the speaker's meaning of a text has no boundaries. As such, the procedure outlined by Barak is unworkable.

To sum up, in the routine application of legal texts, there is no need for legal interpretation. Legal interpretation is a problem-solving activity, and there is no problem in conventional application.

5. LEGAL INTERPRETATION AS A NORMATIVE ACTIVITY

A third approach starting from a certain linguistic (philosophical) foundation defines 'legal interpretation' as the activity that reveals a specific type of meaning within legal texts. The purpose of this section is to illustrate that interpretation is not inherently related to any meaning type. If an activity can reasonably be described as inquiring into the meaning of legal texts, regardless of the type of meaning of the legal texts being explored, it qualifies as an interpretive activity. The question of what kind of meaning legal interpretation should explore is a normative issue, which should not and cannot be answered by clarifying the concept of legal interpretation.

---

49 It is worth noting that in the application of the law, people usually reconstruct the text of the legal regulations according to the need. For example, if the law says, 'if A or B, then C', before applying the provision, the regulation needs to be reconstructed into 'if A, then C' and 'if B, then C'. Although this reconstruction is based on understanding the relevant regulations, it is not an interpretive activity to clarify the meaning.

50 *Supra* note 9, 25.

5.1 Interpretation and the Speaker's Meaning

According to some scholars, only activities that explore legislative intent are considered as legal interpretation. 'You cannot coherently think of yourself as still doing textual interpretation as soon as you appeal to something beyond authorial intention—for example, the original public meaning or evolving principles of justice.'[51] Scholars have put forward three distinct arguments to support this proposition: (1) Apart from the speaker's meaning, the text has no additional meaning. Since interpretation aims to explore the meaning of the text, it can only be an activity that seeks the speaker's meaning. In this context, '[j]ust as intentionalism is not a method in competition with other methods, neither is it a theory in competition with other theories. It is the answer to a theoretical question—what is the meaning of a text? (any text, not a particular text)—but the answer is not itself a theory; it is just the right answer to the question, and therefore the right definition of what interpretation necessarily is, an attempt to specify what some purposive agent meant by these words, marks, sounds, paintings, gestures, etc.'[52] (2) Without presupposing information about the author or relying on authorial intention, it is impossible to ascertain the meaning of a text. Hence, '[i]f we want to make sense of interpretation, then, there is no getting away, even moderately, from the author's intention. Language counts; linguistic rules matter. But we cannot even decide what language a text is written in—and therefore what rules matter, without deciding what language the author intended to write it in—and therefore what rules the author was following.'[53] (3) Legal texts served as the means through which legislators express the norms they created, and interpreting legal texts means clarifying what norms the legislators have established on earth. 'Of course, we can ignore the authorially intended meanings if we do not like them, in which case we have become the authors of the legal norms, not those whose symbols we might appropriate to convey our meanings.'[54]

Cass R. Sunstein has previously provided a counterargument to this claim. In his view, although interpretation in everyday life is to inquire into the speaker's intent, it is based on the practical need for successful communication. However, legal practice serves different objectives.[55] From the author's

---

[51] Walter B. Michaels, 'A Defense of Old Originalism' (2009) 31 (1) Western New England Law Review 21.

[52] Stanley Fish, 'Intention Is All There Is: A Critical Analysis of Aharon Barak's Purposive Interpretation in Law' (2008) 29 (3) Cardozo Law Review 1114.

[53] *Supra* note 12, Stephen Knapp and Walter B. Michaels, 664.

[54] *Supra* note 6, 544.

[55] See Cass R. Sunstein, 'There Is Nothing that Interpretation Just Is' (2015) 30 (2) Constitutional Commentary 194–195.

perspective, Sunstein's counterargument is not very convincing. Of the above three reasons, the first two apply to all texts; thus, the uniqueness of legal practice cannot serve as a valid counterargument. As for the last reason, it relies on the premise that legal texts are a form of communicative text. To refute this, one must demonstrate why legislation cannot be considered a typical communicative act.

However, although Sunstein's counterargument may not be very compelling, it does not necessarily mean that the three arguments mentioned above are correct. Regarding the first argument, the author has extensively discussed it elsewhere, and it will not be reiterated here.[56] The second argument unfolds at the epistemological level, suggesting that without considering authorial intention, we cannot know what language the text is written in or what language rules the author followed, thus making it impossible to determine the meaning of a text. This author thinks this statement is erroneous. Indeed, for a consciously created text, the author always uses a specific language to express their intent and ideas, generally following various rules of that language in the process. However, this does not imply that the readers need to consciously ponder the language and rules the author used before understanding the text he created. As mentioned earlier, the process of comprehending the text typically occurs spontaneously, where readers neither require conscious contemplation of these matters nor need to consciously reflect upon any issues. 'A modular (sub-personal) pragmatic processor which, when all goes well, quickly and automatically delivers speaker meaning (explicators and implicatures).'[57] The third argument regards legislation as a form of communicative action. The issue with this argument lies in the fact that legislation is not a typical form of communicative action. Even if we describe laws as commands, they are not akin to commands issued by A to B, which involve only two parties. Instead, they involve at least three parties: the legislator, the interpreter, and the public. The law addresses both interpreters (as judicial standards) and the public (as behavioral standards), with its primary focus being on the general public. Considering this, interpreters must not only consider what the legislator, as the speaker, intends to convey, but also anticipate how the public will perceive the speaker's expression. Because of this, as Justice Antonin Gregory Scalia emphasized, what matters is not what legislators intend to say, but what the law

56 See Chen Kun, 'Determination of Reference and Legal Interpretation: A Referential Theory Applicable to General Legal Terms' (2016) 38 (5) Chinese Journal of Law 119–120.

57 Robyn Carston, 'Linguistic Meaning, Communicated Meaning, and Cognitive Pragmatics' (2002) 17 (1–2) Mind and Language 146.

indeed says: 'Men may intend what they will, but it is only the laws that they enact that bind us.'[58]

The above arguments are not intended to refute the position of interpretation of intentionalism or endorse the (new) textualism position of interpretation represented by Scalia and others. Instead, they simply suggest that exploring legislative intent is not an inherent requirement of the concept of legal interpretation. Perhaps in some cases, or even generally speaking, legislative intent is not only attainable but also significant—significant enough to outweigh the value of fairness expectations pursued by textualists. Therefore, the exploration of legislative intent should be undertaken. On the other hand, it could also be argued conversely, as advocated by textualists, that legislative history materials are unreliable,[59] and the legislative intent is not of great importance.[60] However, these are factual and normative disagreements that cannot be resolved by analyzing the concept of legal interpretation.

5.2 Interpretation and the 'True Meaning'

Michael S. Moore strongly opposes the interpretation theory of intentionalism and advocates that 'the dead hand of the past ought not to govern [our interpretation], … and any theory of interpretation that demands that it does is a bad theory.'[61] However, unlike other scholars opposing intentionalism, Moore's opposition to intentionalism is built upon his foundation of the realist theories of meaning.

Using 'death' as an example, Moore illustrates the difference between his endorsed realist theories of meaning and the traditional conventionalist theories of meaning. From the perspective of conventionalist theories of meaning, the meaning of 'death' is determined by the descriptive attributes commonly attributed to the word, such as 'cessation of heart function', 'cessation of breathing', or 'loss of consciousness'. Realist theories of meaning, however, do not contend that meaning is determined by linguistic convention. In the context of 'death', realist theories of meaning hold that it refers to a natural kind event with true nature. The term 'death' is applied to those who are 'really dead' rather than those deemed deceased by a linguistic community. As for the

---

58 Antonin Scalia, 'Common-Law Courts in a Civil-Law System: The Role of the United States Federal Courts in Interpreting the Constitution', in Amy Gutmann, A Matter of Interpretation (Princeton University Press, 1998) 17.

59 See Eric Lasky, 'Perplexing Problems with Plain Meaning' (1999) 27 (4) Hofstra Law Review 899.

60 See Frank Easterbrook, 'The Role of Original Intent in Statutory Construction' (1988) 11 (1) Harvard Journal of Law & Public Policy 60.

61 *Supra* note 13, 357.

true nature of 'death' or what qualifies as being 'truly deceased', these are to be unveiled by the best scientific theories. According to Moore, realist theories of meaning appear to be more rational. Firstly, on an intuitive level, we may not know whether a person has died, but there is always a correct answer to this question: either he has died or he has not. This intuition aligns with realist theories of meaning rather than conventionalist theories of meaning. Secondly, suppose we come across a person whose heart has ceased beating, whose breathing has stopped, and who has lost consciousness. According to past beliefs, he is dead. However, if the latest scientific theory informs us that taking a certain action promptly could revive him, intuitively, we could say that the past beliefs were wrong, and he was not dead in fact, rather than saying that the past beliefs were not wrong because their concept of 'death' was different from ours.[62] Since realist theories of meaning are more reasonable and the true meaning of words is determined by the true nature of things, interpreting a word is exploring the true nature of things that the terms refer to. In the process of exploring the true nature of things, what is crucial is accurate facts and moral knowledge, while the intent of the legislators serves only as a 'heuristic device' related to interpretation.[63]

Moore's above argument relies heavily on the assumption of natural kinds. However, most general terms in the legal field are not natural kinds of terms and do not possess any so-called true nature. The reason why Moore's argument seems plausible is that he uses the example of 'death' to discuss that 'death' might indeed be a natural kind of event. In other words, for 'death', there might be some true nature that explains why death is characterized by the cessation of heart and lung functions, together with loss of consciousness. However, for most everyday words such as 'table', 'chair', and similar general legal terms such as 'destruction' or 'legal entity', it is difficult to believe that there is any true nature in the things they refer to that can be used to explain the specific characteristics they each possess.

After realizing this difficulty, Moore further discusses 'functional kinds' and 'moral kinds'. Functional kinds refer to categorizing things based on their functions, considering the function as their true nature. For example, a lawnmower; its true nature would be cutting grass since cutting grass is its function.[64] In legal practice, we can indeed view certain general legal terms as functional kinds of terms, but this approach may lead to absurd consequences. For instance, we could label anything that can cause serious harm as

62 *Supra* note 13, 291–301.

63 *Supra* note 13, 357.

64 See Michael S. Moore, 'Law as a Functional Kind', in Robert P. George, Natural Law Theory: Contemporary Essays (Oxford University Press, 1992) 207–208.

a 'weapon' to address the issue of whether hydrochloric acid, which troubled Arthur Kaufman, is a weapon.[65] However, almost everything can cause severe harm, such as a man's fist, a woman's high heels, or a pet dog. If we were to classify all of these as weapons, it would be absurd, evidently. The reason why function cannot be regarded as a true nature is simple: whether something has a particular function depends not only on the thing itself but also on how it is used. As the saying goes, '[i]f all you have is a hammer, everything looks like a nail'. Conversely, if you want to hammer a nail, then everything will look like a hammer. In daily life, we can take shortcuts, but if functionality serves as true nature within the legal context, it will lead to confusion and chaos.

In addition to functional kinds, Moore also discusses moral kinds. For example, the meaning of 'cruel' does not depend on how people understand 'cruel', but rather on the true nature of the moral kinds to which 'cruel' refers.[66] In the author's view, the problem with moral kinds is even more severe than functional kinds. This is because moral concepts are formed through people's common evaluations. For example, what is the true nature of all 'cruel' action? After all, apart from being evaluated as 'cruel', there seems to be no common characteristic among them. Of course, we could say that their true nature is 'cruelty', but then, how do we determine if an action has this nature 'cruelty'? For all general terms α, we can generally state that the entity it refers to possesses the quality 'α-ness'. However, unless there is an independent path of understanding, this is merely a pretext.

5.3 Linguistic Meaning and Legal Content

Legal interpretation is not an activity aimed at delving into legislative intent, nor is it an activity to unveil the true meaning; rather, it is an activity to clarify the meaning of legal texts. Perhaps in some cases or even generally, legislative intent and true meaning (or other meanings of legal texts) should be considered as standards for interpretation. However, this conclusion should be grounded in people's reflection and balance of the nature and function of law, the institutional rule of judges, as well as political concepts such as democracy and the rule of law, rather than being based on a specific understanding of the concept of legal interpretation. If we were internationalists, what we ought to do is to

65 Kaufman initially classified hydrochloric acid as a 'weapon' due to its potential for causing serious harm, but later felt that 'the limits of permissible analogy were drawn too broadly.' See Kaufman: 'Analogy and *Essence of Things* – A Discussion on Type Theory' (Wu Congzhou tr, 2nd ed., Xuelin Cultural Enterprise 1999) 161.

66 See Michael S. Moore, 'The Interpretive Turn in Modern Theory: A Turn of the Worse?' (1989) 41 (4) Stanford Law Review 882.

present a normative argument to demonstrate the correctness of intentionalism and the incorrectness of other positions of interpretation. This approach should not involve preemptively excluding other positions of interpretation by narrowly construing legal interpretation as solely an inquiry into legislative intent. Legal interpretation always involves normative considerations, going beyond the mere revelation of a specific meaning within legal texts. It is in this sense that legal interpretation is a normative activity.

Now let's examine a different perspective that attempts to deny the normativity of interpretation by the interpretation–construction distinction. For example, in Lawrence B. Solum's view, interpretation involves the revelation of linguistic meaning within legal texts, guided by linguistic facts about patterns of usage. It is considered 'value neutral', or only 'thinly normative'. The construction is normative; it is through construction that the linguistic meaning of legal texts is transformed into legal content.[67]

Despite Solum's confusing terminology, such as using 'legal effect',[68] 'legal doctrine',[69] or 'legal rules'[70] interchangeably when referring to 'legal content', we can still glean a rough understanding of his intended meaning through the various examples he provided. As mentioned earlier, Aharon Barak divides legal interpretation activities into two stages: first, identifying several possible linguistic meanings that the legal texts may carry, and second, selecting one of these various linguistic meanings as the legal meaning.[71] Solum's argument roughly suggests that only the first stage is interpretation, and the second stage is construction. However, there are two points worth noting. Firstly, construction mentioned by him is not confined to determining legal meaning but also encompasses the establishment of the legal effect of legal meaning and adjusting rules based on constitutionality or systemic consistency. This is why Solum uses terms such as 'legal doctrine' or 'legal content'. Since the preceding text has already demonstrated the need to differentiate between interpretation activities and non-interpretive ones, we shall omit this issue here and refrain from further discussion. Secondly, it is not clear whether Solum's notion of linguistic meaning refers to a specific meaning of legal texts or all its possible meanings. His statements about 'the meaning of the language is determined by patterns of usage' seem to point to the conventional meaning of legal texts. However, he also mentioned that semantic content can be understood differently: 'Original-Intentions Originalists may believe that the semantic content of the Constitution was fixed by the intentions of the Framers or ratifiers.

67 *Supra* note 46, 104.
68 *Supra* note 46, 103.
69 *Supra* note 46, 99.
70 *Supra* note 46, 104.
71 *Supra* note 9, 6–7.

Original-public-meaning Originalists may believe that the linguistic meaning of the Constitution is the meaning that the constitutional text had to the competent speakers of American English at the time the Constitution was framed and ratified. Some Living Constitutionalists may believe that the meaning of the Constitution is fixed by contemporary usage at the time interpretation occurs. In other words, there are various theories of constitutional interpretation—in the sense that the interpretation-construction distinction gives that phrase constitutional interpretation—but all of these theories aim at the recovery of the linguistic meaning of the constitutional text.'[72] In this context, it is evident that linguistic meaning refers to all potential meanings of a legal text, and not just all the possible meanings within the semantic scope as articulated by Barak, since Solum mentions the notion of intended meaning. The following passage aims to elucidate that regardless of which interpretation is adopted, it is unreasonable to dismiss the normativity of legal interpretation through the interpretation–construction distinction.

Let us start by examining the first understanding, which is that linguistic meaning refers to conventional meaning. This understanding is quite common in fact. For instance, from Barak's discussions about 'the boundaries of language are the boundaries of interpretation' and 'activities beyond the boundaries of language pertain to non-interpretive activities', it becomes evident that the linguistic meaning Barak refers to aligns with conventional meaning.[73] Similarly, when Hart and Sacks assert that 'language is a social institution",[74] and when Max Radin claims that '[l]anguage has a maximum and a minimum of extension',[75] they all comprehend language within the realm of conventional meaning. It is precisely because Solum sometimes adopts this understanding that he states the vagueness of the text can only be resolved through construction rather than interpretation.[76] If linguistic meaning is not understood solely in terms of conventional meaning, then interpretation aimed at revealing linguistic meaning may not necessarily be incapable of resolving vagueness. For instance, if we interpret the linguistic meaning as the speaker's meaning, we can resolve the vagueness of texts by exploring the speaker's intent. Even in a specific understanding of linguistic meaning, there may not inherently be ontological vagueness. For instance, Moore, grounded in realist theories of

---

72 *Supra* note 46, 101.

73 *Supra* note 9, 18–19.

74 See Henry M. Hart and Albert M. Sacks, The Legal Process (Foundation Press, 1994) 1188.

75 See Max Radin, 'Statutory Interpretation' (1930) 43 (6) Harvard Law Review 866.

76 *Supra* note 46, 106.

meaning, denies the existence of vagueness.[77] Certainly, we can interpret linguistic meaning as conventional meaning, thereby understanding legal interpretation as the activity of revealing the conventional meaning of the legal texts. However, what cannot be denied is that beyond conventional meaning, there are other meanings, including speaker meaning. Given this, the rationale behind such an understanding of linguistic meaning needs justification, which requires defense and cannot be separated from a reflection on normative issues, for example, why conventional meaning is important. In other words, when linguistic meaning is understood in terms of conventional meaning, the interpretation–construction distinction discussed earlier does not eliminate the normativity of legal interpretation; it merely prepositions the normative arguments.

Let us consider the second interpretation, where linguistic meaning refers to all possible meanings of legal texts. In this understanding, by constraining interpretation to the process of revealing different meanings, this approach indeed eliminates the normativity of legal interpretation. However, such a definition of legal interpretation is quite inappropriate.

Firstly, it severely weakens the significance of legal interpretation. The reason legal interpretation deserves attention is that through interpretation activities, the meaning of legal texts is established, the judgments of subsumption are accomplished, specific normative guidance for individual cases is formed, and the major and minor premises of legal reasoning are established. If the outcomes of legal interpretation only reveal the various meanings within legal texts, without indicating which meaning is correct, then the tasks cannot be accomplished. In practice, there is no need for a separate theoretical term that specifically designates the activity of revealing semantic content.

Furthermore, taking a step back, even if a term is necessary, there will be difficulties in determining the scope it refers to. If all processes that reveal potential meanings are considered as 'interpretation' in this sense, then it encompasses both spontaneous, intuitive processes of understanding, as well as conscious, reflective interpretation activities, thereby losing its inherent consistency. However, if only the conscious activities that reveal potential meanings are considered as 'interpretation' in this sense, then since people's grasp of conventional meaning is mostly achieved spontaneously, conventional meaning cannot be one of the alternatives to be considered for subsequent 'construction', and this is evidently absurd.

Finally, the reason why the determination of the scope of 'legal interpretation' under this understanding has encountered difficulties is that this interpretation erroneously depicts the process of ascertaining the meaning of legal

77 *Supra* note 13, 307–309.

texts. In the process of determining the meaning of legal texts, people do not first unveil every potential meaning and then choose based on certain normative considerations. Instead, they follow the "Principle of Least Effort" and only explore relevant meanings when necessary.[78] For instance, only when preliminary information suggests that conventional meaning might be unreasonable would people delve into the speaker's meaning. 'All mainstream interpreters start with the linguistic convention (as to syntax, vocabulary, and other aspects of usage).'[79] Of course, this does not imply that the speaker's meaning is necessarily superior to the conventional meaning. However, if the conventional meaning does not trigger any disputes, then the speaker's meaning, as well as other meanings, would not be considered from the outset. This is not only due to political values such as fair expectation and the stability of law but also because, in general, conventional meaning reflects the legislator's purpose and intent,[80] or at the very least, serves as 'the least unreliable' evidence.[81] This significance of legislative intent is typically defended by invoking democratic values.[82] It can be observed that legal interpretation activities are normative from the outset. Not only does each meaning, including conventional meaning, presuppose relevant values, but also whether a certain meaning requires exploration remains inseparable from normative judgment. In simple terms, legal

---

[78] The principle of *least effort* is a common principle in language communication phenomena. As early as Ferdinand de Saussure's *Course in General Linguistics*, the phenomenon of minimizing pronunciation in language was mentioned. See Ferdinand de Saussure, Course in General Linguistics (Liu Li tr, China Social Sciences Press 2009) 185–187. Pragmatics scholars like Paul Grice and Laurence Horn have analyzed the principle of least effort in pragmatic processes. See Paul Grice, 'Further Notes on Logic and Conversation', in Peter Cole, Syntax and Semantics 9: Pragmatics (Academic Press, 1978) 113–127; Lawrence Horn, 'Toward a New Taxonomy for Pragmatic Inference: Q-based and R-based Implicature', in Deborah Schiffrin, Meaning, Form, and Use in Context: Linguistic Applications (Georgetown University Press, 1984) 11–42. George K. Zipf systematically discussed the principle of least effort in language use and development. See George K. Zipf, Human Behavior and the Principle of Least Effort: An Introduction to Human Ecology (Xue Zhaofeng tr, Shanghai People's Publishing, 2016).

[79] Caleb Nelson, 'What is Textualism' (2005) 91 (2) Virginia Law Review 376.

[80] See John Manning, 'The Absurdity Doctrine' (2003) 116 (8) Harvard Law Review 2398.

[81] See John Manning, 'Textualism and Legislative Intent' (2005) 91 (2) Virginia Law Review 433.

[82] See Paul Brest, 'The Misconceived Quest for the Original Understanding' (1980) 60 (2) Boston University Law Review 204; Raoul Berger, Government by Judiciary (Harvard University Press, 1977) 291.

interpretation is not distinctively divided into the following two stages: first, a descriptive activity that reveals the linguistic meaning, and then a normative activity that determines the legal meaning.

6. CONCLUSION

This chapter tries to further clarify and define the concept of legal interpretation based on consensus. It has been agreed that legal interpretation is an activity related to the meaning of legal texts. The existing divergences mainly lie in: (1) starting from the general meaning of 'interpretation', does interpretation occur in all understanding processes, or only when language conventions cannot provide a clear meaning? (2) starting from the process of legal application, does legal interpretation take place in all legal application processes, or is it only a part of the legal application process as a mystery-solving activity? If legal interpretation is only a mystery-solving activity, what kind of mystery does it solve? (3) starting from the philosophy of language, which meaning of the legal text should be clarified in legal interpretation?

Through detailed analysis, this chapter clarifies in turn that: (1) legal interpretation is a conscious activity, which neither occurs in all understanding processes nor only occurs when language conventions fail to provide a clear meaning but instead occurs when there are problems in spontaneous understanding; (2) legal interpretation is a kind of mystery-solving activity, which only occurs in part of the legal application process. Legal interpretation solves the problem of meaning, rather than the problem of force or application; (3) legal interpretation is a conventional activity and is not inherently related to any interpretive positions. What legal interpretation is one thing, but how it should be conducted is quite another. We can support or oppose a certain interpretive position through some normative arguments, but we cannot predetermine or exclude a certain interpretive position by means of conceptual definition. The answer to the question of interpretation position is ultimately based on people's reflection and weighing on the nature and function of law, the institutional role of judges, and political ideals such as democracy and the rule of law, and cannot be based on language philosophy or any kind of analytical theory. Recognizing this will not only help to study the principles and positions of legal interpretation in depth, but also help to determine what kind of interpretation method is appropriate generally or in individual cases.

3. Reconstructing the regulation of fraud: a pragmatic paradigm

Zhang Songlun

Fraud is one of the oldest of all the abominations of human society.[1] In Ancient Greece, Aristotle distinguished between voluntary and involuntary interactions, the latter including those carried out in secret (e.g., theft, adultery, poisoning, matchmaking, seduction, backstabbing, perjury, etc.) and those carried out by violence (e.g., assault, imprisonment, killing, robbery, maiming, bullying, insulting, etc.).[2] This distinction clearly indicates fraud and coercion. Perhaps influenced by Aristotle,[3] Cicero also poetically juxtaposed the two: fraud is like a fox, and coercion is like a lion.[4] The analogy is not merely literary, but is intended to show that fraud (as well as coercion) can make humans revert to their animal nature, which leads to the detriment of others (*iniuria*).

[1] A corroborating piece of evidence is that ancient laws often required the parties concerned to swear that "they will not deceive". For example, in the case of the Guichard case around 1300 BC, Monsignor testified: "I speak the truth of Pharaoh without falsehood, and if I speak falsely, my nose and ears will be cut off, and I will be sent to the land of Cush …" In the thirteenth century, the Customary Code of Beaune (one of the earliest French statutes) also stated that "he will not deceive …". In the thirteenth century, in the Code of Customs of Béarn (one of the earliest written laws in France), it was also written that the "Custom of Montpellier" required the litigant to "swear that he will never commit fraud or malice". See Wigmore, *A Panorama of the World's Legal Systems*, translated by He Qinhua and others (Shanghai People's Publishing House, 2004) 26, 717–8, re-translated by the author.

[2] Aristotle, *Nicomachean Ethics*, translated by Miao Litian (China Social Science Press, 1999) 99–100.

[3] Cicero himself was deeply influenced by Greek philosophers, including Aristotle; see Xu Yichun: 'Cicero and His Three Treatises', in Cicero, On Old Age, On Friendship, and On Duty (preface), translated by Xu Yichun (The Commercial Press, 2001) 2, 17.

[4] Cicero, *On Obligations*, translated by Wang Huansheng (China University of Political Science and Law Press, 1999) 45.

When fraud was considered in the ancient world, more attention was paid to objective damage, and subjective intent was set aside.[5] In several paragraphs of the Digests, damage to others was the basis of fraud.[6] But Roman jurists were keen enough to see that fraud must be accompanied by intent. Ulpian has pointed out that fraud must be knowing; a person who accepts an object without knowing it does not commit fraud. Conversely, there is no fraud if the other party knows and agrees.[7] Papinian has also said: the interpretation of fraud should be based not only on consequences but also on intentions.[8] In Roman mythology, as the helper of Mercury (the messenger of the gods, and the god of thieves), fraud (Fraus) was released together with malice, greed, etc. from Pandora's box. This shows that fraud has been closely related to malice, which could be seen as the metaphor of the dichotomy between the elements of fraud: is it subjective intent, or is it damage? The starting point for this chapter's scholarly history of the institution of fraud is the Christian era in the West: like many Roman law institutions, the institution of fraud underwent a

---

5 Biscotti, '"Debtors" Fraud in Roman Law: An Opportunity for Some Brief Remarks on the Concept of Fraud', *Fundamina, Vol. 17 (2011)* 4–6.

6 Strictly speaking, it is possible to apply the notice of fraud given by the magistrate, i.e. *actio Pauliana* (Ulpian, *Edict book* 66, D. 42. 8. 1. pr). For example, the loss of usufruct or servitude (as a result of untimely prosecution); the loss of the original holding (Ulpian, *Edict book* 66, D. 42. 8. 42. 8. 3); a person who renounces an inheritance cannot be constituted because he has not forfeited his patrimony (Ulpian, *Edict book* 66, D. 42. 8. 6. 2); a person who knows that the other party will become insolvent, but who has received what is due to him, does not commit fraud (Ulpian, *Edict book* 66, D. 42. 8. 6. 7); and the benefit (the opposite of the loss) becomes the criterion for calculating the amount of compensation: e.g., a bona fide person who receives a gift from a bankrupt is still subject to the notice to the extent of the benefit (Ulpian, *Edict book* 66, D. 42. 8. 6. 11). Similarly, a claim for fraud can be brought for damages: for example, although my possession of a slave does not disappear when the slave is induced to escape, I can still bring a claim for fraud, provided I have suffered a loss (*Proculus*, D. 4. 3. 31).

7 Ulpian, *Edict book* 66, D. 42. 8. 6. 8–9.

8 Papinian, *Questions, book* 32, D. 50. 17.79. Ulpian has also claimed that *actio Pauliana* is equally applicable even if only one of the multiple creditors is defrauded. See Ulpian, *Edict book* 66, D. 42. 8. 6. 10. 7. For the view of modern jurists, see Bonfante, *Istituzioni Di Diritto Romano*, translated by Huang Feng (China University of Political Science and Law Publishing House, 2005) 312. It is worth noting that, although the Digests dealt separately in different paragraphs with fraud (as a claim of aggression) and with the *actio Pauliana* for defrauding creditors, the Romans paid more attention to the sake of the litigation system than the conceptual distinction, and the two terms above both emphasized the elements of damage and intent.

Christian moralized transformation, and the most systematic and insightful view came from Augustine and his two works, *De Mendacio* (*On Lying*) in 395 AD and *Contra Mendacium* (*Against Lying*) 25 years later. His splendid discussion of lies serves unquestionably as a link between the past and the future and is worth discussing.[9]

1. FRAUD IN CHRISTIANITY: MORAL TEACHING ROOTED IN THE HEART

In Augustine's writing, fraud is certainly a sin; at its core is the idea of intentionality: to defraud is "to tell a lie for the purpose of deceiving".[10] Unlike mistakes that come from human infirmity, fraud and lies originate in the conscience;[11] the fault of the liar lies in having the idea of deception in mind.[12] A lie has nothing to do with objective truth; the judgment of whether it is a lie depends on the mind, and the mere desire to lie is sin enough; but if one believes what is said to be true, "it is not a lie".[13] This approach led later theologians (including Thomas Aquinas) and philosophers, as well as civil law scholars.[14] Some Chinese scholars have pointed out, based on the comparative jurisprudence of French law and Japanese law, that fraud, which protects from those with wrongful motives, is an extension of misunderstanding.[15] Actually, this point also goes back to Augustine.

---

9 Denery II goes so far as to state, if lying has a history, it is a history that at first glance seems to have slowed to a crawl under the weight of Augustine's authority. See Denery II, Dallas G., 'Biblical liars and thirteenth-century theologians', in Newhauser, Richard (ed.), *The Seven Deadly Sins: From Communities to Individuals*, (Studies in Medieval and Reformation Traditions) (Brill 2007), 113.

10 Augustine, *Collected Moral Discourses*, translated by Shi Minmin (Joint Publishing, 2009) 173. The following quotations from *On Lying* and *Against Lying* are all from this Chinese translation, so we will not cite the page numbers, but the chapter numbers directly. Here is *Contra Mendacium* (*Against Lying*) 40; *On Lying* 5.

11 Remo Gramigna, 'Augustine on Lying: A Theoretical Framework for the Study of Types of Falsehood', (2013) 4 *Sign Systems Studies, Vol. 41*, 4476.

12 *On Lying*: 3.

13 Ibid., at 3, 4, 34.

14 For example, Flume argues that malicious fraud is any act that consciously causes, reinforces, or maintains the incorrect assumptions of others. See Flume, *Das Rechesgeschäft*, translated by Chi Ying (Law Press, 2013) 644.

15 Liu Yong, 'Reconstruction of the Elements of "Fraud" and Legislative Issues', (2016) 5 *Journal of Southeast University (Philosophy and Social Science Edition)* 67.

But there are serious institutional dilemmas with subjective fraud. First, are all lies culpable? Augustine insisted that lies must be defeated and destroyed by virtue of truth, so all kinds of lies are sins, which even include using a lie to destroy a lie to save the sinner or punish the wicked.[16] But it is Ulpian's invocation we may approve more that a well-intentioned fraud is the same as shrewdness, as in the case of a stratagem devised against an enemy or a robber.[17] According to Augustine, he who lies to expose a blasphemer is even worse than the blasphemer: for the latter blasphemes without knowing it; but the former, knowing the truth, still lies and self-approves their deceit.[18] But how can this be explained by the fact that the Holy Bible also records many cases of hypocrisy on the part of the righteous (e.g., Jacob's claim to be Esau, and Abraham's claim that Sarah was not his wife but his sister)?[19] Augustine argues, first, that some of these are mere concealments of the truth; second, that they are allegories and parables, just as jokes would not be regarded as lies; and, finally, that it is not possible to say that what the saints did can be transposed to moral norms.[20] These defenses are rather pale and even a bit arbitrary for atheists.

Certainly, Augustine cannot be blamed for this, for he was thinking of moral admonition rather than legal responsibility. Augustine only wanted to tell the congregation "what is fraud", and that a good man should never lie even if he is tortured;[21] the fraudster must be a sinner, and that is enough. He does not consider the question of reparation, including revocation, which is accomplished by the late scholastic philosophy,[22] but focuses more on mind than the body, for the chastity of the body dwells in the mind.[23] This is not only because it is written in the Secondary Scripture that "the mouth that belieth slayeth the soul";[24] but also because even a well-intentioned lie leads to the

---

16 *Contra Mendacium* (*Against Lying*) 1, 12.

17 See Ulpian, *Edict book* 11, D. 4. 3. 1. 3.

18 *Supra* note 16, 8.

19 See *Genesis* 18:15; *Exodus* 1:19, 20; *Genesis* 27:19.

20 *Supra* note 16, at 22, 23, 24, 27; note 12, at 2, 7.

21 *Supra* note 12, at 11, 15.

22 See Gordley, *The Philosophical Origins of Modern Contract Theory*, translated by Zhang Jiayong, Law Press, 2006, 110–11. The fraud in common law derives from the action of deceit in common law and action for rescission in equity. See Farnsworth, *The Law of Contract in the United States*, translated by Ge Yunsong and others (China University of Political Science and Law Press, 2004) 240.

23 *Supra* note 16, 39.

24 *Wisdom of Solomon* 1: 11.

disappearance of the truth and opens the way for wrong.[25] Augustine therefore focuses only on the *cor duplex* of the liar: either not telling what he knows to be true (i.e., concealment) or telling what he knows to be false (i.e., perjury);[26] and the detrimental consequences are inconsequential – even if the lie would have beneficial consequences, it should also be forbidden.

Augustine's influence was great in later times,[27] which also included civil law. After the transformation by the late scholastics in the sixteenth century, the subjective element of the defrauded person was added, which thereafter made fraud one of the elements regulating the validity of contracts; in the nineteenth century, the German Civil Code put forward a systematic theory of legal acts in a liberal atmosphere,[28] and fraud in bad faith (along with duress) constituted a validity defect of a legal act on the ground that it improperly affected the freedom of decision of the parties. The fraudulent act (together with coercion) constitutes a defect in the validity of the legal act on the ground that it unduly affects the parties' freedom of decision. This collusion between fraud and autonomy deserves reflection.

---

25 *Supra* note 12, 11. Of course, the reverse is also true, as Holmes argues that a morally innocent statement may also constitute legal fraud. See Holmes Jr., *The Common Law*, translated by Ran Hao and others (China University of Political Science and Law Press, 2006) 285.

26 *Supra* note 12, 3.

27 For example, in his debate with Constant, Kant pointed out that a friend who is being hunted and killed is hiding in your house, so should you lie to the assassin when he questions you? Kant's argument is that one must be honest: the death of the friend, though regrettable, is the work of the assassin; lying is worse. Scholars have argued that Kant's argument here is not an ethical one, but a political one: the idea is that means beyond the law should not be used to reestablish justice without liability for the wrongdoing of others. See Kant, 'On a Supposed Right to Lie from Philanthropy', cited from Geneviève Rousselière, 'On political responsibility in post-revolutionary times: Kant and Constant's debate on lying', *European Journal of Political Theory 2018*, Vol. 17(2) 215, 225. This answer is obviously Augustinian: Augustine himself had pointed out that it is never possible to cause oneself to sin by worrying about the sins of others. Interestingly, Augustine thought the perfect response at this point was "I know where he is, but I will never tell.", *supra* note 12: 24, re-translated by the author.

28 Gordley argues the political values of nineteenth-century liberalism largely determined the content of the rules included in the German Civil Code. See Gordley, von Mehren, *An Introduction to the Comparative Study of Private Law* (Cambridge University Press, 2006) 60.

2. WEAKNESSES AND SHORTCOMINGS: REGULATING FRAUD FOR PRESERVING AUTONOMY

Although inspired by scholasticism, traditional civil law has spontaneously or consciously institutionalized subjectivized fraud: the evils of the fraudster have evolved to be an unjustifiable influence on the victims' freedom of intention.[29] German law, for example, has placed fraud in the general section on the basis of autonomy (legal act), thus moving closer to autonomy (freedom) and further away from damage.[30] Flume goes so far as to argue that the factual component of fraud does not include damage (and its intent) to the person defrauded or to a third party; and that although fraud may produce a mistake, the latter is generally a mistake of motive which is irrevocable.[31] This

---

[29] Faced with the problem of fraud, the late scholastic philosophers (e.g., Conduras and Leucis), drawing on an exposition of the traditional rules, pointed out that fraud destroys the consent of both parties. See *supra* note 22, Gordley's book, 111. This is clearly the predecessor of today's fraud regime, typified by article 1109 of the French Civil Code. It has been argued that the fraud element of the German Civil Code lies in the negative evaluation of the relator's external and objective conduct and is justified on a completely different basis from the other theories of defective representation. See Liu Yong: 'On Concurrence of Contracting Fault and Fraud System – with Fraud's "Intentional" Element as the Center', (2015) 5 *Legal Studies* 62. This seems to be different from the understanding of today's mainstream German academia and is not in line with the liberalism of the German Civil Code legislation.

[30] *Supra* note 14, 631, 646. Of course, some scholars in China believe that the demarcation between motive error and expression error should be eliminated, i.e., to realize the transformation from "dualism" to "monism." See Han Shiyuan: *General Theory of Contract Law* (Law Press, 2018) 264, 271. Domestic scholars, such as Professor Ran Keping, believe that fraud undermines the autonomy of meaning (of the representers) and does not emphasize actual damage. See Ran Keping, *Flawed Meaning: Doctrine and Norms* (Law Press 2018) 276. This approach differs from the common law approach, which places fraud in the context of misrepresentation and distinguishes between fraudulent misrepresentation and no-fault misrepresentation; the other party acting on the basis of the fraudulent misrepresentation will give rise to a tort. See Smith: *The Law of Contrac*t, translated by Zhang Xin (Law Press, 2004) 127.

[31] See Zhu Qingyu, *General Theory of Civil Law* (Peking University Press, 2013) 273; Zhu Guangxin, *Studies on the General Provisions of Contract Law* (University of the People's Republic of China Publishing House, 2018) 294. German scholars have pointed out that fraud in civil law is to safeguard the freedom of decision of the parties, so it will not be like the criminal law crime of fraud, with the loss of property as an element. See Chen Su, Editor-in-Chief,

successfully separates fraud from mistake, placing fraud under freedom of expression, and the key to protecting the defrauded lies in ensuring freedom of formation of meaning, i.e., at the stage of contracting.[32] Nevertheless, fraud can permeate and extend to all kinds and every step of civil legal relationships and is not confined to contracting;[33] and elements of fraud may be contained in various facts: for example, a disparity in price may also constitute "evidence of fraud".[34] Moreover, fraud is inseparable from damages. Just as Shi Shangkuan argues, fraud may not only constitute a tort, but also a damage against customary law, or even a crime of fraud.[35] This makes the fraud in a legal act (contract) slightly awkward.

From morality to liberty, from Christianity to liberalism, the subjectivization path is long enough. But as Sefton-Green argues, the nineteenth-century theory of meaning and the value of "autonomy of meaning" are no longer solid, and we need to shift to more objective standards.[36] Examples are positive fraud (explicitly communicating a false fact) and negative fraud (concealing the truth). This categorization derives from Augustine's "double mind" (*cor duplex*) of the liar,[37] but it is difficult to distinguish at the normative level:

Commentary on the General Principles of Civil Law (vol. two) (Law Press, 2017) 1069.

32 The common law emphasizes abuses in the contracting process rather than the substance of the agreement. See *supra* note 22, Farnsworth's book, 239.

33 For example, in listed companies, there is an element of fraud in the occasions of misappropriation of assets, malfeasance, theft of trade secrets, or bribery, etc., and it is clearly not limited to contracting. See Yang Dan, *Financial Reporting Fraud and Corporate Governance of Listed Companies* (China Publishing Group Oriental Publishing Center, 2016) 35.

34 *Supra* note 28, p. 465. This view goes back at least as far as the medieval jurists, who held that the defense of fraud applied if the price was more or less than half the fair price. See Zimmermann, Whittaker edited, *Good Faith in European Contract Law*, translated by Ding Guangyu and others (Law Press, 2005) 82–83.

35 See Shi Shangkuan, *General Introduction to Civil Law* (China University of Political Science and Law Press, 2000) 440–41. For a similar view, see Xu Zhijun and Zhang Chuanwei, 'The Definition of Fraud', (2006) *4 Politics and Law Forum*, 91; and scholars believe that fraud is regulated by both the legal act system and the tort system, with the former protecting autonomy of meaning and the latter filling in for damages. See Yang Wei: 'A Brief Discussion on the Tort Liability of Fraud', (2010) 3 *Jinan Journal (Philosophy and Social Science Edition)* 205.

36 In Scandinavian law, for example, contracts will be invalidated for fraud not on the basis of defective intent, but on the basis of regulation of bad faith or abuse of freedom of contract. Ruth Sefton-Green, ed., *Mistake, Fraud and Duties to Inform in European Contract Law* (Cambridge University Press, 2005) 2–3, 13.

37 Gillian R. Evans, *Augustine on Evil* (Cambridge University Press, 1982) 67.

silence without disclosing a fact equals a statement of the opposite: for example, not disclosing that a house is infested with pests is the same as asserting that it is not infested with pests. This is also the standpoint of the Restatement (Second) of the Law of Contracts: if a party knows that "[a] person's non-disclosure of a fact known to him is equivalent to an assertion that the fact does not exist in the following cases only … [b] where he knows that disclosure of the fact would correct a mistake of the other party as to a basic assumption on which that party is making the contract and if non-disclosure of the fact amounts to a failure to act in good faith and in accordance with reasonable standards of fair dealing …", the failure to disclose the fact is tantamount to a statement that the fact does not exist. It is perhaps the reason that American courts are moderating, weakening or even departing from the "no duty to disclose" rule, holding that non-disclosure of a fact is tantamount to a representation that the fact does not exist.[38]

Further, while it is autonomy (of the person defrauded) that is protected by the traditional fraud regimes, legislatures and courts often insert their own value judgments: the reliance that the law seeks to preserve is the one that it deems to be "justified".[39] The revocability induced by fraud lies in the fact that the autonomy has been "improperly influenced", but actually "unlawfully influenced" has always been a factor in the application of § 123 of the German Civil Code.[40] Thus, over-exaggerated advertising and general commercial boasting normally do not constitute fraud;[41] even false advertising, which is subject to administrative penalties, has been held by Chinese courts that it did not constitute contractual fraud.[42] The German Supreme Court has even

---

38 See Restatement (Second) of Contracts, art. 161, para. B, *supra* note 22, Farnsworth's book, 245–7.

39 Larenz, *Methodenlehre der Rechtswissenschaft*, translated by Chen Ai-e (The Commercial Press, 2003) 351.

40 *Supra* note 14, 630; Chinese scholars hold similar views, *supra* note 30, Han Shiyuan's book, 257. Savini supported the element of illegality and rejected the inclusion of an intent to disadvantage the interests of the relative party in the fraud element; however, criminal law scholar Liszt argued that the concept of malice should be included due to the differences between civil and criminal law. See *supra* note 29, Liu Yong's article, 62–3. This goes back to an older academic tradition like the discussion above.

41 Supra note 31, Zhu Qingyu's book, 274; Civil Judgment No. 297 of Quanzhou Intermediate People's Court of Fujian Province (2014) Quan Min Chu Zi No. 297.

42 See Zhengzhou Intermediate People's Court of Henan Province (2009) Zhengmin Erfeng Zi No. 1826 Civil Judgment, and Taizhou Intermediate People's Court of Jiangsu Province (2015) Taizhong People's Final Zi No. 00293 Civil Judgment. It is noteworthy that courts in China have made similar arguments in a number of cases that when faced with high-priced goods, the defrauded person

held that bad faith fraud is not committed if the fraudster seeks to maximize the benefit to the person being defrauded.[43] At common law, in the famous case of *Laidlaw v. Organ*,[44] Farnsworth argues that there is also some justification for requiring disclosure of information: since access to such information should not be encouraged in the circumstances of the case.[45] Conversely, "truth" beyond what is generally expected may also constitute fraud. Cooter and Ulen provide a vivid example of a plaintiff who purchased a "reliable method" for killing grasshoppers and received two wooden boards, saying that the grasshoppers could be killed by being squeezed between the boards.[46] This, of course, is also fraud. So, the liberty protected by the court is the one which the court considers reasonable rather than that of the person defrauded.[47] Thus, the word "truth" in Article 148 of the Chinese Civil Code is more accurate, which emphasizes the judgment of the parties to exclude the wrongful interference of others ("I really wanted it to be so"), which precisely reflects the value judgment of the law.

In summary, even if autonomy is affected by fraud, it is not the reason for the State and the law to oppose fraud: the courts and the law can always override

---

should "make comprehensive considerations before deciding whether or not to purchase".

43 *Supra* note 14, 630.

44 See 15 U.S. (2 Wheat.) (1817). The facts of the case were as follows: whether the plaintiff could claim fraud on the part of the defendant, who had been privy to the armistice and had purchased a large quantity of tobacco from the plaintiff, and whose price had risen so high as a result of the announcement of the armistice. Justice Marshall held that the plaintiff did not have a duty to inform; the German law also holds a similar view: no duty to inform does not constitute illegal fraud. In fact, the setting of the duty to inform certainly represents a value judgment of the law.

45 *Supra* note 22, Farnsworth's book, 245. An economic objection to the outcome of the case is that what the defendants did was rent-seeking, and that the cost of the expenditures to obtain information about the truce was wasteful. See Friedman, *Law's Order: What Economics Has to Do with Law and Why It Matters*, translated by Yang Xinxin (Law Press, 2004) 200.

46 Cooter and Ulen, *Law and Economics*, translated by Zhang Jun (Shanghai People's Publishing House, 1994) 293–4. There is a similar meme in the traditional Chinese crosstalk show 'The ancestral secret formula': the ancestral secret formula for relieving the itch on the skin is a slip of paper with the words "scratching yourself" written on it.

47 Thus, some scholars argue that true voluntariness is impossible because market standards and values must necessarily permeate the contract. See Wang Shaoyu, *The Expanding Problem of Competing Torts and Contracts – A Perspective on Common Law* (Peking University Press, 2010) 122.

the "free will" of the parties without hesitation. So, the fraud regime should focus on the role of state power in combating fraud.

3. THE ROLE OF STATE AUTHORITY IN COMBATING FRAUD

Why are states and laws needed to combat fraud? One view is that fraud is a real investment in misinformation which is totally useless to society and should not be remunerated.[48] Besides the difficulty of identifying what is "totally useless to society" due to its vagueness, it does not follow that information that is totally useless to society is necessarily unremunerated or unprotected: a typical example is a trade secret (and useless patents or copyrighted works) – it may not always be socially useful to recognize the information as a trade secret (sometimes there is a net benefit to society if it is disclosed), but the law still provides a reward (protection). Friedman therefore proposes a modified version: the law should not guarantee information-based profits if the person possessing information closely related to the value of the subject matter has an incentive to block the information so that the net loss becomes a net gain.[49] In addition to operational difficulties (including the identification of "net gain" and "closely related"), this solution lacks generalizability: because some defrauded person is willing to participate in the defrauded situation even he or she knows it (for he or she believes that his or her loss can be compensated by others' greater loss, such as in the pyramid scheme, or gambling), but the law would still recognize fraud. We need a more ambitious perspective, i.e. an institutionalist perspective.

The state and the law are neither necessary nor sufficient conditions for combating fraud. Laws cannot eliminate all fraud, and the absence of laws does not mean that fraud is inevitably rampant; social mechanisms, including morality, profit in the long run, and private penalties, etc., are sufficient to suppress most fraud and foster cooperation.[50] So why is there a system of fraud

48 Posner, *Economic Analysis of Law*, translated by Jiang Zhaokang (Encyclopedia of China Press, 1997) 140.

49 *Supra* note 45, Friedman's book, 201–2. This view is implicit in the recognition by American courts that sellers have a duty to disclose material facts that they know or ought to know and that the buyer would not be able to discover through ordinary care and diligence. See *Holcomb v. Zinke*, 365 N.W.2d 507, 512 (N.D. 1985).

50 It is a time-honored instinctive reaction to emphasize the importance of contractual morality (natural law) and to use morality as the basis for anti-fraud norms. See Mather, *Contract Law and Morality,* translated by Dai Mengyong and others (China University of Political Science and Law Press, 2005) 242–9. Individual

(in the empirical sense)? It is easy to see that fraud tends to be more profitable in short-term, one-off transactions (the so-called "one-shot deals");[51] in other words, the "invisible hand" can hardly provide sufficient protection for the interests of the parties in the first transaction until a long-term stable order is formed. Transaction formation with asymmetric information requires effective guarantees to send incentive signals, which neither promises nor credibility can achieve at the outset of a transaction. The problem of adverse selection caused by fraud cannot be avoided in the absence of a pilot and front-loaded credit facilitation mechanism.[52] More importantly, fraud and the general level of integrity in society are related in a complicated way: the higher the general level of integrity in society, the greater the potential gain for fraudsters in a specific industry ("the other side will believe anything they say"), which in turn creates incentives for more people to engage in different kinds of fraud. From this point of view, fraud is a kind of entropy, and the rule against fraud is essentially an acceleration rule: that is, the use of public power as a guarantee to ensure that in the market that has not yet been or cannot be accumulated into a long-term order, the enforcement and punishment to accelerate the formation of trust, in order to ensure the perfect operation of the market.

However, we must also recognize that there are tensions between public power, which is the center of the law, and the market. Although the state and the market are likely to work together to combat fraud because it can impede or even undermine transactions and cooperation, there can be competition and even tensions between the two in the fight against fraud. Self-enforcement and punishment mechanisms emerge in periods when public power is not strong

---

interests (especially interests gained in the future) can make fraud an unwise practice, see Erickson, *Order Without Law: How Neighbors Settle Disputes*, translated by Su Li (China University of Political Science and Law Press, 2003) 67–8; for a more Chinese example, see Yan Yunxiang, *The Flow of Gifts*, translated by Li Fangchun and others (Shanghai People's Publishing House, 2017) 132–9. As for punishment, as Sang Benqian argues, punishment is the basis and prerequisite for cooperation and trust, but law is not the only or the most efficient mechanism. See Sang Benqian, *Monitoring and Punishment among Private Persons* (Shandong People's Publishing House, 2005) 254, 301.

51 See North, *Structures and Change in Economic History*, translated by Li Yiping, (Commercial Press, 2007) 42–3. For an empirical study, see the examination of the medieval trade system by American scholars, Greif, *Institutions and the Path to the Modern Economy*, translated by Zheng Jianghuai and others (CITIC Publishing House, 2008) 43.

52 On adverse selection, see Stiglitz, Walsh, *Economics*, translated by Huang Xiaofeng and others (People's University of China Press, 2010) 336–41.

enough.[53] Because integrity is an expensive and scarce consumable, the lower the private integrity, the greater the trust in the state. The fact that private individuals turn to the government for fraud (including fraud prevention) reduces the government's search costs for the fraudster and increases the credibility of the public authority and the existence of additional rents.[54] Thus, the law would be willing to monopolize the identification and punishment of fraud, and even has incentives to expand the strength and application of the fraud regime. A typical example is the intentional purchase of the defective products, and Chinese courts even held that "trading with the knowledge of fraud and then bringing claims for compensation" is "using litigation as a means and the courts as a tool", which can seriously undermine judicial authority.[55] This kind of view reflects the fact that excessive private reliance can challenge the authority of the government, so the state has put in place mechanisms to encourage the proactive breaking of personal reliance: for example, reporting systems and reward systems.

It is not the monopoly of the law that should be criticized here, but we should be aware there is a limit to what the law can do. In addition to agency risk, growth in numbers and complexity can reduce the functionality of courts and systems, so law and courts cannot be seen as an all-powerful black box.[56] Fraud regimes require more sophisticated legal techniques, and the traditional approach, juxtaposed with coercion, is poor in practice.

---

53 An empirical examination shows that the emphasis on self-enforcement and punishment in village contracts in the late Qing Dynasty and early Republican period arose precisely from the weakness of the central authority at this time because of war and regime change. See Madeleine Zelin and others ed., *Contracts and Property in Early Modern China*, translated by Li Chao and others (Zhejiang University Press, 2011).

54 For example, mandatory publicity in property law: it is precisely because of the presupposition that governmental publicity is more reliable and less prone to fraud than individual promises that mandatory insurance must be put in place to obtain additional rents (including taxes). On the cost of compulsory publicity, see Zhang Songlun, 'An Economic Analysis of the Publicity of Property Rights' (2017) 6 *Zuel Law Journal*, 99–100.

55 See Beijing Third Intermediate People's Court (2017) Beijing 03 Civil Final Civil Judgment (No. 13090). For a contrary judgment, see Qingdao Intermediate People's Court of Shandong Province (2019) Lu 02 Civil Final No. 263 Civil Judgment.

56 See Komesar, *The Law's Limits*, translated by Shen Weixing and others (Commercial Press, 2007) 166–7, 183.

4. THE BREAK BETWEEN FRAUD AND COERCION IN THE MODERN ERA: FROM THE POINT OF VIEW OF CONDUCT

Fraud is present in many typical wrongful acts (such as adultery, breach of contract, and even theft[57]) – much like coercion; and today, the law's regulation (and even sanctioning) of fraud is rich and complex – again, much like coercion. It is perhaps for this reason that fraud and coercion have always appeared in pairs and continue to be so due to the strong influence of Aristotle and German law. Although the structure of Roman law actions for fraud and coercion differed markedly,[58] and fraud and coercion differed in terms of their content (i.e., the creation of "fear" versus "mistake"), their constituent elements, their exclusion periods, and their effects on third parties,[59] but they both undermine autonomy. However, the commonality of the acts does not justify the same norms: even if both affect the freedom of the parties (which is in itself rather doubtful), it does not justify the application of the same legal mechanisms (i.e., the invalidity of the legal act or of the contract by revocation). The author has pointed out that the institution of coercion actually represents a means of combating and restricting illegal autonomous enforcement by the public power in order to preserve its own authority,[60] but what about fraud? In order to clarify this question, we have to abandon for the moment the positivism of Rechtsdogmatik and face the act itself.

Fraud and coercion both involve the use of information about the individual person, but whereas coercion is a forceful interference based on information about the coerced person, fraud is a direct interference with false information provided to the defrauded person. This means that coercion is typically immediate, whereas fraud is delayed: by creating a state of legitimacy, the person being defrauded (at the time of the fraud) does not realize that he is being defrauded; whereas the person being coerced is aware of the threat from the outset. The coercer is therefore more concerned with the coerced person's personal resistance, especially immediate resistance (obviously in physical coercion), whereas the fraudster is concerned with the other person's acceptance of the "deception".

---

57 Open theft without deception would be more like robbery; hence, in ancient China, there is a distinction between "Dao (盜, theft)" and "Zei (賊, burglary)."

58 The claim of fraud is characterized as *in personam*, whereas the claim of duress is *in rem*. See Xue Jun, 'Third-Party Fraud and Third-Party Duress', (2011) 1 *Chinese Journal of Law*, 60.

59 Lin Chenger, *General Principles of Civil Law* (Law Press, 2008) 403.

60 Zhang Songlun, An Economic Analysis of the Coercion Regime (2018) 3 *Peking University Law Journal*, 632–50.

Thus, fraud is unique compared to coercion in the following ways: first, coercion may contain fraud (e.g., the fable of fox borrowing tiger's majesty and might), but fraud does not contain coercion (otherwise it would be coercion). Fraud will be more common, whereas coercion will be more specific – just as everyone after all has told a few lies, but not everyone has, will (or can) coerce others. Secondly, some behavior originally does not have the content of fraud, and even the parties may not have the malicious intent of fraud, but in specific areas and occasions it may still constitute fraud for special reasons. For example, in insolvency, regardless of the intention of the parties, it may constitute a fraudulent transfer of property as long as the debtor's property and the ability to repay debts are diminished to the detriment of the creditors.[61] Finally, and most importantly, the weakness of the coerced person does not deter or diminish the wrongfulness of the coercive act; but the personal status of the person defrauded affects the liability for fraud: in Ancient Greece, the person who was defrauded because of being too simple (stupid) was responsible for his or her own actions;[62] In more recent law, factors such as the status of the parties and their experience may cause the corresponding liability for certain fraudulent acts to be discharged or exonerated.[63] These circumstances are impossible in the coercion regime.

In traditional civil law, coercion is considered to be worse than fraud on the grounds that the former causes greater harm to autonomy.[64] But Cicero argues that fraud is more despicable than coercion. Quoting Gaius Aquilius, he points out that fraud is "pretending to be one thing but doing another" (*aliud simulatum, aliud actum*); it is the most evil of all wrongs to make oneself appear

---

[61] Therefore, it is called the tendency of 'objectification of subjective elements' by scholars. See Xu Defeng, *On Bankruptcy Law* (Peking University Press, 2015) 407–14; Zhang Yanli, *Research on Legal Regulation of Bankruptcy Fraud* (Peking University Press, 2008) 84–6.

[62] *Supra* note 5, 5.

[63] For example, in *Cobbe v. Yeoman's Row Management Ltd* ([2008] UKHL 55, [2008] 1 WLR 1752, HL), the plaintiff and the defendant had reached an oral agreement and were encouraged by the defendant to make the necessary preparations (obtaining planning permission for the building) at considerable expense when the defendant changed its mind. The court denied the plaintiff's claim, noting that although the defendant's behavior was unethical, the plaintiff should have foreseen the risk of withdrawing from the contract because the plaintiff was an "experienced developer." In contrast, the liability for fraud changes when the person being defrauded has a specific status (e.g., consumer, lawyer, accountant, notary, etc.) (e.g., when punitive damages are involved under Article 55(2) of Law of the People's Republic of China on the Protection of Rights and Interests of Consumers, the law also imposes special obligations).

[64] *Supra* note 14, 631–2.

noble when one is in fact evil.[65] As successors of this point of view, Augustine quotes the Bible in *On Lying*: "thou hatest all workers of iniquity./Thou shalt destroy them that speak leasing: the LORD will abhor the bloody and deceitful man."[66] The Bible usually interprets the second half of the sentence as the first, so that a lie is specifically sinning; and since "thou shalt destroy" is obviously worse than "thou hatest", a lie is much worse than sinning; there is no authority to justify lying.[67] In Dante's Divine Comedy, fraud is a sin peculiar to mankind and is more abhorrent to God, and "the fraudulent are in the lowest hell and suffer greater misery".[68]

Those who emphasize that coercion is worse are addressing the impact on the victim's autonomy, while those who argue that fraud is worse are addressing the moral character of the perpetrator. The fact that the two are so hard to compare seems to suggest that "preserving autonomy" may not be the only approach (or even the right approach). The reason for this is the richness and multilayered nature of fraud:[69] if there is one side to the truth, there are a thousand sides to the lie.[70] This is why we should pay attention to the particularized qualities of both parties to a fraud, and especially of the person who has been defrauded, and to make different legal judgments in light of the specific circumstances.

5. MULTI-LEVEL FRAUD REGIMES: FROM THE PERSPECTIVE OF THE PERSON BEING DEFRAUDED

Fraud is too difficult to define due to its diversity in content. As scholars have argued, a precise and technical definition of fraud allows "tricksters" to learn how to circumvent the law.[71] Given the tension between the factual diversity of fraud and normative abstraction, the more refined the concept of fraud, the greater the openness to lawlessness; on the contrary, the more ambiguous the

---

65 *Supra* note 4, at 45, 239.

66 *Psalms* 5: 5–6.

67 *Supra* note 12, 9.

68 In Dante's hierarchy of hell, the fraudster is worse than the murderer, and only "superior" to the traitor and the betrayer. See Dante, *The Divine Comedy*, translated by Tian Dewang (People's Literature Publishing House, 1997), 75.

69 Augustine then identifies eight kinds of lies; for details, see *supra* note 12: 17.

70 See Michel de Montaigne, *Des Menteurs On Liars*, in W. Carew Hazlitt ed., *The Essays of Michel Eyquem de Montaigne,* Great Books of the Western World, Vol. 25 (Benton, 1952) 16.

71 *Supra* note 50, Mather's book, 218–19.

concept of fraud, the better it facilitates the state's ability to scrutinize and judge the legitimacy of individual reliance, thereby implementing the state's overall control over the economy and society. More importantly, no one can avoid fraud totally. In the case of real estate transactions, for example, it is not possible or necessary for a seller or buyer to know 100% of the rights;[72] therefore, in the absence of other information, and from the point of view *ex post facto*, legality and illegality may be one step away at the turn of a so-called victim's mind: the person who subsequently discovers and claims to be defrauded is just the same person who previously consented, but then reversed himself because he realized the mistake; and, unlike coercion, the defrauded person can avoid the fraud at minimal cost ("I'm not doing business with you anymore!"). This is especially true in non-monopolized markets.

Thus, fraud is often a reason for ordinary people to show that they do not wish to continue trading and to claim compensation.[73] The judgment of fraud must therefore be inductive, not deductive, based on the assertions of the parties. The basis of plausibility will be different for different (including potential) fraud victims and for judges. When the defrauded person is excessively shrewd, this is the intentional purchase of the defective products; and "whether the intentional purchase of the defective products constitutes fraud" is a pseudo-question. The defrauder's fraud and the defraudee's knowledge are clearly not at the same stage: the premise that the fraud becomes a fraud is precisely that the defraudee does not know that the other person is defrauding at the time of the act, so the intentional purchase of the defective products is certainly fraud (for the defrauder) and certainly not fraud (for the defrauded person).[74] In turn,

---

72 Even if the title is a marketable title, not all doubts need be removed. See *Malloy & Smith, Real Estate Transactions, Problems, Cases, and Materials* (Aspen Law & Business 1998), 324; *Conklin v. Davi*, 388 A.2d 598 (N.J. 1978); Singer, *Property Law: Policy, Rules, and Practice* (CITIC Publishing House 2003), 910.

73 One piece of supporting evidence is that fraud has been used by plaintiffs as a synonym for breach of the principle of honesty and good faith in a number of court decisions in China. See Zhang Zhiqiang v. Xuzhou Suning Electrical Appliance Co., Supreme People's Court (2000) Civil Judgment No. 155.

74 However, this does not justify the crackdown on professional hunters for counterfeiters. Some scholars believe that professional hunters tend to choose large shopping malls or supermarkets that have lower prosecution costs, are relatively easy to fix, and emphasize reputation, and because the management of these enterprises is more standardized, it is easy to create a situation in which bad money drives out good money in the long run. See Zhao Peng, 'Rethinking Administrative Law on Punitive Damages' (2018) 1 *Chinese Journal of Law* 41. The premise of this assertion is valid, but the conclusion is inconceivable. For a functionalist analysis of knowingly buying fake, see Xiong Bingwan, 'Form and

when the defrauded person is excessively "stupid": e.g., when they obstinately participate in a scam (even one that is patently illegal or against good morals), do they have standing to subsequently claim that they have been defrauded? Do they have standing to subsequently claim that they have been defrauded? Should the reaction of the "defrauded person" at different stages of the transaction affect the final outcome of the law?

It should be noted that the person defrauded will often be imputable for the occurrence of the fraud: "The victims of fraud are in most cases guilty of some degree of imprudence, and the necessity of remedies by the law is impaired."[75] As the Phaedrus dictum: people want to be deceived (*Vulgus vult decipi*); today, the public is prone to participate in, or condone, wrongful acts of deception.[76] Actually, the victim of a fraud will actively intervene in the fraud, either out of dissatisfaction with the legitimate market, such as joining a pyramid scheme because working too hard or the money earned is too slow/little, or because of the new circumstances that have induced it, such as the illegal behavior of investors in the securities markets since the twenty-first century. For example, the frequency of investor misconduct in securities markets has increased since the twenty-first century.[77] Should all these victims of fraud be (or be eligible to be) protected?

Criminal law is much more radical than civil law on this issue. According to Viktimodogmatik, which seeks to respond to the normative needs of victims, the criminal protectability and necessity to protect the victim is one of the factors defining wrongfulness, and the most important and in-depth discussion is the crime of fraud (which Mr Che Hao refers to as the "main battlefield").[78] The German scholar Amelung argues that a victim of fraud who has suspicions – at least to the extent of a specific suspicion – but still participates at

---

Function of Law: Taking the Case of "Intentional Purchase of Defective Products" as an Analytical Example', (2017) 2 Peking University Law Journal 330–39.

[75] Shen Hai'en, *Power in Private Law: A New Launch of the Gestaltungsrecht* (Peking University Press, 2011), p. 135.

[76] Nars, *Swindling Billions*, translated by Huang Funing (Law Press, 2013) 28.

[77] Statistically, the proportion of investors who are illegitimate has risen from 21.7% at the end of the last century to 37.72% nowadays. See Xing Huiqiang, *Empirical Research on Securities Fraud Regulation* (China Legal Press, 2016) 4, 7.

[78] See Shen Liuhua, 'A Preliminary Study of Victim Creed in German Criminal Law', (2011) 1 *Criminal Law Review* (Peking University Press, 2011) 201, 203, 225. When scholars in China initially studied the doctrine of Viktimodogmatik, it was also in relation to the crime of fraud, see Che Hao, 'From the South China Tiger Photograph Case to the Responsibility of Victims in the Crime of Fraud', (2008) 9 *Law Science Magazine* 51.

his own risk and his interests should not be protected by criminal law. Earlier, Naucke argued that extremely simple, poorly executed, and easily detected frauds should be excluded from the elements of fraud.[79] The German scholar Frisch, however, questioned Amelung's principle of subsidiary protection: why does it exist only for relational crimes such as fraud (to which can be added a number of sexual offenses), but not for other types of crimes?[80] In response to this challenge, some scholars have turned to the right of self-determination, arguing that the latter and self-responsibility are two sides of the same coin, that the individual choice of the victim should be respected, and that there is room for the application of criminal law to be recognized within the limits of the individual's legal interests.[81] However, it is a luxury to speak of self-determination in criminal law: in many cases, the crime is established even though the victims have not been "victimized" (e.g., in the case of the crime of group licentiousness) because the state presupposes itself to be the victim of the crime. This is one of the biggest differences between criminal law and civil law: the state/power may dominate the private subject and become a party to the legal relationship. So why can't criminal law ignore "victimization" and create a crime purely for the purpose of combating fraud, no matter how ridiculous the act may be?

Only economics can answer the question: granting indiscriminate protection to all victims of fraud would not only waste judicial costs, but also unduly indulge parties' irrational judgments about risk.[82] According to the Viktimodogmatik of criminal law, the crime of fraud should not be committed when the fraud is too poorly executed or when the victim has (or should have had) doubts. Drawing on this conclusion, a fraud should not be committed when it is too obvious and contrary to morality. If the victim is an active

---

79 See Che Hao: 'Victim Consent and Victim Self-Inflicted Risks in Negligent Offenses', (2014) 5 *Politics and Law* 6–7; Sun Li, *Study on the Objective Elements of the Crime of Fraud* (China University of Political Science and Law Press, 2016) 17.

80 *Supra* note 9, Che Hao's article, 5.

81 Che Hao, *Local Shaping of Criminal Law Doctrine* (Law Press, 2017) 56–9; *Supra* note 79, Che Hao's article, 31–2.

82 Because it means that the person concerned will have "reliance" before choosing: the opportunity to undo his previous behavior, however absurd and stupid it may be, through the law in the name of being defrauded. From an ex post point of view, this is a protection for the person concerned; but from an ex ante point of view, this protection undoubtedly reduces the cost of "stupid behavior," and will lead to more people being less careful in making choices, thus resulting in a waste of society's resources as a whole.

participant in the scheme, he should not be entitled to relief.[83] Interpretive theory either recognizes the fraud victim's own fault in bearing the loss, based on Article 157 of the Chinese Civil Code, or permits restitution but creates additional public law liability (such as a fine) for the "victim". The multilayered system of fraud means that the conduct of the fraudster and the fraud victim cannot be equated, and therefore does not prevent the creation of separate legal liability for the fraudster at the same time.

6. THE FRAUD REGIME AS A REMEDY

Since fraud is put in the system of legal acts (contracts) (leading to contracts being void or voidable), the following task is to explain the affinity between fraud and tort. The so-called "Supreme Court" of Taiwan, China has pointed out in its judgment that since the legal act is not invalid before revocation, the seller still enjoys the claim of the price, and the total amount of the property has not been reduced, so it is difficult to constitute a tort because there is no damage. Wang Zejian opposed the view above, arguing that fraud may cause others to lose the opportunity to enter into a better contract, which constitutes an infringement of a protected right (the right to liberty); moreover, the two-year statute of limitations (for torts) is longer than the one-year period of exclusion, which is advantageous for the protection of the victim.[84] But these arguments are too weak: a breach of contract often results in the loss of a better contracting opportunity for others, such as refusing to return a leased property in possession at the end of the lease term, which has been recognized by both the courts and academics in Taiwan, China as constituting a delay in payment;[85] but it cannot be incorporated into tort liability. It is a mistake of reversing cause and effect to recognize that fraud may constitute a tort based on the difference between the statute of limitations and the period of exclusion: the correct way is that fraud (for other reasons) may constitute a tort subject to

---

83 The basis for this conclusion can be found in the legal proverb of equity, "He who comes to equity must come with clean hands". As J. Murphy pointed out in *Precision Instrument Manufacturing Co v. Automotive Maintenance Machinery Co*: "The maxim 'he who comes into equity must come with clean hands' closes the doors of a court of equity to one tainted with inequitableness or bad faith relative to the matter in which he seeks relief, however improper may have been the behavior of the defendant" (324 US 806, 814 (1945)).

84 See Wang Zejian, *A Study of Civil Law Doctrine and Jurisprudence* (Peking University Press, 2015) 255–9. For a similar view, see *supra* note 31, Zhu Qingyu's book, 278.

85 See Qiu Congzhi, *Newly Revised Treatise on the Law of Debt* (Volume 1) (People's University of China Publishing House, 2006) 317.

the general statute of limitations; and the regimes for avoidance of contract and tort damages are inherently different.[86]

Much of the above dilemma stems from the dichotomy between contract and tort. It should be noted that fraud in contract often causes detriment to others, and that the reversal of fraud triggers restitution, often to the same goal of torts. In fact, fraud is present in all wrongful acts: either to defraud others or to defraud the public authority (the government). Thus, some countries allow fraud to be claimed as damages without revocation;[87] while some other countries put misrepresentation with the element of fraud directly under the law of torts.[88] Since the split between fraud in autonomy (contract) and damages (tort) originates from an ancient academic genealogy, and the strict distinction between tort and contract law has been constantly criticized,[89] it is only logical that modern law should reconceptualize and redesign the fraud regime.

By claiming fraud on the part of the other party, the parties are in fact denying (their previous) market trust by placing reliance on public authority: the essence of revocation of a contract (legal act) is to stop applying market trust (the contract) and to invoke legal trust (the rules of positive law). The right of avoidance is a safety valve of the law and the power to intervene in market reliance; therefore, it is necessary to have a corresponding period of exclusion: this is a cost-saving mechanism for the law, in the same way as the statute of

---

86 Although it is true that some States and territories do so in practice, see *supra* note 14, 633. However, this reasoning is hardly convincing: it would be tantamount to overriding the exclusionary period for the right of avoidance; if the one-year exclusionary period is too short, the law should be amended to extend it, rather than recognizing that fraud can constitute a tort on such grounds.

87 *Supra* note 36, 26.

88 The logic of the common law is that this obligation does not come from a contractual agreement, but from a provision of law. Cardozo pointed out that "Growing out of a contract, it has none the less an origin not exclusively contractual … the duty is imposed by law." *Glanzer v. Shepard*, 233 N.Y. 236 (1922) (retranslated from Chinese translation). However, the United States Uniform Commercial Code also recognizes the avoidance of contracts in cases of gross fraud and holds that avoidance does not preclude damages (in the tort sense) because "Remedies for material misrepresentation or fraud include all remedies available under this Article for non-fraudulent breach. Neither rescission or a claim for rescission of the contract for sale nor rejection or return of the goods shall bar or be deemed inconsistent with a claim for damages or other remedy." *supra* note 22, Farnsworth's book, 259.

89 For an overview and discussion of this issue, see Zhang Jiayong, *A Study of Adjustment Models in the Intermediate Areas of Contract and Tort Law* (Peking University Press, 2016) 4–5.

limitations.[90] On the other hand, if the parties have not developed sufficient trust in the first place, it is natural that there is no need or possibility for the revocation regime to intervene. Therefore, there is no need to make the contract (legal act) and its validity an antecedent judgment: contract avoidance, tort compensation, and criminal liability should be complementary, not mutually exclusive, and not necessarily concomitant.[91]

Fraud is an assertion by the parties in a specific context, a trigger mechanism for legal intervention and relief, so neither intent nor damage is the element of fraud; however, they are the signs of fraud as well as the basis on which the parties' reliance has been breached. Fraud may be prejudicial – both in terms of actual rights or interests, and in terms of the inability to contract or to continue performance because of the breach of reliance, leading to the inability to seek an equivalent transaction at the same cost; but it may also be that no actual prejudice arises from fraud, but only from intent. The increasing complexity of the "duty to inform" in modern countries is in fact a reflection of the tendency for fraud to be specific, case-by-case and objective: it also confirms and exacerbates the blurring of the boundaries between tort and contract. From tort law to contract law, the degree of reliance is progressive and varies as the duty of care progresses;[92] for fraud in between, the rule of *culpa in contrahendo* applies. It has been argued that the latter stems from the narrow qualification of German tort law,[93] which is partly true, for the problem is not unique to Germany.[94] For at its root, negligence in contracting (or no matter

[90] As Geng Lin has pointed out, the statute of limitations and the period of exclusion are not distinct, but are in fact measures of legislative policy that highlight the different needs for the protection of the relevant state of affairs. See Geng Lin, 'On the Exclusion Period', (2016) 3 *Peking University Law Journal*, 613–45.

[91] *Supra* note 31, Chen Su's Book, 1069.

[92] Medicius, *Allgemeiner Teil des BGB*, translated by Du Jinglin and others (Law Press, 2004), 95; *supra* note 89, 106–7.

[93] See Li Zhongyuan, 'Questioning the Independence of Contractual Negligence Liability', (2008) 7 *Law Science* 132–44.

[94] There is a need for such a rule in almost all countries of the world. For example, the French case of a person who accepted a position with a new company but the latter canceled it, Cour de cassation, ch. soc., 22 March 1972, D.S. 1972, 468; the American case of a promise followed by a withdrawal of the lease, See Channel Home Centers v. Grossman, 7 F.2d 291 (3rd Cir. 1986); and the defendant made a promise to purchase the plaintiff's store, which resulted in the plaintiff's sale of other businesses and purchase of a home elsewhere, then the defendant refused to do so. See *Hoffman v. Red Owl Stores, Inc.* 133 N.W.2d 267 (Wis. 1965). Relevant provisions are found in the European Contract Law Rules of the European Commission on Contract Law (the Lando Rules) and in the rules of the International Association for the Unification of Private Law (The UNIDROIT

what it is called) stems from the tension between the linear relationship from tort law to contract law and the reality that fraud is a specter that runs through the entire transaction and does not stop for the formation of a contract. Even if one recognizes the linear logic above, which is in fact very doubtful, one cannot assume that economic reliance will follow the same linear pattern and that reliance during the conclusion of the contract will sometimes not be less than the contract itself. It is therefore counterproductive to say that liability for breach of contract is a "rights-protective" regime:[95] it is because the reliance of the parties at the stage of the breach of contract is often not sufficient for the law to intervene (or else it would increase the costs of the law) that a loss of rights (benefits) is required as a symptom of fraud (*culpa in contrahendo*); however, when the reliance interest is sufficiently strong (e.g., to become a trade secret),[96] it can break the bounds of validity of the contract (e.g., Article 501 of Chinese Civil Code).[97]

We should understand the issue of fraud as an issue of remedies:[98] i.e. different remedies which are provided by the law for different situations. These remedies should not be fixed or uniform, and they need to be judged on a case-by-case basis. The fraud regime is certainly a mechanism for avoiding the risk that "whoever makes a decision in a haphazard manner will also be held responsible";[99] however, if it is necessary to redress the harm done to the aggrieved person, tort can also be utilized as the proper instrument. At the extreme, if the fraudster's conduct constitutes a crime, this may trigger

---

Principles). *Supra* note 28, 429, 435, 443, 447. Indeed, the issues of negligence in contracting and the validity of an offer (promise) can easily become two sides of the same coin, so that the emergence of negligence in contracting cannot be entirely attributed to the "narrowness" of German tort law.

95 This may have been influenced by German law, which initially required damage to property and was subsequently extended to interests in the modernization of the law of debt. See *supra* note 29, Liu Yong's article, 62.

96 A corroboration of this is that, with the trend towards property rights in trade secrets, Article 123 of the Chinese Civil Code recognizes "trade secrets" as objects of intellectual property rights.

97 Mr. Sun Weifei pointed out that the provisions of Article 43 of the Contract Law were clearly indifferent to whether the contract was formed or came into effect. See Sun Weifei, 'Commentary on Article 42 of the Contract Law (Liability for Contractual Negligence)' (2018) 1 *Jurist*, 183.

98 Professor Han Shiyuan argues that the fraud regime addresses the validity of the representation and (unlike) *culpa in contrahendo* which provides a remedy. See *supra* note 30, Han Shiyuan's book, 167. This separates fraud from remedies artificially: this is particularly evident given that avoidance (and restitution) following fraud inherently carries an element of remedies.

99 *Supra* note 31, Zhu Qingyu's Book, 272–3.

criminal law, but it does not necessarily preclude the remedies from civil law. This touches on a much-discussed question: is a contract that constitutes a crime of fraud still valid? Professor Ye Mingyi argues that the fate of the contract is not linked to the guilt or innocence of the contracting party, and that it is the fraudulent act (in the case of fraud) that constitutes the crime, not the contract; therefore, only if the fraudulently concluded contract directly infringes on the interests of the state should the contract be considered null and void.[100] This conclusion is correct, but the process of arguing is flawed: because contracts suspected of being fraudulent are, of course, normally valid as a category (often loans), but the criminal law judgment of guilt is aimed at a specific contract, which is certainly not enforceable (i.e. invalid). The key point is that the strike by law against the fraudster (the crime of fraud) is not the same as the strike against the person being defrauded (also the guarantor of the contract), and the invalidity of the contract is directed against the former. However, the latter may still be afforded legal protection in the form of valid contract.

Whether revocable (Articles 149 and 150 of the Chinese Civil Code) or invalid (Article 146 of the Civil Code and Article 26 of the Labor Contract Law, etc.), the law does not qualitatively differentiate between the specific situation of the person who has been defrauded, but rather places it in the quantitative part of the law: i.e., in the second half of Article 157 of the Civil Code, "the loss thus incurred upon the other party shall be compensated by the party at fault", so that the person who has been defrauded may also have been defrauded without exercising the necessary care, and thus bear secondary responsibility.[101] Therefore, the person defrauded may also be held secondarily liable for not exercising the necessary care.[102] This originates from and reflects the idea of a multi-layered remedy for fraud, but the use of intent and negligence to locate liability is easily confused with the principle of attribution of liability in torts, and has given rise to some unthinkable concepts, such as negligent fraud.[103]

---

[100] See Ye Mingyi, 'The Civil Law Regime of Contract Fraud', (2012) 1 *China Legal Science* 133–4.

[101] Some scholars have argued that this article triggers liability for negligent contracting, *supra* note 30, Han Shiyuan's book, 322. For a critique of this view, see Li Yu, *Essentials of the General Principles of Civil Law* (Law Press, 2017) 740–41.

[102] Ibid. Li Yu's book, 743.

[103] It has been argued that the duty to provide information constitutes negligent fraud because the intent to defraud is incompatible with the normative purpose of protecting freedom of intentional decision. See *supra* note 29, Liu Yong's article, 62. For a similar academic view, see *supra* note 30, Ran Keping's book, 286.

It is undesirable to equate the "intent" of fraud with the intent of tort,[104] not to mention that "negligent" fraud is very absurd. The duty to inform is not the "negligent-ization" of fraud, but rather the objectification of fraud through "breach of contract": it is expressly provided for (or contracted for) by statute (or contract), and the fraud is more clearly manifested.

7. THE FUTURE OF THE FRAUD REGIME: RETURNING TO THE ROMAN LAW MODEL

This article is biased towards the legislative theory. The axiomatic model has many advantages, but it is inappropriate for the fraud regime. Instead, a more modern alternative is to go back to the old beginnings: the Roman law of fraud as a "bailout" for the "exhaustion of other remedies",[105] demonstrates a remarkable practical rationality. In other words: the "specific obligation (duty) + including clause" is the rational model to be adopted in modern fraud regimes: it leaves ample room for dealing separately with the fraudster and the fraud victim, while at the same time guaranteeing legislative (as well as judicial) precision in the strike against fraud.

Thus, the real challenge of fraud is left to legislators and to the judiciary (who legislate at the margins of the law). The law needs to recognize what constitutes fraud in different areas and on a case-by-case basis. Legislation needs to identify objective standards of fraud and remedies in specific types of transactions. The more rational institute of fraud of the future will consist of an infinite number of specific fraud norms; if there is a unifying clause, it will be a clause left to the judge's discretion in the absence of other remedies.

---

104 For example, Mr Zhang Jiayong points out that "intent" (Article 42 of the Contract Law) only requires knowledge of the wrongfulness of the act and cannot be equated with "intent" in the sense of the standard of attribution. See *supra* note 89, 129.

105 See Ulpian, *Edict book* 11, D. 4. 3. 5; D. 4. 3. 7. 3; D. 4. 3. 7. 3. And the fraud claim requires that the scam be "large and obvious" (D. 4. 3. 7. 3).

4. The protection of the obligatory right and its doctrinal construction in tort law

Shi Hongpeng

1. INTRODUCTION

In line with the tradition set forth in Article 6(1) of the Chinese Tort Liability Law and Article 106(2) of the General Principles of Civil Law, Article 1165(1) of the Chinese Civil Code adopts an abstract and general legislative model for the general provisions on tort liability. Although legislation has consistently recognized the protection of both rights and interests in tort law, many scholars still draw inspiration from the German legal tradition and advocate for the separate protection of rights and interests through interpretation.[1] Within this context, the topic of pure economic loss in tort law remedies has been a consistent subject of discussion in comparative law and domestic literature. However, there has been no consensus on the composition of the constituent elements of its damages. This lack of consensus arises partly from the fact that pure economic loss itself is a broadly defined concept, and even within a legal framework, controversies concerning the compensability of different types of

[1] See Yu Fei, 'Method to Distinguish between Right and Interest in Tort Law' (2011) 4 *Chinese Journal of Law*, 118–119; Sun Weifei, 'Rights and Legal Interests in the Law of Tort Liability', in Wang Hongliang et al. eds, *Studies on Private Law in China and Germany*, Volume 11, Peking University Press, 2015, p. 320; Zhu Hu, 'The Distinct Protection of Different Legal Interests in Tort Law: Thought and Technique' (2015) 5 *Journal of Comparative Law*, 45–50; Zhu Yan, General Theory of the Law of Tort Liability – General Introduction, Law Publishing House, 2011 edition, pp. 161–162; Cheng Xiao, *Tort Liability Law,* second edition, The Law Press 2015, pp. 191–196; Zhang Xinbao, *Tort Liability Law*, fourth edition, People's University of China Press 2016, p. 4.

pure economic loss can arise based on the same norm.[2] This implies that even if an obligatory right were considered a type of pure economic interest,[3] a specific examination of this type is still necessary. To strike a balance between the protection of legal interests and the freedom of action, obligatory rights, as a type of interest, should be distinguished from other absolute rights in terms of the composition of constituent elements of damages.[4] However, beyond the violation of protective norms which intend to safeguard obligatory rights, there is no consensus in tort law theories regarding the general constituent elements of damages resulting from the infringement of obligatory rights. There is disagreement on whether intent is necessary for subjective fault or whether gross negligence is also included, and whether the violation of public order and good morals is necessary for establishing illegality.[5] The diversity of conclusions and the arbitrary nature of arguments have further contributed to judicial

---

2 See Mauro Busani, Vernon Valentine Palmer, eds, Pure Economic Loss in European Law, translated by Zhang Xiaoyi and Zhong Hongming, Law Press, 2005 edition, p. 394.

3 This is a fairly mainstream view. See Yu Fei, 'Method to Distinguish between Right and Interest in Tort Law' (2011) 4 *Chinese Journal of Law*, 106. There are also scholars who claim that third-party infringement of obligatory rights causes pure economic loss, see Cao Dengfeng, 'China's Tort Composition Mode of Tort Liability Law: Focusing on the Positioning and Functional Analysis of "Civil Interest"' (2013) 6, *Chinese Journal of Law*, 102; Ye Mingyi, 'Distinction and Overlap between Contractual Liabilities and Tort Liabilities' (2018) 1 *SJTU Law Review*, 14.

4 See the Civil Law Office of the Law System Working Committee of the Standing Committee of the National People's Congress, "Explanation of the Provisions of the Tort Liability Law of the People's Republic of China, Legislative Rationale, and Relevant Provisions", Peking University Press, 2010 edition, p. 8; Wang Liming, "Research on the Tort Liability Law (Upper Volume)" (second edition), People's University of China Press, 2016 edition, p. 91.

5 Some scholars advocate that the third-party infringement of obligatory rights is necessary for intent, but not for the element of being contrary to good morals, e.g., Cheng Xiao, *Tort Liability Law,* second edition, Law Press 2015, p. 186. Some scholars advocate that the establishment of a third-party infringement claim requires the tortfeasor's intentional reneging on good morals, such as Wang Liming, 'The Scope of Protection by General Provision in Tort Law' (2009) 3 *The Jurist*, 28; Ge Yunsong, 'Compensation for Purely Economic Losses and the General Provisions of Tort' (2009) 5, *Peking University Law Journal*, 728; Ran Keping, 'The Formation of "Malicious Collusion" and "Concealing an Illegal Purpose under the Disguise of Illegitimate Acts" in the General Provision of Civil Code' (2017) 4, *Modern Law Science*, 74.

confusion, especially as the number of cases related to third-party infringement of obligatory rights[6] has increased in recent years.[7]

In fact, there are even differing views on whether obligatory rights should be defined as interests or rights. In China's current common textbooks on tort law, some scholars clearly advocate that obligatory rights fall under the category of non-enumerated rights in Article 2(2) of the Tort Liability Law.[8] Some scholars directly argue that obligatory rights belong to the category of interests.[9]

---

6 The author conducted a full-text search for judgment documents containing the keywords "obligatory right" and "infringement" or "tort" in the database of "WKFirst" (https://law.wkinfo.com.cn/). Taking the judgments since 2020 as an example, among the 3,995 judgments with the subject matter of "dispute over tortious liability", the substance of 68 judgments involves the infringement of obligatory rights by a third party.

7 At least in the decisions made by the Supreme Court or the cases in the Gazette of the Supreme People's Court of the People's Republic of China, some of the main points of the decisions advocate that the tort law protection of obligatory rights is premised on the fact that the aggressor knew or should have known of the existence of the obligation, and that the damaging conduct violated the laws, regulations, and other normative legal documents aimed at protecting the obligatory right, or violated public order and good morals, such as the judgment of "Jilin Small and Medium-sized Enterprises Credit Guarantee Group Co. Ltd. v. China Great Wall Asset Management Company Limited, Jilin Branch and Other Companies' Creditor Interests Liability Dispute", see *Gazette of the Supreme People's Court of the People's Republic of China* (2019) 3. Some decisions assert that a third party who is obliged to assist the court in taking preservation measures, if the third party refuses to assist the court in taking preservation measures or takes other measures to obstruct the preservation, maliciously infringing on the claims of the applicant for preservation, thus causing the final judgment to be unenforceable and the applicant's obligatory rights to be unfulfilled and suffering damages, the third party shall be liable to the applicant for damages in tort, e.g., the ruling of "Shanghai Puxin Investment Management Consulting Co. v. BOCI Securities Co. Bulletin", see *Gazette of the Supreme People's Court of the People's Republic of China* (2014) 10. The two cases are similar in their conclusions, recognizing the limited protection of obligatory rights in tort law, but not similar in their statements of the constituent elements. In contrast, the Supreme Court has also stated in a number of cases that "mere contractual claims between contractual counterparties fall within the scope of contract law, not tort liability law", see the Judicial Opinion of No. 15 of Retrial Civil Cases of Supreme People's Court (最高法民再15号) (2016).

8 See Yang Lixin, *Tort Liability Law,* third edition, Peking University Press 2018, p. 20.

9 See Zhang Xinbao, *Tort Liability Law*, fourth edition, People's University of China Press 2016, p. 5.

Others suggest that obligatory rights can only be protected when there is an intentional breach of good morals and other special elements, indirectly implying that obligatory rights are a type of interest.[10] There are also scholars who emphasize the necessity of intent as one of the constituent elements but do not clearly specify whether obligatory rights belong to the category of rights or interests.[11]

The question of whether obligatory rights can be protected by tort law depends primarily on the characterization of rights in tort law. In this regard, the theory that the rights in tort law must possess the characteristics of "attributed contents" (*Zuweisungsgehalt*), "excludability" (*Ausschlußfunktion),* and "typical social publicity", as introduced by the German civil law scholar Fabricius to illustrate the characteristics of rights in Article 823(1) of the BGB, and hasn't become a prevailing view in the theories of German civil law till today,[12] has been widely accepted by most Chinese scholars and even some judges at various levels[13] after its introduction into China by pioneering legal experts.[14] However, the characteristics of "right" in tort law, particularly whether "typical social publicity" is necessary, remain debatable. In general,

[10] See Zhu Yan, General Theory of the Law of Tort Liability – General Introduction, The Law Press, 2011, pp. 161–162.

[11] See Cheng Xiao, *Tort Liability Law*, second edition, The Law Press 2015, pp. 184–186.

[12] Compare Gerhard Wagner, Kommentar zum § 823, in: *Münchener Kommentar zum BGB*, eighth edition, Munich: C. H. Beck, 2020, para. 305; Johannes Hager, Kommentar zum § 823, in: *J. von Staudingers Kommentar zum BGB*, Berlin: de Gruyter, 2017, para. B124.

[13] See Wang Zegian, Tort Law, China University of Political Science and Law Press, 2001 edition, p. 181; Sun Peng, Research on Hot Issues of Contract Law, Mass Publishing House, 2001 edition, p. 248; Yu Fei, 'Method to Distinguish between Right and Interest in Tort Law' (2011) 4 *Chinese Journal of Law*, pp. 110–111.

[14] Some of the literature directly invokes the expression "typical social publicity", for example, Li Yongjun, General Principles of Civil Law, China Legal Publishing House, 2018, p. 543; Wang Liming, Essence of Civil and Commercial Law, The Commercial Press, 2018, p. 448; Xie Hongfei, 'Default Liability and Tort Liability Competing Theory of Reconstitution', in Long Weiqiu and Wang Wenjie, editors, Frontiers of Cross-Strait Civil and Commercial Law (4th series), The Law Press, 2015, p. 567; Cheng Xiao, *Tort Liability Law,* second edition, The Law Press 2015, p. 185; Zhang Jiayong, Study on Adjustment Mode of Intermediate Fields of Contract Law and Tort Law-Centred on the Empirical Analysis of Institutional Interaction, Peking University Press, 2016, p. 357. In addition, a large number of judgments have formally or substantively adopted the jurisprudence of the typical social publicity and formed corresponding judgments.

the question of whether obligatory rights are a type of right and the basis on which the remedy of tort damages can be recognized have not yet been fully examined.

As the dispute over whether a distinction between unlawfulness and fault should be made concerning the constituent elements of tort liability remains unsolved in tort law theory,[15] this chapter, constrained by its subject matter, will not provide any comments on that issue. However, since judges sometimes need to indirectly assess the social appropriateness of an act through the objective legal order requirements in cases related to the infringement of obligatory rights, a specific discussion of unlawfulness may enhance the clarity of this chapter. Therefore, this chapter still makes the necessary distinction between fault and unlawfulness.

2. JURISPRUDENTIAL RECONSTRUCTION OF THE THEORY OF RIGHT IN TORT LAW

At first glance, there seems to be a shift in perspective between the general theory of rights in private law and the theory of rights in the law of torts, due to the different doctrinal functions performed by the concept of rights. Generally, what we emphasize in the case of rights is the possibility for the subject to "act in a certain way" based on empowerment within the framework of the legal order.[16] In legal relationships, the attributed contents of rights not only determine the content of duties or constraints but also establish the normative basis for evaluating illegality through the infringement of rights or the violation of duties. However, in tort law, as its core involves remedies and sanctions after the infringement of rights and interests, the underlying tort liabilities must take into account the balance between the protection of legal interests and the liberty of action as a legal ethical consideration. As a result, the typical social publicity of rights is taken into account in the current doctrine when examining and determining rights in the sense of tort law.[17] In this

[15] On this see Cheng Xiao, *Tort Liability Law,* second edition, The Law Press 2015, pp. 260–263.

[16] Compare Karl Larenz, 'Zur Struktur hsubjektiver Rechte', in: *Festgabe für Johannes Sontis*, Munich: Beck, 1977, p. 147.

[17] See Yu Fei, 'Method to Distinguish between Right and Interest in Tort Law' (2011) 4 *Chinese Journal of Law*, pp. 110–111; Fritz Fabricius, "Zur Dogmatik des" sonstigen Recht "gemäß § 823 Abs. 1 BGB", *Archiv für die civilistische Praxis*, 160 (1961), 273, 291.

dichotomous perspective, obligatory rights are usually regarded as an interest in the name of a right in tort law, while not as a right due to the lack of typical social publicity.[18]

For a given violation, the subjective fault of the perpetrator would be evaluated by an independent criterion. That is to say, what matters is not the so-called typical social publicity, but the possibility of individualized publicity. As for unlawfulness, what matters is the violation of protective law or public order and morality, rather than typical social publicity. In the case of infringement or nuisance of rights as part of the objective legal order, the attributed contents and structure of the rights directly provide the criterion for judging unlawfulness; the typical social publicity and other external prerequisites are of no use. While it is true that some rights do not have the possibility of being infringed by their nature and therefore cannot be brought under the protection of tort law, the abrupt division of the rights theory of private law into two parts only because of the special legal policy considerations of tort law, and the special characteristics of the rights calling for a paradoxical structure of constituent elements for tort liability, necessitate a re-evaluation of the need for the existence of the element of typical social publicity. For this reason, this chapter takes a re-examination of the theory of rights in tort law as the starting point to explore the correct way to view obligatory rights.

2.1 The Right Protected by Tort Law Should Have its Attributed Content and Excludability

Owning a right by a subject implies, first of all, that the legal order has attributed a certain content of interest to that particular subject. This structure is known as the "attributed contents" of a right.[19] Attributed contents essentially emphasize the fact that a right should have a defined content of interest and boundaries.[20] Therefore, not only property, intellectual property rights, personality rights, and identity rights, but even formative rights can also be attrib-

---

18 See Yu Fei, 'Method to Distinguish between Right and Interest in Tort Law' (2011) 4 *Chinese Journal of Law*, p. 106; Ge Yunsong, 'Compensation for Purely Economic Losses and the General Provisions of Tort' (2009) 5, *Peking University Law Journal*, p. 694.

19 Compare Anne Röthel, "Die Lehre vom Zuweisungsgehalt", *Juristische Ausbildung* 10 (2018), 1004, 1005. Also referred to as "Zuordnungsfunktion" ("Function of Attribution"), see Claus-Wilhelm Canaris, Der Schutz obligatorischer Forderungen nach §823 I BGB, in: *Festschrift für Erich Steffen zum 65. Geburtstag*, Berlin: De Gruyter, 1995, p. 90.

20 Compare Larenz/Wolf, *Allgemeiner Teil des Bürgerlichen Rechts*, ninth edition, Munich: C. H. Beck, 2004, p. 243ff.

uted with corresponding attributed contents, e.g., Article 240 of the Chinese Civil Code for ownership rights. According to Article 118, obligatory rights have their own attributed contents and boundaries as well.

In addition to attributed contents, another basis for the protection of rights in tort law lies in the exclusionary function.[21] Attributed contents exist as the basis and prerequisite for excludability because "only when the law attributes to a subject a defined and clearly delimited content of interest is there a clear line of demarcation between that subject and the potential infringer".[22] Here, based on the principle of equality of obligatory rights, the same interest of a certain performance can exist over multiple obligatory rights without exclusivity between each other; the obligatory right is thus usually considered to lack excludability, although the interest of performance can always be attributed to a particular subject. The problem here is that excludability is mixed with exclusivity, and in such a background, a wrongful conclusion that obligatory rights have no excludability was drawn. This will be criticized later.

2.2 Rights Protected by Tort Law Are Not Necessary to Have Typical Socially Publicity

As the discussion on attributed contents shows, the essence of the infringement of rights lies in the infringement of the legal interests protected by the rights. Take ownership, the prototype of the concept of rights in tort law, as an example; the existence of rights cannot be separated from the existence of the tangible object. Even if we extend the observation to the right of personality, there are still many legal interests of personality that exist based on the legal position of the subject, which are inextricably linked to the right of personality, even though there is no tangible object external to the subject itself. These examples reveal that the externalization of rights ensures that third parties are aware of the rights and prevents them from being infringed. Based on the model of rights such as ownership, Fabricius proposes that "typical social publicity" is a key characteristic of rights in tort law. In essence, typical social publicity is "the obvious identifiability of the legal interest based on social and cultural perceptions",[23] i.e., "the conceptual reflection of the object, based on custom and experience, which originates in the ordinary senses, and which

---

21 Compare Larenz/Canaris, *Lehrbuch des Schuldrechts: Besonderer Teil*, 2. Halbband, thirteenth edition, Munich: C. H. Beck'sche Verlagsbuchhandlung, 1994, p. 374.

22 See Yu Fei, 'Method to Distinguish between Right and Interest in Tort Law' (2011) 4 *Chinese Journal of Law*, 109.

23 See Fritz Fabricius, Zur Dogmatik des "sonstigen Recht" gemäß § 823 Abs. 1 BGB, *Archiv für die civilistische Praxis*, 160 (1961), 273, 291.

allows the public to establish the idea of the existence of the legal interest".[24] This assertion of Fabricius is obviously appealing since it is easy to conclude that, based on an inductive approach, rights, which range from property rights to specific personality rights and to incorporeal property rights, such as intellectual property rights, should have a typical social publicity. But can this legal cognition based on induction stand up to further scrutiny by existing civil law doctrines?

The requirement of typical social publicity to rights can be broken down into two perspectives. First, the typical social publicity of a right presupposes that the right and its attributed content are recognized by social and cultural ideas (including legal ideas). Second, the right should be objectively and typically identifiable. As far as the latter is concerned, the "object" on which typical social publicity is based does not need to be physical or perceptible,[25] but to achieve such identifiability, it is necessary to have some kind of external object that can be perceived and grasped. Obligatory rights have always been recognized by the legal order, thus fulfilling the first level of the "requirement" of typical social publicity. On the latter level, taking into account the fact that, in the usual obligatory relationship, neither the obligation undertaken nor the act of performance can be accomplished is public, and that only the parties to the obligatory relationship can be aware of the existence of the right. Therefore, Fabricius considers that the obligatory right lacks the typical social publicity.[26]

However, the requirement of typical social publicity is based on the function of guaranteeing the liberty of action. Scholars have argued that, from the perspective of the victim, "rights in tort law should be socially typically public, a feature like that is important for safeguarding the reasonable expectations of the victim and guaranteeing his or her liberty of action".[27] However, the guarantee of liberty of action can, at best, provide value guidance for argumentation and cannot exist as a rule-based product in itself. Even when examined in the light of the function of guaranteeing liberty of action, the typical social publicity does not constitute a sufficient or necessary condition for the protection of rights. In the former case, if typical social publicity is a self-sufficient condition for the guarantee of liberty of action, it needs to be analyzed in terms of the typical social publicity in a socio-cultural sense of the right itself, i.e., that the need for protection of a certain right is recognized in socio-cultural perspectives, as well as in terms of the identifiability of the right itself. Thus, in the case of, for example, a general personality right, which, given that it

24 Ibid., 291.
25 Ibid., 292–293.
26 Ibid., 301.
27 See Yu Fei, 'Method to Distinguish between Right and Interest in Tort Law' (2011) 4 *Chinese Journal of Law*, 108.

is recognized and perceivable as an external personality interest of the legal order, is not a sufficient condition for the protection of rights. Therefore, in cases such as general personality rights, given their recognition by the legal order and their perceived extrinsic personality interests, they should be recognized as having a typical social public nature. In practice, however, the protection of general personality rights can still only be ascertained through a case-by-case weighing of interests against the guarantee of liberty of action. What really matters in terms of its necessity as a guarantee of liberty of action is not the so-called typical social publicity, but the specific publicity of the right – if the behaver in the individual case cannot recognize the existence of the right, there is no subjective fault. Accordingly, typical social publicity in the sense of the second perspective above is no longer necessary. In fact, the specific construction of the right in terms of its attributed contents and excludability would make typical social publicity superfluous: on the one hand, the attributed content of the right determines the fact of infringement; on the other hand, the excludability of the right reflects, in other words, the special permission or authorization of conduct by the legal order and ultimately determines the boundaries of the liberty of action. This is true for rights with certain attributed contents, as well as for interests that require a case-by-case weighing of interests to determine their protectability. Because for the latter, it is nothing more than that the boundaries of the protection of the infringed interest are to be determined in individual cases by the liberty of action (e.g., freedom of expression), and that the excludability, which depends on a case-by-case weighing, is the true basis of the preventive claims such as cessation of the infringement, exclusion of the obstruction, and abatement of the danger. Also, because it is the excludability that essentially determines the duty of conduct, the excludability is the true source of the judgment of unlawfulness.[28] The theory that the infringement of a right indicates the unlawfulness of the conduct in comparative tort law literature is also based on the full existence

---

[28] It is for this reason that in some cases of infringement of the interest in the realization of an obligatory right (e.g. infringement of the right of tenancy), many judgments have directly recognized the protection through the tort, without relying on a special element of illegality. The justification of such position lies in the fact that the obligatory right serves as a right to provide the foundation for damage, and possession as a state that can exclude the infringement of the private force. Meanwhile, possession, as a state, not only excludes private invasion but also creates a legal status similar to that of a right in rem in relation to third parties outside the lease relationship, thus providing an exclusive function for the entire right. For more information on the construction of the lease right, see also Lei Qiuyu, 'The Civil Interpretation of Acting against Third Party of Tenant Right' (2019) 5 *The Jurist* 97.

of excludability that the right normally possesses, rather than on the typical social publicity of the right.[29]

Of course, as a conceptual tool for renewing the category of "rights" in tort law, the concept of typical social publicity at least attempts to establish a channel of communication between the legal order and the public's feelings about the law so that emergent interests can be guided by typical social publicity to be further considered as rights within the scope of protection of the law of torts in the course of judicial practice. In modern society, however, it is, in fact, difficult to find interests that are recognized by tort law on the one hand, but whose attributive content and excludability cannot be ascertained on the other hand, so the doctrinal and legal policy contributions of typical social publicity are of limited significance.

3. THE DUAL NATURE OF THE OBLIGATORY RIGHT AS RIGHT AND INTEREST IN TORT LAW AND ITS DAMAGE PATTERNS

The doctrinal worthlessness of typical social publicity implies that we cannot dismiss the potential existence of an obligatory right merely because it lacks typical social exposure. The nature of the obligatory right, as a legal interest or right, warrants further analysis.

3.1 The Obligatory Right as a Right in the Sense of Attribution

In comparison to other absolute rights, an obligatory right is a form of relative right. However, it is inadequate to reject the possibility of tort remedies when a third party infringes upon an obligatory right.[30] On one hand, according to traditional empirical legal provisions, Article 2(2) of the Chinese Tort Liability Law encompasses rights with a relative nature, such as guardianship and shares, within its scope of protection. This position is likely to be the interpretative foundation for the scope of protection outlined in Article 1165(1) of the Chinese Civil Code. On the other hand, the exclusivity of absolute rights differs from the excludability of rights. The former implies that no more than

29 For a contrary view see Fritz Fabricius, "Zur Dogmatik des" sonstigen Recht "gemäß § 823 Abs. 1 BGB", *Archiv für die civilistische Praxis*, 160 (1961), 273, 295.

30 For opposing views, see e.g. Fikentscher/Heinemann, *Schuldrecht,* tenth edition, Berlin: De Gruyter, 2006, p. 764; Dieter Medicus, Besitzschutz durch Anspruche auf Schadensersatz, *Archiv für die civilistische Praxis*, 165 (1965), 115, 117; Wu Xiangxiang, 'On Damages for Infringement of Possession' (2013) 3 *Peking University Law Journal*, 612.

two rights with incompatible contents can coexist on a given object simultaneously.[31] The latter focuses on the right holder's ability to assert a preventive claim and secure a litigation remedy against third-party infringement.[32] Consequently, an obligatory right can still be a protected right in tort law as long as it possesses both attributed content and excludability. This determination is advantageous because, due to its exclusionary function, infringement of an obligatory right in the sense of attribution ("attribution of obligatory right") does not necessitate a violation of public order, good morals, or protective laws to argue unlawfulness.

In cases involving rights with property value, the grant of a right to a subject implies exclusive property claims and the exclusive competence to perform specific acts. Scholars have referred to these two aspects as "property entitlement" (Vermögensberechtigung) and "action permission" (Aktionsberechtigung).[33] Of these aspects, the property aspect is undoubtedly more fundamental. An obligatory right, in the sense of a property right, emphasizes the attribution of the right to a specific subject, as opposed to the creditor's claim of performance against the debtor.[34] If we exclude the realization aspect of the obligatory right, the right itself, as a property object, can still be subject to derogation or loss in tort law. The obligatory right, as a product of mental concepts, can only be diminished or lost through legal or litigation acts, especially acts of disposal. Consequently, both disposal and acceptance of performance can lead to the extinction of the obligatory right, making them typical forms of infringement of the attribution of the obligatory right. In contrast, the obligatory right would not be infringed by the request of a non-rights-holder or by private remedies.[35] These infringements include assignments, pledges, releases, and the collection of obligatory rights.[36] The attributed contents of obligatory rights are also

---

31 See Cui Jianyuan, *Property Law*, fourth edition, People's University of China Press, 2017, p. 18.

32 See Claus-Wilhelm Canaris, Der Schutz obligatorischer Forderungen nach §823 I BGB, in: *Festschrift für Erich Steffen zum 65. Geburtstag*, Berlin: De Gruyter, 1995, p. 90.

33 Compare Karl Larenz, "Zur Struktur hsubjektiver Rechte", in: *Festgabe für Johannes Sontis*, Munich: Beck, 1977, p. 140.

34 See Yuan Guo He, 'Disposition Consciousness in Fraud: Necessity and Contents' (2021) 3 *Chinese Journal of Law* 137.

35 The interruption of the statute of limitations as a result of the request can certainly have an impact on the interest in the realization of the obligatory right, but it has nothing to do with infringement. See Yang Wei, 'Comments on Article 195 of the Civil Code (Outside Litigation Request; Obligation Recognition)' (2021) 4 *The Jurist* 177.

36 The authority to collect is attributed to the creditor; this is the premise of receiving the liquidation, and receiving the liquidation is still essentially a kind

evident in the law of unjust enrichment, where the effective disposition and collection of another's obligatory rights give rise to a claim for restitution. The rationale for such a claim stems from the attribution of authority and corresponding interests to the creditor.

Obligatory rights are not exclusive rights, but they possess excludability. Once an obligatory right has been attributed to a specific creditor, this legal position must be respected by all others. In terms of attribution, obligatory rights are "absolute" concerning unspecified third parties,[37] while relativity exists concerning the debtor. Absolute attribution implies that unspecified third parties are obligated not to infringe upon the attribution of the obligatory right, and their infringement is therefore unlawful. If this unlawfulness aligns with the unlawfulness in the constituent elements of the right to removal of obstacles and the right to elimination of danger, and if the purpose of such preventive claims in the legal system is to prevent actual damage and compensate for the inadequacy of protection in tort law, then the excludability of the obligatory right in the sense of attribution is endorsed in civil law.[38] Consequently, the creditor may still exercise the right of prevention in case of infringement of the attribution of the claim. The rights of prevention, in the sense of "removal of obstacles" and "elimination of danger" as modes of civil liabilities, are of general validity and are not limited to rights in rem.[39] Through the systematic positioning of the Tort Liability Section in the Chinese Civil Code, it can naturally be applied to the infringement of absolute attribution of obligatory rights.[40]

---

of disposal of the obligatory right. There is no lack of relevant cases in judicial practice, such as "Beijing Shan Bai Li Heng Land Co., Ltd. and Wang Xueying application for bankruptcy and reorganisation, tort liability disputes", No. 27 First Instance Civil Judgement from Jinmen Intermediate People's Court of Hubei Province (鄂08民初27号) (2020).

37 See Han Shiyuan, General Theory of Contract Law (4th ed.), The Law Press, 2018, p. 898; Karl Larenz, *Lehrbuch des Schuldrechts: Allgermeiner Teil*, Vol. 1, fourteenth edition, Munich: C. H. Beck'sche Verlagsbuchhandlung, 1987, p. 574.

38 Compare Claus-Wilhelm Canaris, Der Schutz obligatorischer Forderungen nach §823 I BGB, in: *Festschrift für Erich Steffen zum 65. Geburtstag*, Berlin: De Gruyter, 1995, p. 90f.

39 See Zhang Gu, 'The Tort Liability Law and its System under the Influence of Two Concepts', in *Proceedings of the Seminar on Contemporary Civil and Commercial Theoretical Innovation and Legislative Foresight and the First Cross-Strait Forum on the Frontiers of Civil and Commercial Law in 2011,* p. 694.

40 See Xu Xiaofeng, 'Third Party's Nuisance Liability for Infringement of Obligatory Rights' (2005) 2 *The Taiwan Law Review* 122–127. Judicial practice has also recognized this opinion, see "Ji Jun, Ji Lanying and Zhao Shiwei tort

The excludability of obligatory rights in substantive law is also reflected in enforcement law. For example, when an obligatory right is frozen and enforced by a judicial organ, a genuine creditor may file an enforcement objection. In this regard, Article 25(1) of the Provisions of the Supreme People's Court on Several Issues concerning the Handling of Enforcement Opposition and Reconsideration Cases by People's Courts stipulates that "other properties and rights, [...] if not registered, the people's court shall decide according to a contract or any other evidence proving property ownership or right holders". This explicitly recognizes that a third party may bring an objection suit against execution, a recognition supported by judicial practice[41] and theoretical studies. For instance, when an agent holds an obligatory right against a nominee due to the agent's actions, the nominee may still exercise the right of repossession or file an enforcement objection when the obligatory right held by the agent is facing enforcement.[42]

As mentioned earlier, if a legal position possesses both attributed contents and excludability, it can be considered the "right" in tort law. Consequently, the tort remedies for the infringement of the attribution of obligatory rights cannot simply apply the constituent elements of damages for the infringement of interests. Instead, they need to consider damages for the infringement of the attribution of obligatory rights, which still need to be correctly determined.

3.2 An Obligatory Right as an Interest in its Possibility of Being Implemented

The realization of an obligatory right is mediated by performance, which falls under the general rules of obligation law or contract law. Tort law does not actively contribute to the realization of an obligatory right. Specifically, the debtor's willingness to perform, the object of the performance, and the liability assets securing the realization of the obligatory right are not attributed to the obligatory right and therefore lack excludability. Consequently, the obligatory right in the sense of realization is only a kind of interest. However, since performance is a purposeful and conscious act of the perpetrator to increase the interests of others, which objectively includes a special sacrifice of the perpetrator, the existence of the obligatory right still provides the possibility of increasing the overall property for the creditor. For such a right aiming at

liability dispute", No. 11362 Final Civil Judgment of Xi'an Intermediate People's Court of Shaanxi Province (陕01民终11362号) (2020).

41 See the No. 43 Enforcement Written Order of the Execution Ruling of the Hefei Intermediate People's Court of Anhui Province (皖01执异43号) (2018).

42 See Zhu Hu, 'Exceptions to Disclosed Agency and their Corresponding Effects' (2019) 4 *Chinese Journal of Law* 96.

realization through performance, the infringement of that right occurs when the performance cannot be realized due to the injurious behavior of a third party. Specifically, infringement of an obligatory right as an interest includes the following three situations:

3.2.1 Interest realized by voluntary performance: will driving in obligatory rights

As a rule, only in the case of non-performance of a debt does a primary obligation of performance transform into a secondary obligation of damages. The realization of the latter and other debts accompanied by liability depends on the liability assets and is not affected by the inducing behavior of third parties. Therefore, the will-driving function of the obligatory rights, which is contained in the debtor's will for performance, is only relevant in cases related to the primary obligation to performance. Accordingly, the form of infringement of this interest is expressed in the form of inducing a breach of obligation.

In the case of induced default, the failure to realize the obligatory rights is due, on the one hand, to the debtor's non-performance and, on the other hand, to the persuasive conduct of the third party, both of which ultimately result in the same damage. In other words, after the formation of the obligation, the debtor's duty to perform is based on the existence of a special bond, and the act of performance will be motivated by the will contained in the claim. Although third parties are not bound to the obligation, this "will-driving" nature of the obligation would ultimately lead to its realization without the intervention of third parties.[43] Just as the law of torts regulates abetment, in cases such as induced default, where the third person's intervention in the debtor's will gives rise to or reinforces the debtor's default, the appropriateness of the constituent element depends on the act of inducement on the one hand, and the eventual default of the debtor on the other hand. The debtor's breach of its obligation to perform does not sever the causal link between the third person's act and the occurrence of the damage.

3.2.2 Interests in its possibility of being implemented in obligatory rights realized by enforcement: liability assets for securing the realization

Security rights, designed to secure obligatory rights, constitute an independent object of protection under tort law. Evaluating them as an infringement of the interest of obligatory rights is not useful. The ultimate realization of obligatory

---

[43] Compare Helmut Koziol, *Beeinträchtigung des fremden Forderungsrechts*, Vienna: Springer-Verlag, 1967, p. 154ff.; Horst-Eberhard Henke, *Dos sog. Relativität des Schuldverhältnisses*, Berlin: Dunker & Humblot, 1989, p. 65.

rights depends, to a large extent, on the adequacy of liability assets. For the creditor, the infringement of the interest in the realization of obligatory rights may be based on factual tort or a legal act. In the case of wrongful infringement of an individual property right, the property owner's claim for damages against the aggressor likewise forms part of his or her liability assets. The total amount of the liability assets is not diminished, so there is no damage in a legal sense for the creditor. Consequently, damage exists objectively only if the third party, through the assignment of the debtor's property, renders the liability assets insufficient to satisfy the claim.

3.2.3 Basis for the realization of the primary interests of obligatory rights through performance: the object of the performance

Although the content of the obligation is performance, the obligatory right is not a right of domination over the property or person of the debtor. Neither the object of performance nor the person of the debtor is the subject of the obligatory right, so that in the orientation of the interest in its possibility of being implemented, there is only an interest in the realization of the right. If the object of performance or the person of the debtor is harmed, there is a possibility of establishing corresponding tort liability, which may also lead to the non-realization of the interests of obligatory rights. As seen, the normative impairment of the interest in obligatory rights still exists.[44]

In summary, from the perspective of the rights theory of tort law, the different aspects of obligatory rights constitute rights and interests respectively. This means that the broad category of "infringement of obligatory rights" needs to be examined separately in the law of torts, both in terms of its constituent elements and in terms of the calculation of damages, in order to determine what constitutes the respective liability for damages.

---

44 For a favorable view, see also Chen Huabin, A General Introduction to the Law of Obligations, The Law Press, 2012, p. 171. However, the German scholar Professor Gerhard Otto has cited a counterexample to oppose this view: A destroyed the goods which should be delivered to C by B based on the contractual relationship between them. If A in this case needs to be bound by the contractual relationship between B and C, then A will be liable for the damage C suffered, even when A is the owner of the goods. Compare Gerhard Otto, Schadensersatz nach §823 I BGB wegen Verletzung der der Schadensersatz nach §823 I BGB wegen Verletzung der "Forderungszuständigkeit"?, *Juristische Zeitung*, 1969, 253, 253. However, the fallacy of this fine case lies in the fact that, even if the perpetrator is motivated by an apostasy, his actions can be justified by safeguarding his own legitimate interests. Compare Jürgen Oechsler, Kommentar zum § 826, in: *J. von Staudingers Kommentar zum BGB*, Berlin: de Gruyter, 2009, Rn. 53.

4. REALITY AND NECESSITY OF TORT LIABILITY FOR THE INFRINGEMENT OF OBLIGATORY RIGHTS

It is indisputable that the protection of obligatory rights in tort law pays attention not only to the specific constituent elements but also to the reality and necessity of such protection within the legal system of obligations. This involves addressing two questions: firstly, whether the tort remedies for obligatory rights align with the existing legal framework of obligations, and secondly, whether these tort remedies provide systemic benefits.

4.1 The Correctness of Tort Remedies for Infringement of the Attribution of the Obligatory Right and its Complementary Functions

4.1.1 System coherence between tort remedies and assignment

According to the German civil law scholar *Otto*, the acceptance of performance by a non-creditor (e.g., assignor) in an assignment, thus infringing the attribution of the claim, is not prohibited by Article 407 of the German Civil Code.[45] On the basis of Article 546(1) of the Chinese Civil Code, the assignment without notice is not effective against the debtor. According to the dominant theory of civil law, this provision serves to protect the debtor by ensuring correct liquidation.[46] The notion that the original assignor's acceptance of performance leads to the extinction of the obligatory right is a reflection of relieving the bona fide debtor, not due to the assignor's authority to accept. Therefore, if the debtor is held liable for damages due to incorrect liquidation resulting from the infringement of the attribution of obligatory rights, it would conflict with the special protections afforded to the debtor through the assignment institution.[47]

However, the liberation of the debtor from incorrect liquidation does not absolve the original assignor. The acceptance of performance, leading to the extinction of the obligation, is treated similarly to an act of disposal in terms

---

45 Ibid., 254.

46 See Han Shiyuan, General Theory of Contract Law (4th ed.), The Law Press, 2018, p. 616; Wang Hongliang, General Theory of Law of Obligations, Peking University Press, 2016, p. 461; Zhu Hu, 'The Protection of Assignee's Status in the Assignment of Claims: The System Integration of the Rules in Civil Code' (2020) 4 *The Jurist* 14; Xu Duiyu: "Comments on Article 80 of the Contract Law (Notice of Assignment)" (2019) 1 *The Jurist* 185.

47 Compare Dieter Medicus, *Bürgerliches Recht*, twenty-first edition, Cologne/Berlin/Munich: Carl Heymanns Verlag, 2007, p. 369f.

of legal effects,[48] even if not in its original sense.[49] Even with the liquidation and extinction in effect, the legal nature as an unauthorized disposal remains unchanged. A similar legal balancing act exists in the system of good faith acquisition: to protect the bona fide transferee, the right to property changes, but the disposer remains liable for unjust enrichment or tort damages. Just as the effect of a bona fide acquisition is not due to a valid act of disposition, the reason why the original creditor receives the performance and extinguishes the obligatory right in the case of assignments is not due to the fact that he or she has the authority to receive the performance, but due to a special provision of the enacting law. It is untenable to argue that the original assignor's infringement of the attribution of the obligatory right is not prohibited by the legal order from the fact that article 546(1) of the Chinese Civil Code and its doctrinal observations do not contain a prohibition on the original assignor's acceptance of the performance. Denying tort liabilities for the infringement of obligatory rights in this manner is akin to denying the tort liabilities of a transferor in bona fide acquisitions.

4.1.2 Competing and complementary protection of attribution of obligatory rights in tort law

The pursuit of tort remedies for infringement of the attribution of obligatory rights must be considered in relation to remedies in the law of unjust enrichment and contract law. According to *Medicus*, recognizing the absolute status of the attribution of obligatory rights and applying Article 823(1) of the BGB may not be necessary, as remedies based on Article 816(2) of unjust enrichment and the causal relationship of the assignment (e.g., sale) may suffice in cases like assignments.[50] However, Medicus' argument does not negate the possibility of competing claims for restitution of unjust enrichment and tort claims for damages.[51] Especially from the point of view of practical needs, it

48 Compare Looschelders, *Schuldrecht: Allgemeiner Teil,* sixteenth edition, Munich: Vahlen, 2018, p. 132.

49 Compare Fezer, Kommentar zum § 362, in: *Münchener Kommentar zum BGB*, eighth edition, Munich: C. H. Beck, 2019, Rn. 11.

50 Compare Gerhard Otto, Schadensersatz nach §823 I BGB wegen Verletzung der der Schadensersatz nach §823 I BGB wegen Verletzung der "Forderungszuständigkeit"?, *Juristische Zeitung*, 1969, 253, 253.

51 See Shi Shangkuan, General Introduction to the Law of Obligations, China University of Political Science and Law Press, 2000, p. 89; Cui Jianyuan, Han Shiyuan, Yu Min, The Law of Obligations, Tsinghua University Press, 2010, p. 208 (written by Cui Jianyuan). There are even some views that advocate the subsidiary of the right to claim for the return of unjust enrichment in comparative law. See Wang Zegian: Unjust Enrichment, Peking University Press, 2009, p. 210.

is still necessary to remedy the infringement of the attribution of obligatory rights through tort law. This is because the beneficiary may raise the defense that he or she has ceased to benefit (art. 986 of the BGB), thus preventing the claim from being realized.[52] Remedies through tort law are necessary to compensate for the lack of remedies in the law of unjust enrichment and are even inherent in achieving consistency in the evaluation of the legal order.

In principle, infringement of the attribution of obligatory rights occurs whenever a performance made by the debtor to the quasi-possessor of the rights has a liquidating effect,[53] or the quasi-possessor of the rights engages in a valid act of disposition of the rights. While contractual remedies take precedence where a contractual relationship exists between the quasi-possessor and the true creditor, such a relationship may not exist in all cases of infringement of the attribution of obligatory rights. For example, an obligatory right may have been assigned several times, and without notice to the debtor by either the assignor or the assignee, the debtor has satisfied the first assignor; or the holder of bearer securities has tendered them to the debtor and has accepted them;[54] or even a departed corporate officer made a claim against the debtor of a company, and the debtor validly asserts a representation, and so on.

4.2 The Functions of Sanction and Remedy of Tort Law Besides Contractual Remedies

It is indeed accurate that contract law often ensures the realization of interests associated with an obligatory right. In cases where the violation of this interest results from the debtor's breach of contract, contract law stands ready to provide the necessary remedies, irrespective of whether priority is explicitly given to contract law.[55] When the breach of contract stems from actions by a third party, Articles 577 and 593 of the Chinese Civil Code establish the debtor's

---

[52] See Wang Hongliang, 'The System and Application of the Basis of the Right to Claim for the Return of Unjust Enrichment' (2021) 3 *The Jurist* 39.

[53] For the scope of a quasi-possessor of an obligatory right and the constituent elements for the occurrence of the effects of satisfaction, see Qimuti, 'On the effects of the debtor's satisfaction of a quasi-possessor of a claim' (2013) 3 *Law Science* 88–95.

[54] Compare Claus-Wilhelm Canaris, Der Schutz obligatorischer Forderungen nach §823 I BGB, in: *Festschrift für Erich Steffen zum 65. Geburtstag*, Berlin: De Gruyter, 1995, p. 88.

[55] Those who advocate the priority of contractual liability, such as Esser/Schmidt, *Schuldrecht: Allgemeiner Teil*, 2. Teilband, eighth edition, Heidelberg: C.F. Müller, 2000, p. 158. Same position in the French law and the position of the judicial practice in Taiwan, China. For an argument in favor of the "mutual

liability for breach of contract due to the actions of that third party. However, it is crucial to recognize that the debtor's liability for breach of contract is rooted in contractual remedies. In instances where a third party's infringement of the interest in an obligatory right occurs simultaneously with both unlawfulness and necessary fault, unless to avoid double benefit to the creditor, excluding the creditor based on the third party's liability for damages in tort law is not precluded. To underscore the regulation of tort law regarding third-party infringement of the interest in an obligatory right on top of contractual remedies is, in essence, an endeavor to meet the inherent objectives of the sanctioning function and remedy of tort law.

Concerning its sanctioning function, the third party typically lacks a contractual relationship with the creditor. Disregarding the regulation of tort law in cases where damage results from an act characterized by illegality and fault would inevitably lead to inconsistent legal evaluations of similar behaviors. As for its remedial function, tort law plays a crucial role in protecting interests in obligatory rights when contractual remedies may prove insufficient: on the one hand, in circumstances like destroying the driving function of the obligatory rights and infringement of the debtor's person or the object of performance and so on, the debtor who breaches the duty may not have sufficient property to guarantee the realization of the creditor's interests, even if we recognize the damages claims; on the other hand, in the case of the improperly reduced liability assets, in which the damage to the creditor results from the fact that the debtor's liability assets are not enough to meet the creditor's claim, the last resort of remedy can only be the compensation of the tortfeasor.[56] Especially, in these cases, the creditor's rights of revocatory or subrogation may not be able to provide adequate remedy. Because the creditor's right of revocatory applies only to the debtor's legal action, and there is a strict time limit, strict composition of the elements.[57] Similarly, if the right of revocatory proves insufficient,

influence of claims", see Ye Mingyi, 'Comments on Article 122 of the Contract Law (Competing Liabilities)' (2019) 2 *The Jurist* 180.

[56] For relevant examples, see No. 1375 First Instance Civil Judgement of Nanhu District People's Court, Jiaxing, Zhejiang Province (浙0402民初1375号) (2020).

[57] For example, if the debtor transfers the property to a third party in bad faith, and that third party creates a burden on the property for another person in good faith, the creditor's right of avoidance cannot be effective against that other person. Relevant examples can be found in Shanghai First Intermediate People's Court (2009) 沪一中民二（民）终字第898号 Civil Judgement, No. 3986 First Instance Civil Judgement of Cangnan County People's Court, Zhejiang Province (浙0327民初3986号) (2020), No. 2800 First Instance Civil Judgement of Yongkang County People's Court, Zhejiang Province (浙0784民初2800号) (2020),

the remedy function of the right of subrogation may also fail, given that subrogation is contingent on the functioning of the rights of revocatory.

5. UNLAWFULNESS AND FAULT IN THE PROTECTION OF THE OBLIGATORY RIGHT UNDER TORT LAW

The dual nature of the obligatory right as right and interest has already been elucidated. What really needs to be analyzed further in terms of the tort law protection of obligatory right is the unlawfulness of the infringing act and the determination of fault, whereas the infringing act itself and the causation between act and damage are of no special particularity.

5.1 Unlawfulness as a Constituent Element of the Infringement of the Obligatory Right

5.1.1 Infringement of attribution of the obligatory right directly indicates the unlawfulness

As previously discussed, the legal order defines a right, endowing it with specific attributed content and excludability. The coherence of the legal order mandates that tort law recognizes the right-holder's interest as a superior institutional interest deserving protection over the liberty of action within the context of the attributed content of the right.[58] Thus, a right simultaneously bans the behavior of others, and any infringement constitutes a breach of duty, thereby constituting an unlawful act.[59]

In the realm of tort law, the doctrine of unlawfulness places emphasis on the wrongfulness of the result, yet its foundation remains rooted in the wrongfulness of the act itself. This wrongfulness is a purely objective attribution of responsibility within civil law,[60] contingent upon where the prohibition is situated in the legal order. When an obligatory right, construed in terms of attribution, possesses excludability, it imposes a legal obligation on others not to cause harm. Consequently, the act of infringing the attribution of the obligatory right is deemed unlawful. The institutional binding force of an obligatory

etc. For a similar view, see Han Shiyuan, General Theory of Contract Law (4th ed.), The Law Press, 2018, p. 900.

58 See Liang Shangshang, 'Logic in Weighing System Interests' (2012) 4 *China Legal Science* 74.

59 See Shi Shangkuan, General Introduction to the Law of Obligations, China University of Political Science and Law Press, 2000, p. 125.

60 See Wang Qianwei, 'The Concept of "illegality" in the Law of Civil Damages (II)' (2001) 9 *Chengchi University Law Review* 202.

right, especially in terms of attribution as a right in tort law, and its rule-setting requirements based on principles of equality and interchangeability, dictate that, in tort law, the priority of this right over liberty of action should persist. This holds true even if the right is not deemed a "typical social public" right in a general sense. Therefore, regardless of an individual's failure to recognize the existence of a specific right (resulting in a lack of subjective fault), the direct infringement of a legal interest prioritized by the law of torts is still considered unlawful. In this regard, the infringement of the attribution of an obligatory right may lack negligence but is unmistakably and directly labeled as unlawful.

5.1.2 The construction of unlawfulness of the infringement of the interest in the obligatory right

A. The construction of unlawfulness when undermining the will-driving function of the obligatory right

The complexity of contractual relationships and the potential inducement of a breach by third parties require careful consideration within the framework of tort law. If a debtor's willingness to fulfill a prior contract is influenced by entering into a subsequent contractual relationship with a third party (e.g., multiple sales) involving the same performance, the third party's behavior may be considered a legitimate competitive act and not automatically deemed unlawful.[61] Even if the will-driving function of the obligatory right is compromised, and harm befalls the creditor, it does not inherently signify unlawfulness. To

[61] In contrast, in French tort law, when a creditor has already acquired an obligatory right, the third party is under an obligation not to enter into a contract with the debtor that may prevent the fulfillment of the prior creditor's claim. When the third party knows the existence of the prior obligatory right, but still concludes a contract with the same debtor, the third party and the debtor together will constitute the infringement of the interests of the obligatory right with "collusion" and may have the consequence of tort damages in Article 1382 of the French Civil Code. See Li Shigang, French contract law reform – a comparative study of three drafts, The Law Press, 2014, 176–177; Yin Tian, French modern contract law: the conflict and balance between freedom of contract and social justice, The Law Press, 2009, p. 294. However, this viewpoint in French judicial practice is rather particular; it has its deep historical origins (e.g., the restrictions on the freedom of laborers to choose their employment under the medieval guild system) and has been influenced to a large extent by the later controversy between individualist and socialist philosophies. See Vernon V. Palmer, 'A Comparative Study (From a Common Law Perspective) of the French Action for Wrongful Interference with Contract', *The American Journal of Comparative Law*, Vol. 40, 1992, pp. 313–321, 333.

address such situations, tort law must resort to special rules preventing actions originally justified by the liberty of action from infringing on the interests of others. Prohibitions against such behavior extend beyond basic contractual obligations and include special rules against human behavior, such as those outlined in Article 148 (fraud) and Article 150 (duress) of the Chinese Civil Code,[62] and other provisions related to public order and good morality.[63] The application of these principles, especially in cases of inducement to breach, requires further discussion.[64]

Abetment is the basic behavioral pattern for inducing a breach of contract. Generally, the unlawfulness of the abetment is either independently proved or is based on the transmission of the unlawfulness of the act committed. In the case of abetment by a third party, however, neither source of unlawfulness exists. In the case of the former, on the one hand, if the act of competing at a high price does not have the nature of being contrary to good morals, the abetment of such an act should not be subject to different value judgments depending on the difference in motivation; on the other hand, the act of abetment itself cannot be assessed as a violation of public order and good morality. Because abetment may also involve urging others to perform and other positive content, even if it involves negative content, abetment in the sense of social life is, despite its moral condemnation, legally not to be blamed. As the dominant doctrine has denied the legitimacy of helping the breach of contract, it is unjust to treat the abetment that has a similar nature in a totally different way.

According to the general theory of criminal law and tort law about abetment, abetment itself does not have any unlawfulness, which rather lies in the transmission through the illegal behavior of the original offender.[65] The difference, however, is that in the case of criminal acts and torts in general,

---

62 See Li Yu, Essentials of the General Principles of the Civil Law: A Collection of Normative Interpretations of Discourses and Criticisms, The Law Press, 2017, pp. 583–584, 600.

63 See Liang Shangshang, 'The Commensurability Problem of Qualitative Interests Weighing and Its Solution' (2014) 4 *Tribune of Political Science and Law* 11.

64 As for the case of malicious collusion to the detriment of the legitimate interests of others (including the interests of obligatory right), the general view is that it constitutes a violation of public order and good morals. See Li Yu, Essentials of the General Principles of the Civil Law: A Collection of Normative Interpretations of Discourses and Criticisms, The Law Press, 2017, p. 700; Jürgen Oechsler, Kommentar zum § 826, in: *J. von Staudingers Kommentar zum BGB*, Berlin: de Gruyter, 2009, Rn. 224.

65 See Ma Kechang and others, editors, The Complete Book of Criminal Law, Shanghai Science and Technology Literature Publishing House, 1993, p. 659 (by Ma Kechang); Hans Heinrich Jessek and Thomas Weigandt, Textbook of German

the interests protected by the enacting law are of a temporal nature, and the abettor is under the same obligation not to contribute to the fulfillment of the constituent elements. The debtor's breach of contract is also unlawful, but the obligation created between the parties is only a specific behavioral norm or a standard of conduct that exists only between the parties of the obligation. In terms of the overall legal order, this kind of behavioral norm or standard of conduct is "neutral", which is different from the general tort law.[66] In other words, the unlawfulness of breach of contract is only meaningful to the parties to the contract and does not have the function of instigating the unlawfulness of behavior in general tort law.

Besides abetment, the behavior of a third party may act in a way that is contrary to good morals if the third party uses culpable means to make the debtor change his or her will of performance. For example, a third party induces a breach of contract by releasing the debtor from the duty to pay damages for his breach of contract. Here, it is not the subjective intention to break a prior contract that makes the behavior contrary to good morals, but the fact that, through excessive means, the institutional obligation to pay damages loses its function of deterring breach of contract, thus completely destroying the real mechanism of the "sanctity of the contract".[67] From the perspective of the damages, being contrary to good morals should likewise render the construction of a potential third-party contract of interest ineffective, thus necessitating a remedy through tort law. Similarly, abetting a breach of a special duty of loyalty that is part of the institutional interest, such as the duty of loyalty

Criminal Law (Upper), translated by Xu Jiusheng, China Legal Publishing House, 2017, p. 446.

66 See Chen Zhongwu, The Objects of Protection of Contractual and Tort Liability, New Academic Forest 2008, pp. 203–204; Oechsler, Kommentar zum § 826, in: *J. von Staudingers Kommentar zum BGB*, Berlin: de Gruyter, 2009, Rn.225; Josef Esser, *Schuldrecht,* Vol. 2, third edition, Karlsruhe: Verlag C. H. Müller, 1969, p. 395f.

67 Compare BGH NJW 1981, 2186; Oechsler, Kommentar zum § 826, in: *J. von Staudingers Kommentar zum BGB*, Berlin: de Gruyter, 2009, para. 227. The central argument of the dissenting opinion is that the conduct of the third person reinforces the possibility of the fulfillment of the duty of damages, and in this case it seems to be a contradiction in terms to still regard it as an aberration of good morals. Compare Helmut Köhler, Die "Beteiligung an fremdem Vertragsbruch" – ein unerlaubte Handlung?, in: *Festschrift für Claus Wilhelm Canaris zum 70. Geburtstag*, Vol. 1, Munich: Verlag C.H. Beck, 2007, p. 596f. This is not a tenable point, since the infringement of the interest of the obligatory right has relevance to the primary obligation to perform, and it is on this point that infringement is evaluated by the corresponding unlawfulness, while without any direct connection to the concrete consequences.

of the worker to the employer, as implied in article 91 of the Chinese Labour Contract Law,[68] would also constitute in its nature a breach of public order and good morality.

Being contrary to good morals in relation to the infringement of obligatory rights cannot be used directly to regulate the competitive market behavior. For the case of platform anchors being "poached" by other platforms,[69] the behavior of the new platform does not violate public order and good morality from the perspective of infringing on the interests in the obligatory rights. However, since the behavior of the anchors usually constitutes the platform's market competition, the behavior of the platform should be further considered through a positive weighing of interests to determine the impact of the behavior on the order of competition, the development of the industry and many other factors.

B. Unlawfulness of infringement of the interest in the obligatory rights through undue diminution of the liability assets

As noted earlier, infringement of individual property does not result in a diminution of the liability assets. Even if a third party "infringes" the liability assets with the purpose of infringement of the obligatory right, thus reflecting a violation of good morals, the creditor has not suffered damage as a result.[70] Therefore, the cases to be considered are merely those in which the debtor's liability assets are reduced by a legal act. Normally, cases of this type are also subject to the creditor's right of avoidance. However, as mentioned above, there is no reason to exclude tort remedies as a matter of course when the creditor has been harmed and the third party's behavior is unlawful. On top of that, not all acts that meet the requirements for the creditor's right of avoidance are unlawful on the part of the third party; otherwise, all fraudulent acts should be assessed as invalid. It follows that the acquisition of property or a property interest by a third party that infringes the creditor's interest cannot in itself directly invoke unlawfulness. Since the behavior of infringement is limited to the bilateral legal act, for example, in the cases where a debtor gratuitously disposes of its property rights by waiving an obligation owed to the debtor, waiving the security provided for the obligation, gratuitously transferring property,

68 See Xu Jianyu, 'The Faithful Obligation of Employees in Labor Law' (2014) 6 *Tsinghua University Law Journal* 121–123.

69 See No. 4950 Final Civil Judgment of Wuhan Intermediate People's Court, Hubei Province (鄂01民终第4950号) (2017).

70 The norms in special laws that protect the liability assets always have other purposes as well. For example, the duty of shareholders not to abscond with their capital contributions, as set out in article 36 of the Chinese Companies Law, arises from the fact that the capital contributions of the shareholders constitute not only the company's liability assets but also the company's business assets.

and other unreasonable means, the unlawfulness of the act is either based on the debtor and the third party's bad faith conspiracy, or based on the conduct of the violation of the public order and good morality. As far as the latter is concerned, when the perpetrator has the intention to cause damage, the autonomy of private law and the security of the transaction can no longer justify his behavior,[71] and the purpose of the liability assets to protect the creditor is thus undermined, so that his behavior constitutes an abuse of the institution and thus has the attribute of being contrary to public order and morality.

C. *Offences against the object of performance or against the person of the debtor*

There is no connection between the unlawfulness based on the violation of the object of performance or of the person of the debtor and the unlawfulness based on the violation of the interest in the obligatory rights, which is merely an indirect violation dependent on the former, and its unlawfulness can only be dependent on the breach of the duty to maintain safety. However, the duty to maintain safety does not protect all rights and interests in tort without limitation. The interests are protected only to the extent that there is a protective norm of interest; otherwise, the duty to maintain safety protects only absolute rights in principle.[72] Therefore, the unlawfulness of a violation of an object or person, and thus of an obligatory right, still needs to be proved by a violation of public order and good morality. In this regard, if a third party commits an offense against the object of performance or against the person with the purpose of infringing an obligatory right, the means are disproportionate to the purpose and there may be a violation of public order and good morality.

5.2 The Fault in the Infringement of the Obligatory Right

5.2.1 General subjective element of infringement of the attribution of an obligatory right: intent or negligence

As already mentioned, the element of typical social publicity has its significance in terms of legal policy. Since only when the right is perceptible to the general public, a claim for damages resulting from the infringement of a right would not have the effect of restricting the general liberty of action. However, the attribution of the obligatory right as a kind of right reveals that

---

71 See Dai Mengyong, 'Juridical Act and Public Order and Good Morals' (2020) 1 *The Jurist* 30.

72 See Li Hao, The Theory of Duty to Maintain Safety: An Interpretation of the Structural Changes in German Tort Law, Peking University Press, 2008, pp. 175–176; Larenz/Canaris, *Lehrbuch des Schuldrechts: Besonderer Teil*, 2. Halbband, thirteenth edition, Munich: C. H. Beck'sche Verlagsbuchhandlung, 1994, p. 406.

the protection of the attribution takes precedence over liberty of action in the hierarchy of values of the legal order. Thus, if the infringer knew the existence of the other's legal interests and their action resulted in damage, then the liability of the infringer for damages does not deter the liberty of action. In terms of negligent infringement of the attribution of obligatory rights, even if the fact that the violation of the law that causes damage is often found to be prima facie evidence of the existence of the victim's negligence,[73] the violation of the law of the conduct of the victim only establishes the violation of the external objective duty of care,[74] which is different from the internal subjective standard of care used to determine the fault.[75] The lack of subjective due care presupposes the infringer's awareness of the existence of the obligatory rights, which is always the case in individual circumstances, since the infringement of the attribution of the obligatory right should be done in the form of a legal act. Only in those cases where the tortfeasor mistakenly took another person's obligatory right as his own, which belongs to the category of errors of knowledge of the constituent elements, the judgment of the violation of duty of due care might need to be considered. The question of what constitutes the standard of due care in a relationship is to be resolved by objectifying negligence. There is no negligence if no one in the group has the means to recognize the attribution of the obligatory right and the tortfeasor accepts the performance in this situation.

5.2.2 General subjective elements of infringement of the interest in the obligatory rights: intent and exceptional negligence

In the case of special protective norms relating to the specific obligatory rights,[76] the unlawfulness of the act may be established and prima facie evidence of a breach of the duty of care exists. In such cases, the scope of damages can be limited by the fact that the protective norm itself contains the purpose of protecting the interests of a specific subject, and the potential

---

73 See Zeng Shixiong, Principles of Damages Law, China University of Political Science and Law Press, 2001, p. 92.

74 See Erwin Deutsch and Hans-Jürgen Ahrens, German Tort Law – Torts, Damages and Pain Relief, translated by Ye Mingyi and Wen Dajun, People's University of China Press, 2016, p. 59.

75 See Zhang Gu, 'Negligence and Negligence as One's Own Liability – A Commentary from the Perspective of Structural Symmetry', in *Studies in Chinese and German Private Law*, Vol. 4, Peking University Press, 2008, p. 38.

76 For example, article 43 of the Notary Law, article 1 of the Several Provisions of the Supreme People's Court on the Trial of Relevant Civil Cases Involving Notarial Activities, and article 4 of the Several Provisions of the Supreme People's Court on the Trial of Compensation Cases for Civil Tort Involving Accounting Firms Engaging in the Audit Business.

aggressor can take precautions when facing a clear norm, so that reasonable breaches of law and policy do not unduly restrict his or her liberty of action. Thus, it is not inappropriate to extend the subjective element of infringement of the interest in an obligatory right to negligence. Similarly, although no *lex specialis* norm exists, if there is a transactional contact or a special bonding relationship whereby the creditor places special reliance on a third party, the duty to maintain safety should serve as a medium to bring negligent behavior within the scope of the regulation.

In addition to the mentioned cases, the judgment of unlawfulness of the infringement of the interest in the obligatory rights often depends on the violation of public order and good morals or other prohibitions in general civil law (e.g. article 539 of the Civil Code). Here, the subjective fault of the aggressor is evident if he or she has the intention to cause damage. Moreover, the purpose of the judgment of unlawfulness is to dissolve the justification of liberty of action, which makes the establishment of unlawfulness unaffected when there is only a misconception in the perception of unlawfulness (e.g. a mistaken belief that the act is not contrary to good morals), but not a misconception in the perception of the facts underlying the assessment of the act as unlawfulness, which would otherwise have the effect of justifying the wrongful act by the individual's misperception.[77] This is different from the general tort of intent, which requires that the aggressor be aware of the breach of duty (unlawfulness); otherwise, his behavior would be merely negligent.[78]

For the attribute of violation of public order and good morality in the case of infringement of the interests in an obligatory right, the misconception of the facts underlying the judgment of unlawfulness will preclude the judgment from being contrary to public order and good morality.[79] In this regard, we should not confuse "ought to have known" as a factual judgment (presumption of knowing) with "ought to have known but did not know" as a normative judgment (gross negligence), which cannot give rise to ultimate liability for damages here. This is because, although the existence of an obligatory right is certain, requiring third parties to identify it in ordinary social intercourse would undoubtedly constitute a restriction on liberty of action.

---

77 Compare Jürgen Oechsler, Kommentar zum § 826, in: *J. von Staudingers Kommentar zum BGB*, Berlin: de Gruyter, 2009, Rn. 61.

78 See Zhu Yan, General Theory of the Law of Tort Liability – General Introduction, Law Publishing House, 2011 edition, p. 278; Karl Larenz, *Lehrbuch des Schuldrechts: Allgermeiner Teil*, Vol. 1, fourteenth edition, Munich: C. H. Beck 'sche Verlagsbuchhandlung, 1987, p. 280.

79 Compare Dirk Looschelders, *Schuldrecht: Besonderer Teil*, fourteenth edition, Munich: Vahlen, 2019, p. 533.

5. The generative logic of the system of the cooling-off period before divorce and its reflection

Ma Zhiyong

INTRODUCTION

On 28 May 2020, the National People's Congress of the People's Republic of China deliberated and passed the *Civil Code*, Article 1077 of which establishes the legality of the system of cooling-off periods in divorce.[1] This system has received continuous attention ever since it was drafted into the Draft Civil Code. Each time there is a change in this provision in the Draft Civil Code, it is widely discussed. Those in favor of this system argued that in the past the threshold for registered divorce had been very low and there had been no concern for the interests of the weaker party in the family, leading to the abuse of registered divorce and causing an increase in the number of wanton divorces, which consequently undermined family unity and social stability and had a significant negative impact on society and the family, while the cooling-off period before divorce could reduce wanton divorces and preserve family stability.[2] Those against it suggested that forcing the vast majority to pay for the marital problems of a very small number of people, and prolonging suffering in marriages that have already been confirmed as failures, is likely to be con-

1 Article 1077 of the *Civil Code of the People's Republic of China* states: Where either spouse is unwilling to divorce, he or she may, within 30 days from the day on which the marriage registration authority receives the application for divorce registration, withdraw the application for divorce registration from the marriage registration authority. Within 30 days after the expiration of the period as prescribed in the preceding paragraph, both parties shall apply for divorce certificates in person at the marriage registration authority. If no application is filed, the divorce registration application shall be deemed to have been withdrawn.

2 See Ma Yinan, 'Divorce Cooling-off Period is a Limit and Restriction on Wanton Divorce' (2020) 4 *Journal of Chinese Women's Studies* 105.

trary to the system's good intentions.[3] Moreover, at a time when divorce is not easy in China, the cooling-off period before divorce has created more fear of marriage, and it may not necessarily reduce the divorce rate, but it is likely to increase the rate of non-marriage.[4]

Why has the divorce cooling-off period system aroused such a wide debate? How should we perceive this system? Most previous studies have focused on the current state of the system, analyzing it by focusing on the cross-sectional dimension of the system. For example, some scholars have analyzed the values underlying the system of a cooling-off period before divorce, arguing that such a system is consistent with the nature of the marriage based on affection, since impulsive, non-deliberate behavior is not love.[5] Other scholars have also analyzed the specific application of the system of a cooling-off period before divorce in practice, pointing out that the purpose of setting such a period is to balance the values of freedom of divorce and family stability. The value orientation of the provisions prescribing this system is family ethics, and the value judgment that ethical values are superior to the freedom of divorce is the first and most important criterion for the application of the provisions.[6] There are also scholars who have analyzed foreign systems that are similar to the system of a cooling-off period before divorce, such as the Korean system of the deliberation period for divorce and the British system of the reflection and consideration period, with a view to drawing on their institutional experience.[7]

These horizontal analyses of the cooling-off period before divorce have given us a basic grasp of the outlines of the system. However, these analyses are based on a more contemporary understanding of this system, ignoring the historical logic behind the formation of the system and the question of the ultimate effectiveness of the system that has been formed in accordance with

3 See Wang Shu, 'National People's Congress Deputy Jiang Shengnan: Suggested That the Draft Civil Code Delete the "Divorce Cooling-off Period"' (BJNews 19 May 2020) <https://www.bjnews.com.cn/detail/158988705815022.html> accessed 5 June 2021.

4 See '"Divorce cooling-off period" Again Overwhelm: Why 40000 Comments Unanimously Raised Their Hands Against It' (Peng Pai News 16 May 2020) <https://m.thepaper.cn/newsDetail_forward_7425545> accessed 5 June 2021.

5 See Jiang Dawei, 'The Social Base and Legislative Expression of Divorce Calm Period in the Marriage and Family Law' (2020) 4 *Journal of Huaqiao University (Philosophy & Social Sciences)* 126–7.

6 See Xia Qin, 'Interpretation of the Cooling-off Period for the Registration of Divorce in the Civil Code' (2020) 5 *The Jurist* 34–8.

7 See Yang Lixin, Jiang Xiaohua 'The Legislative Evaluation of Divorce Cooling-off Period in the Draft of Marriage and Family Law in the Civil Code' (2019) 6 *He Nan Social Sciences* 38–40.

that historical logic. This makes it difficult for previous studies to explain why such a heated debate about the system of a cooling-off period before divorce has arisen, and thus it is difficult to gain a truly in-depth understanding of this system, and may even lead to misinterpretation and misunderstanding of the system in the process of its specific application. For example, some scholars have argued that the cooling-off period before divorce provision should be universally applied as a basic behavioral and adjudicative norm.[8] Comparatively speaking, from the perspective of historical perspective, to return to the origin of the construction of such a system, to explore the process of the system formation, and to clarify the problem from the source, will help us deeply understand and better grasp the presence and future of the system of the cooling-off period before divorce. To this end, this chapter takes the two different conceptions of "ethical obligations" and "free choice of spouses" behind marriage as the entry point, describes the evolution of the contemporary marriage institution and analyzes the institutional logic behind the evolution, so as to show the whole chain of the generation of the system of a cooling-off period before divorce. On the basis of the basic understanding of the formation history of the system of a cooling-off period before divorce and the consideration of the current situation of the family, this chapter attempts to analyze the potential difficulties that this system may encounter in the future, and to propose a possible response to them.

1. THE TWO CONCEPTIONS BEHIND MARRIAGE: "ETHICAL OBLIGATIONS" AND "FREE CHOICE OF SPOUSES"

Since China has been drawn into the process of modernization, attitudes towards marriage have diverged. The marriage based on the conception of "ethical obligations", which used to be regarded as a matter of two clans, serving and subordinating to the continuation of the family, has been undermined by the conception of "free choice of spouses" from the West, which emphasizes the mutual affection of couples and the freedom of marriage. At the end of the nineteenth century, some reformist women were active in introducing the marriage and love situation of Western countries to Chinese people. For example, the article *Noble Marriages* published by the Journal of Women's Studies on 27 August 1898 criticized Chinese marital forms by way of comparison, claiming that Chinese marriages deprived the individual's right of making his or her own choices, so that "Phoenix and crow, mismatched in

[8] See Xia Qin, 'Interpretation of the Cooling-off Period for the Registration of Divorce in the Civil Code' (2020) 5 *The Jurist* 36–7.

woe, lifelong regret in tow", while in the West, people have the right to choose their own spouses, and "they are then forever bound to each other".[9] After the New Culture Movement, this attitude towards marriage produced a more obvious polarization. Since then, any attitude towards marriage has been more or less influenced by the ideas of "ethical obligations" and "free choice of spouses". In this section, I will specifically explain the implications of the "ethical obligations" and "free choice of spouses" of marriage.

1.1 "Ethical Obligations"

The idea of "ethical obligations", which focuses on the duties and responsibilities of both men and women towards the family, derives from the Confucian philosophy of familyism, which regards the family as an ethical community and is committed to defending the unity and stability of the family. The traditional idea of Confucianism focuses on family ethics, emphasizes the tradition of filial piety and seniority rules, and requires people of different status to practice different rites. With regard to the five most important social relationships – emperor and subjects, father and son, husband and wife, the elderly and the young in a family, and friends – Confucianism prescribes different rites[10] and requires everyone to fulfill the appropriate rites according to his or her status, so as to achieve the Confucian ideal that "There are principles of courtesy and righteousness between emperors and subjects, distinctions between men and women within marriages, hierarchical orders between elders and youngsters, and the virtue of honesty and trustworthiness among friends".[11] The "ethical obligations" of marriage were formed on the basis of maintaining the rites of "family ethics". This section will elaborate on the idea of "ethical obligations" in three aspects: the conclusion of marriage, the maintenance of marriage, and the dissolution of marriage.

Firstly, with regard to the conclusion of marriage, it is regarded as a matter of the two clans rather than of the individual man and woman. Marriage has very little to do with individuals; it is not a natural result of the free will of

---

[9] See He Liping, *Women's Rights in the Republic of China under the Influence of the Western Wave* (JiuZhou Press 2009) 134.

[10] See T'ung-Tsu Ch'ü, *Law and Society in Traditional China* (The Commercial Press 2011) 318–24.

[11] Qian Mu, Tang Junyi and Liang Qichao have all explained the process of the formation of the ethical norms promoted by Confucianism. See Qian Mu, *Twelve Lectures on Chinese Culture* (Gui Zhou People's Press 2019) 24; Tang Junyi, *Cultural Consciousness and Moral Reason* (Social Sciences Academic Press 2005) 29–36; Liang Qichao, *History of Pre-Qin Political Thought* (Yue Lu Press 2010) 88–92.

two people who are in love with each other, but it is the fulfillment of the rite of the children to show filial piety to their parents and to carry on the family line, so that the family may continue.[12] In *the Book of Li Chi*, it is said, "The marriage is a rite that will unite the two families, and is related to the worship of the patriarchal temples and family lineage, so the junzi attaches great importance to it." The ancients entered into marriages with the focus on the woman's ability to bear children for the inheritance of lineages, and they emphasized the economic and business cooperation between the man and the woman, rather than whether the two parties were in love with each other. For men, marriage is not for individuals, but for clans; for women, marriage is not for themselves, but for entering the husband's family. This conception of marriage, which ignores the affectional connection between men and women and emphasizes family ties, is still prevalent in some places today. For example, there are still many people in society who emphasize the importance of "a marriage between families of equal social rank" and regard marriage as "living together in partnership". Another example is the "two-sided marriage", which is popular in the provinces of Jiangsu and Zhejiang in China.[13] This form of marriage occurs mainly when both spouses are the only child, and since both are the only descendants of their respective families, these two people will inevitably face the problem of whose clan inheritance is broken when they get married. The "two-sided marriage" is a compromise between the two parties in order to continue their respective family.

Secondly, with regard to the maintenance of marriage, the "ethical obligations" regulate marital relationships on the basis of the idea that men are superior to women. Under this idea, women are seen as always under the will and authority of men and in a subordinate position. *The Da Dai Li Chi – Ben Ming* says: A woman is a person who subordinates to others by way of rites. Therefore, there is no reason for a woman to be arbitrary; instead, she never dares to do anything of her own will, for she has to observe the principle of the "three obediences", which means that she follows her father at home, her husband when she marries, and her eldest son when her husband dies. At that time, this was considered to be a rite for women to follow. This male-dominated relationship is reflected in all aspects of marital life. For example, the family internal division of labor is the "men are mainly responsible for making

12 See Feng Youlan, *Series of Books by the Historian of Philosophy* (People's Publishing House 1998) 106.

13 "Two-sided marriage" is characterized by the fact that a couple has two children by prior agreement, each of whom follows the last name of the couple and is eventually raised by each of the two families of origin. See Mao Yisheng, Chen Shuyi, '"Two-Sided Marriage" Common in Jiangsu and Zhejiang? The Hidden Worries Have Emerged' *Jie Fang Daily* (Shang Hai 30 December 2020) 14.

money and socializing outside the home, and women are mainly responsible for taking care of the family" model, and the fact that the woman does not have the final authority in matters within the family and is subject to the patriarch when her will conflicts with that of the patriarch. Another example is that, in cases of spousal violence and homicide, the laws of ancient China were based on the principle of aggression between superiority and inferiority and imposed enhancing and lightening punishments respectively; i.e., a wife who assaults her husband receives a heavier punishment, while a husband who assaults his wife receives a lighter punishment.[14] The ancients generally regarded a husband's violence against his wife as something unavoidable and justified for managing a family. On the other hand, when a wife assaults her husband it is considered an intolerable crime, which is not only punished by the law with a heavy punishment but also criticized by public opinion as a "shrew" and "not observing women's morals". This idea of male superiority and female subordination is still alive today, even after thousands of years. For example, many people still advocate for the traditional roles of men as breadwinners and women as homemakers, and the idea of asking women to tolerate, compromise, and make sacrifices for the sake of the family is still prevalent in some places today, and a member of the National Committee of the Chinese People's Political Consultative Conference even put forward the proposal of "encouraging women to return to family life from workplace".[15] The recurrent problem of domestic violence is also related to the traditional idea of marriage in which men are superior to women.

Finally, with regard to the dissolution of marriage, the "ethical obligations" assert that as long as it is not particularly harmful, couples should stay together in any kind of marriage. This orientation also adopts a restrictive attitude towards divorce and emphasizes individuals' responsibilities and obligations to the family.[16] Marriage and family law, which is based on the idea of "ethical obligations", regulates the dissolution of marriage to a large extent not on the basis of the existence of conjugal love between the two parties, but on the fulfillment of the duties and obligations of each of them within the family. Even if there is no affectional connection, as long as both parties fulfill their respective duties and obligations, they are not allowed to divorce. Any marriage can be dissolved only if there is a "legitimate reason", commonly referred

---

14 See T'ung-Tsu Ch'ü, *Law and Society in Traditional China* (The Commercial Press 2011) 135–6.

15 See Li Dong, Zhang Ying, Shi Shanwei, Yu Mengjiang and He Tao, '"Encouraging Women to Return to the Family" – Our Interview with Women's Studies Expert Zhang Xiaomei' *Guang Zhou Daily* (Guang Zhou 8 March 2011) 6.

16 See Tang Junyi, *Cultural Consciousness and Moral Reason* (Social Sciences Academic Press 2005) 26.

to as the "seven legal circumstances of divorce" in ancient Chinese culture. In the absence of the "seven legal circumstances for divorce", the husband is subject to criminal punishment and the law does not recognize the validity of the divorce, requiring the forced departure of the wife to be remedied and the couple to be reunited.[17] A typical character in this aspect is Chen Shimei, the main male character in the traditional theatre piece The Beheading of an Ungrateful Husband. Nowadays, people still hold a negative view of the party in a marriage who is "abandoning the old for the new" and abandons his wife who has shared her husband's hard lot, calling him a "contemporary Chen Shimei" and morally condemning him. Moreover, it is also common for people to aspire to and celebrate a married life that continues until old age. Expressions like "a day as a couple, a hundred days of grace" and "better to demolish ten temples than to ruin one marriage" continue to have many proponents today.

Under the idea of "ethical obligations", marriage relationships are guided by ethical norms rather than individual will, aiming to achieve a state where both partners in the marriage care for and assume responsibility for each other. Marriage itself is also considered a state that should be stable and long-lasting. At the same time, this idea of marriage emphasizes the importance of maintaining family stability, the closeness of the relationships between family members and the unity of the family, and the sense of closeness fostered by this family culture, which is the basis for social cohesion. This is an aspect of the "ethical obligations" that merits acknowledgment. However, while prioritizing family stability, the idea of "ethical obligations" has, to a large extent, limited the personalities and freedoms of the family members and prevented the development of the human personality. Moreover, the structure in this marriage relationship is hierarchical, which emphasizes distinctions in status and

[17] Besides the mentioned seven circumstances, another circumstance under which a marriage could be dissolved was the so-called i-chüeh 义绝, "breaking the bond of the matrimonial relationship". It included such acts as a husband's beating or killing members of his wife's family; a wife's beating or killing members of her husband's family; a wife having illicit intercourse with her husband's relatives in the first, second, third, or fourth degree; and a husband having illicit intercourse with his wife's mother; or a wife's murder of her husband. Under T'ang and Sung law, a husband was punished with a year and a half's imprisonment if he divorced a wife who had not violated any of the seven conditions for divorce or the rules of i-chüeh, 义绝. And the punishment was one hundred strokes if he divorced a wife who had violated one of the seven conditions for divorce but had fulfilled any of the three conditions under which a divorce was not permissible. Under Ming and Ch'ing law, the punishment for a husband was eighty and sixty strokes under the two above-mentioned conditions respectively. See T'ung-Tsu Ch'ü, *Law and Society in Traditional China* (The Commercial Press 2011) 135–6.

gender, and upholds the unequal relationship between men and women. These became the focus of criticism by the sense of "free choice of spouses".

1.2 "Free Choice of Spouses"

The idea of "free choice of spouses" asserts that love is the foundation of marriage and emphasizes that the affectional connection between spouses is at the heart of the marriage and lasts throughout its duration. This idea originates from Western theories of marriage and family based on the equality of individuals, which spread during the modern process of Western learning. In contrast to the traditional Confucian stance that individuals must accept the roles assigned to them in family relationships according to generation, age, degrees of consanguinity, gender, etc., the individualism stance emphasizes human desires and the natural rights of human beings. It detaches the individual from predefined family roles and no longer prioritizes duties and responsibilities, but it emphasizes respect for each person and asserts that each individual should decide, to the greatest extent possible, how to live his or her own life. The individual takes precedence over the community as the supreme entity.[18] When applied to marriage, this philosophy gives rise to the idea of "free choice of spouses", which values personal happiness, spousal emotions, and the pursuit of one's own life. In contemporary China, this idea of marriage has been formed and developed primarily in the context of the various marriage policies and regulations of the Communist Party of China.

Firstly, in terms of the conclusion of marriage, it is believed that marriage is a union of free individuals, and that only marriages resulting from free love are genuine, correct, and meaningful.[19] Here, people highlight the decisive role of the affection between a man and a woman in the conclusion of a marriage, and advocate that marriages united by love are morally acceptable. Thus, marriage is only seen as the business of the individuals involved, and this idea opposes interference in marriage from parents or other external interference. In 1925, the Fourth National Congress of the Communist Party of China passed the Resolution on the Women's Movement, which explicitly proposed "freedom of marriage and divorce" and advocated "breaking the rites that enslave women".[20] Article 2 of the *Regulations on Marriage in the*

---

[18] See Sun Xiangchen, 'Individual Rights in Modern Time and "Individual" in Confucian Tradition' (2017) 3 *Literature, History, and Philosophy* 92–4.

[19] See Qiao Ruilin, 'The Building of Free Community and the Changes of Daily Life – Research on Budapest Schools' Theories on Marriage, Family and Women's Liberation' (2019) 8 *Academic Exchange* 8–10.

[20] 'Resolutions on the women's movement' in Party Literature Research Ce ntre, CCCPC, Archives Bureau, CCCPC (eds), *Selected Important Documents*

Shanxi-Gansu-Ningxia Border Region, decreed in 1939, re-emphasizes that "marriage shall be based on the principle of their own free will".[21]

Secondly, in terms of the maintenance of marriage, the idea of "free choice of spouses" holds that a marriage based on love should continue to maintain and prioritize love, and emphasizes the harmony of the couple's emotional affection for each other. Compared to the idea of "ethical obligations", the idea of "free choice of spouses" diminishes the sense of cooperation between spouses in economic and business matters and highlights the love and affection between husband and wife. Individuals no longer submerge themselves in their families for the sake of family continuity, and maintaining family stability is no longer the primary purpose of marriage. People put more emphasis on individual feelings in their marriages. Accordingly, with regard to interpersonal relationships within marriage, the idea of "free choice of spouses" favors free negotiation on the basis of equality and rejects the ideas that men are superior to women and the model of "male lord outside homemaking women", with particular emphasis on the protection of women's interests. In 1927, *the Resolution on Rural Women's Problems* adopted by the First Provincial Peasants' Congress in Jiangxi clearly pointed out that, "Rural women, in addition to working hard every day in their homes, need to undertake cooking, bringing up their children, taking care of the household, and doing all the other chores. In many places they also have to go to chop wood, plough, and do the same kind of work as the men, but they have very few rights." In order to liberate women, this conference proposed: "Article 4. Women workers should receive equal wages for the same work as men. Article 5. Abusing child brides and daughters-in-law, drowning female fetuses, imposing ear-piercing on women, imposing foot-binding on women, etc., is strictly prohibited."[22]

Finally, in terms of the dissolution of marriage, the conception of "free choice of spouses" insists that the breakdown of the mutual affection should be the only criterion for the dissolution of a marriage. Divorce is not subject to those "legitimate reasons" under the idea of "ethical obligations", and the criterion of divorce is not based on fault. The moral judgment on the act of divorce tends to be neutral. As soon as the love and affection between both

---

since the Founding of the Communist Party of China (1921–1949) (Volume 2) (Central Party Literature Press 2011) 253.

21 Zhang Xipo, *History of Marriage Legislation in China* (People's Publishing House 2004) 257–8.

22 See 'Declaration and Resolution of the First Provincial Farmers' Congress of Jiangxi Province' in Party History Research Center of the CPC Central Committee (eds), *Reference Materials on the History of the Communist Party of China (II): The Period of the First Revolutionary Civil War* (People's Publishing House 1979) 438.

parties in the marriage relationship have disappeared, even if one of the parties has fulfilled his or her obligations in the family, the marriage shall be dissolved at that time if the other party initiates the dissolution of the marriage. Under the idea of "free choice of spouses", love is the foundation of marriage; when the mutual affection disappears, the marriage will naturally lose the necessity to be maintained. This is essentially a form of "divorce freedom". As early as during the Chinese Agrarian Revolutionary War, Article 9 of the *Marriage Regulations of the Chinese Soviet Republic*, decreed in 1931, stipulated that: "Divorce is free, and divorce shall be granted where both the man and the woman agree to divorce; any man or woman who insists on divorce shall be divorced immediately." In 1932, Xiang Ying, then vice-chairman of the Central Executive Committee of the Chinese Soviet Republic, responded to a letter "questioning the freedom of divorce" with a clear statement: "If one of the parties insists on getting a divorce, the divorce should be allowed without any doubt. … If there is an excuse with no reason, this is nothing more than a disguise against marriage freedom, which is, in fact, in favor of the existence of the old system of oppressing women."[23]

Under the idea of "free choice of spouses", marriage is based on the love between a man and a woman and the principle of respect for the free will of the individual. This allows the development of individuality and the equalization of marital relations. Furthermore, marriage and family legislation based on the idea of "free choice of spouses" provides strong protection for women's interests and a gradual reduction in gender discrimination. This is a commendable aspect of the conception of "free choice of spouses". However, at the same time, it is necessary to acknowledge that, due to the focus on the individual's feelings in marriage and the emphasis on the freedom of divorce, in the context of imperfect social security, this jeopardizes the fulfillment of the functions of the family in terms of production, consumption, nursing, and child-rearing, and puts an excessive burden on the individual, which ultimately leads to the instability of society. Moreover, the justification of the family ethic has been questioned, and family members are no longer bound by the obligation to family unity, which has led to an impact on the cherished values of caring, reciprocity, and altruism in the family, with the negative consequence of a tendency towards extreme utilitarian egocentrism. These are the aspects of the idea of "free choice of spouses" that have been criticized.

---

[23] Zhang Xipo, *History of Marriage Legislation in China* (People's Publishing House 2004) 138.

2. THE VALUE ORIENTATION OF THE MARRIAGE INSTITUTION IN COMTEMPORARY CHINA: A PRAGMATIC ATTITUDE TOWARDS MARRIAGE

Different notions of marriage shape different marriage institutions. Institutions based on the idea of "ethical obligations", which stress the preservation of marital stability and family unity, may be subject to individual "alienation" during their implementation.[24] Institutions rooted in the idea of "free choice of spouses" focus on protecting the individual's rights, but the ethical value of the family may be neglected. Both the idea of "ethical obligations" and the idea of "free choice of spouses" have their respective advantages and disadvantages. The construction of the marriage institution in contemporary China is in constant change between the two ideas, adopting a pragmatic attitude towards marriage and attempting to solve the different problems that the institution has faced in different periods. Historians distinguish between the past, the present, and the future, arguing that the problems of the present are the result of past behavior and that the future is subject to the behavior of people in the present.[25] The logic behind the "cooling-off period before divorce" system can be traced back to events that occurred before its establishment. Thus, clarifying the story of the system before its establishment is the key to understanding the current system of the cooling-off period before divorce and predicting what happened afterward. This section will illustrate the true historical process of the system of a cooling-off period before divorce by describing the evolution of the value of Chinese Marriage Law at different times, especially the evolution of the divorce provisions.

2.1 Out with the Old and in with the New: *The Marriage Law* (1950) Establishes the Value of "Free Choice of Spouses"

On 13 April 1950, the Seventh Plenary Session of the Central People's Government Commission passed the first Marriage Law of the new People's Republic of China. As noted above, since its foundation, the Communist Party of China has been striving to overthrow the feudal marriage system based on the conception of "free choice of spouses" of marriage, which viewed obligations as a foundation and limited the free will of both men and women.

---

[24] See Zhang Jianyuan, 'Familyism or Individualism? – The Reconstruction of Jurisprudence of Family Law Principles in Contemporary China' (2020) 2 *Law and Social Development* 138.

[25] See Zhou Yumin, 'Approach to the Historical Truth in the River of History' (2018) 5 *Journal of Shanghai Normal University (Philosophy & Social Sciences Edition)* 162–4.

Instead, the Party aimed to establish a new marriage system in which men and women, on the premise of equality and freedom of choice, regard love and affection as marital criteria and guarantee the autonomy of spouses to divorce. Either *the Marriage Regulations of the Chinese Soviet Republic*, which were applied in the Jiangxi Soviet Area in 1931, or *the Marriage Regulations of the Shanxi-Gansu-Ning Border Region*, which were applied in the Shanxi-Gansu-Ning Border Region in 1939, were specific attempts by the Communist Party of China to reform the marriage system. *The Marriage Law,* implemented in 1950, continued the Communist Party of China's vision of reforming, which is the result of a nationwide legislative activity of breaking the old and establishing the new after the Communist Party of China had gained power.

Article 18(1) of *the Marriage Law* of 1950 states: "Divorce shall be granted if both men and women voluntarily divorce. If one party insists on divorce and mediation by the local people's government and judicial authorities is ineffective, the divorce shall also be granted." This clause inherits the spirit of the legislation behind article 9 of *the Marriage Regulations of the Chinese Soviet Republic*, which stipulates that divorce is unconditional. There was intense debate surrounding this article during the drafting of *the Marriage Law*. A large majority of people opposed this provision, suggesting that marriage is a significant life event and excessive divorce freedom would be detrimental to social stability. Particularly in the rural areas, the freedom of divorce inevitably affects the vital interests of some farmers, who would likely become an opposition force to policies. In addition, some are concerned that there may be a small number of officers who, after moving to the city, abandon their original spouse under the excuse of freedom of divorce and have another new lover.[26] Thus, they proposed that divorce should be subject to certain conditions and the divorce shall be granted only if the conditions are met. On the other hand, a small group of people, including Deng Yingchao, were strongly in favor of divorce without any conditions. Deng Yingchao said, "The most oppressed people in Chinese society are women, and women suffer the most on the issue of marriage. … Women asking for a divorce are often not allowed to do so. The notion that 'Divorce can be granted as long as one party insists' is mainly based on women's interests. Today's Marriage Law is prescribed in principle, and by destroying the old and establishing the new, it is necessary to confront the inequality between men and women and give women protection."[27] By the time the draft Marriage Law was completed, a consensus on this matter was not reached.

---

[26] See Huang Chuanhui, Marriage in the World – Chronicles of the Three Marriage Laws of the People's Republic of China (Wen Hui Press 2004) 42.

[27] Ibid., 44.

On 21 January 1950, the draft Marriage Law was submitted to the Central Committee of the Communist Party of China by the Central Committee of Women's Movement, accompanied by a personal letter from Deng Yingchao. This letter pointed out the disagreement within the drafting group on Article 18 and requested the Party Central Committee to give a final decision. The legislation eventually adopted the views of Deng Yingchao and others. On 28 January, the Commission of Legislative Affairs submitted to the Central Committee of the Communist Party of China an amendment explaining that: "Freedom of divorce and marriage is one of the basic requirements for the liberation of women in the new democratic revolution, which is opposed to feudalism. The existence of situations in which divorce and remarriage are not free in Chinese society only proves that the regulations on marriage must be of a thoroughly liberating nature in order to break through the deep-rooted shackles of the old society and to create family relations suitable for the new social system of new relations of production, rather than the opposite."[28] In terms of divorce practice after the implementation of *the Marriage Law* (1950), statistics show that in 1952, in divorce cases in the provinces of Shanxi, Guizhou and Hubei, the rates of permitted divorces were respectively 70.01 percent, 98.4 percent and 89.5 percent, and there was a climax of divorces in 1953.[29]

In this light, *the Marriage Law* (1950) essentially embraced the concept of "freedom of divorce", i.e., in the matter of divorce, both the party at fault and the party not at fault have the right to divorce; both the party at fault and the innocent party had the right to initiate divorce. The criteria for determining whether a divorce is granted only depend on the likelihood of the couple continuing to live together and their emotional connection, rather than on other conditions. With regard to the attitude towards marriage, *the Marriage Law* (1950) clearly stresses love as the essence of marriage, emphasizes the decisive role of love in the conclusion, maintenance, and dissolution of marriage, and highlights the freedom of the individual, with relatively little regard for the individual's duties and responsibilities within the family. However, it should also be noted that *the Marriage Law* (1950) not only established the value orientation of "free choice of spouses", especially in the matter of divorce, but also adopted the doctrine of "divorce freedom", which at that time was aimed more at abolishing the old marriage system, with strong political connotations. On 14 May 1950, Deng Yingchao pointed out in her *Report on the Marriage*

---

28 Ibid., 47–8.

29 See Liu Shijie, Liu Yalin, *Study on Divorce Trials* (Chong Qing University Press 1998) 67.

Law that "our present task is to give people full freedom of marriage and to destroy the old system completely".[30]

2.2 Deviations in Implementation: From 1957 to 1978

The value of "free choice of spouses" established in *the Marriage Law* (1950) has not been consistently applied in practice, and the idea of "free divorce" has been almost completely ignored during this period, due to the influence of "Left Inclination". On 2 July 1957, Dong Biwu, in his *Report on the Work of the Supreme People's Court* at the Fourth Session of the First National People's Congress, pointed out that, after the implementation of *the Marriage Law* (1950), there was a gradual decrease in the number of cases of divorce conflicts on the basis of feudal marital relations, while at the same time there was an increase in the number of hasty marriages, wanton divorces, and instances of not providing for elderly family members.[31] These were considered to be an unhealthy consequence of "divorce freedom". In the absence of comprehensive social security measures, society had limited capacity to bear the consequences of divorce, and the functions of nursing, child-rearing, economic organization, and education still need to be carried out to a large extent by the family. The mentioned phenomena such as wanton divorces destroy the stability of the family to a certain extent and also affect the subsequent socialist construction.

Based on this understanding, the courts' perception of divorce began to shift towards the idea of "ethical obligations" in the judicial practice at that time. However, the object of the obligation has shifted from the "family" to the "state". Divorce is no longer based on incompatibility, but on whether the reasons for divorce are "justified". The content of the reasons has accordingly changed from the "seven legal circumstances of divorce" in traditional society to the political requirements for individuals at that time, for example, opposing the idea of capitalist marriage views and drawing a clear line with the "rightists", "counter-revolutionaries" and "landlords and rich peasants". The Fifth National Judicial Conference, held in 1960, pointed out that "the current divorce cases reflect to a large extent the contradiction between the

---

[30] Deng Yingchao, 'Report on the Marriage Law' in Party Literature Resear ch Centre, CCCPC (eds), *Deng Yingchao Collection* (People's Publishing House 1994) 78.

[31] Dong Biwu, 'Report on the Work of the Supreme People's Court' in Legislative Affairs Office of the State Council of the People's Republic of China, Regulations of the People's Republic of China editorial board (eds), *Regulations of the People's Republic of China (July–December 1957)* (Law Press China 1958) 276.

two ideologies of the proletariat and the capitalists. The courts should handle divorce cases in the same way as they handle other cases, 'analyzing them from the class viewpoint'."[32] For example, the Higher People's Court of Sichuan Province proposed in 1960 that, in cases where divorce was submitted on the basis of capitalist ideology, the party with capitalist ideology should be seriously criticized and patiently educated, and generally not allowed to divorce, while if the innocent party agrees to the divorce, it should be granted.[33]

During the Great Cultural Revolution that began in 1966, political considerations took precedence in marital relationships, and marriage has been in the service of politics. For those who were recognized as "counter-revolutionaries" or subjected to struggle sessions at the time, as long as their spouses adhered to "distinguishing boundaries" and insisted on divorce, regardless of the state of their marital relationships, they were generally granted divorce. For those who classified as the "five black categories" (a definition of five groups of poorly behaved people put forward in the 1950s for landlords; rich peasants; counter-revolutionaries; saboteurs; and rightists) filing for divorce, it is usually not granted, even if the couple's relationship breaks down. For those deemed "politically problematic", even if their spouses did not request a divorce, they could still be forced to divorce on the grounds of "revolutionary necessity".[34]

2.3 Subsequent Adaptations: From *The Marriage Law* Published in 1980 to the Amended One in 2001

After experiencing the prevailing doctrine of "freedom of divorce" based on the idea of "free choice of spouses" and the doctrine of "fault-based divorce" governed by the idea of "ethical obligations", the Marriage Law passed in 1980 and its subsequent amendments attempted to take a middle path in choosing marital values. That is to say, the institution of marriage is designed to be based on love and to satisfy people's requests for feeling love. But at the same time, its value orientation is also appropriately shifted towards the idea of "ethical obligations" and imposes restrictions on divorce in order to meet the challenge of family disintegration brought about by the freedom of divorce. This is reflected in the fact that, on the one hand, the will of the couple to divorce

32 Editorial Board of the Contemporary China series, *Trial Work in Contemporary China – Volume 2* (Contemporary China Publishing House 1993) 37.

33 See Liu Shijie, Liu Yalin, *Study on Divorce Trials* (Chong Qing University Press 1998) 74–5.

34 Editorial Board of the Contemporary China series, *Trial Work in Contemporary China – Volume 2* (Contemporary China Publishing House 1993) 39.

is respected and breakdown of the mutual affection is conceived as the lawful criterion for divorce. On the other hand, breakdown of the mutual affection is interpreted as a flexible conception involving substantive moral requests, like caring for the weaker party in the marriage, preserving the ethical values of the family, and condemning the party at fault. All these are included in the consideration of divorce.

The Marriage Law (1980) kept the principle of freedom of divorce established by *the Marriage Law* (1950). Given the lessons learned from the overly restrictive implementation of the divorce criteria since 1957, Peng Zhen, when *the Marriage Law* was being amended, stated: "With regard to the divorces. We have quite a lot of experience in this matter. In any case, it is always a principle that men and women are free to marry and divorce."[35] Article 25 of *the Marriage Law* (1980) explicitly sets that breakdown of the mutual affection no longer exists as the criterion for divorce,[36] rejecting the criterion of "Justifiable Reasons", which had been applied to divorce since the "the thoughtful trends of Left Inclination".

With *the Marriage Law (1980)* returning to accept the guidance of the idea of "free choice of spouses", divorce because of bad behaviors, such as keeping a mistress, third-party involvement in marriage, wanton divorce, and other unhealthy phenomena, has once again become the focus of public attention. In Guangdong province and other economically developed areas, there were even cases of keeping mistresses publicly for personal enjoyment, apparently challenging social ethics and moralities.[37] In order to prevent such unhealthy consequences, during the period of amending the Marriage Law published in 2001, a debate arose as to whether the legal condition for divorce should be defined as "the breakdown of mutual affection" or "breach of marital relationship". Scholars who favor "breach of marital relationship" believe that, in terms of the ground of marriage, although affection should be the ethical foundation of it, people are still subject to various social conditions (e.g., economy, status, domicile, etc.) when choosing a spouse. That is to say that

---

35 Writing group for the biography of Peng Zhen, *Peng Zhen Chronicle (1979–1997) (vol. 5)* (Central Party Literature Press 2012) 57.

36 Article 25 of the *Marriage Law of the People's Republic of China (1980)* states: If one party alone desires a divorce, the organization concerned may carry out mediation or the party may appeal directly to a people's court to start divorce proceedings. In dealing with a divorce case, the people's court should carry out mediation; divorce shall be granted if mediation fails because mutual affection no longer exists.

37 You Zhilong, 'Rule of Law and Reform in the Family' in Guangdong Province Law Society (eds), *Moving Forward with the Law* (People's Publishing House 2018) 529–30.

marriage is not entirely based on affection. In view of the legal characteristics of marriage, the family, which is centered on marriage, carries out a variety of social functions, and its dissolution inevitably involves the interests of the family members and society; therefore, when stipulating the lawful reasons for divorce in the Marriage Law, in addition to taking into account the affectional factors, it is also necessary to deliberately allow for the interests of the family and society.[38] Nevertheless, scholars arguing in favor of "breakdown of mutual affection" suggest that it is a result of the destruction of feudalism in Chinese marriage, as well as a result of decades of experience in civil trials in line with Chinese reality.[39] They also believe that the claims that the stability of marriage is linked to the stability of society entail a danger of reviving the dross of traditional ethics repressing human nature.[40]

Although the final legislation adopted the expression "alienation of mutual affection", the actual judicial interpretation of it tends to favor the "breach of marital relationship" and emphasizes the protection of family ethics and moralities. *The Marriage Law* (2001) absorbed the Opinions of the Supreme People's Court on "breakdown of mutual affection" (1989) and stipulated five legal reasons for divorce in Article 32. However, *the Marriage Law* (2001) also establishes, in Article 46, a system of compensation for divorce damages, which gives the party not at fault the right to claim compensation for damages caused by the party at fault and punishes behaviors incompatible with family ethics. From the perspective of judicial practice, the courts, in determining whether there is "alienation of mutual affection", also give priority to family unity guided by the idea of "ethical obligations", highlighting the protection of family ethics. This is demonstrated by the fact that when the court hears divorce cases, most of them are resolved eventually by a judgment rejecting the appeal for divorce, a mediation intended for repairing the marital relationship, or a withdrawal initiated by the plaintiffs. In view of this fact, judges often deny the "breakdown of mutual affection", such as "complying with family-orientation", "caring for each other" and "trusting each other". Judges

---

38 See Zhang Xianyu, 'The Principle of Breaching of Marital Relationship Should be the Legitimate Reason for Divorce' in Li Yinhe, Ma Yinan (eds), *Marriage Law Amendment Debate* (Guangming Daily Publishing House 1999) 132–3.

39 See Li Zhongfang, 'Adherence to the Principle of the Alienation of Mutual Affection in Divorce' in Li Yinhe Ma Yinan (eds), *Marriage Law Amendment Debate* (Guangming Daily Publishing House 1999) 170–71.

40 See Xiao Jianxue, 'Against Attaching Divorce Conditions "in addition to the Principle of the Alienation of Mutual Affection"' in Li Yinhe Ma Yinan (eds), *Marriage Law Amendment Debate* (Guangming Daily Publishing House 1999) 173.

also remind couples that they should cherish each other and make deliberate decisions on divorce while stressing that family members should "respect each other and love each other", "understand each other", and "give each other a chance to correct their behaviors".[41] If one of the parties still persists in divorce, then divorce may only be allowed in a second lawsuit after six months.

2.4 The Logic behind the System of a Cooling-Off Period before Divorce

The above historical perspective and analysis of the divorce provisions in *the Marriage Law* from 1950 to 2001 suggests that the legal practice of the marital system in our state entails a pragmatic logic. This means that, from the point of view of the state, neither family unity, which is defended by the idea of "ethical obligations", nor the freedom of individuals, which is defended by the idea of "free choice of spouses", has independent significance in themselves. The state does not regard them as ends in themselves, but rather as flexible choices between the two ideas when the marital system is confronted with different situations. Whether the marital system is constructed on the basis of the idea of "ethical obligations" or the idea of "free choice of spouses", the state is motivated only by strategic reasons, with the ultimate aim of solving the current problems faced by the marital system. Flexible choices emerging in the reform of the marital system are considered justified as long as the problems it faces are solved, even if they conflict with the values of the previous legislation. For example, *the Marriage Law* (1950) insists on the idea of "free choice of spouses" because it was conducive to breaking the system of feudal marriage at that time and liberated women. However, from 1957 to 1978, the legal practice of the marriage law immediately shifted the original orientation to the idea of "ethical obligations", as it was more compatible with the "ideology of Left Inclination". After 1978, in response to the political movement of rectifying leftist ideology, *the Marriage* Law (1980) once again reconstructed its marital system on the basis of the idea of "free choice of spouses". In order to prevent the unhealthy consequences of completely free divorce, *the Marriage* Law (2001) has developed a "practical morality" deriving from the experience gained since the implementation of the new marital system in 1950, and the contemporary system of marriage is structured on the basis of the orientation of "practical morality".[42]

---

[41] See Zhao Liuyang, '"Privatization" of Marriage in China? Divorce of Women in Contemporary Chinese Legal Practice' (2019) 2 *Open Times* 91–3.

[42] See Philip C. C. Huang, 'Morality and Law: China's Past and Present' (2015) 1 *Open Times* 84–5.

The system of a cooling-off period before divorce is a derivation of the logic of practicality at the present time. On 30 July 2003, the State Council passed the *Regulation on Marriage Registration*, implemented on 1 October of the same year, and the *Regulation on Marriage Registration Management (1994)* was repealed at the same time. The new *Regulation on Marriage Registration* abolished the provisions of "a letter of introduction provided by the unit, villagers' committee or residents' committee" and "a one-month review period for divorce". According to Article 13 of the *Regulation on Marriage Registration (2003)*,[43] a divorce registration shall be conducted on the spot after a formal examination and inquiry carried out by the marriage registration organ if the application for registration of divorce meets the three conditions that (a) the couple is on the spot in person; (b) the couple is voluntary, and (c) they have reached an agreement on such issues as child upbringing, property and debts. Thus, it seems that the new *Regulation on Marriage Registration* adopts the idea of "free choice of spouses" as for marriage, emphasizing the autonomy of the individuals, and the decision to divorce or not to divorce is entirely up to the individuals themselves. As we have seen from the previous section on the evolution of provisions providing divorce, in cases of litigious divorces, the proceedings impose certain restrictions on divorce. But even if so, the idea of "free choice of spouses" has made a negative difference to divorce, challenging our cherished family ethics – caring, reciprocity, and altruism. Actually, it is judges that preserve the ethical values of the family in legal practice in a pragmatic way. However, the current system of divorce registration, which has neither the limitations of the contentious procedures nor the role of a "judge" to stress the family ethics and make them assured, will produce more negative consequences of divorce, such as wanton divorce. In order to address the many negative impacts brought about by registered divorce, on the occasion of drafting *the Civil Code*, the state, with reference to the idea of "practical morality" developed in litigious divorces, appropriately shifted towards the idea of "ethical obligations" and set up a cooling-off period of 30 days for "registered divorce", in order to reduce wanton divorces and maintain family stability.

Although constructing the marriage system in accordance with the logic of pragmatism will, to a certain extent, solve the problems that the marital system faces at this time, we can witness the development history of *the Marriage*

[43] Article 13 of the *Regulations on Marriage Registration*, passed and implemented in 2003, states: The marriage registration organ shall examine the certificates and certification presented by the applicants for divorce registration and inquire of them about relevant facts. For the applicants who wish to get divorced of their own free will, if an agreement has been reached on such issues as child upbringing, property and debts, registration shall be conducted on the spot, with a divorce certificate being issued to them.

Law, which has been shifting repeatedly between the ideas of "free choice of spouses" and "ethical obligations" since 1950, that such a way of solving the problems in the field of marriage and family will inevitably result in a double squeeze and will produce a number of unexpected consequences deviating from the originally designed purposes of the system. There is no exception in the system of a cooling-off period before divorce.

3. THE WEAKENING OF INSTITUTIONAL FUNCTIONS STEMMING FROM THE NON-EXPECTED CONSEQUENCES CAUSED BY THE COOLING-OFF PERIODS BEFORE DIVORCE

The system of a cooling-off period before divorce is well intentioned as it seeks to maintain family stability and reduce the negative consequences the idea of "free choice of spouses" leads to and prevent families from breaking up. However, in terms of the specifics of the cooling-off period before divorce, it does not provide for exceptions but rather indiscriminately imposes restrictions on almost all parties applying for the registered divorce. This may ignore other interests that exist in marriage and family, leading to unexpected consequences, such as aggravating the disadvantages faced by women in the family and overlooking the burdens faced by family members. These unexpected consequences can weaken or even directly dissolve the institutional functions of the cooling-off period before divorce. This section will illustrate the concrete manifestations of unexpected consequences and their weakening of the functions the system of a cooling-off period before divorce takes up.

3.1 Cooling-Off Period before Divorce has Exacerbated Disadvantages Faced by Women

The Explanations of the Draft Civil Code of the People's Republic of China explains the applicability of the cooling-off period before divorce: "In practice, there has been increasing cases of wanton divorces, which is not conducive to the stability of the marriage and family. Thus, the draft provides for a cooling-off period of thirty days after submission of the application for divorce registration, during which either party may withdraw the application for divorce from the registration authority.'[44] It can be seen that the system

[44] Wang Chen, 'The Explanations of the Draft Civil Code of the People's Republic of China' in the General Offices of the National People's Congress Standing Committee (eds), *Documents of the Third Session of the Thirteenth National People's Congress of the People's Republic of China* (People's Publishing House 2020) 384.

of a cooling-off period before divorce is intended to address the problem of wanton divorces. However, it appears from Article 1077 of *the Civil Code* that such a system does not distinguish between wanton divorces and other divorces, and in fact imposes restrictions on all divorcing couples. Further, the system of a cooling-off period before divorce emphasizes the importance of family interests. When an individual submits an application for divorce registration, the system of a cooling-off period is not based on the idea of "free choice of spouses" which emphasizes individuals' rights, but rather on the idea of "ethical obligations" such as "tolerance" and "mutual love and respect", and requiring the individuals to make certain compromises and concessions for satisfying the purpose of maintaining family stability. This does to some extent address the problems arising from wanton divorces and makes those parties involved in wanton divorces aware of their obligations and responsibilities in the marriage. However, this one-size-fits-all approach, which gives priority to family stability in all divorce cases, also ignores the dilemma faced by women in the family and makes no difference to protecting women's interests.

Firstly, as many women are both mentally and materially independent nowadays, they are initiators in divorce cases today. The Supreme People's Court has issued the *data on divorce cases in 2017*, which shows that 73.4 percent of the first-instance divorce cases in China were instituted by female plaintiffs, and the vast majority of men in these cases were reluctant to divorce their wives. According to the data, 91.09 percent of cases involve a fact that one party insists on breaking the marriage while the other rejects a divorce.[45] This is related to family modernization. The research of family sociology points to a fact that the family has undergone a shift from the familyism to the individualism in the course of industrialization and urbanization. As a result of the emphasis on gender equality in the educational system, occupational institutions, the legal system, and so forth, women's lives are no longer confined to household affairs, and they are no longer dependent on men for supporting themselves. More and more women are becoming quite independent, having their own hobbies, plans, and options, and they no longer regard themselves as subordinate to the family. Owing to the overall rise of women's economic status, many women today no longer conceive marriage as an access to financial security, as generations before them did, and nor do they necessarily consider it their only spiritual sustenance.[46] In such cases, if a marriage doesn't turn

45 'Judicial Big Data Report on Divorce Cases' (Supreme People's Court 23 March 2018) <http://www.court.gov.cn/fabu-xiangqing-87622.html> accessed 5 June 2021.

46 See William Josiah Goode, *The family* (2nd ed, Prentice Hall, New Delhi, 1989) 115–25.

out the way they want it to, they would rather choose a divorce than endure endless conflicts.

Secondly, in terms of the specific situation of marriage today, women's legal rights and interests are often violated in reality, but under the influence of the idea of "ethical obligations", there are often no effective remedies. Based on the idea of "ethical obligations", the social gender view of "men are superior to women" still prevails. There are still a lot of women who are in a subordinate position in the family and are even beaten up and insulted by their husbands. Consider, for example, the fact that women are subjected to domestic violence. The *Executive Report of the Third Survey on the Status of Chinese Women*, published after a joint survey by the All China Women's Federation and the National Bureau of Statistics, shows that "24.7 percent of women have suffered from different forms of domestic violence, like insults, assaults, restriction of personal liberty, marital rape".[47] However, the conceptions of the family that prevail widely in society, like that "Lovers' quarrels are soon mended" and "a day together as husband and wife means endless devotion the rest of your life", have led people to treat domestic violence in a way that makes the rights of victims unprotectable and allows the perpetrators to go unpunished. That is to say, people blurred the boundary between right and wrong. And in the context filled with discourses like "being a couple is not easy" and "marital life has to go on", they more or less consciously minimize the harmful impacts of domestic violence and ignore the interests of the women who have suffered from the unjust treatment. Moreover, in practice, the Supreme People's Court published the *Data on Divorce Cases in 2017*, which showed that 91.43 percent of the first-instance cases involving domestic violence imply that it is men who impose violence on women.[48] However, the judicial recognition of domestically violent actions is not commonly easy. For example, in the first half of 2016, the People's Court of Banan District in Chongqing province heard 46 cases involving domestic violence, but only three of them explicitly recognized the acts implying domestic violence as protecting women's rights and interests.[49]

---

[47] Project Group of the 3rd Survey on the Status of Chinese Women, 'Executive Report of the 3rd Survey on the Status of Chinese Women Project Group of the 3rd Survey on the Status of Chinese Women' (2011) 6 *Collection of Women's Studies* 14.

[48] 'Judicial Big Data Report on Divorce Cases' (Supreme People's Court 23 March 2018) <http://www.court.gov.cn/fabu-xiangqing-87622.html> accessed 5 June 2021.

[49] Tu En, 'Inconsistent Standards of Judgment Make It Difficult to Support Claims of Domestic Violence' *People's Courts Daily* (Bei Jing 15 August 2016) 6.

Numerous empirical research studies on how courts deal with divorce cases also reveal the fact that women's rights and interests are ignored in the practice of divorce proceedings. For example, the research of Xin He and Kwai Hang Ng on how judges deal with cases involving domestic violence during the process of judicial mediation points out that in the court investigation stage, even if domestic violence against women's rights and interests is raised, argued about, or even confirmed to exist, a judge still tries his best to shape a less hostile atmosphere where the judge must avoid condemning words and strategically removes some legal facts involving domestic violence. As a matter of fact, the compromises the judges are dedicated to achieving between divorcing spouses undeniably violate women's right to freedom of divorce undeniably.[50]

Thus, women subject to the prevailing idea of "ethical obligations" in marriage do not have full freedom and are in a disadvantageous position in marriage. The system of a cooling-off period before divorce, set up to limit wanton divorce by emphasizing duties and responsibilities in marital fields, does not appropriately classify the manner in which restrictions are imposed, but rather extends such restrictions to all applicants requesting divorce. This may threaten or dissolve women's dedication to gender equality. As can be expected, China will continue to promote the dissemination and implementation of the idea of gender equality. Under this trend, however, what the system of a cooling-off period before divorce expresses is the idea of serving family merely by means of women's tolerance, obedience, and sacrifices. Such an idea will diminish their sensibility of approval for gender equality. Therefore, the justification for the system of a cooling-off period before divorce is being challenged.

3.2 The System of a Cooling-Off Period before Divorce Aggravates Family Members' Burdens

The design purpose of the cooling-off period before divorce is to "resolve marital crises and maintain family stability". *The Interpretation of the Civil Code of the People's Republic of China (Book Five Marriage and Family)* explains that "the cooling-off period before divorce is conceived as a better approach to resolving marital crisis, providing people with a period of time to think calmly and treat marital relationships cautiously, and to maintain family stability".[51] The reasons for maintaining the stability of the family are as follows: on the

[50] See Xin He, Kwai Hang Ng 'In the Name of Harmony: The Erasure of Domestic Violence in China's Judicial Mediation' (2013) 1 *International Journal of Law, Policy and the Family* 97–115.

[51] Yang Lixin, Guo Mingrui, *The Interpretation of the Civil Code of the People's Republic of China (Book Five Marriage and Family)* (People's Publishing House 2020) 96.

one hand, as mentioned above, we cherish the values of love, reciprocity, and altruism in the family; on the other hand, many theoretical and empirical research have shown that, both in the past and at present, the family has incomparable advantages in elderly care, raising children, social governance, and so on. However, *the Regulation on Marriage Registration (2003)* makes the registered divorces effective only on the basis of the will of individuals. This legislation, based on orientation towards absolute "free choice of spouses", has led some people to disregard family responsibilities and has made the family fragile. From this point of view, the implementation of the system of a cooling-off period before divorce is an attempt to protect the increasingly fragile family by adding the procedures of divorce and emphasizing the individual's responsibility towards the family. However, if we concentrate on the whole field of family law and take into account the family-sociology research on family policy, we can see that even if the ignorance of women's interests revealed above is rectified, such a provision of the cooling-off period may still fail to achieve the expected consequences of preserving family stability. Because it is quite likely to omit the burdens family members need to take up, bringing about the intensified trend of non-marriage and infertility.

Firstly, according to the research on family policy, while the protection of the family emphasizes the family responsibilities of social individuals, it should also stress governmental assistance in helping these individuals to fulfill their responsibilities. The rise and development of family policy research are related to family change. Although there is much academic debate about the pattern and extent of family change and the specific aspects of the family that have changed,[52] it is certain that the family has undergone an irreversible change from familyism to individualism in the process of industrialization and urbanization. The changed family scale tends to be smaller; the couple relationship has become the core of marriage, and the couple as well as intergenerational relationships tend to be more equal; the traditional functions of the family, such as economic support, childbearing, raising children, and emotional comfort, have been weakened, and the ability of the family to take responsibility has been greatly challenged. At this time, the proposal that family responsibilities should be assigned exclusively to family members has been increasingly challenged. In the process of responding to such social changes in the family field, new arguments in relation to the family, such as neoliberalism, social

---

52 Models of family change, for example, range from William J. Goode's modernization of the family (i.e., the view that economic development is the main engine of family change), to C. K. Yang's model of state intervention, to Martin King Whyte's model of cultural transmission. See Martin King Whyte, 'Confronting Puzzles in Understanding Chinese Family Change: A Personal Reflection', (2020) 3 *Chinese Journal of Sociology*, 339–63.

democracy, structural functionalism, and social conflict theory, have emerged. They emphasize the government's inevitable responsibility for supplying and regulating family welfare, arguing that family responsibilities should be taken up not only by family members but also by the government.[53] Of course, despite the fact that there are different views among scholars on such issues as the manner in which the government should assume responsibility for the family and the boundaries between governmental responsibilities and family ones, there is still a basic consensus among scholars that family problems cannot be attributed simply to spiritual factors such as the expansion of individualism or moral decay, and that social factors in terms of changes in family structure and the increasing geographical mobility of families and their members also play an important role.[54] Thus, the protection of the family should also be considered in both the individual dimension and social one.

Secondly, in the Chinese context, the state places greater emphasis on individual responsibilities for the family and provides relatively little governmental support for the family. On the one hand, the Chinese family has also undergone a shift from the familyism to the individualism, but as can be seen from the above review of marital values, the state has never given up emphasizing the individual's responsibilities for the family. In practice, the state has in fact continued to strengthen intergenerational family relations and rely on the law to enhance family responsibilities. This is clearly reflected in the changes of the provisions prescribing the duties of family members in the Marriage Law. *The Marriage Law (1980)* provides a special chapter for "Family Relations", which not only specifies in Article 15 the obligations of children to support parents and the obligations of parents to upbring and educate children,[55] but also in Articles 22 and 23,[56] that include the relationships between grandparents and grandchildren, and between siblings. The two articles stipulate that

---

[53] See Lü Yajun, *Research on the European Family Policies at the EU Level* (Economic Science Press 2009) 36–46.

[54] See Zhang Xiulan, Xu Yuebin, 'Formulating a Developmental Family Policy in China' (2003) 6 *Social Sciences in China* 86–8.

[55] Article 15 paragraph 1 of the *Marriage Law of the People's Republic of China (1980)* states: Parents shall have the duty to bring up and educate their children; children shall have the duty to support and assist their parents.

[56] Article 22 of the *Marriage Law of the People's Republic of China (1980)* states: Grandparents who can afford it shall have the duty to bring up their grandchildren who are minors and whose parents are dead. Grandchildren who can afford it shall have the duty to support their grandparents whose children are dead. Article 23 states: Elder brothers or elder sisters who can afford it shall have the duty to bring up their younger brothers or sisters who are minors if their parents are dead or have no means to bring them up.

grandparents and grandchildren, even if there is an intermediate generation between them, are obliged to support each other, and also elder brothers and sisters are obliged to support younger brothers and sisters. In contrast to Article 13 of *the Marriage Law (1950)*, which regulates the relationship between parents and children – "Parents shall be under the obligation of upbringing and educating their children, and the children shall also be under the obligation of supporting their parents" – it can be seen that the *Marriage Law (1980)* not only specifies the forms of the obligation of supporting each other between family members, but also imposes this obligation on grandchildren and siblings which should have been undertaken merely by the children and parents. *The Marriage Law (2001)* keeps the provisions prescribing the obligation to support family members provided in the *1980 Marriage Law*, and its Article 29 further specifies the obligation of younger brothers and sisters to support their elder brothers and sisters.[57] Under this system, the obligations to support each other between family members may, indeed, cover all members of the family. On the other hand, a number of researches on family policies in China have shown that our policies related to family welfare mainly depend on assistance and subsidy, with a relatively small scope of coverage. The policy of supporting family is aimed at socially vulnerable groups, such as the "low-income households" in rural areas, and incomplete families with orphaned or disabled children, while structurally healthy families depend to a large extent on self-support.[58] A noteworthy result owing to this kind of policy is that an individual with a healthy family relies primarily on himself or herself to take his or her family responsibilities. In contrast to an incomplete family, it receives less support from the state. This is to some extent not a reward but a punishment on individuals undertaking family responsibilities.

The above analyses imply that the protection for the family in the past was based only on the individual aspect and thus attributed structural problems such as family instability only to the individual. Omitting the challenges arising from the structural factors of society on the family has also led to an unexpected consequence, namely, that the more we emphasize the protection for the family, the more we objectively increase the burdens of its members. As

---

57 Article 29 of the *Marriage Law of the People's Republic of China (2001)* states: Capable elder brothers and sisters shall be under the obligation of supporting their younger brothers and sisters whose parents have deceased or whose parents are incapable of supporting them. The younger brothers and sisters who have been brought up by the elder brothers and sisters shall be under the obligation of supporting their elder brothers and sisters who are without labor capabilities and without sources of living necessities.

58 See Hu Zhan, Peng Xizhe, 'China's Family Policies in the Context of Family Changes' (2012) 2 *Population Research* 5–6.

mentioned earlier, similarly, the system of a cooling-off period before divorce is also based on the individual dimension to protect the family, while there are no governmental subsidies depending on new nation policies to support the family at the present time. Then, the system of a cooling-off period before divorce, despite its good intentions, may objectively aggravate the burdens faced by family members in practice. In this sense, many objections to the system of a cooling-off period before divorce are credible. As some opponents have claimed, while accusing young people of being impulsive and irresponsible, we should perhaps look into the lives of young people nowadays and grasp what kind of future they are facing, "To stabilize family life? But for young people nowadays, 'working for 12 hours a day and 6 days a week, or even 24 hours a day and 7 days a week' is already the routine, and it is hard for them to spend time at home. If so, they are even unlikely to enjoy normal family life."[59] Therefore, it is reasonable in a sense to admit that the system of a cooling-off period before divorce tends to cause the increasing rates of celibacy, as people may choose not to get married in order to escape from excessive family burdens.

4. LEGAL REPONSES TO THE SYSTEM OF A COOLING-OFF PERIOD BEFORE DIVORCE

The sociological analyses of family reveal that the cooling-off period before divorce may have some unexpected consequences, but this does not mean that this cooling-off period should be abolished. This chapter reveals the unexpected consequences of the system of a cooling-off period before divorce, but it is not intended to deny such a system. Instead, it systematically analyzes this system on the basis of the complexity of the law itself, in order to provide theoretical support for the system functioning in practice. In this regard, the concern here is how the value-justified system of a cooling-off period before divorce can function properly in practice. Limiting the scope of application of the provision of the cooling-off period before divorce in accordance with the purposive limitation approach in filling legal loopholes, as well as developing corresponding supporting policies for families, are the legal responses to the issues caused by the system of a cooling-off period before divorce.

---

[59] 'Cannot Keep People Calm During "Divorce Cooling-off Period"' (Peng Pai News 2 June 2020) <https://m.thepaper.cn/newsDetail_forward_7664104> accessed 5 June 2021.

4.1 Limiting the Scope of Application of the Provision of the Cooling-Off Period before Divorce by Virtue of Purpose Limitation

In terms of legal provisions, there is a hidden legal loophole in article 1077 of the Civil Code, which sets up the cooling-off period before divorce. A legal loophole is a concept in legal interpretations referring to an incompleteness in the positive law system that affects the ideal functions the positive law possesses and is contrary to the legislative intent.[60] How to determine whether there is a legal loophole? Huang Maorong has made a thorough and comprehensive analysis, "As long as a fact of life is justly assessed as a matter that does not belong to extra-legal space … then a loophole exists in the law with respect to that fact of life if the law (A) does not prescribe such a fact comprehensively, or (B) contradicts the prescriptions which regulates it, or (C) fails to prescribe it at all, whether or not the law regulates types of cases similar to, or (D) improperly prescribes it."[61] As far as the cooling-off period before divorce is concerned, firstly, it involves the registration of divorce, a matter that is naturally regulated by the law. Secondly, as shown in the previous part of the analysis, this cooling-off period puts women in a more adverse situation, which is not conducive to gender equality. This is naturally belonging to the D situation mentioned above. In addition, according to the differences the legal loopholes manifest, scholars have differentiated loopholes into obvious ones and hidden ones so as to apply different methods of filling loopholes. One of the common manifestations of hidden loopholes is an excessively broad scope of application including facts that should not be included.[62] As can be seen from the previous analyses, it is precisely because the law does not clearly define the scope of application of the cooling-off period before divorce and inappropriately includes divorcing parties not derived from wanton divorces which leads to the dilemma of protecting women's interests. Therefore, the loophole here of the system of a cooling-off period before divorce is a hidden legal loophole.

After affirming the existence of a legal loophole, it is necessary to further choose the appropriate way to fill the loophole. Theoretically, there are two ways, namely, the legislative and judicial ways. Here, however, since the cooling-off period before divorce is normally applied to registered divorces, it has

---

60 See Liang Huixing, *Civil Law Interpretation* (4th edn, Law Press China 2015) 253.

61 Huang Maorong, *Legal Methodology and Modern Civil Law* (China University of Political Science and Law Press 2001) 348.

62 See Wang Liming, *Introduction to Legal Interpretation – A Civil Law Perspective* (Law Press China 2009) 469–70.

nothing to do with the courts. Thus, we can exclude the possibility of filling the loophole relying on judicial means. The only feasible way to fill the legal loophole I refer to here is that the Standing Committee of the National People's Congress provides legislative interpretation for further defining the specific meaning of such a provision prescribing a cooling-off period before divorce.[63]

For different types of legal loopholes, there are different methods of the application of legal interpretations to fill the loopholes. Purpose limitation is one of the methods for hiding legal loopholes and is an appropriate way to fill the legal loophole of the system of the cooling-off period before divorce. It means: "Considering the negligence of the legislator in not explicitly excluding the situation that the literal meaning of a legal provision should encompass a certain type of case, which should have been excluded according to the legislative purpose and the will to ensure the coherent and consistent implementation of the legislative intent, this specific type of case is consequently excluded from the scope of applicability of that legal provision."[64] Accordingly, as mentioned earlier, the official legislative instructions clearly mention that the cooling-off period before divorce is set up for responding to the problem of wanton divorce, so the scope of application of the system should be merely limited to the category of wanton divorce, in accordance with the purpose of the legislation. Furthermore, the term "application for divorce registration" in Article 1077 of *the Civil Code* should be interpreted restrictively to refer only to the application for registered divorce on the basis of recklessness and impulsive grounds.

After limiting the applicable object of Article 1077 of *the Civil Code* to wanton divorce by virtue of legal interpretation, the question of how to identify wanton divorce in practice remains. Wanton divorce is a commonly used term, and there needs to be a process of legal conceptualization when it is converted into legal practice. Indeed, it is difficult to immediately define clearly wanton divorce in a legal context here. In practice, however, it is still possible to identify the term by typology. On the one hand, there are types of cases in practice that exclude the application of the cooling-off period before divorce, due to public order and mandatory regulations, etc. These cases include: one party is diagnosed with a disease which is regarded by medical science as a factor unfit for marriage after marriage, one party is suffering from a disease which is regarded by medical science as unfit for marriage, sexual incapacity, revocable marriages that have exceeded the time limit set for legal dissolution

---

63 See Commission for Legislative Affairs of the Standing Committee of the National People's Congress, *The Interpretation of the Legislation Law of the People's Republic of China* (Law Press China 2015) 152–4.

64 See Liang Huixing, *Civil Law Interpretation* (4th edn, Law Press China 2015) 276.

of the marriage, bigamy, marital cohabitation, domestic violence, desertion of any family member, maltreatment, and arranged marriages.[65] We can, firstly, exclude these types of cases from wanton divorce. On the other hand, we can comprehensively determine whether a person's application for registered divorce is wanton or imprudent, in terms of their marriage duration, status in the process of divorce, reasons for divorce, and awareness of the consequences of divorce.

4.2 Constructing Developmental Family Policies

From the external perspective of the law, in order to make the system of a cooling-off period before divorce achieve the purpose of maintaining family stability, the government is required to share necessary responsibilities to assist families in alleviating the burdens of family members. In this regard, family policy research has provided us with useful references. Scholars of the research on family policies have proposed constructing a developmental family policy in China. Developmental family policy treats family policy as a social investment. It argues that all families need to be supported and that the developmental policy supports non-impoverished families from a preventive perspective. It is pointed out that the roots of the problems resulting from poverty, unemployment, juvenile crime, and domestic violence, etc., lie in the dysfunctioning of the family and that family policy should therefore prevent the functions of the family from being disrupted rather than provide alternative or compensatory assistance after its functions have been damaged.[66]

With regard to the construction of developmental family policies in China, firstly, the government should change its idea of family policy-making from remedial orientation to a developmental orientation, rather than focusing only on "dysfunctional families" and working on relief afterwards. Moreover, the formulation of family policies should shift its guiding principles from meeting the most basic survival needs of families to constructing the functions of families, hence actively enhancing the development capacities of the family itself.[67] For example, since the government has not explicitly acknowledged that a family policy was implemented in China in the past, in achieving a change in the idea of family policy making, a special family policy institution should be set up for integrating various social resources and promoting the

---

65 See Xia Qin, 'Interpretation of the Cooling-off Period for the Registration of Divorce in the Civil Code' (2020) 5 *The Jurist* 37.

66 See Lü Qing, Zhao Xianghong, *Family Policy* (Social Sciences Academic Press (China) 2012) 56.

67 See Wu Fan, 'Family Changes and Policy Reflections in China in the Context of the Second Population Transition' (2012) 2 *Social Sciences In Guangdong* 29.

construction of a family-policy system in China.[68] Secondly, the government should provide families with necessary financial support and strengthen the assistance on the family functions of supporting the older generation and taking care of the younger generation. This is because both caring for the elderly and raising children are quite costly for most families in China at the present time. The government can recognize these costs through tax policy and take supportive measures in the area of basic social services so as to reduce the cost of raising children for families and alleviate the social burdens on family members financially.[69] Thirdly, the government should encourage or require employers to establish a specific kind of work system that is conducive to individuals taking up their family responsibilities, hence creating an environment that supports individuals in taking up their family responsibilities. Because many kinds of family needs are often contingent, they in many cases conflict with the requirements of our work. In the absence of relevant family-policy supplies, couples are forced to seek a private solution, negotiated and compromised internally by themselves. In modern societies that emphasize equality between genders, conflicts between spouses tend to intensify during such negotiations. After all, whoever compromises is bound to face an unfavorable situation in their career. This is not only harmful to family stability, but also reduces work efficiency. As such, the government can encourage enterprises to establish flexible working hours and flexible leave arrangements, and provide these enterprises with corresponding policy incentives and subsidies.[70]

5. CONCLUSION

The problems exposed by the system of a cooling-off period before divorce are a typical manifestation of the difficulties faced by marriage and family nowadays. The State's pragmatic approach to dealing with problems in such a field seems, on the surface, to address the problems specifically at present, but actually fails to take into account the diversity of interests that exist in the modern family. From the perspective of legal effectiveness, it is likely to conflict with the original intent of the legal system, resulting in consequences that people are unwilling to accept. Moreover, under the domination of the logic of practicality, the boundaries of power between the State, the family,

---

[68] See Hu Zhan, Peng Xizhe, 'China's Family Policies in the Context of Family Changes' (2012) 2 *Population Research* 7.

[69] See Zhang Xiulan, Xu Yuebin, 'Formulating a Developmental Family Policy in China' (2003) 6 *Social Sciences in China* 96.

[70] See Peng Xizhe, Hu Zhan, 'The Contemporary Transition of the Chinese Family and the Reconstruction of Family Policy' (2015) 12 *Social Sciences in China* 130.

and the individual are always blurry. In such a situation, we may actually have difficulty in protecting family values and indeed individual values coherently. Since the law itself is an intricate and subtle project involving all aspects and fields of society, no matter what this law project is designed or constructed for, or how it operates in practical milieus, it will ultimately play a role in people's daily lives and make a difference to their future destinies. Therefore, in solving problems in the sphere of marriage and family, we should introduce integrative thinking; only by adopting a comprehensive view of the factors involved in a legal system will the legal system not only have ideological and conceptual significance but also be practically operative.

6. The deviation-style interaction between public opinion and criminal law: narratives of individually lowering the age of criminal liability in China

Zhu Xiaoyan

INTRODUCTION

Whether to reduce the age of criminal liability is an important issue in the management of juvenile delinquency in China, which has caused a long-term theoretical opposition and practical dispute. However, with the online public opinion triggered by hot cases such as the murder of a 13-year-old boy in Dalian, and the individual lowering of the age of criminal liability in Criminal Law Amendment Act XI, the narrative background of setting the minimum age of criminal liability has quietly changed. The 'Dalian 13-year-old boy homicide case' marked a turning point, as the societal demand to lower the age of criminal liability and harshly punish delinquent juveniles quickly evolved into a highly consensual public opinion through the dissemination of information and emotional transmission on large-scale social networking platforms like Sina Micro-Blog. In the face of the 'clamoring' expectation of law revision, the 'Criminal Law Amendment Act XI' partially responded to this significant social concern by individually lowering the age of criminal liability. This highly functionalist way of thinking makes criminal law temporarily get rid of the pressure of public opinion but carries the unprecedented function of juvenile delinquency.

It can be seen that the demand of public opinion and the response of criminal law to reduce the age of criminal liability have developed into a pair of closely related, different, and even contradictory forces, which are gradually embedded in the increasingly complex governance pattern of juvenile delinquency. It also deeply affects the implementation effect of the newly revised 'Juvenile

Protection Law' and 'Juvenile Delinquency Prevention Law'. Therefore, the demand of public opinion and the response of criminal law to reduce the age of criminal liability is not only a major practical issue that needs to be deeply interpreted through empirical analysis, but also a theoretical issue that needs to be reinterpreted with the help of new observation perspectives and new research methods.

1. LITERATURE REVIEW AND TOPIC DECONSTRUCTION

1.1 Review and Reflection of Relevant Literature

The individualized adjustment of the age of criminal liability in Criminal Law Amendment Act XI marks the arrival of the era of criminal law intervening in the management of juvenile delinquency and wrongdoing. The theoretical research on the setting of the minimum age of criminal liability has gradually shifted from the classic debate on whether to lower the age of criminal liability to the debate on how to perfect the management of juvenile delinquency under the premise of criminal law intervention. On the whole, the existing research is committed to clarifying the relationship between punishment and comprehensive correction and realizing the modernization goal of independence and specialization of juvenile justice in China, which has deep consensus, by balancing protection, punishment, and prevention.[1] Specifically, in terms of top-level design, existing studies believe that the management of juvenile delinquency should strengthen the concept of 'tolerance but not connivance' and form a two-way protection system that takes into account both minors in contact with the law and social security order.[2] In terms of supporting measures, existing studies believe that the governance of juvenile delinquency should optimize the co-governance model led by the state and multi-participation of society,[3] improve the hierarchical intervention and comprehensive

[1] See Yao Jianlong, 'The Dilemma and Outlet of Juvenile Law: On the Revision of the Law on the Protection of Minors and the Law on the Prevention of Juvenile Delinquency' (2019) 1 *Youth Research* 1–15.

[2] See Liu Shuangyang, 'From Detention and Correction to Special Correction Education: Review and Shaping of the Treatment Mechanism of Minors Who Violate Law' (2021) 1 *Yunnan Social Sciences* 92–99.

[3] See Sun Qian, 'The construction of Chinese Juvenile Justice System Path' (2021) 6 *Journal of Politics and Law* 2–14.

correction system,[4] and pay attention to the reintegration of offending minors and society.[5]

However, as mentioned above, the appeal of public opinion and the response of criminal law to lower the age of criminal liability have played an important role in the governance pattern of juvenile crime and wrong behavior. If vicious cases committed by young minors occur again in the future, under the premise of repeated pressure from public opinion and the absence of normative barriers to criminal law intervention, it is difficult for case handling organs to make final decisions that meet existing research expectations and conform to the logic of juvenile justice.[6] Therefore, the vast majority of existing studies regard the governance of juvenile delinquency as a highly closed system that fully follows the logic of juvenile justice, in fact, self-shielding the potential role of public opinion and failing to capture the complexity of the interaction between public opinion demands and criminal law responses behind this major public governance issue. When the understanding of the governance pattern of juvenile delinquency in China is not comprehensive, if the theoretical research enters directly into the discussion of practical criticism and measures construction, it will inevitably face the estrangement between the theoretical preconception and the governance reality, and there will be insufficient localization consciousness.

At the same time, some existing studies have noticed the interaction between public opinion appeals and criminal law responses, and tried to explain the legislative intent of lowering the age of criminal liability based on the 'pressure-response' model. Such studies believe that a series of extreme cases have touched the sensitive nerves of the public, forming online public opinion pressure mainly to reduce the age of criminal liability,[7] and the limited reduction of the age of criminal liability in the criminal law is an example of responding

4 See Deng WanXin, Mo HongXian, 'Age Boundary Reconstruction under the Background of Coordination Mechanism of the Juvenile Criminal Liability' (2021) 3 *Journal of Learning and Practice* 75.

5 See Liu Yanhong, Ruan ChenXin, 'Establishment and Development of the Concept of Judicial Protection for Delinquent Minors from the Perspective of New Law' (2021) 1 *Yunnan Social Sciences* 83–91.

6 See Gabriella Hauber Flip, Mendes Motta, 'News Media and Connectivity in Deliberative Systems; Reflections on the Debate about the Brazilian Age of Criminal Liability' vol. 15 (2021) 1 *Brazilian Political Science Review* 1–3.

7 See Zhang Yijian, 'The Main Provisions of the Eleventh Amendment to Criminal Law and the Development of Criminal Legislation' (2021) 1 *China Law Review* 51–59.

to public concerns.[8] This amendment can meet the practical needs of punishing and preventing juvenile crimes,[9] ease the rigidity of the minimum age standard of criminal liability, and enhance the ability to respond and space to respond of the criminal law to public opinion.[10]

However, although this kind of research has achieved a shift in perspective, it still focuses on the fuzzy description of social public opinion, and the few empirical studies are also limited to statistical forms such as questionnaire survey,[11] ignoring the unique derivative structure of online public opinion in the context of digital society. Large-scale social media platforms such as Sina Weibo (Micro-Blog) have significantly reshaped the way in which the public participates in major public governance issues. Public opinion is easily transformed into network sentiment with clear demands and focused viewpoints, often magnified through hot searches and trending topics.[12] The contemporary evolution of the behavior pattern of public participation in social governance issues will gradually subvert the inherent cognition of public opinion in theoretical research. Under the new background of 'network sentiment', the previous stereotypical research impression of 'spontaneity, blindness, and fragmentation'[13] can neither help to uncover the true veil of 'public opinion sets stage and network sentiment plays drama', nor can it accurately describe the complex demands behind online public opinion with reasonable research perspectives and methods.

---

[8] See Zhou Guangquan, 'Progress of Criminal Legislation and Judicial Prospect – General Comment on the Eleventh Amendment to Criminal Law' (2021) 1 *Science of Law* 18–35.

[9] See Chen Weilu, 'Prevention of Juvenile Delinquency and Revision of Minimum Age of Criminal Responsibility' (2021) 2 *China Youth Research* 52–57.

[10] See Peng Xinlin, 'Rationality of Criminal Liability Age Limit Individual Cut' (2021) The Democracy and Legal System Times.

[11] See Su Mingyue, Zheng Xiaoyu, 'Reduced Criminal Liability Age from the Polls and Legislative Changes' (2021) 9 *Journal of Social Governance* 29–32; See Fu Liping, 'Can the Age of Criminal Liability for Minors Be Lowered? An Empirical Study Based on 1010 Questionnaires' (2019) Human Rights Research (Journal of Human Rights) 285–289.

[12] See Anastasia Powell, Gregory Stratton, Robin Cameron, *Digital Criminology: Crime and Justice in Digital Society* (New York: Routledge 2018) 138–157.

[13] See Liu Xianquan, 'Criminal Legislation Should Refrain from Emotions – from the Perspective of the Ninth Amendment to Criminal Law' (2016) 1 *Law Review* 87–88.

1.2 Theoretical Innovation and Thought Design

Combining the deficiency of existing theoretical research with the reality of juvenile delinquency management in China, this chapter will try to promote the research of this problem from two aspects of research perspective and method.

From the perspective of research, this chapter takes the interactive structure of 'public opinion appeal – criminal law response' as the origin of observing the lowering of the age of criminal liability. The appeal of public opinion to reduce the age of criminal liability and the response of criminal law show a 'problem chain' which includes four aspects: what to respond to, how to respond, effect of response, and how to improve the response. What to respond to, that is, what is the public opinion appeal of the criminal law to reduce the age of criminal liability? How to respond, that is, what techniques and strategies the criminal law adopts to respond to public opinion appeals? Effect of response, that is, does the unique mode of criminal law response achieve the desired result? Improvement of response, that is, under the existing response strategy and response mode, how can the public participation in juvenile delinquency be improved? The problem chain formed by the interconnection and continuity of these four aspects jointly shapes the basic framework of public opinion demands and criminal law responses. With the help of these aspects, we can see the complex struggle between internal legal factors and extralegal pressure, and deeply understand the vision and reality, functions and boundaries, advantages and loads of the strategy of responding to online public opinion pressure through criminal legislation. Then we can explore the way of harmonious coexistence between criminal law and comprehensive treatment of juvenile crime and wrongdoing.

The objective attribute of the research problem determines the subjective selection of the research method. The first question is 'what to respond to', which is the beginning of the whole problem chain. In this chapter, the online public opinion of Sina Weibo is selected as a representative sample of public opinion demands for lowering the age of criminal liability, and Long Short-Term Memory (LSTM) is introduced to classify the emotions of massive comment texts, and the count function is used to count high-frequency words. By digitizing high-frequency words with different emotional tendencies the institutional demands of public opinion are presented. The second question is 'How to respond', which needs to take the aforementioned online public opinion as a sample to analyze in depth which online public opinion appeals behind the Criminal Law Amendment Act XI have been responded to and what strategies have been adopted. The third question is 'respond to what'. It is still necessary to use the LSTM to classify the emotions of the network public opinion after the amendment and use the count function to count high-frequency words to summarize different emotional reactions of different emotional tendencies, so as to see the response effect of the criminal law in lowering the age of criminal liability, as well as to provide targets for how to further guide public opinion in criminal law; the fourth question is 'what is the perfect response?', which, on the basis of data analysis and theoretical abstraction, explores the way to improve criminal law response according to the deviation between public opinion demands and the response effect.

In this chapter, the innovation of research methods lies in the introduction of LSTM, which not only hopes to complete an in-depth dialogue between criminal law and social science with the help of the wave of 'technology empowerment', but also strives to contribute knowledge increment to the innovation of empirical research methods of law in the theoretical transformation of 'digital law'. To be specific, first, the introduction of LSTM can lift the fuzzy veil of social public opinion and remove the disciplinary barriers faced by criminal law research in observing public opinion, so as to realize the cross-disciplinary perspectives in the discussion of the complex issue of lowering the age of criminal liability. LSTM is a classical intelligent recurrent neural network structure, which is suitable for processing and predicting important events with relatively long intervals and delays in time series in massive texts, and effectively capturing the emotionally prominent parts.[14] It can deal intensively with the research obstacles that traditional criminal law research has difficulty in overcoming, such as online public opinion digital noise, short comment sentences, text irregularities, etc., and digitally present the specific trend of public opinion. With the support of natural science methods, the research of criminal law can effectively get rid of the fuzzy cognition of social public opinion and form an in-depth dialogue with public opinion, political science, sociology, and other social science factors behind public opinion, so as to produce knowledge products with more practical insight and persuasion.[15] Second, with the appropriate application scenario of lowering the age of criminal liability, the significance of introducing the methodology of LSTM is also to promote the innovation of legal empirical research methods from statistics to big data. Under the background that digital survival and digital governance are deeply embedded in social development, if legal empirical research is still limited to artificial statistical methods, specific regression models, and the number of

---

[14] See Chen Ling, Song YanXin, 'LSTM Sentiment Analysis Based on Public Emotional Context: A Case Study of Typhoon Lekima' (2020) 6 *Modern Information* 99.

[15] See Che Hao, 'Jurisprudence and Social Science: Taking Criminal Jurisprudence as An Example' (2021) 5 *China Law Review* 137–138; See Bai Jianjun, 'On the Doctrine of Criminal Law and Empirical Research' (2021) 3 *Law Studies* 120–123.

hundreds of thousands of samples,[16] it may not be able to effectively present the practical logic behind the deep integration of law and technological society behind such issues as lowering the age of criminal liability.[17] The introduction and experiment of LSTM is expected to highlight the many advantages of big data technology in information acquisition channels, in-depth data analysis and digital description ability, and promote legal research to be more social scientific, incorporating more artificial intelligence, and more accustomed to exploring the laws of the legal world from big data, aiming to realize the method relay from statistics based on manual to big data under machine technology.[18]

2. DATA PROCESSING AND METHOD APPLICATION

2.1 Research Objects and Data Sources

In this chapter, comments on Sina Weibo trending '#Dalian 11-year-old girl murdered#' and '#police report Dalian 10-year-old girl murdered#' were selected as data samples of public opinion demands before the law amendment; the comments of '#Criminal Law Amendment Act XI reduce the statutory minimum age of criminal liability to 12 years old#' and '#adjustments to the scope of criminal liability for younger minors#' were selected as data samples of public opinion appeals after the amendment.

The selection of the aforementioned data samples stems from the unique derivative structure of online public opinion on lowering the age of criminal liability. In October 2019, the 'homicide case of a 13-year-old boy in Dalian' for the first time detonated the topic of lowering the age of criminal liability on the Weibo platform in the form of 'continuous hot searches', forming a huge pressure of online public opinion. Moreover, these online public opinions are highly concentrated in the hot searches '#Dalian 11-year-old girl murdered #' and '#police report Dalian 10-year-old girl murdered#' (see Table 6.1). And it is highly concentrated in the hot searches '#Criminal Law Amendment Act XI reduces the statutory minimum age of criminal liability to 12 years old #' and '# adjustment of the scope of criminal liability for young minors#' (see Table 6.2). In addition, compared with other social media platforms such as WeChat, QQ, Bilibili and Hupu, Sina Weibo puts more emphasis on topic focus and point of view clustering of hot events. It can skillfully use discussion

16 See Zhou Xiang, 'As the Research Method of Law of Big Data Technology' (2021) 6 *Journal of Jurists* 61–65.

17 See Shen WeiXing, Liu Yun, 'New Paradigm of Legal Research: Connotation, Category and Method of Computational Jurisprudence' (2020) 5 *Legal Studies* 20.

18 See *supra* note 16, 61.

Table 6.1 *The top 5 trending searches on Sina Weibo about 'murder of a 13-year-old boy in Dalian'*

Hot search name	Reading quantity	Discussion volume
#11 year old girl killed in Dalian#	1.4 billion	28.6 thousand
#Police report murder of 10-year-old girl in Dalian#	1.1 billion	15.2 thousand
#Girl killed in Dalian wrote to parents#	310 million	Two hundred thousand
#Dalian girl killed#	270 million	Forty-nine thousand
#Why do minors commit crimes at a younger age#	270 million	Three hundred thousand

Source: SinaWeibo website edition, statistical time as of January 7, 2021.

Table 6.2 *The top 5 hot searches on Sina Weibo about the topic of 'Lowering the age of criminal liability in the Criminal Law Amendment'*

Hot search name	Reading quantity	Discussion volume
#The scope of criminal liability for young minors has been adjusted#	930 million	Seventy thousand
#Amendments to the Criminal Law lower the statutory minimum age of criminal liability to 12 years#	190 million	Forty thousand
#The revision of the Criminal law intends to fine-tune the scope of criminal liability for minors#	47,495,000	3630
#Age of criminal liability lowered to 12 years#	25,949,000	2957
#Age of criminal liability lowered to 12 years#	3,676,000	187

Source: Sina Weibo website edition, statistical time as of January 7, 2021.

mechanisms with in-depth interactive functions such as hot search and explosive topics, and quickly integrate scattered public opinions in the market into online public opinions that can influence public policy choices. In the digital social media environment, Sina Weibo has become one of the important platforms to reflect the demands of public opinion.[19] Therefore, the above four hot searches from Sina Weibo have sufficient sample representativeness.

2.2 Data Collection and Data Processing

In the process of data collection, Scrapy crawler software is used to collect comment data of Sina Weibo hot searches '#Dalian 11-year-old girl murdered#' and '#police report Dalian 10-year-old girl murdered#' (hereinafter referred to as 'network public opinion samples before the law revision'), and a total of 10,053 comment data have been obtained. The comment data of Sina Weibo hot searches '#Criminal Law amendment lowered the legal minimum age of criminal liability to 12 years old#' and '#Adjustment of the scope of criminal liability for young minors#' (hereinafter referred to as 'sample of online public opinion after the revised law') were collected, and a total of 9,706 comment data were obtained.[20]

In the process of data processing, this chapter uses regular expressions to remove punctuation, null values, expressions, and advertising data to get the comment corpus. Through manual screening, the comments that do not have sentiment analysis value, such as greetings, forwarding Weibo blogs, @ unknown Weibo users, irrelevant topics, etc., are removed. In order to further improve the accuracy of data screening, this chapter adds an additional 'modification and restoration' procedure in the process of manual screening and restores the comments of sentiment analysis value with wrong characters and sensitive words according to the original meaning of the comments, in order to minimize the loss of valid data. After triple screening, a total of 9,615 valid comment data were retained in the online public opinion samples before the revised law, and 4,443 valid comment data were retained in the online public opinion samples after the revised law.

---

19 See Cui Yanchen, Zhang Peng, Lan Yuexin, Wu Lizhi, 'A Time Series-oriented Analysis of Public Opinion Derived from Weibo Emergencies: A Case Study of Public Opinion Derived from the "6.22" Nanny Arson Case in Hangzhou' (2019) 3 *Intelligence Science* 121–128.

20 Statistical period as of January 7, 2021. Since the crawler can only crawl the comment text of the first 50 pages of each hot search, the crawl comment data will be lower than the actual data. However, the web version of Sina Micro-Blog usually puts popular microblogs with large V reposts or a high number of comments and likes in the top position, and the relevant comment text is also concentrated in these popular microblogs. Therefore, this statistical result is still representative.

2.3 Algorithm Steps and Data Results

Sina Weibo comment text is generally presented as short text data, and its main emotional tendencies and institutional demands are concentrated in specific vocabulary.[21] Therefore, in order to effectively extract key information from tens of thousands of review texts, it is necessary to use appropriate data processing methods to effectively extract and combine words in review texts. The data processing process of Sina Weibo comment text is as follows:

Step 1: word segmentation and transformation. In this chapter, the jieba word segmentation script is used to segment the filtered review text, the short text data is reasonably divided into multiple terms, and Word2vec is used to convert the text of lexical categories into word vectors. The purpose of this process is to convert different words into different numerical values, so as to facilitate the subsequent data operation of the comment text.

Step 2: emotion classification, that is, using LSTM to conduct corpus training on massive review texts, extract different emotional features expressed by different words, and classify emotions according to these features. The main algorithm process is shown in the following Formula 1, where *W* is the calculated weight, *WT* is the matrix, *X* is the independent variable, *b* is the bias, and *y* is the result. After the input of independent variable *X*, *y* can digitally present the probabilistic relationship between different word vectors and different emotions in the comment text, so that the emotions of netizens in the comment text can be quantified into three categories: positive emotion, negative emotion and neutral emotion. The results are shown in Table 6.3. Vertically, by comparing the difference in the proportion of positive emotion, negative emotion and neutral emotion before and after the revision of the law, we can perceive the overall emotional change of online public opinion and further judge the actual effect of criminal law response. Horizontally, different emotional tendencies often represent different incident feedback and institutional demands; negative emotional comments have the strongest feedback and demands for lowering the age of criminal liability; positive emotions can most directly reflect the positive attitude of public opinion, and neutral emotions can represent the rational voice of public opinion to a certain extent.

Formula 1: $y = \frac{1}{1+e^{-\left(w^T X+b\right)}}$

---

21 See Zhang Liu, Wang Xiwei, Wang Duo, Wei Yanan, 'A Study on the Emotional Evolution Map of Public Opinion in Universities under the Weibo Environment: A Case Study of "Academic Misconduct in Universities" on Sina Weibo' (2019) 10 *Modern Information* 123.

Table 6.3 Emotional distribution and proportion of online public opinion samples before and after the amendment

Affective type Sample condition	Sample of online public opinion before the amendment (Quantity)	Sample of online public opinion before the amendment (Proportion)	Sample of online public opinion after the amendment (Quantity)	Sample of online public opinion after the amendment (Proportion)
Negative emotion	7717	80.26%	2838	63.88%
Neutral emotion	717	7.46%	460	10.35%
Positive emotion	1181	12.28%	1145	25.77%

Step 3: high-frequency word statistics, that is, the count function is used to classify and count the words with the highest frequency in the comments with different emotional tendencies. After the count function is used to obtain the statistical results of high-frequency words, this chapter removes irrelevant high-frequency words such as 'should', 'one' and 'Dalian', and obtains the top 10 high-frequency words of positive emotion, neutral emotion and negative emotion respectively (see Table 6.4 and Table 6.5). This link can provide effective data support for accurate analysis of the focus of attention of different online public opinions, integration of their implied institutional demands, and focus on showing the demands and emotional changes of social public opinions before and after the amendment.

3. PUBLIC OPINION RESPONSE OF SENSATIONAL CASES: THE EMOTIONAL MAP AND APPEAL INTEGRATION OF COMPLEX PUBLIC ISSUES

Before the revision of the law, public opinion on Sina Weibo concentrated on expressing expectations for the function of criminal law, strong negation of protecting minors, and deep doubts about the age of criminal liability (see Table 6.4).[22] Unlike the stereotypical characterization of 'spontaneity, blindness, and

[22] On the whole, high-frequency words with negative emotions show an overwhelming quantity advantage in frequency. Although neutral emotions and positive emotions are relatively stable in emotional expression, high-frequency words such as 'hope', 'amendment', 'law' and 'protection' euphemistically express the disagreement of these commentary texts on the criminal law's excessive indulgence of delinquent minors, which is generally consistent with the demands of

Table 6.4 Top 10 high-frequency words of various emotions in online public opinion comments before the amendment

Number	Frequently used negative words	Frequency of negative words	Frequently used neutral words	Frequency of neutral words	Frequently used forward direction words	Frequency of forward direction words
One	Minor	1164	Protection	51	Child	97
Two	Protection	1316	Underage	49	Support	68
Three	Law	1105	Parents	27	Protection	64
Four	Child	982	14	23	Underage	63
Five	Murder	825	Hope	22	Girl	44
Six	Parent	726	Edit	22	Parents	42
Seven	Age	688	Law	18	Age	31
Eight	14	612	Age	17	Child	25
Nine	Crime	533	Boy	15	Law	25
Ten	Society	368	Girl	14	Education	25

Table 6.5 Top 10 high-frequency words of all kinds of emotions in the online public opinion comments after the law revision

Number	High-frequency negative direction word	Frequency of negative direction word	High-frequency neutral word	Frequency of neutral word	High-frequency forward direction word	Frequency of forward direction word
1	Age	515	Age	34	Support	399
2	Minor	435	12	30	At last	81
3	12	169	Children	25	Children	51
4	Protect	158	Crime	21	12	43
5	Homicide	153	10	17	Adjust	42
6	Death penalty	134	Law	17	Attention	33
7	Hope	125	Support	15	Age	30
8	10	119	Past	12	Cheer	27
9	Criminal law	109	Education	12	Minor	26
10	Kid	104	Parents	12	Hope	24

fragmentation' made by traditional criminal law theory towards public opinion, network demand for lowering the age of criminal liability in the context of the digital society not only arises from the shortcomings of the legal system, but also reflects the general anxiety induced by extreme cases and amplified through interactive discussions on Sina Weibo. It shows structural characteristics of rational demands and irrational reactions intertwined.

3.1 Huge Functional Expectations for Criminal Law

The public opinion on Sina Weibo has huge functional expectations for criminal law in the management of juvenile delinquency and wrong behavior; it is reflected in high-frequency words such as 'society', 'parents', and 'killing'.

From the perspective of social defense, public opinion on Sina Weibo believes that the lack of punishment and measures such as education and probation are difficult to implement in practice, leading to the fact that the offending minors have obtained legal forgiveness without paying any price. Based on this concern, the public opinion on Sina Weibo expects to penalize offending minors by means of punishment, so as to achieve the governance effect and emotional comfort of preventing crime and maintaining social security. Typical comments included 'He caused too much harm to society; if this punishment is not severe, there will be more minors like him' (comment text No. 7659). The advocated measures of strengthening family education, enhancing school participation and ordering discipline before the revision of criminal law can essentially be referred to as 'soft governance strategies'. While these diversified measures are worth promoting, the virtualization of punishment actually weakens the effectiveness of soft strategies. Some juvenile offenders may even take advantage of the 'age limitation' in the law to commit severe crimes, leading the juvenile justice system to fall into the dilemma of 'raising them before punishing, feeding them before killing'.

The two high-frequency words 'society' and 'murder' reflect the expectation of public opinion on Sina Weibo to use criminal means to narrow the gulf in social justice. Typical commentary text such as 'All intentional homicides are subject to the death penalty!' 'It's not just unfair to the victims! It's unfair to society!' (comment text No. 109, No. 7255). Demands of social opinion on Sina Weibo for the entry of criminal law with the implementation of social justice contradict theoretical positions such as the minimization of criminal law participation in crime governance, but it does not completely represent the stubbornness and ignorance of social opinion. Since offending minors seriously

---

social public opinion on negative emotions. Therefore, the analysis of public opinion appeals in this part mainly focuses on negative emotion.

challenges the bottom line of social ethics and morals, endangers social security, and harms the legal feelings of the public, public opinion instinctively makes a stressful emotional response based on its own thinking mode and value judgment. The functional expectation and emotional dependence of strengthening crime prevention and implementing social justice are naturally generated in criminal law. To some degree, the emotional tendency to advocate the realization of social justice through criminal law is not to improve legal provisions themselves, but to rediscover and consolidate the common norms that society relies on through punishment.[23]

The emergence of the high-frequency word 'parents' reflects the emotional tendency and institutional appeal of social public opinion on Sina Weibo that expects the criminal law to make up for the absence of guardian responsibility. Typical comments like 'Shouldn't parents like this bear criminal liability?' and 'Parents should be arrested and sentenced together' (comment text No. 207, No. 551) illustrate this. The lack of family intervention, such as improper education and growth care, is indeed a major issue in the management of offending minors, but compared with the great expectation of social defense and social justice of the high-frequency word 'society', there are still a lot of irrational factors in the reasoning logic of criminal law intervention and 'child's debt being paid by the parents'. Moreover, extreme emotional tendencies such as 'killing for life, it is natural. If age is not enough, let parents pay with their life' and 'parents should be executed by shooting' (comment text No. 169, No. 224) are not only not diluted in the massive commentary text but instead amplified through interactions such as likes, shares, and replies. Demands for using penalties to achieve social defense and social justice are mixed together, and eventually develop into the pressure of network public opinion that the criminal law has to face and respond to.

3.2 Extreme Rejection of the Concept of Protection

Regarding the important value balance between protection and punishment in the management of juvenile delinquency, public opinion on Sina Weibo points to the ground on one side that using criminal law to punish offending minors severely and extremely rejects the concept of protection, which is specifically reflected in high-frequency words such as 'minors', 'protection' and 'law'. Moreover, these high-frequency words often appear in the same comments. Many high-frequency words relate to each other and support each other (see Table 6.4). These emotional tendencies are not only influenced by

---

[23] See Michel Foucault, 'Discipline and Punishment: The Birth of the Prison'; Life, New Findings and Sanlian Bookstore 2019 edition, 103–120.

the traditional Chinese criminal policies of 'caring for the young' and 'showing pity for the weak' on the public psychology,[24] but also closely related to the reform of the concept of emphasizing protection and light punishment in contemporary China.

The issue of prioritizing the interests between the perpetrator and the victim, public opinion on Sina Weibo tends to strengthen the protection of the victim and reduce the protection of the perpetrator, especially when both the perpetrator and the victim are children. The core position behind this emotional tendency is that the post-disposal method of heavy protection and light punishment only emphasizes the protection of the interests of the offending minors in essence, and even satisfies the protection of the interests of the offending minors at the expense of the interests of the minor victims, resulting in serious interest imbalance. Typical commentary reads, 'Why no criminal charges? This is protection' (comment text, No. 585). It can be seen that the institutional demands behind these emotional reactions are mainly to change excessive protection into severe sanctions, especially to significantly restrict the personal freedom of the offending minors by means of punishment, so that they can leave the comfort zone of the family of origin and bear the pain equivalent to their behavior, in order to exchange enough moral sanctions and emotional relief in the hypothetical scenario of the victim.

Regarding the question of which is the priority between the interests of minors and the interests of society as a whole, the mainstream public opinion on Sina Weibo believes that the protection concept allows minors to continuously use 'age advantage' to commit crimes, so the overall interests of society should be aimed at reducing protection and strengthening punishment. Typical commentary text is 'Protect minors today, tomorrow they will kill us' (comment text No. 33). Many commentary texts also express the negation of the personality of the offending minors and the extremely pessimistic attitude towards correctability of the offending minors. Typical comments such as 'minors are so calm to commit crimes so calmly with stronger psychological qualities than adults. Should we let them harm the innocent after they become adults?' (Comment text, article 875). It can be seen that in the protection of the interests between perpetrators and victims, and the value tradeoff between minors and society, the one-sided emphasis on the concept of protection by law enforcement agencies has triggered strong punitive demands in public opinion. Prior to the promulgation of the Criminal Law Amendment Act XI, the criminal law had long adhered to the criminal policy of 'education first, punishment as a supplement'; the lenient judicial treatment of offending minors

---

24 See Jing Fenghua, 'The logic of "Being weak": The legal genealogy of the Murder Cases of Children in Qing Dynasty' (2017) 6 *The Jurists* 73–74.

was covered in a series of system designs.[25] In contrast, the concept of punishment and its supporting measures have been ignored relatively, leading to the unprincipled protection of some minors who commit severe crimes, which not only contradicts the traditional Chinese concept of substantive justice of 'caring for the young' and 'protecting the weak', but also induces the cognitive gap between criminal law norms and public opinion.[26] Therefore, the 'murder case of a 13-year-old boy in Dalian' is like the last straw that broke the camel's back, driving the public opinion on Sina Weibo to an emotional extreme towards the strong rejection of protection.

3.3 Explicitly Negate the Normative Setting of the Minimum Age of Criminal Liability

As for the standard about the age of criminal liability in Article 17 of the Criminal Law, public opinion on Sina Weibo believes that the minimum age of criminal liability should be adjusted, and some propositions even demand the restriction of the age of criminal liability should be abolished. Such appeals are concentrated in high-frequency words such as '14', 'age' and 'child', which clearly reflect the conflict between the professional provisions of criminal law and the simple emotions of the public.

Overall, public opinion on Sina Weibo believes that the age of criminal liability in the criminal law should be lowered in a timely manner. Such as 'He could calmly ask the dead girl's father, which was too mature to look like a child at all.' 'Children are becoming more and more mature nowadays. Even elementary school students know things that adults should know. If the law is not amended according to this trend, more minors will engage in crimes.' (comment text No.543, No.593). In general, public opinion shows the legitimate questioning of the one-size-fits-all approach of the criminal liability provision to cope with a rapidly changing society. According to the simple understanding of public opinion, improvement of living conditions and the optimization of diet structure have resulted in earlier physical development in children. Moreover, the prevalence of smartphones and the integration of digital life have significantly increased children's cognitive abilities. Hence, criminal law must lower the age of criminal liability to cope with the above changes according to public opinion. On the contrary, more complex and specialized factors such as whether lowering the age of criminal liability has sufficient empirical support, whether it can achieve crime governance efficacy, and

---

25 See Wang, Zhenhui, 'Perfection of Judicial System for Juvenile Delinquents' (2020) 4 *Journal of State Procurators College* 134–137.

26 See *supra* note 25, 84–86.

whether it violates the Convention on the Rights of the Child are not within the scope of public opinion.

It is worth noting that some social opinions on Sina Weibo believe that the restriction of the age of criminal liability should be completely abolished. Typical comment text such as 'No matter how old or young a child is, killing someone proves that they must have cognitive abilities, and the degree of precocity of children can no longer be viewed with the eyes of the past' (comment text No. 126). It can be seen that the public opinion appeal for adjusting the setting of the minimum age of criminal liability is not completely dependent on professional knowledge, but deeply based on the interpretation system of common sense and human nature. In the view of the public, 'I killed people. I will pay with my life' is a social norm known to all ages, and younger minors naturally have the ability to identify and control intentional homicide and its results, so they can be punished with penalties. In contrast, the normative setting of the age of criminal liability has often been packaged as 'education as the main, punishment as the supplement' and 'the principle of the best interests of children'. Although this rational and scientific face is understandable to the legal professional group, it is too rigid and cold in the cognition of public opinion. Even against the most basic common sense and human nature.[27] In the case that there is already a certain gap between law and reason, public opinion is more dissatisfied with age settings. The reason is that society not only believes that criminal law neglects the minors' physiological development, but also believes that criminal law lacks exceptional space for handling severe behaviors such as intentional homicide.

4. ACTIVE INTERVENTION AND SIDEWAYS RESPONSE: CRIMINAL LAW AMENDMENTS PRESERVE LIMITED GOVERNANCE PATTERNS

In the complex institutional environment of existing governance patterns, political systems, and legal frameworks, criminal law creatively adopts three strategies including decentralized response under the premise of active governance, introducing a discursive substitution to avoid the protection versus punishment debate, and lowering the age of criminal liability with multiple restrictions. These strategies aim to establish an organic communication and mutual adaptation between diverse public opinion demands and modern juvenile justice. Through the complex logic of active intervention and side response, legislators

27 See Wang Yong, 'No killing, No killing: A study on the Guidance of Public Opinion in the Judicial Control of Death Penalty' (2017) 3 *Journal of Law* 72.

hope that the diversified demands of public opinion and the modernization of juvenile justice could organically communicate and adapt to each other.

4.1 Decentralized Response under the Premise of Active Governance

Facing the public's huge expectations, criminal law not only bears the burden of governing juvenile delinquency, but also pays attention to social governance measures, in order to scatter people's attention and reduce criminal law's pressure from public opinion.

Driven by the strong demands of public opinion and other factors, it is imperative for the criminal law to carry the function of governing juvenile delinquency. Hence, lowering the age of criminal liability is not only a contemporary extension of positive criminal legislation but also a response to the implementation of policies centered around the people and their values.[28] However, facing the reality that the juvenile justice system is not complete and public opinion itself is mixed with different preferences, the expansion of the criminal law function will face structural governance risks. How to reasonably reduce the excessive expectation of public opinion on the function of criminal law has become the core concern of the Criminal Law Amendment Act XI.

If we slightly arrange the time axis in the process of Criminal Law Amendment Act XI, it will be obvious that many significant events relating to juvenile delinquency took place around the promulgation of Criminal Law Amendment Act XI. After the second draft of the Criminal Law Amendment Act XI on October 13, 2020, the Standing Committee of the National People's Congress amended and adopted 'Juvenile Protection Law' on October 17, 2020. Prior to the official adoption of Criminal Law Amendment Act XI on December 18, 2020, the National Bureau of Statistics released a data monitoring report about the 2019 Outline for the Development of Children in China (2011-2020) which shows an obvious decline in juvenile delinquency. In 2019, there were 43,000 juvenile offenders in China, a decrease of 25,000 compared to 2010, representing a 36.9% reduction. The number of juvenile crimes accounted for 2.59 percent of the crimes in the same period, showing a 4.19% decline compared with 2010.[29] On December 26, 2020, on the day of the adoption of the Criminal Law Amendment Act XI to the Criminal Law,

---

[28] See Hu Yunteng, Xu Wenwen, 'Explanation of Several Problems in the Amendment to Criminal Law (XI)' (2021) 2 *Research on Rule of* Law 5 9.

[29] See National Bureau of Statistics, 'Outline for the Development of Chinese Children (2011–2020)' <http://www.stats.gov.cn/tjsj/zxfb/202012/t20201218_1810128.html> accessed 27 March 2021.

the Standing Committee of the National People's Congress revised and passed 'Juvenile Delinquency Prevention Law'.

Such dense time nodes and diverse responses reflect a decentralized response strategy of criminal law to the sensitive topic of lowering the age of criminal liability. Under the situation that criminal law has to respond to the important social concerns and intervene in the governance of juvenile delinquency, a straightforward strategy of limiting the functions of criminal law could result in terrible risks of public disapproval. The unique institutional environment has shaped the relatively passive role arrangement for criminal law. Hence, legislators have to take the opportunity of the revision of 'Juvenile Protection Law' and 'Juvenile Delinquency Prevention Law' to embed the response of criminal law into the promulgation of non-criminal law positively, so public excessive attention and functional load towards criminal law were dispersed. To a certain extent, this decentralized response strategy achieves a repositioning of criminal law to moderately limit its functions and exercise cautious intervention.

4.2 The Replacement of the Discursive System between Can't 'Release Simply' and Can't 'Punish Simply'

Faced with the rejection of the protection by public opinion, criminal law uses the response discourse that you can't 'release simply' and 'punish simply', avoids the sensitive topic of how to choose between protection and punishment with the help of a smooth movement of different words in the same topic, showing legislators hope to find the idea sharing and value consensus between public opinion and the response of criminal law.[30]

The response discourse that you can't 'release simply' requires that the criminal law in the face of a small number of very serious crimes committed by minors, to avoid the emergence of obvious regulatory loopholes. Following the murder case of the 13-year-old boy in Dalian, the Supreme People's Procuratorate stated on December 21, 2019 that minors who are suspected of committing a crime but have not reached the age for criminal liability should be punished and corrected in accordance with the law instead of being 'released simply'.[31] In the process of deliberating the Criminal Law Amendment Act XI, legislators followed this system of discourse, pointing out that 'the consensus

[30] See Yang Xuedong, Ji Zhixuan, 'Term-sharing vs. Concept-sharing in Political Discourse Construction: Taking Zhili as a Case' (2021) 1 *Journal of Nanjing University (Philosophy, Humanities and Social Sciences)* 74.

[31] See Xinhua net 'The Supreme People's Procuratorate's Response to Young Minors' Violations and Crimes: Can't Just Let It Go' <http://www.X1nhuanet.com/legal/2019-12/21/c_1125371547.htm> accessed 28 March 2021.

is that it should be regulated, not only to correct crimes but also to protect the interests of victims'.[32] Obviously, criminal law is indirectly aligning itself with the value of punishment through the discourse system of you can't 'release simply', and there is a new distribution of value balancing between the interests of offenders and the victims. However, criminal law simply emphasizes the position of punishment without any range, especially the Criminal Law Amendment Act XI raises the age of sexual consent and further strengthens the punishment of the crime of sexually assaulting minors,[33] therefore the criminal law needs to establish a new discourse system in order to connect with the response discourse that you can't 'punish simply', and to maintain the uniformity of the position between criminal law and criminal policy.[34]

Therefore, the criminal law emphasizes 'can't punish simply' at the same time. The emphasis of the response of 'can't punish simply' lies in that the imposition of punishment should be restrained and conform to the objective law of governing juvenile delinquency, and in line with 'education first, punishment as a supplement' and the policy of education, persuasion and redemption. Similar to the discursive function, the discursive use of 'can't punish simply' aims to prevent excessive use of force of criminal law, but it does not delimit the specific range of punishment. In short, the replacement of the discourse system between 'release simply' and 'punishment simply' has the same advantages: although the criminal law partially recognizes the severe demands of public opinion, it does not slide to the extreme of the harsh law; without touching the sensitive nerve of public opinion, the concept of punishment control is also retained.

4.3 Lowering the Age with Multiple Restrictions

On the level of concrete norm setting, criminal law neither adopts the principle of maliciously supplementing the age of criminal liability nor lowers the age of criminal liability in an all-round way. Instead, criminal law creatively adopts an individual adjustment mode of 'lowering the age with multiple

---

32 See Standing Committee of the National People's Congress, 'Amendment (XI) to the Criminal Law (Draft) (Second Draft for Review) Provisions on Crimes Involving Minors' <http://www.npc.gov.cn/npc/c30834/202010/933421416c12433a8bdc24e61fc2825a.shtml> accessed 28 March 2021.

33 See Zhao Junfu, 'Judicial Regulation of Sexual Offenses against a Child in the Context of Amendment to Criminal Law: Idea, Techniques and Institutional Application' (2021) 6 *Political Science and Law* 26–38.

34 See Sun Wanhuai, 'The Moral Resort of the Criminal Law Amendment' (2021) 1 *Oriental Law* 112.

restrictions'.[35] This particular adjustment termed 'extremely prudent' officially has a dual meaning. According to the changes in the social situation and the deliberation of multiple opinions,[36] criminal law in a timely manner reduces the age of criminal liability and effectively connects with the Civil Code,[37] to protect the overall interests of minors.[38] In addition, the range of criminal law intervention should be reduced as far as possible through multiple restrictions to prevent the governance of minors from falling into the dilemma of excessive criminalization.[39]

Paragraph 3 of Article 17 of the Revised Criminal Law stipulates, 'If a person who has reached the age of 12 but not the age of 14 commits intentional homicide or intentional injury, thus causing death to another person, or causes serious injury or severe disability to another person by especially cruel means, with serious circumstances, shall bear criminal liability by the examination of the Supreme People's Procuratorate for prosecution.' The revision first significantly lowers the age of criminal liability to the age of 12. It can be seen that in the face of public criticism regarding the excessive rigidity of the age, criminal law acknowledges the social reality of the earlier physical and mental development of minors after careful consideration,[40] and accepts the public demand for lowering the age of criminal liability to punish juvenile offenders.

While the age of criminal liability has been greatly lowered, the criminal law has very carefully stipulated the restrictions of specific situations and special procedures. The specific situations include three restrictions of acts, consequences, and circumstances: First is limited to acts of intentional homicide or intentional injury committed by minors; second is limited to death or serious injury or serious disability caused by particularly cruel means, and the

---

[35] See Li Chuan, 'The Basis and Application of the Revision of Age of Criminal Responsibility from the Perspective of the Theory of Penalty Responsibility' (2021) 4 *Global Law Review* 100.

[36] See Wenhua Peng, Liangfu, 'Discussion on Minimum Age of Criminal Responsibility for the 11th Amendment to Criminal Law' (2021) 1 *Issues on Juvenile Crimes and Delinquency* 29–30.

[37] See Guo Hua, 'On the Connection between the Adjustment of the Age of Criminal Responsibility of Minors in the Criminal Law Amendment Act XI and Other Laws' (2021) 4 *Juvenile Delinquency Prevention Research* 29–30.

[38] Wang Denghui, 'On the Basic Problems of Reducing the Age of Criminal Responsibility of Minors' (2020) 4 *Journal of Southwest University of Political Science and Law* 86–88.

[39] See Wang *Aili, 'Explanation of the Articles, Legislative Grounds and the Relevant Provisions of the Criminal Law of the People's Republic of* China' (Peking University Press 2021) 36–38.

[40] See Feng Fei, 'Timely Contingency of the Age of Criminal *Responsibility' Social Sciences Weekly* (October 29, 2020).

term 'particularly cruel means' is generally limited to acts that cause extreme suffering to the victim and greatly exceed morality and ethics; third is required to reach a bad extent including deep subjective malignancy and extremely bad social influence. Procedural restrictions refer to the approval of the Supreme People's Procuratorate. This unique setting is to reserve flexible judgment space of the following three restrictions of behavior, consequences, and circumstances to the Supreme People's Procuratorate.[41] This litigation institution should judge whether a minor needs to bear criminal liability substantially.[42] In the context of institutional function transformation, the Supreme People's Procuratorate needs to bear the function of 'lubricant' between public opinion and criminal law response, so as to avoid the irreconcilable conflict again.

5. MIXED PROSPECTS FOR RESPONSES: INTERACTION BIAS BETWEEN STRUCTURAL APPEALS AND PARTIAL RESPONSES

According to the emotional changes of public opinion towards lowering the age of criminal liability (see Table 6.3), the proportion of negative emotion decreased by 16.38% after amending the law, while the proportion of positive emotion increased to 25.7%. Although the topic attributes of 'Dalian 13-year-old Boy Murder Case' and 'Lowering the Age of Criminal Liability' are not the same, it is still commendable that there is a positive emotional change. Anyway, the individual lowering of the age satisfies some expectations of public opinion, partially alleviating the long-term high-pressure situation for criminal law, and the social emotion begins to connect with criminal law by the individual lowering of the age of criminal liability.

However, according to the data in Table 6.5, it seems that we should not be overly optimistic about the effect of lowering the age of criminal liability. First of all, the high-frequency positive affective words are mostly words with strong emotional tendency, such as 'support', 'finally', 'concern' and 'cheer'. These words affirm the event of lowering the age of criminal liability itself rather than provide substantial evaluations of the strategies used by criminal law's response. The increase of positive affective words doesn't represent the effectiveness of criminal law's response. Neutral emotional high-frequency words such as 'past', 'education', and 'parents' involve the retroactivity of

---

41 Jiang Min, 'The Justifiable Foundation and Judicial Application of the Newly Added Clause of Minimum Age of Criminal Responsibility in the Amendment (XI) to the Criminal Law' (2021) 3 *Criminal Science* 30.

42 Liu Xian-quan, Lu Yimin, 'Interpretation and Reflection on the Eleventh Amendment of Criminal Law' (2021) 1 *Journal of Soochow University (Philosophy & Social Science Edition)* 33.

norms, educational correction, and family education, but the absolute quantity of these words is low and may not be representative enough. What is concerning is that among the high-frequency words associated with negative emotions such as '12', 'death penalty', '10', and 'criminal law'. In the analysis of 'how to respond', negative high-frequency words will continue to serve as a theoretical prism to reflect the misunderstanding and deviation between structural public appeals and partial criminal law responses.

5.1 The Function Expectation of Criminal Law Does Not Decrease but Increase under the Decentralized Response Strategy

The new high-frequency words such as 'criminal law', '12', and '10' embody the public opinion's preference for the punishment function of criminal law. First of all, the high-frequency term 'criminal law' reflects the hope that strengthening the guardian's responsibility through punishment has not dispersed, a typical commentary text such as 'It is the fault of the father and the mother if a child is not taught. I hope criminal law can also impose responsibility on guardians' (comment text No. 9628). Secondly, the two high-frequency words '12' and '10' clearly express that the public opinion on Sina Weibo is not satisfied with the lowering of the age of criminal liability, but instead harbors fantasies of expanding the function of criminal law. In the eyes of public opinion, since the criminal law has been involved in the governance of juvenile delinquency, then it should fully unleash its harsh punitive aspect. Typical comment are texts such as 'Ten is fine, 12 is too easy!' and 'It should be ten, boys nowadays understand everything in the fifth or sixth grade' etc. (comment text No. 10352 and No. 10216).

The expectation of the function of criminal law is rising, which reflects the deviation between the functional demand of public opinion and the decentralized response of criminal law; this tendency may induce a series of negative chain reactions. From the perspective of the demand side, public opinion will entrust the function of social defense and the obligation of the guardian to the criminal law. On the supply side, facing the huge structural functional expectation, criminal law formulates a dispersive response strategy, hoping to disperse the focus of public opinion and loosen the load of its own function by the amendment of 'Juvenile Protection Law' and 'Juvenile Delinquency Prevention Law', as well as disclosing juvenile crime data. However, this strategy does not systematically answer the core question of the function and role of criminal law in the governance of juvenile delinquency, but may induce the public to have functional expectations of criminal law intervention.[43] On the contrary, under the reality of the deviation between supply and demand, excessive functional expectation is likely to put more pressure on criminal law, force criminal law to make concessions, and cause the consequences of emotional legislation and populism judicature.[44] Especially in the circumstance that 'Juvenile Protection Law' and 'Juvenile Delinquency Prevention Law' have made significant progress in juvenile delinquency, strengthening the connection between public opinion and criminal law's response may improperly hinder the systematic and comprehensive governance of juvenile offenders.

5.2 Circuitous Discourse Can't Reverse the Imbalance of Acceptance between Protection and Punishment

The number of high-frequency words such as 'hope' and 'protection' remains high after revision, and the emergence of new high-frequency words like 'death penalty' indicates a strengthening hostility towards the idea of protection. Words such as 'hope' and 'protect' show a strong rejection of protection among public opinion on Sina Weibo. Comments such as 'hope that the law protects the victims, not the offenders' reappear after the amendment (comment text No. 9788). With the involvement of criminal law, the term 'death penalty' has taken on a subtle populist bent, reflecting the increasing hostility of social opinion on Sina Weibo to the idea of protection. Typical comment text such as 'Age is not a reason to exonerate! Those who commit intentional homicide should be sentenced to death penalty!' and 'I hope, for cases with serious circumstances, the trial should be based on motive; the death penalty should be considered', etc. (comment text, No. 10283, No. 11052). It can be seen that the application of the discourse system, which cannot be 'released simply' or 'punished simply', has not substantially improved the emotional inclination of social public opinion towards the rejection of protection and the reverence for punishment.

The reason why the imbalance of recognition between protection and punishment can't be reversed is that criminal law replaces the structural system appeal with fuzzy words, which can't really narrow the inherent cognitive bias between protection and punishment. Can't 'release simply' or 'punish simply' avoid the positive conflict with public opinion, but it only outlines the non-conniving and non-strict intervention framework, and does not really answer the question of how to balance the interests of the victim and the offender. On

43 Wang Qiangjun, 'Rational Reflection on the Early Intervention of Criminal Law' (2021) 3 *China Legal Science* 236.

44 Liu Jiong, 'Protect the Weak through Criminal Law: Observation and Rethinking Based on the Theory of Menschenbild' (2017) 2 *Science of Law* 36–7.

the premise that the vague response cannot match structured demands, it is reasonable that public opinion has continuous hostility to protection and excessive praise towards punishment.

5.3 The Alienation Risk of Restrictive Norms under the Lack of Consensus

As for the specific amendment of the age of criminal liability, the public opinion on Sina Weibo is almost 'one-sided' in doubt. First of all, two new high-frequency words '12' and '10' not only reflect the excessive expectation of the function for criminal law, but also express reasonable questions about the lowering range of age. The word 'age' ranks first in the negative emotional high-frequency words and even expresses the call to remove the age limit thoroughly. Typical comments such as 'The age limit should be lifted for cases of intentional homicide, intentional injury which have severe social impact' and 'No age limit, murder is compensation for life', etc. (comment text, No. 11254 and No. 10651). Secondly, the emergence of high-frequency words such as 'criminal law' and 'murder' also implies that public opinion on Sina Weibo questions the legitimacy of the restrictive provisions. 'All murderers should be sentenced to death penalty' and 'Murder, rape, wounding, criminal law should be followed without exception' (comment text, No. 10685, No. 10723) shows that in the cognitive intuition of public opinion, there is a direct connection between homicide and criminal liability. Whether it constitutes 'bad circumstances' in the sense of criminal law and whether to accept the important procedural restriction of 'prosecution approved by the Supreme People's Procuratorate' can't shake the simple ethical principle of 'killing for life'.

The regulation of the age of criminal liability is questioned due to the lack of necessary consensus between public opinion and professional rules. It is undeniable that criminal legislation has its unique formulation technology and operation logic, but focusing on the perspective of professional knowledge and making many restrictions is inevitable to bear the possible misunderstanding and suspicion from public opinion. It is foreseeable that when the judicial organs explain 'using special cruel means' and 'bad circumstances', the interpretation space will be relatively limited, and the difficulty of the interpretation will increase.[45] In the face of the potential pressure of penalty populism, the filtering and restriction mechanism of 'Supreme People's Procuratorate's approval of prosecution' may not be able to effectively assume the function of

---

45 See Wang Deng hui, 'Justification and Judicial Application of the Downward Adjustment of the Minimum age of Criminal Responsibility under the Amendment to the Criminal Law (XI)' (2021) 4 *Journal of Southwest University of Political Science & Law* 116–118.

balancing emotion and law, and even have the alienation risk of active prosecution or forced prosecution.

6. CONCLUSION: SEEKING THE 'CUCKOO–MANDARIN DUCK' MODEL OF PUBLIC OPINION APPEAL AND CRIMINAL LAW RESPONSE

In the digital age, the public opinion appeal of lowering the age of criminal liability has obvious structured characteristics; that is, the rational demands and irrational demands are deeply mixed and dependent on each other. Although some response strategies of criminal law can partially avoid confrontational conflicts with public opinion to a certain extent, this response process essentially follows the 'cuckoo model' where social public opinion takes the lead and the criminal law responds passively.[46] There are many deficiencies in these aspects such as response ability, response strategy and response content, which cannot systematically guide the structured public opinion, even abnormally interacting with the social public opinion in the track of deviation. In order to effectively respond to social public opinion in a systematic manner, it must go beyond the 'cuckoo model' in which social public opinion takes the lead and the criminal law responds passively, and explore the 'cuckoo–mandarin duck model' in which criminal law actively guides and public opinion actively interacts on the evolution logic of public opinion.[47]

---

[46] The cuckoo model here refers to a model in which the state and government respond to public opinion on important public governance issues, which is characterized by public opinion first, the state and government responding passively, and the substantive interaction between public opinion and the state and government not being high. Although this response model can temporarily calm the pressure of network public opinion, the network of public opinion in the institutional demand has not been a fundamental solution, like the cuckoo blood. See Weng Shihong, Ye Xiaoyun, 'An Analysis on the Government Response to Internet Political Participation for Decision-making: Taking Protest-Against PX in Ningbo as an Example' (2013) 4 *Journal of Public Management* 28.

[47] The 'mandarin duck model' is an ideal interactive model, characterized by a high degree of participation of public opinion and a high degree of response from the state and government. See Weng Shihong, Gu Lime, 'The Response Modes of Government Decision-making to Internet Political Participation' (2012) 8 *Chinese Public* Administration 40. More specifically, 'Cuckoo–Mandarin Duck Model' refers to the optimization process of public governance from 'public opinion first, state or government passive response' to 'state, government and public opinion highly interactive'. See Zheng Shiming, Lan Yu Xiao, Li Feng 'The Interactive Logic of Online Public Opinion and Government Response – Based on the Data Analysis of the "Leadership Message Board" during the COVID-19 Pandemic'

First, from the perspective of function, public opinion demand and criminal law response for reducing the age of criminal liability is an issue of bridging the gap between supply and demand; criminal law must lower the excessive expectations of public opinion in a reasonable manner while providing governance products to strengthen crime prevention and social justice. On the demand side, criminal law urgently needs to rely on the systematic juvenile delinquency data to guide the public to develop a rational cognition of criminal law's function. In the period of social transformation, the core factor of juvenile crime in China is the lack of social support affected by population mobility, mainly manifested as seeking financial crimes, becoming criminal tools, forming gang crimes, and being victims due to being left-behind, etc.[48] Hence, with the improvement of the economic development level and of the social trust mechanism,[49] the juvenile crime is also expected to be effectively suppressed.[50] These views are almost recognized by the practical and theoretical circles. On this basis, the disclosure of juvenile crime data can start from the influencing factors and explain the actual role of non-penalty factors such as population flow and social support in the occurrence of crimes, describing delinquent minors as both disrupters of social order and victims of insufficient social support. If the effectiveness of comprehensive governance measures such as social construction, economic development, and family intervention can be strongly supported by crime governance data, the relative limitations of criminal law's functions can be reasonably highlighted. Protecting citizens' right to know, to participate, to express, and to supervise through solid criminal data disclosure,[51] leading the public to have a rational cognition of criminal law's function is feasible at the methodological level. On the supply side, it is opportune to improve the actual effect of special correction measures from the perspective of punishment substitution measures by the revision of'Juvenile

(2021) 3 *Journal of Public Management* 35. It is urgent for the criminal law to change its relatively passive status and improve the quality of interaction with public opinion. Therefore, the 'cuckoo–mandarin duck model' is an excellent model reference.

48 See Wang Guangcong, 'On the Rationality of Juvenile Criminal Justice from the Perspective of Criminology' (2020) 4 *Journal of Chinese Youth Social Science* 136.

49 See Jin Jiang, Shi Yangjing, Zhu Libo, 'The Barriers of Identity: Population Diversity, Social Trust and Crime' (2020) 4 *Chinese Journal of Sociology* 210–213.

50 See Liu Cheng, 'The School Bullying Behaviors in Primary and Middle Schools and Their Influencing Factors' (2020) 6 *Youth Studies* 33.

51 See Shan Yong, Ruan Chongjun, 'The Role of Social Governance Map to the Three Type Development of Overall Governance System – Taking Urban Brain for Example' (2021) 1 *Studies on Socialism with Chinese Characteristics* 69.

Protection Law' and 'Juvenile Delinquency Prevention Law'. Empirical studies have shown that if the state scientifically and reasonably designs alternative measures with effective governance function, then the vast majority of the public will no longer absolutely support and be infatuated with punishment.[52] Based on the consideration of loosening criminal law's function, it is urgently necessary to support the correction education measures to strengthen their function of social justice and crime prevention.[53]

Secondly, emphasizing the concept of punishment cultivates the idea of protection. The reason why public opinion is extremely hostile to the concept of protection is that past practices in juvenile delinquency excessively emphasized protection and neglected punishment, thus stimulating confrontational thinking in public opinion due to the deviation in concepts. Therefore, the criminal law should neither excessively emphasize protection nor adopt a displacement strategy to shift the topic. Instead, criminal law should start from the concept of punishment, continuously show the tendency of not condoning extremely serious delinquent acts committed by minors, and provide society with a sense of security and trust, creating the possibility for deep communication between criminal law and public opinion. After social public opinion gradually becomes more accommodating, the public opinion is guided to accept the protection concept corresponding to the concept of punishment. And criminal law can form the governance concept of minor crime and wrong behavior which is the heavy and the light.[54] In fact, only by deeply understanding the structural demands of public opinion can criminal law provide an appropriate discourse system and institutional resources to lay a necessary social psychological foundation for the modernization of juvenile delinquency.

Third, make full use of the open structure of legal resources and non-legal resources in the social consensus[55] to support the existing criminal law norms. Based on the legislative purpose of the age of criminal liability, criminal law should find a scientific and reasonable legitimate basis for the minimum age line to prove that the existing age of criminal liability system can accommodate the

---

52 See Liang Genlin, Chen Eryan 'Public Opinions on Death Penalty in China: Measurement, Interpretation and Communication' (2020) 5 *Peking University Law Journal* 1263–1264.

53 See Wang Zhenhui, Lin Miao, 'Campus Bullying Phenomenon Observation and Governance Path Remodeling' (2021) 3 *China Youth Study* 103–109.

54 See Wang Yong, 'On the Idea of "Graded Administration" for Controlling Juvenile Delinquency' (2020) 3 *Jilin University Journal Social Sciences Edition* 142.

55 See Hou Mingming, 'The Risks and Solutions from the Ways and Strategies of China's Judicial Response to Society' (2020) 1 *Studies in Law and Business* 128.

continuous development of minors.[56] Many empirical studies show that minors have a high judgment ability in understanding the wrongfulness of criminal behavior and distinguishing between criminal behavior and mischievous behavior.[57] However, the judgment ability of minors is easily damaged by family, school, and other factors; as a result, their psychological and physiological development level lags behind the degree of development needed to make mature decisions.[58] Juvenile delinquency can certainly draw on the reasonable components of these studies. It can conduct regional or even nationwide public announcements to clarify the uniqueness of the physical and mental development process of juveniles to public opinion. This will build a bridge of communication and understanding between the specialized provisions of criminal law and the public's understanding, allowing for a legitimate recognition of individual lowering of the age of criminal liability. Furthermore, according to the objective law of juvenile criminal justice, combined with the general standards of theoretical and practical circles of 'extremely cruel means' and 'bad circumstances' in other provisions of criminal law, the basis for judging 'extremely cruel means' and 'egregious circumstances' in Article 17 of the Criminal Law will be gradually refined. Drawing on the meaning of other provisions of the Criminal Law will not only keep the criminal law's internal system coherent, but also will strengthen the age of criminal liability's legitimacy and rationality with the aid of the existing legal authority. This will proactively address potential normative blind spots that may generate public opinion risks, eliminate potential obstacles for the Supreme People's Procuratorate, and ultimately maximize the compatibility with the principles of juvenile justice and the best interests of the children.

Through the biased interaction between public opinion and the criminal law response, the issue of lowering the age of criminal liability goes beyond the traditional debate of whether criminal law should intervene and closely aligns with the concept of 'rule of law as a way of life'. 'For the country, observing the customs and understanding the fundamentals of the country are necessary for law. Do not observe the customs, do not observe the country, then

---

[56] See Gao Yanan, 'The Minimum Age of Criminal Responsibility in the Theory of Capacity Development of Minors' (2020) 9 *China Youth Study* 39–45.

[57] See Wagland Paul, Bussey Kay, 'Appreciating the Wrongfulness of Criminal Conduct: Implications for the Age of Criminal Responsibility' Vol. 12 (2017) 1 *Legal and Criminology Psychology* 130–149.

[58] See Carrie S. Fried, N. Dickon Reppucci, 'Special Issues on Children, Families, and the Law Criminal Decision Making: The Development of Adolescent Judgment, Criminal Responsibility, and Culpability' Vol. 15 (2001) 1 *Law and Human Behavior* 45–61.

its legislation and civil disorder will be destroyed.'[59] If criminal law wants to effectively intervene in the modern governance of juvenile delinquency, it must deeply embed itself in the local context of reducing the age of criminal liability and proceed steadily on the premise of fully understanding public opinion. Based on such a narrative structure and interactive logic, this chapter introduces LSTM to complete the in-depth dialogue between criminal law and social science from the perspective of superposition of natural science and social science. It must be acknowledged that this intelligent recurrent neural network structure may have certain objective errors in analyzing emotional tendencies. The researchers also have subjective preferences in selecting hot search samples and setting emotional tendency thresholds. These limitations determine that the empirical research process and results of this chapter are still subjective. Indeed, digital society has significantly reshaped the public's participation in public governance issues. Combined with the unique attention-grabbing effect of criminal cases, how criminal law responds to public opinion remains an important theoretical topic for modernization governance. For the legal empirical research method, this issue also provides a new opportunity for social science to reasonably absorb and apply natural science under the background of 'new liberal arts'.

59 Shang Yang, *Book of Lord Shang* (written in Warring States Period, Translation and annotation by Shi Lei, (Zhonghua Book Company 2016) 75.

7. The penalty of administrative joint violation under the principle of culpability

Zhang Xuefu

1. INTRODUCTION

Dealing with cases of plural actors jointly committing unlawful acts has always been a challenge in the field of administrative penalties in China. The 2021 revised Law of the PRC on Administrative Penalty (hereinafter referred to as the Administrative Penalty Law) does not overtly address this issue, and related theoretical research is insufficient. Among a rising number of cases involving joint illegal actions, especially in the fields of health, anti-monopoly, finance and securities, and public security management, two main issues emerged in the handling of such cases: first, how to identify a joint violation, and second, how to issue penalties to the actors involved in the joint violation.[1] These two issues correspond to two parts of the theory of administrative joint violations: the criteria for identification of joint violations and rules of penalty decisions. The former aims to determine whether the actors should be held liable for illegal actions, while the latter focuses on deciding the specific type of legal responsibilities that the actors should bear.

Regarding the criteria for determining joint violations, the controversy lies in whether it is necessary for the actors to bear joint subjective faults, resulting in three different viewpoints. The first viewpoint draws on the theory of the 'four elements framework' of criminal liability in China's Criminal Law and states that the establishment of joint violations requires multiple actors (subject) to commit illegal acts jointly (mens rea) based on joint intent (actus

[1] See Shi Nan, 'Analysis on Administrative Penalty on Joint Illegal Act by AML Enforcement Agencies-Focusing on Legal Remedy of Two Cases' (2018) 1 *Competition Policy Research* 39–48; Yao Yu, 'Analyzing Administrative Penalties for Joint Violations of Health and Family Planning Laws' (2017) 4 *Chinese Journal of Health Inspection* 391–394.

reus), thereby infringing upon the administrative order (object).[2] According to this viewpoint, joint intent is required for the construction of joint violations. The second viewpoint denies the position of subjective fault as a constitutive element of administrative violations, which in turn denies the view that the establishment of joint violation shall be predicated on joint subjective fault.[3] The third viewpoint essentially differs from the previous two by drawing on the three-tiered structure of criminal liability and points out that 'for the identification of joint violations, it is only necessary to judge whether the unlawful acts by the actors bear relevance or connection ... without considering whether there is joint intent as the mens rea.'[4] This viewpoint does not invalidate the principle of culpability but examines joint violations in terms of elements of violations and unlawfulness, leaving the examination of subjective fault (mens rea) in the discussion of culpability,[5] which, in fact, weakens the role of subjective factors in determining joint violations.

Despite the difference in formulations, there are essentially two main positions regarding the rules for examining joint violations: one is 'joint liability for joint conduct,' which holds that the actors should bear joint liability as a whole for administrative penalties. For the rationales for taking this position, in addition to the convenience of execution of administrative penalties and the inspiration from civil law,[6] some scholars have also pointed out that this is the inevitable result of applying the aforementioned first criterion for identifying joint violations, that is, once joint violations are established, joint liability naturally follows due to the same cause of culpability, and therefore can only be punished as a collective act.[7] The other position is 'separate liability for joint conduct,' which holds that the actors should bear respective responsibilities with administrative authority, imposing separate penalties on each actor within the scope of administrative punishment.[8]

---

2 See Yang Jiejun, *Order, Power, and Legal Control: A Study of Administrative Penalty Law* (Sichuan University Press, 1999) 228–229.

3 See Wang Yongqing, 'On the Rules for Administrative Penalty' (1993) 4 *Chinese Journal of Law* 42.

4 Xiong Zhanglin, 'On the Basic Stand of Amending Administrative Punishment Law' (2019) 1 *Contemporary Law Review* 108.

5 See Xiong Zhanglin, 'Yardstick and Judgement Rules of Joint Illegal Activities' (2015) 3 *Legal Science* 155.

6 See Yu Hongyuan, 'What Constitutes Joint Violations in Administrative Penalties for Inspection and Quarantine' (2014) 1 *China Port Science and Technology* 42.

7 See Xiong Zhanglin, *supra* note 5, 155.

8 See Gao Lijun, 'Administrative Penalty of Joint Illegal Activities' (2011) 8 *Fujian Quality & Technology Supervision* 36–37.

The above controversies have undercut the consistency of administrative penalties issuance in practice, resulting in 'different penalties for the same case.' In this regard, this chapter intends to apply the 'principle of culpability' to construct a theory of joint violations and clarify existing viewpoints. The principle of culpability states that only when the actors have the capacity and conditions of responsibility when committing acts that violate administrative order, can administrative authorities impose punishment.[9] Although Article 33, Paragraph 2 of the 2021 Administrative Penalty Law touches upon this principle, the following text shall explain in detail the reason why the above-mentioned article proves difficult to serve as a legislative basis for the principle of culpability.

Existing theories still need to be improved when examined from the perspective of the principle of individual responsibility. Firstly, regarding the criteria for joint violation determination, the aforementioned second viewpoint fundamentally excludes the application of individual responsibility in deciding administrative penalties, which leads to logical obstacles when identifying joint violations. Whereas the first viewpoint takes joint intent as a constituent element of joint violations, it constructs such criteria based on the 'four elements of crime framework' for criminal liability determination, which, in doing so, cannot guarantee consistent application of the principle of individual responsibility and leads to contradictions between criteria of violation identification and rules of penalty decisions. The third viewpoint only considers the subjective fault of the actors in determining culpability, completely excluding subjective factors in the identification of joint violations, which can result in false conclusions in judging cases involving simultaneous offenses and conspiracy to commit illegal acts, and so on. Secondly, regarding the rules for determination, the application of the principle of culpability can explain the rationale for applying separate penalties and account for special occasions in applying penalty rules for joint violations. Therefore, this chaper aims to construct a theory of joint violations based on the principle of culpability.

2. CONTROVERSIES OVER THE THEORY OF JOINT ADMINISTRATIVE VIOLATIONS IN PRACTICE

The theory of joint administrative violations can be divided into two parts: the 'criteria of identification' and the 'rules of penalty decisions,' which can be construed in the same way as the distinction between the theory of criminal offenses and the theory of penalties in criminal law. When approaching an

[9] See Wang Guisong, 'On the Culpability Principle of Administrative Penalty' (2020) 6 *Political Science and Law* 2.

illegal act, the 'criteria of identification' are first applied to determine whether the parties involved have violated the law and which specific acts of violation have been carried out. The 'rules for penalty decisions' are applied then to determine what kind of administrative liability the parties involved should bear. This is a necessary thinking process for administrative authorities in making judgments. In practice, there are controversies around the criteria for identifying joint administrative violations and the rules for penalty decisions. Most of the current research on the subject has provided explanations from the perspective of administrative law enforcement practice. Building on previous works, this chapter attempts to illustrate further the controversy regarding the criteria for identifying joint violations and the rules for penalty decision-making and how they have led to inconsistencies in administrative law enforcement and judicial judgments from a new perspective — 'contradictory judicial judgments.'[10] For this purpose, this chapter analyzes 156 judicial opinions collected from the 'PKULaw' database.

2.1 Controversies over the Criteria for Determining Joint Violations

As mentioned above, the controversy regarding the criteria for determining joint violations lies in whether it is necessary for the actors to have 'joint intent.' This affects the conclusion on whether the actors have participated in the joint illegal activity. Among the 156 judicial opinions, 42 explicitly confirm that joint violations require joint intent as a prerequisite, two explicitly deny the need to consider subjective intent when determining joint violations, while 112 judicial opinions do not mention subjective intent when analyzing the legality of administrative penalties. It is not clear whether those judicial opinions with no express stance on subjective intent hold that the construction of joint violations does not require joint intent and therefore an analysis isn't necessary, or because they recognize the administrative authorities' determination of joint intent in these cases and therefore didn't present an analysis.

---

[10] The specific retrieval method is as follows: Set 'administrative penalty' as the cause of action, with 'joint violations' as the keyword, retrieve cases concluded from January 1, 2018, to June 30, 2021. A total of 177 adjudicative documents were obtained. After a case-by-case reading and eliminating irrelevant cases, a total of 156 valid judicial opinions were accessed. The term 'irrelevant cases' refers to judicial opinions where the phrase 'joint violations' appears, but the case facts are unrelated to joint violations. Such opinions mainly fall into two categories: first, when the court cites legal provisions for other purposes and the provisions coincidentally include the phrase 'joint violations'; second, when the administrative counterpart asserts that the administrative organs jointly undertaking administrative actions constitute 'joint violations.'

Even so, based solely on the data, there is inconsistency in judicial opinions on whether joint intent is required in determining joint violations, or at least, the determination of the existence of joint intent is an unnecessary step in making judicial decisions.

A more thorough case study with an expanded scope of research shall give a prominent picture of the inconsistency in judicial decisions, as observed in the following two types of cases:

The first type involves cases with joint actions but without joint intent. The differences in judicial judgments lie in whether joint violations can be established based solely on the joint actions by the actors. In *Wang Guangxia v. Public Security Bureau of Wuwei County* (case for appeal of administration management of public security), the appellate court determined that although the two actors had jointly assaulted the victim, there was no evidence proving that they had the intention of liaison, so their actions constituted no joint offense.[11] This indicates that the court considers joint intent to be a necessary element for establishing joint violations. In contrast, in the earlier case of *Zhang Xudong v. Public Security Bureau of Jiashan County* (case on the dispute over an administrative penalty of public security), the court recognized that both the plaintiff and the third party had obstructed the police in the performance of their duties. The trial court ruled that although there was no evidence to prove that the two individuals had collusion, 'since both individuals appeared at the scene of the incident for the same reason and separately committed acts that hindered the police in the performance of their duties, it should be deemed as a joint violation.' The appellate court also supported this decision.[12] It can be drawn from this case that the courts concerned held that joint violations can be established based solely on joint actions.

The second type involves cases with only joint intent but no joint actions. The differences in judicial decisions lie in whether individuals who have joint intent but do not participate in joint actions should be considered as one party of joint violation. In the *Xue Wencong et al. v. China Securities Regulatory Commission* (case for appeal), Xue Wencong and others were punished by administrative authorities for market manipulation. Xue Wencong argued that he did not engage in manipulative activities regarding the target stock, thus

---

11 See Wang Guangxia *v.* Public Security Bureau of Wuwei County for appeal of administration management of public security, No. 146 Final Administrative Judgment of Intermediate People's Court of Wuhu City of Anhui Province (皖02行终146号), (2018).

12 See Zhang Xudong *v.* Public Security Bureau of Jiashan County for dispute over an administrative penalty of public security, No. 13 Final Administrative Judgment of Intermediate People's Court of Jiaxing City of Zhejiang Province (浙嘉行终13号), (2013).

did not commit an administrative violation. However, the court considered that he participated in discussions of illegal trading strategies with the other violators, which contributed to joint intent, making him a participant in the joint violation.[13] On the other hand, in *Yang Sizi, Yang Muxiang et al. v. Wuhu Municipal People's Government* (case for appeal of administration management of public security), Yang Sizi and Yang Muxiang sued the administrative authorities because they did not penalize the third party involved in the joint assault against them. The court held that since the third party did not participate in the joint assault, they did not constitute joint violations with the other actors. In this decision, the court only considered the actions of the third party and did not take into account whether there was joint intent between the third party and the other violators.[14]

2.2 Controversies over the Rules for Penalty Decisions in Joint Violations

Regarding the rules for penalty decision-making in joint violations, the dispute lies in whether to apply the principle of 'joint liability for joint conduct' or 'separate liability for joint conduct.' As mentioned above, 'separate liability for joint conduct' means that each actor involved in the violation bears their responsibility respectively within the scope of punishment, while 'joint liability for joint conduct' requires the individuals to share joint responsibility within the scope of punishment. For example, if the legislation stipulates a fine of 500 to 1,000 yuan for a specific violation, when two people commit a joint violation, under the principle of 'separate liability for joint conduct' each person should bear a fine of 500 to 1,000 yuan, regardless of whether the total fine exceeds the upper limit of 1,000 yuan. Under the principle of 'separate liability for joint conduct', on the other hand, the two people would share the fine within the range of 500 to 1,000 yuan. It is evident that the differences in penalty decision rules directly affect the severity of the punishment imposed on the actors. In addition, under the guidance of the principle of 'separate liability for joint conduct', some administrative authorities list all the punishments for each actor involved in a single penalty decision document, forming a single penalty decision. However, other administrative authorities issue

13 See Xue Wencong et al. *v.* China Securities Regulatory Commission for appeal, No. 1928 Final Administrative Judgment of The High People's Court of Beijing Municipality (京行终1928号), (2019).

14 See Yang Sizi, Yang Muxiang et al. *v.* Wuhu Municipal People's Government for appeal of administration management of public security, No. 63 Final Administrative Judgment of Intermediate people's Court of Wuhu City of Anhui Province (皖02行终63号), (2020).

separate penalty decision documents with independent document numbers for each individual, resulting in multiple penalty decisions, which can affect the remedies available to the parties involved.

Disputes over the rules for penalty decision-making in joint violations are difficult to demonstrate through quantitative research on judicial documents because relative points are usually not explicitly stated in the documents. Therefore, we can only infer from the 'traces' in the wording of the documents, such as whether different document numbers for penalty decisions are mentioned or whether different punishments are imposed on the parties involved. By applying this method to analyze the 156 sampled judicial opinions, it is found that 87 opinions adopted the principle of 'separate liability for joint conduct,' 12 opinions adopted the view of 'joint liability for joint conduct,' and that 57 opinions could not be classified as either. Although this data can demonstrate the contradictions in court judgments, such conclusions are not precise enough. Therefore, this chapter uses individual case analysis instead to illustrate the inconsistencies in court judgments. Some courts follow the principle of 'separate liability for joint conduct.' For example, in the case of '*Administrative Adjudication regarding Application for Enforcement of a land penalty decision filed by the Land and Resources Bureau of Dali County*,' the court explicitly stated that for the joint violations committed by three individuals, the punishment should be decided separately based on the facts, circumstances, their part in the illegal activity, and the degree of social harm caused by their joint actions.[15] This ruling negates the practice of administrative authorities issuing joint penalties for joint offenses. However, there are also courts that explicitly advocate 'joint penalty for joint violation'. For instance, in '*Guangzhou Zengcheng Lvchuangbao Farm v. Forestry and Landscape Bureau of Zengcheng District, Guangzhou* (case for judgment of forestry administrative management),' the court considers that the penalty decision issued by the administrative authority requiring the parties involved to bear joint fines is legal and valid.[16]

---

[15] See application for enforcement of penalty decision of land filed by the Land and Resources Bureau of Dali County, No. 22 First Instance Administrative Judgment of People's Primary Court of Dali County of Shaanxi Province (陕0523行初 22号), (2018).

[16] See Guangzhou Zengcheng Lvchuangbao Farm *v.* Forestry and Landscape Bureau of Zengcheng District, Guangzhou for judgment of forestry administrative management, No. 2357 First Instance Administrative Judgment of The First Railway Transportation Primary Court of Guangzhou City of Guangdong Province (粤7101行初2357号), (2017).

2.3 Root of the Controversy: Ambiguity in the Theory of Joint Administrative Violations

The reason for the aforementioned disputes is that there are controversies surrounding the theory of joint administrative violations in China, and there is no uniform standard in regulations applicable to administrative authorities when handling joint administrative violation cases. Such insufficiency of the theory of joint administrative violations can be traced back to the fact that administrative penalties in China have not fully embraced the principle of culpability.

The principle of culpability requires that individuals have the capacity and conditions for responsibility when committing illegal acts for administrative authorities to impose penalties.[17] Capacity for responsibility refers to the ability of individuals to discern and control their own actions, which has been explicitly recognized in the Administrative Penalty Law. However, there is still divergence regarding the conditions for responsibility, that is, the individual's subjective fault as the prerequisite for imposing an administrative penalty. Although Paragraph 2, Article 33 of the 2021 revised Administrative Penalty Law stipulates, 'No administrative penalty shall be imposed on a party who has sufficient evidence to prove that he has no subjective fault,' this provision still proves difficult to serve as the legislative basis for the principle of culpability for two reasons. Firstly, examined from the perspective of systemic interpretation, this provision is under the part that regulates rules on issuing a lighter penalty, mitigating or exempting penalties, so it is not clear whether the presence of subjective fault is a constitutive element of the administrative penalty or a condition for exempting penalties. Secondly, Paragraph 3 of Article 33 of the same provision also states that administrative organs shall educate parties who commit violations of law but are exempted from administrative penalties according to the law. Education means making individuals recognize their misconduct and correct it. If there is no subjective fault in wrongdoing by the administrative counterpart, then why is such education necessary? These contradictions show that the newly revised Administrative Penalty Law has not fully embraced the principle of culpability. As a result, the debate over whether administrative penalties shall be based on the principle of culpability continues in academic discussions.[18]

However, the ongoing academic discussion on culpability often falls into a misconception: the current arguments mainly focus on the level of values when discussing culpability, some arguing for the principle of culpability in

---

17 See *supra* note 9, 2.

18 See Cheng Xiezhong, 'Clarify the Attribution Principle of Subjective Fault, Enhance Rule of Law in Administrative Penalty' (2021) 4 *Chinese Rule of Law 85–87.*

consideration of the protection of citizens' rights and dignity,[19] others arguing against it for the reason of administrative inefficiency.[20] These arguments overlook the role of culpability in constructing a systemic theory and law enforcement practice. Whether administrative penalties should embrace the principle of culpability is not only a matter of value choice but also is related to the integrity and logical consistency of the theoretical system on administrative penalties, and more importantly, whether many basic regulations on administrative penalties can be effectively implemented in individual cases, thus directly affecting the ability of administrative authorities to enforce the law lawfully and effectively. For example, some scholars have pointed out that the theoretical construction and practical application of the rules on exemption for administrative liability should be based on the principle of culpability.[21] The core argument of this chapter is that the construction of the theory of joint administrative violations should be based on the principle of culpability, and that administrative authorities can only handle joint violation cases legally and reasonably by considering the subjective fault of the parties involved.

3. THE ROLE OF JOINT ADMINISTRATIVE VIOLATION THEORY

The imperfection of the joint administrative violation theory led to differences in practice. What role does this theory play in handling administrative penalty cases? Seeing that administrative organs issue a large number of administrative penalty decisions, and that the extent of infringement on legally protected interests by administrative law violations is relatively less severe than that of criminal offenses, therefore, in consideration of the burden of workload on administrative authorities, is it necessary to introduce such a complex system of joint violation theory into administrative penalty? Furthermore, even if the value of the joint administrative violation theory is to be recognized, why shall it be based on the principle of culpability? By examining the syllogism reasoning process by administrative authorities in imposing penalties for joint misconduct cases, the role of the joint violation theory is evident at each step of the reasoning, and its application is closely related to the principle of culpability. The so-called 'syllogism' reasoning for imposing administrative penalties refers to the process of interpreting applicable laws for the major premise,

---

19 See *supra* note 9, 2.

20 See Li Honglei, 'On the Improvement of China's Administrative Punishment System: Comment on the Administrative Punishment Law of P.R.C. (Revised Draft)' (2020) 6 *Studies in Law and Business* 8.

21 See Zhang Qingbo, 'Review on Subjective Element of Behaviors Deserved to Be Punished by Administrative Sanction' (2020) 10 *Law Science* 82–92.

investigating case facts for the minor premise, and finally 'subsuming' the major premise into the minor premise, thus forming a penalty decision by exercising discretion.[22] In joint violation cases, the minor premise of 'multiple parties jointly committing the misconduct' pertains to factual investigation and is not the subject of legal reasoning. Once the minor premise is established, the role of the joint violation theory based on the principle of culpability is reflected in the subsequent reasoning steps:

3.1 The Role in Establishing the Major Premise: Explaining and Supplementing the Elements of Illegal Activities

After clarifying the minor premise, which is the fact that multiple parties commit illegal conduct, the administrative enforcer needs to 'find and interpret the law' to determine whether the legislation has made stipulations regarding the activity concerned. This also reflects the principle that administrative penalties should be imposed in accordance with the law, which requires that the elements of the penalty should be legally prescribed, and the actual illegal activities be consistent with the elements of conduct required by the law.[23] In other words, the elements of administrative misconduct should be prescribed by the normative documents issued by administrative organs with the authority to set penalties, and the penalty should be imposed only when the conduct of the violators meets the elements prescribed by the law. However, it shall be noted that legislation cannot cover every detail comprehensively, and legislative language is often vague. Therefore, in applying the law, administrative authorities need to interpret the law and even supplement elements not specified in the legislation through explanation of the law. Based on the requirements of legal universality and consistency, the interpretation by enforcers must not be arbitrary or deviate from the intent of the legislation. Thus, legal interpretation must follow the interpretation methodology and legal theories.[24]

In joint violation cases, although the legislation does not explicitly prescribe 'more than two parties jointly commit violation with subjective intent to violate the law' as necessary for the determination of certain types of administrative illegal activities, the lack of such condition would result in logical impossibility or exclusion of these activities as acts culpable under administrative penalty law. To address this, it is necessary to supplement the constituent elements of the misconduct with the joint violation theory based on the principle of

22 See Hartmut Maurer, *Allgemeines Verwaltungsrecht*, translated by Gao Jiawei (Law Press, 2000) 123.

23 See Chen Qingxiu, *Administrative Penalty Law* (Law Press, 2016) 32–41.

24 See Chen Jinzhao, 'Legal Methodology in Judicial Process' (2002) 4 *Law and Social Development* 32–33.

culpability to explain that the legislation intends to require 'jointness'. Sorting out relevant laws, it can be found that the following three types of administrative violations are concerned:

The first type is organized group illegal activities. For establishing such violations, two conditions shall be met. The first is a gathered 'group', indicating plural parties thus naturally constructing joint actions. The second condition is 'organized', that is, there must be joint intent between the multiple parties, and communication of intent to take actions in order to achieve the illegal result. Thus, the situation where multiple actors commit the same actions at the same time and location by coincidence cannot be classified as the above kind of violation. This also highlights the importance of the principle of culpability to the theory of joint violation, for without considering the subjective state of actors, it proves difficult to identify if there is any 'organization' of such an action. For example, in China's Anti-Monopoly Law, Articles 13 and 14 respectively stipulate administrative violations, namely, horizontal and vertical monopoly agreements. Although the legislation does not specify the conditions for reaching monopoly agreements, applying the joint violation theory based on culpability allows us to infer that the conclusion of a monopoly agreement requires that, subjectively, multiple parties communicate with mutual intent to take action, which also reflects the 'consensus' nature of the agreement itself. Objectively, it is required that the participants jointly implement actions that exclude or restrict competition. Based on this interpretation, it can be inferred that: firstly, if there is only one party, it is impossible to form a monopoly agreement and can only be considered an abuse of a dominant market position; secondly, even if multiple parties are involved, without mutual intent between them, a mere coincidental implementation of actions such as changing prices cannot be considered a monopoly agreement, and the acts of each party should be evaluated respectively; finally, if one party reaches a monopoly agreement with other parties but does not engage in monopoly acts, the party should still be held responsible for the harmful consequences caused by the joint agreement.

The second category comprises the acts of aiding and abetting that are independently classified as punishable offenses. In China's administrative legislation, certain acts of instigating and assisting are specifically stipulated as punishable offenses, along with corresponding penalties. In criminal law, this arrangement is referred to as 'principalization of accomplice'. Though there is no corresponding category in administrative penalty theories, such kinds of regulations are massive in practice. For instance, Article 14 of the administrative regulation 'Measures for the Investigation and Punishment of Unpermitted and Unlicensed Business Operations' stipulates that anyone who knowingly provides assistance, such as providing a place of operation or transportation facilities, to someone engaged in unlicensed operations, etc., shall be penalized. In the interpretation of this provision, the theory of joint violation based on the principle of responsibility should be applied as follows: First, although the legislation only penalizes the party providing assistance, the establishment of 'assistance' necessarily involves multiple parties, constituting a joint violation. Second, purely providing assistance, such as renting a property or transporting goods, does not itself bear illegality; rather, the reason for penalizing the assisting party is that their acts facilitate the realization of the illegal consequences of unlicensed operations. Therefore, the illegal outcome can be attributed to the assisting party, and this judgment requires the application of the theory of joint violation. Third, if the actor provides assistance without knowing that the assisted party is engaging in unlicensed operations, the assisting party shall not commit an offense. In such cases, the principle of responsibility should be applied to determine whether the actor subjectively intended to facilitate or condone the realization of the illegal consequences through their assistance, in consideration of the actor's subjective fault.

The third category is 'reciprocal violations,' which refers to violations committed by two or more parties in a mutual illegal activity where one is the subject of the other and vice versa, such as prostitution and whoring, or as stipulated in Article 99 of the Road Traffic Safety Law, driving a motor vehicle without a license and providing a motor vehicle to an unlicensed person. Regarding 'reciprocal violations,' the legislation or regulations may only penalize one party or choose to prescribe the same or different penalties for both parties. Applying such regulations requires interpretation based on the principle of culpability to draw the conclusion that relevant articles require the involvement of multiple actors, and that they subjectively know the other party's acts.

It should be noted that this supplementary interpretation does not contradict the principle of 'penalty according to the law.' In criminal law practices, which are subject to stricter restrictions under the principle of legality, it is recognized that adopting a logical interpretation method to supplement the interpretation of blank or simple clauses of crime.[25] By the same token, in administrative penalties where less severe offenses are concerned, using the theory of joint violation based on the principle of responsibility to interpret and supplement the elements of unlawful behavior is acceptable and necessary.

---

[25] See Zhang Mingkai, *Criminal Law (Volume I)* (Law Press, 2016) 115.

3.2 Role in Subsumption: Identifying the Parties Involved in the Major Premise

In the process of subsumption in joint offense cases, one particular issue arises: most administrative regulations are targeted at single violators. Therefore, when applying the major premise of legal norms to the minor premise of 'multiple parties committing offenses,' it is necessary to determine which parties fall within the scope of the punitive provisions, and such is the issue of whom to attribute the unlawful consequences. If the judgment is incorrect, it may lead to an inappropriate expansion or contraction of the scope of punishment. To illustrate this, let us take the *Lou v. Public Security Bureau* (case for appeal of administration management of public security) (hereinafter referred to as the *Lou* case) as an example. In the *Lou* case, the manager of a certain company, Wang A, was suspected of instructing He, Wang B, and Dong to restrain the victim, Lou, and seize the official seal carried by Lou. Under manager Wang A's orders, He, Wang B, and Dong intercepted Lou. Then, Wang B and Dong controlled the victim Lou in a vehicle while He stood by as a lookout. The public security authority imposed administrative penalties on Wang B and Dong for unlawfully restricting personal freedom. However, the victim Lou believed that He and Wang A should also be punished and thus initiated a lawsuit.[26]

Without considering the investigation and verification of the case facts, the core issue of this case lies in determining which individuals' actions fall within the scope of 'unlawfully restricting personal freedom' and should therefore be the subjects of administrative punishment. The above actors can be divided into three categories: (1) Wang A, who only instructed others to restrict Lou's personal freedom but did not perform any specific actions; (2) He, who executed the interception and surveillance without physically confining Lou in the vehicle; (3) Wang B and Dong, who both actively and intentionally restricted Lou's personal freedom by taking him into the vehicle. The specific classification is illustrated in Table 7.1. There are three different viewpoints on this case.

The first viewpoint chooses not to apply the theory of joint violations. Without applying the theory of joint offenses, each individual's actions and the

---

26 This example originates from Lou Jianlv *v.* Public Security Bureau of Longhua District, Shenzhen for appeal of administration management of public security, No. 100 Final Administrative Judgment of The Intermediate People's Court of Shenzhen (粤03行终100号), (2019). The parties in this case have disputes over the conclusion of facts; for the convenience of readers, this chapter simplifies the case facts and omits controversial parts. Therefore, comments on the characters in the example from this chapter do not represent descriptions of the real parties concerned in this case.

Table 7.1 Analysis of subjective state and objective actions of actors in the Lou *case*

Category	Actors	Subjective State	Objective Actions
Category I	Wang A	Subjectively intentional	None
Category II	He	Subjectively intentional	Partial actions
Category III	Wang B, Dong	Subjectively intentional	All actions

consequences they caused can only be evaluated separately and independently. Therefore, Wang B and Dong, the individuals in category III, directly caused the unlawful restriction of Lou's personal freedom, constituting administrative violations. He, in category II, performed the interception and surveillance, which, when considered independently, did not directly lead to the infringement of legal interests. Also, as the action of surveillance is not by itself a punishable offense in administrative law, there's no administrative violation constituted. As for Wang A in category I, he only instructed others to restrict Lou's personal freedom, and mere instructions cannot possibly produce unlawful consequences. Moreover, administrative regulations do not punish malicious intent expressed through mere instructing. Therefore, he shall not be subjected to an administrative penalty.

The second viewpoint is to follow the theory of joint violations without considering subjective fault. In this case, only He from category II and Wang B and Dong from category III are suspected of administrative violations because their objective actions contributed to the unlawful consequences. However, for Wang A from category I, without adopting the principle of culpability, his subjective intent cannot be evaluated as he did not carry out any objective actions; therefore, he cannot be held accountable.

The third viewpoint applies the theory of joint violations based on the principle of culpability. In this case, all three categories of individuals should be held responsible for the final unlawful consequences. The theory of joint offenses aims to 'determine which parties the unlawful consequences should be attributed to,' thereby evaluating the actions of multiple offenders as a whole.[27] The individuals in all three categories share the common subjective intent to unlawfully restrict personal freedom of Lou and contribute to the unlawful consequences through their psychological or objective actions. Hence, all three actors should be held accountable for the final unlawful results.

By comparing the above viewpoints, quite contrary to the argument that 'applying the principle of culpability would inappropriately narrow the scope

27 See Zhang Mingkai, 'Joint Crime is a Form of Law Violation' (2010) 13 *People's Procuratorial Semimonthly* 7–8.

of punishment,' it is evident that only by applying the culpability-based theory of joint violations can the actions of each individual be comprehensively evaluated, thus avoiding omission of the subjects of punishment. In the example case mentioned above, Wang A, the planner and instigator of the unlawful acts, is the main cause of the offense and has the most severe subjective malice. He executed the interception and also encouraged Wang B and Dong's direct offense by acting as a lookout. Without holding the first and second categories of individuals accountable, it not only contradicts the common understanding of the public but also fails to meet the need to maintain administrative order. Therefore, in the corresponding real-life judgment, the court did not support the public security authorities' choice of not investigating the actors in the first and second categories but instead demanded that the public security authorities conduct further investigations.

3.3 Role in Determining Penalty Decisions: Conditions for Imposing a Heavier or Aggravated Penalty

After the subsumption process, that is, after confirming the actions by the actors in the minor premise correspond to the constituent elements of violation prescribed by the major premise, the next step is to decide the actual punishment. The determination of penalty results is the process of administrative authorities exercising discretionary power, which must adhere to the principle of proportionality. During this process, the liability-based theory of joint violations plays a role in deciding whether to impose a heavier or aggravated penalty.

According to the law, when multiple people jointly commit an administrative violation, they often face more severe punishment. For example, Paragraph 1 of Article 43 of the Public Security Administration Punishments Law of PRC stipulates the penalty for 'beating others,' while Paragraph 2 of Article 43 sets forth aggravated penalties for 'beating or injuring others by forming a group.' This is mainly based on the following reasons: first, from the perspective of the consequences of harm, administrative punishment emphasizes the protection of public order and other legal interests. Compared with individual offenders' violation of public order and legal interests, multiple offenders assisting one another can make their actions more destructive and cause greater harm. Second, from the standpoint of subjective malice of offenders, due to the influence of group psychology, joint offenders' collective planning and action reinforce each other's subjective malice, thus increasing the likelihood of their committing unlawful acts. Therefore, harsher punishment is required to serve as a deterrent.

This also reflects the role of the responsibility-based theory of joint violations. Firstly, to determine whether the parties involved in the joint offense are subject to heavier or aggravated punishment, the theory of joint violations must be applied. Secondly, the reason for imposing heavier punishment on joint offenders also involves the consideration of subjective factors; that is, joint offenders' subjective malice is enhanced during the joint offense process due to group psychology, making them more likely to commit unlawful acts.

4. CRITERIA FOR DETERMINING JOINT VIOLATIONS BASED ON THE PRINCIPLE OF CULPABILITY

As discussed above, the application of the theory of joint administrative violations runs through the entire process of syllogism reasoning in administrative punishment. So, how do we construct the theory of joint violations based on the principle of culpability? The theory of joint violations consists of 'criteria for identification' and 'rules for penalty decisions.' Only after determining the 'criteria for identification' and establishing that multiple actors engaged in joint violations can we consider the 'rules for penalty decisions.' Therefore, this section first discusses the criteria for identifying joint violations.

4.1 The Essence of Criteria for Identification of Joint Violations

To construct the criteria for determining joint violations, we first need to consider its essence: What are the elements of the standard of proof that serve to identify a joint violation? In other words, what elements are required to be 'joint' by the 'standard of proof' of joint violations?

When there is only one actor involved, the identification of whether they should be subject to administrative punishment mainly depends on whether their actions meet the statutory requirements for constituting administrative violations, that is, whether they satisfy the 'major premise.' The constitutive elements of different administrative violations vary, but by using systematic thinking for summarization and generalization, we can establish the general constitutive elements of administrative violations.[28] In this regard, the academics mainly present two different theories: the 'three-tiered theory' and the 'four-element theory.' The 'four-element theory' posits that for an individual's violation to be subject to punishment, four elements shall be fulfilled: subjective elements, objective elements, subjective fault elements, and objective fault elements.[29] On the other hand, the 'three-tiered theory' suggests that

---

[28] See Xiong Zhanglin, 'On the Model of Acts Deserve Administrative Penalty' (2021) 5 *Legal Science* 70–72.

[29] See Jiang Bixin, 'On the Constitutive Elements of Acts Culpable of Administrative Penalty' (1996) 6 *Journal of Law Application* 3.

the actions subject to punishment should meet three levels of requirements: elements of illegality (the conduct satisfies the constitutive elements as prescribed by legislation), defense (that there is no such defense as justification and excuses), and culpability (the actor possesses the capacity to bear responsibility and subjective fault). These three levels form a layered structure, and only when the former is met can the latter be examined.[30] Other theories are mostly variations of the aforementioned two theories. Regardless of which theory is adopted, only when an individual's conduct satisfies all constitutive elements will they be subject to administrative punishment. When multiple actors are involved, their collective actions contribute to the realization of the illegal consequence, whereas for each participant, they often only implement one part of all the constitutive elements. For example, in a joint illegal logging activity, each participant might perform different acts such as directing, keeping watch, cutting, and transporting. So, should each participant be held responsible for the entire illegal consequence? This requires a determination of whether these actors constitute joint violations, thereby making each participant responsible for the final illegal outcome. Though each participant's actions in a joint action may differ, a joint violation will be established if the parties share at least some aspects in common or have jointly fulfilled some of the constitutive elements of the administrative violation. The question of what elements shall be jointly fulfilled to constitute a joint violation is the question to be addressed by the criteria for identifying joint violations.

From the above discussion, it can be understood that the essence of the criteria for determining joint violations is to judge, for all the constitutive elements of the administrative violation, whether multiple actors collectively construct the necessary constitutive elements for such violation, so as to determine whether multiple actors constitute joint violations.

4.2 A More Rational 'Standard of the Joint Act'

Since the criteria for determining joint violations are primarily used to judge whether multiple actors collectively possess the necessary constitutive elements, which elements must be classified as joint? There are two different viewpoints: the 'joint violation standard' and the 'joint conduct standard,' originating from criminal law theories of 'joint criminality theory' and 'joint violation theory,' respectively. It can be seen that discussions on administrative joint violations draw heavily from criminal law theories, and that borrowing

---

30 See Xiong Zhanglin, 'Administrative Illegal Action's Tatbestandsmäßigkeit' (2015) Autumn Volume, *Nanjing University Law Journal* (Law Press, 2015) 193–207.

criminal law theory in administrative punishment research is quite common. The rationale for this is that criminal theories are more developed, and on the other hand, the substantial distinction between administrative punishment and criminal law has been narrowing due to the development of society, clearing the barriers for theoretical reference.[31] However, such borrowing must take into consideration the distinctive features of administrative punishment.

The 'joint violation standard' stipulates that joint violation is established when multiple actors bear commonality regarding the following two aspects: First, they must conduct common actions; second, they must bear common responsibility, which requires the actors to possess common subjective fault. This viewpoint is derived from the 'joint criminality theory' in criminal law, which states that the possibility of establishing joint crime starts only after plural actors jointly commit actions for the purpose of achieving uniform intentional offense.[32] Based on this, when answering the question of 'which aspects are common between all offenders,' joint criminality theory asserts that there should not only be mutual actions in the objective aspect, but also mutual subjective liability.[33] What is worth noting is that there is a promoting and discarding process in administrative joint violation theory's borrowing of the joint criminality theory in criminal law. In criminal law, joint criminality theory further diverges into two theories, namely, 'all-joint criminality theory' and 'partial joint criminality theory'. The former holds that the actors must have the same criminal intent to commit the offense, while the latter suggests that if there is an overlap in the criminal intent among the actors, they jointly commit the offense within the overlapped scope. For instance, if a person intentionally kills someone, and another person intentionally injures someone, they jointly commit the offense of intentional injury within the scope of the intent of injury. In criminal practice, the 'all-joint criminality theory' is not widely accepted due to its inflexibility, and the 'partial joint criminality theory' becomes the prevailing view in judicial judgments.[34] However, in administrative punishment, the issue of overlapping subjective intent is often absent. Therefore, the distinction between the two stances is not as apparent. But if such a situation arises, considering that the 'all-joint criminality theory' has been abandoned, it is advisable to adopt the perspective of the 'partial joint criminality theory.'

---

31 See Hong Jiayin, 'Administrative Penalty', in Weng Yuesheng, *Administrative Law (Volume I)* (China Legal Publishing House, 2009) 830.

32 See Qian Yeliu, *The Foundation and Development of Joint Offense Theory* (China University of Political Science and Law Press, 2014) 73.

33 See Gao Mingxuan & Ma Kechang, *Criminal Law (5th Edition)* (Peking University Press & Higher Education Press, 2011) 165–166.

34 See *supra* note 32, 77.

On the other hand, the 'standard of the joint act' originates from the 'joint conduct theory' in criminal law, which takes the 'three-tiered theory' of criminal construction as a premise. Since the 'three-tiered theory' of criminal construction posits that criminal construction should satisfy three levels: 'elements of violations,' 'defense,' and 'culpability,' judgment must be made in sequence for each level. Hence, it is possible for the case where plural offenders jointly satisfy the wrongdoing requirement, and are subsequently judged on their culpability respectively by examining for each offender what kind of crime is committed and whether they should be subject to criminal liability.[35] Based on the 'joint conduct theory' in criminal law, we can establish the 'joint conduct standard' in administrative punishment, which considers that the administrative counterparts only have joint intent regarding the construction of illegal activity, and therefore courts should determine whether each violator should be subject to administrative punishment and what types of administrative penalty should be applied.

Which of the above two viewpoints is more reasonable? Unlike the complex relationship between the 'joint criminality theory' and the 'joint conduct theory' in criminal law, the application of 'joint conduct standard' in administrative punishment is more reasonable, mainly for two reasons:

Firstly, it can address cases involving jointly committed violations by individuals with no capacity for responsibility. For example, if an individual with capacity for responsibility (Person A) incites a group of individuals under the age of 14 to assault a victim, according to the 'joint violation standard,' as the minors have no capacity of liability, there is no common subjective element between Person A and the minors; thus, they do not commit joint violation. In this case, the minors are not subject to administrative punishment due to their lack of capacity forliability, and Person A is only considered to have 'individually assaulted someone'; thus, the provision of Paragraph 1 of Article 43 of the Public Security Administration Punishments Law of PRC shall apply. Whereas under the 'joint conduct standard', it can be established that Person A and the minors jointly committed the act of assault, and they should all bear responsibility for the illegal outcome. However, at the level of culpability, even though they committed a violation, the minors are not held accountable because of their lack of capacity for liability. Meanwhile, Person A is held accountable for assault by forming a group and bears the capacity for responsibility for the act of joint assault. Comparing the two approaches, the 'joint violation standard' results in two issues: First, it is against the principle of fairness. Regardless of whether inciting minors with no capacity for liability or inciting individuals with capacity for liability, they all jointly committed

35 See *supra* note 27, 7–8.

the act of assault, and the consequences of infringement on legally protected interests are the same. However, under the 'joint violation standard,' a person who incites minors with no capacity for liability shall be categorized as having committed individual assault, while a person who incites individuals capable of bearing liability shall be categorized as having committed joint assault, resulting in not only different treatment for the same cases but also contradicting verification of the same facts. Second, it contradicts the principle of proportionality in punishment. It is generally recognized that organizing minors under the age of 14 to participate in joint assault not only violates the rights of the victims but also negatively affects the healthy growth of minors, with a greater subjective malignancy and a more severe social impact. However, if the 'joint violation standard' is adopted, such behavior might receive a lighter punishment, leading to an unbalanced penalty and potential of encouraging the use of minors as 'hatched men' in illegal activities. From this perspective, the 'joint conduct standard' should be used in determining joint violations.

Secondly, there is the matching between the criteria for identification and the rules for penalty decisions. If the 'joint violation standard' is adopted, the actors must inevitably constitute the same illegal act and violate the same penalty, bearing joint liability, i.e., 'joint penalty for joint offense.' This not only contradicts the common practice of imposing 'separate penalties for joint acts' but also rules out the possibility of issuing corresponding penalties according to the respective malice of each actor,[36] which means that the principle of culpability cannot be implemented consistently throughout the whole process of administrative penalty implementation.

4.3 Application of the Principle of Culpability in the 'Joint Conduct Standard' in Administrative Punishment

When adopting the 'joint conduct standard' as the criteria for determining joint violations, it is crucial to emphasize the application of the principle of culpability. Some argue that since the 'joint conduct standard' only requires an objective connection between the actions by plural actors, there is no need to consider subjective intent when determining whether joint violations exist.[37] However, this viewpoint is debatable. In fact, although the 'joint conduct standard' seems to focus only on the actors' actual behavior without considering subjective elements, its construction and application still involve the principle of individual theory.

---

36 See *supra* note 5, 156.

37 See *supra* note 5, 155.

Firstly, the theoretical basis of the 'joint conduct standard' directs that 'act is joint, whereas responsibility is individual,' thus distinguishing between the questions 'whether the actors jointly commit violations' and 'what kind of responsibility each actor should bear.' This avoids confusion regarding the responsibilities of different actors and ensures that each actor bears responsibility according to their individual subjective fault. From this perspective, the 'joint conduct standard' relies on the separation of objective behavior and subjective responsibility while emphasizing the individualization of subjective responsibility, in which way the principle of culpability can be better implemented.

Secondly, the application of the 'joint conduct standard' does not exclude the exploration of subjective responsibility. Under the 'absolute joint conduct standard,' it is to be concluded that joint violations can still be constituted even without any connection of intention. This viewpoint originates from the absolute 'joint conduct standard' in criminal law, which has been abandoned and moderated due to its problems.[38] First, an absolute 'joint conduct standard' would lead to confusion between 'joint violation' and 'simultaneous offense.'[39] 'Simultaneous offense' refers to the situation where 'even though multiple people can complement each other in objective respect, due to the fact that they have no knowledge of others' infringement on legal interests, thus unintentionally infringing on the same legal interests coincidentally.'[40] This situation also exists in administrative punishment. For example, as mentioned earlier, several main operators in a specific market independently raise prices without any intentional connection, but they achieve similar effects to horizontal monopoly. If subjective intent is not considered at all, it would be impossible to determine whether they reach a monopoly agreement. Secondly, the absolute 'joint conduct standard' may have omissions in handling conspiratorial administrative violations, as exemplified in the case of the *Lou* Case. Applying the 'joint conduct standard' without considering the intentional connection between the actors would make it impossible to punish manager Wang A.

Therefore, the 'joint conduct standard' is not solely based on objective behavior, but still requires a causal relationship between the actors at the subjective level. Thus, it still needs to explore the actors' subjective state. However, compared to the 'joint violation standard,' the 'joint conduct standard' has more

---

[38] See Li Hong, *Thoughts on Issues Concerning General Provisions of Criminal Law* (China Renmin University Press, 2007) 478.

[39] See Liu Yanhong, 'Systematic Thought of Substantive Criminal Law' (2014) 4 *Law Review* 67.

[40] See Guo Yan & Jia Yu, 'The Advocate of the Behavioral Common Theory' (2016) 2 *Journal of National Prosecutors College* 106.

lenient requirements, which can be specifically manifested in the following two points:

Firstly, the requirement of the 'joint conduct standard' regarding the intentional connection between the actors is based on 'knowing,' meaning that if an actor knows that others are contributing to the realization of his or her illegal outcome, there is an intentional connection. Compared to the 'joint violation standard,' on the one hand, it does not require all actors to be aware of each other's actions. It is sufficient if the main participants are aware of the joint involvement of others in the illegal activities. On the other hand, the requirement of knowing does not necessitate all actors pursuing the same illegal outcome, but only requires one actor to be aware that another's action objectively contributes to the realization of their illegal outcome.[41] Secondly, the 'joint conduct standard' does not limit the subjective state of the actors to only intent but also includes negligence. The 'joint violation standard' requires actors to have a shared intent, excluding joint violations of negligence. By applying the 'joint conduct standard,' joint violations can be established when all actors hold a negligent mentality or when one actor holds a negligent mentality and the other holds an intentional mentality. In the former case, it might involve multiple actors with an obligation of care who are mutually aware of each other's obligations but cause harm due to negligence or excessive confidence. In the latter case, it might involve an actor with an obligation of care who knows that another actor is intentionally causing harm but fails to prevent it. In the criminal law field, Article 25 of the Criminal Code denies the possibility of joint negligence offenses. Essentially, whether to recognize joint negligence offenses is a policy choice. Rejecting joint negligence crimes allows for more stringent restrictions on criminal penalties, but it also increases the difficulty of investigation and evidence showing for the prosecution, as the prosecution needs to prove that the actor's state of mind was intentional rather than negligent.[42] In comparison to criminal law, administrative punishment is less invasive, and considering the frequency of administrative penalties and the requirement for administrative efficiency, it is not appropriate to burden administrative authorities with excessive investigation responsibilities to distinguish between intentional and negligent behavior. Therefore, recognizing joint negligence violations is more reasonable in administrative punishment.

---

41 See Liao Yinan, *Administrative Penalty Law (2nd Edition)* (Angle Publishing Co., Ltd., 2017) 144.

42 See Zheng Hui, 'The Purpose Exploration of Joint Crime' (2019) 2 *Chinese Criminology Review* 31–32.

4.4 The Specificity of the 'Joint Conduct Standard' in Administrative Punishment

From the above discussion, it is evident that the 'joint conduct standard' can be adopted to determine administrative joint violations. Although the 'joint conduct standard' originates from the 'joint conduct theory' in criminal law, its application in administrative punishment has its particularities, mainly reflected in the following:

Firstly, in criminal law, there are so-called 'conspiratorial principal offenders,' referring to suspects who have not taken concrete steps to implement criminal acts but only participated in planning.[43] Therefore, in criminal law, they are undoubtedly considered joint criminals. While in administrative punishment, there is a contention that administrative penalties generally apply to minor violations of social order, so they can be limited to 'joint implementers,' i.e., denying that the conspirators should be penalized.[44] This viewpoint confuses the identification of joint violations and penalty decision-making. In the identification of joint violations, based on the 'joint conduct standard,' co-conspirators participate in illegal acts in the way of psychological connections, assisting or even dominating the realization of the illegal outcome; thus, they shall be recognized as joint violators. Whether co-conspirators should be exempted from punishment due to minor infringement is another question in joint violation adjudication. Even if co-conspirators are ultimately not punished, it does not mean that they are not joint violators. In practice, co-conspirators are often organizers and dominating parties of illegal activities, bearing the primary responsibility for illegal outcomes, so they often face heavier punishment.

Secondly, in criminal law, there are instigators and accomplices, but in administrative punishment, there is controversy over how to punish instigators and accomplices. Two opposing viewpoints exist: one argues that administrative punishment deals with minor violations of social order, the culpability of which is generally lower compared to those in criminal law. Since the actions of instigation and assistance are less severe than direct implementation, there is no need to punish instigators and accomplices in administrative punishment.[45] This viewpoint essentially exempts instigators and accomplices from liability. The other viewpoint argues that due to the frequency of administrative punishment and the need to reduce the burden on administrative authorities, there is no need to deliberately distinguish instigation and assistance from direct

43 See *supra* note 23, 164.
44 See *supra* note 23, 164–165.
45 See *supra* note 23, 167.

implementation. Instead, they suggest directly imposing punishment based on the act of direct implementation, known as the 'single actor' theory.[46] This viewpoint essentially increases the liability of instigators and accomplices.

To resolve this, it is necessary to distinguish between the identification and penalty decision-making of actions of instigation and assistance. At the identification level, based on the 'joint conduct standard,' instigation and assistance have a positive impact both psychologically and objectively on the realization of illegal outcomes, thus to which the illegal outcomes can be attributed; that is to say, instigators and accomplices can be deemed as joint violators. As to adjudication regarding penalty decisions, the specific degree of punishment for instigators and accomplices can be at the discretion of the administrative authority within the statutory scope. Furthermore, it is essential to emphasize that in the case where the law prescribes corresponding penalties for certain instigative and assistive actions, they should be punished according to the specific provisions of the law.

5. RULES FOR ADMINISTRATIVE PENALTY DECISIONS OF JOINT VIOLATIONS BASED ON THE PRINCIPLE OF CULPABILITY

In cases involving joint illegal acts, after applying the criteria for identification of joint violations to establish the fact that multiple actors commit joint illegal activities, the next step is to consider what kind of liability each actor should bear, which is the question to be resolved by the rules for administrative penalty decisions. As mentioned above, there are two viewpoints concerning this matter: 'joint liability for joint conduct' and 'separate liability for joint conduct.' The application of the principle of culpability should be utilized to determine the most appropriate approach.

5.1 'Separate Liability for Joint Conduct' Based on the Principle of Culpability

For most administrative penalties, the principle of 'separate liability for joint conduct' should be applied. This means that the liabilities of each participant should be separately determined, and each participant should be issued an independent penalty decision with a distinct document number.

---

[46] See *supra* note 41, 144.

5.1.1 Respective determination of legal liabilities for each actor

Respective determination of legal liabilities for each actor is the core of the principle of 'separate liability for joint conduct.' Adopting this principle is not only a policy choice but also a natural consequence of applying the 'joint conduct standard' and adhering to the principle of culpability, reflected in the following two aspects:

First, in regard to the determination of illegal acts, different criteria for joint illegal acts will lead to differences in the rule of penalty decisions. If the 'joint violation standard' is applied, multiple actors will only violate the same article of law and be subject to the same penalty. At this point, the possibility of applying 'joint liability for joint conduct' exists. However, this approach would contradict the principle of proportionality, as the penalties imposed would not match the subjective malignancy and harmfulness of each participant's behavior. Whereas if the 'joint conduct standard' is applied, although the participants jointly engage in 'one' illegal act, the specific administrative violation committed by each individual would differ, resulting in different penalty regulations being applied. For example, as mentioned earlier, person A operates without a license, and person B provides the operating venue. In this case, although both jointly engage in the activity of illegal operation, person A violates the provision of Article 13 of the Measures for the Investigation and Punishment of Unpermitted and Unlicensed Business Operations while person B violates the provision of Article 14 of the same regulation. As their actual violations differ, the reasons for their administrative penalties and the liabilities they should bear also differ. In this situation, 'joint liability for joint conduct' is not applicable, and only the 'separate liability for joint conduct' is appropriate. It should be noted that although one main contention of this article is that the principle of culpability should still be applied in following the 'joint conduct standard,' the subjective requirement is only for one actor to have knowledge of the others' actions, but not that all actors act with the joint intention of the same illegal activities. That is to say, to emphasize the principle of culpability in the 'joint conduct standard' would not lead to the case in which only one single legal regulation can be applied when imposing punishment on each actor.

Second, in regard to the determination of penalty liability, administrative penalties emphasize their punitive aspect, which differs from the compensatory feature in civil liability where joint tortfeasors may share liability, and the compensation sum is limited to the loss suffered by the victim. In light of the punitive nature of administrative penalties, the determination of penalties should not only consider the extent of the damage caused by the violation but also take into account the subjective malignancy and social harm of the conduct. Therefore, under the principle of 'separate liability for joint conduct,' the total penalties imposed on joint participants may exceed the upper limit of the penalty range. This does not violate the principle of proportionality, as the term 'fault' in the proportion between fault and penalty refers not to the damages caused by the violation but to the fault and harmfulness of each individual's conduct. This interpretation is consistent with current legislation, as joint illegal acts are often regarded as an aggravating element for punishment. Compared to the violation committed by a single participant, joint participants often receive more severe penalties. If 'joint liability for joint conduct' were applied, with each participant sharing the penalty liability, the penalty burden for each participant would be lighter when more individuals engage in the specific violation. This, in essence, would 'encourage' joint illegal acts and lead to a higher occurrence of group offenses, which would not serve the legislative purpose of combating joint illegal acts.

5.1.2 Issuing independent penalty decision with distinct document numbers

Under the principle of 'separate liability for joint conduct,' there is also some debate regarding how to issue penalty decisions in practice. Some administrative authorities list the penalties for each participant in a single decision, while others issue separate penalty decisions with distinct document numbers for each participant. The difference in this approach can affect the remedies available to the participants. This chapter suggests that the latter method is preferable.

First, from the perspective of the number of administrative actions, under the situation of 'separate liability for joint conduct,' the penalties imposed on each participant may only have a partial consistency regarding the minor premise (i.e., the actual illegal activity they carried out) but could have differences in the major premise of applicable law or the ultimate penalty decision. Therefore, the penalties issued to each actor are not the same administrative action, but only several administrative actions of the same category. Following the practice of 'a distinct document number recording one administrative action,' administrative agencies should issue multiple decisions with distinct document numbers.

Second, from the perspective of remedies available to participants, issuing separate penalty decisions with distinct document numbers is more conducive to dispute resolution and the protection of the rights of participants. The reason for this is that current rules regarding joint litigation and joint review in China are not well defined; issuing a single document for multiple participants would lead to complex joint administrative review and joint litigation cases, which would hinder effective dispute resolution.

In joint litigation cases, courts usually determine the number of administrative actions based on the number of document serial numbers of administrative penalty decisions. This is used to ascertain whether the administrative authority made one administrative action or multiple actions of the same type, ultimately determining whether a compulsory joinder or permissive joinder should apply. If the administrative authority issues a single document with one document number for multiple participants, it effectively creates a compulsory joinder litigation. In practice, there are complex situations where some participants sue first, while others sue later, or some participants sue while others request a review simultaneously. This not only increases the difficulty of court proceedings but also leads to the increasing occurrence of group events. From the perspective of participants, complex and prolonged procedures are not conducive to obtaining remedies. Conversely, if separate penalty decisions with distinct document numbers are issued to participants, the court can treat the case as a permissive joinder litigation. At this point, each administrative penalty is an independent administrative action, and theoretically speaking, can be decided by the court respectively, avoiding conflicts in judgments resulting from participants of the same case initiating different procedures. Of course, in permissive joinder litigation, the court's determination of the joint facts should not be contradictory, but this can be resolved through the theory of res judicata of decided facts, i.e., if multiple plaintiffs sue successively, the facts determined in the previous lawsuit should be recognized in the later trial.[47] Therefore, in joint illegal acts cases, the court's determination of joint illegal acts has binding force on each plaintiff, but the court can render separate judgments on the penalty responsibility of each participant, ensuring consistency in judgments and better protection of the rights of parties.

5.2 Special Circumstances in the Penalty Decision-Making of Administrative Joint Violations

While the rule for penalty decisions of joint illegal acts should adhere to the principle of 'separate liability for joint conduct' to meet the requirements of the principle of culpability and that of practice, in specific situations, special rules may be applied due to the complexity and diversity of administrative management.

5.2.1 Where legislation mandates joint liability for participants

In criminal law, 'separate liability for joint conduct' is strictly applied, based on the fact that penalties in criminal legislation are stipulated for individual offenders. However, in administrative penalties, some legislation may impose joint and several liability on participants. In this case, 'joint liability for joint

---

[47] See Weng Xiaobin, 'On the Effect of Judged Facts' (2006) 4 *China Legal Science* 180–189.

conduct' should be followed. It is easy to determine if such liability is explicitly stipulated by legislation. However, it is often the case that legislation does not directly prescribe regarding this matter, such as when interpretation of legal regulations is required. This can be done in two steps: first, applying the principle of proportionality to judge whether the direct application of the legal norms would result in significant unfairness;[48] second, applying the teleological interpretation to determine whether the legislative purpose is to establish joint and several liability.

5.2.2 Where participants are treated as a single entity

Treating participants as a single entity is a theoretical approach for dealing with violations involving multiple participants, fundamentally different from joint violation theory.[49] If multiple participants constitute a single entity, joint violations cannot be established, and therefore the rule of joint illegal acts is not applicable. Strictly speaking, single entity theory is not the subject matter to be addressed by this chapter; however, in appearance, the treatment of participants as a single entity and the rule of joint illegal acts may show similarities; thus, clarification is still needed. A single entity refers to multiple participants forming a whole due to a certain relationship of rights and obligations, allowing them to be treated as a fictional single entity and their joint conduct to be viewed as the conduct of the fictional single entity. At this point, there is only 'one' participant in the illegal act rather than 'multiple' participants, and therefore, the issue of joint illegal acts does not arise.

A typical example of a single entity is the 'single economic entity' theory in antitrust law. Under this theory, multiple participants engaged in monopolistic behavior are regarded as a 'single economic entity,'[50] and while each participant maintains independent legal status, they do not compete with each other but form a coalition.[51] Common scenarios include relationships between the parent company and its subsidiaries and among parties involved in monopolistic agreements and so on. To give another example, in the case of an individual partnership that has not obtained a business license in accordance with the law, as stipulated in Article 15 of the 2018 Interpretation of the Supreme People's Court on Application of the Administrative Litigation Law of the People's Republic of China, shall such a situation arise in administrative penalties, the partnership should be treated as a single legal entity.

---

48 See *supra* note 23, 177.

49 See Liu Wuchao, 'Rethink on the Fine Rules for Monopoly Agreements and its Implementation' (2014) 5 *Chinese Public Administration* 110–111.

50 See *supra* note 1, 44.

51 See *supra* note 49, 110–111.

A single entity is a legal fiction whereby the legislature regards the participants as having a unified subjective intention and acting collectively as a cohesive entity in their external conduct. As a result, this entity is treated as a single party for the purpose of imposing penalties, emphasizing a closer association compared to joint illegal conduct. However, in appearance, punitive decisions concerning a single entity will separately specify each participant comprising the single entity and require them to bear joint liability. This resembles the 'joint liability for joint conduct' approach applied in cases of joint unlawful conduct. This clarification is provided to avoid confusion.

6. CONCLUSIONS

In conclusion, this chapter has discussed the criteria for identifying joint administrative violations and the rule of penalty decisions for such violations. Regarding the identification criteria, the chapter proposes the adoption of the 'joint conduct standard' based on the principle of culpability, ensuring accuracy and logical consistency in the recognition of joint illegal acts. This approach not only avoids the obstacles faced in implementing the absolute joint conduct standard in handling simultaneous offenses and conspiracies but also addresses the disconnection between the criteria for identification and penalty decisions found in the 'joint violation theory' and the omission of handling joint illegal acts involving individuals without capacity for responsibility. Moreover, by adopting such 'joint conduct standard' under the principle of culpability, the problem of logical barriers in determining joint illegal acts caused by the complete denial of responsibility is also prevented. On this basis, the chapter attempts to demonstrate the reasonableness of 'separate liability for joint conduct' as the rule for handling joint illegal acts and points out that when acting under the guidance of 'separate liability of joint conduct,' administrative authorities should issue separate penalty decisions with distinct document numbers for each participant for the purpose of ensuring convenient remedies for the participants. Additionally, the chapter provides clarification on special circumstances in the handling of joint violations. While the choice to adopt the principle of culpability in administrative penalties may appear to be a choice of values, it indeed has significant implications for the systematic theoretical construction and administrative law enforcement practices. This suggests that discussions on administrative penalties should not only focus on value choices but also conduct technical and detailed studies on actual law systems.

8. Singapore Convention on Mediation and the legislation of China's commercial mediation from the perspective of contextualism: a study on the mediation models

Xiong Hao

1. INTRODUCTION[1]

In 2018, after decades of negotiations and legislative discussions, the United Nations Commission on International Trade Law completed the drafting of the United Nations Convention on International Settlement Agreements Resulting from Mediation. The Convention is also known as the Singapore Convention on Mediation because it was signed in Singapore in 2019. By now, 53 countries have signed the Convention and 6 countries have ratified it.[2] "It creates a harmonized framework for cost-effective and prompt enforcement of international mediated settlement agreements, aiming to render mediation more efficient and attractive to commercial parties globally."[3] In the meantime, "[i]t

1 This chapter is the periodic outcome of the 2022 Shanghai Philosophy and Social Science Planning Annual Project "Study on the Development of Shanghai's Modern Commercial Mediation System from the Perspective of Singapore Convention on Mediation" (2022BFX007) and the National Social Science Fund Major Project "Research on the Modernization of Civil Judicial Procedures" (21&ZD206). When revising and perfecting this chapter, the author has received valuable advice and patient help from the editor-in-chief of *The Jurist* and anonymous external review experts, for which the author expresses his sincere gratitude.

2 See "2018 Singapore Convention on Mediation, International Arbitration", https://www.international-arbitration-attorney.com/2018-singapore-convention-on-mediation/, accessed 18 July 2021.

3 "Singapore Convention on Mediation", https://www.singaporeconvention.org/convention/about, accessed 25 September 2022.

is important that international commercial disputes in Asia be settled quickly and efficiently, given the expectation of an increase in the number of disputes in Asia with trade initiatives.'[4] Some researchers thus believe that the advent of the Convention marks a new stage of international commercial mediation which has an institutionalized and unified international legal mechanism, compared with the previous barbaric expansion of practice and multifarious rules.[5]

With a long history of mediation and widespread global interests, China actively participated in the draft of the Singapore Convention on Mediation and signed the Convention in 2019 as one of the first signatories. However, there are still many obstacles when China implements the Convention in its domestic mediation system, which could be solved, in most of the Chinese academic opinion, by adding norms as a part of the move to perfect the legal system. For example, some researchers suggest supplementing four categories of regulations to ensure that China's applicable laws could keep in line with the Convention, namely, specific procedural rules for applying for relief from settlement agreements, guidelines for mediation and mediators, proper law for settlement agreements, and regulations on the mediation of disputes.[6] Similarly, other scholars suggest that China needs to clearly stipulate the qualifications and abilities required for professional mediators, mediation norms, appointment and dismissal conditions, professional ethics, and disclosure standards. In the meantime, it is necessary to establish or perfect punishment rules for false mediation, eventually making up for the shortage of mediator norms under the current legal system.[7] There are also suggestions that China should put priority on judicial supervision of international mediation agreements and break through the confidentiality requirements of mediation procedures through public policy review, that is, reviewing and circumventing acts in international mediation agreements that may seriously infringe upon the

---

4 Eunice Chua, 'The Singapore Convention on Mediation-A Brighter Future for Asian Dispute Resolution' (2019) 9 (2) *Asian Journal of International Law* 204.

5 See Chen Meng, 'Establishment of China's Commercial Mediation Rules under the Background of the Singapore Convention on Mediation' (2021) 3 *Commercial Arbitration and Mediation* 17.

6 Ibid., 17.

7 See Bao Kangyun, 'The 'Latecomer Advantage' of the Singapore Convention on Mediation and China's Position' (2020) 6 *Wuhan University International Law Review* 35; Yang Anqi and Yang Shudong, 'The Practical Dilemma to Implement Singapore Convention on Mediation in China's Commercial Mediation System and the Ways to Solve it' (2022) 2 *Journal of Henan University of Economics and Law* 80.

substantive justice and basic interests of the State through substantive safeguards for the basic principles of law, fundamental interests of society, and good customs.[8] These suggestions are reasonable and do provide solid support for the localization of the Convention in China, yet insufficient regulations and norms are not the fundamental barrier that hinders the Convention from taking effect in China. Solely perceiving the challenges from a normative perspective mirrors a methodological misunderstanding, which attributes the obstacles of implementing international laws in China to a mere mismatch of regulations and systems. In such a methodological perspective, the social background, cultural habits, context of meaning, and ideology in which norms are implanted are ignored. In fact, dispute resolution should be seen as a kind of local knowledge and a cultural process, and its effectiveness depends on the integration of the rules and the social context in which they are embedded.[9]

During China's legalization of international rules, it is essential to reach the conformity between rules and context. Theoretically, such conformity between external rules and internal context can be subsumed by the concept of "cultural legitimacy", a prerequisite for the effective localization of international rules. It means, even though certain rights and norms have been procedurally recognized internationally, their authenticity and effectiveness still need to be examined from the perspective of "cultural legitimacy" to see whether they are accepted by the local society.[10] The rights, obligations, and practice methods confirmed at the text level from international norms need to be compatible with the local cultural context, reality, and time and space conditions, and the content of the norms needs to reflect the local society where they are embedded. Although the research path of normative jurisprudence or legal positivism is more universally recognized in the study of international law, it does not exclude the methodology of sociology of law or legal contextualism. According to Professor Gregory Shaffer and Professor Tom Ginsburg in 2012, "this scholarship tended to assume, rather than examine, the efficacy of international law and cooperation".[11] Thus, the international law study needs a "New Empirical Turn". It doesn't mean to construct a new grand narrative,

[8] See Sun Nanxiang, 'The Ratification and Implementation of the Singapore Convention on Mediation in China' (2021) 2 *Legal Studies* 171.

[9] See Guo Xinghua ed., *Legal Sociology Course* (Renmin University of China Press, 2015) 194–195.

[10] See Abdullahi Ahmed An-Na'im, 'Problems of Universal Cultural Legitimacy for Human Rights', in A. An-Na'im and F. Deng, eds., *Human Rights in Africa: Cross-Cultural Perspectives* (The Brookings Institution, 1990) 333–334.

[11] See Gregory Shaffer and Tom Ginsburg, 'The Empirical Turn in International Legal Scholarship' (2012) 106 (1) *The American Journal of International Law* 2–3.

but to establish a medium-range theory which focuses on the conditions and prerequisites for international law to play its true role in different realities. In this way, academic analysis can be set in the three dimensions of "empirical findings", "abstract theorizing" and "real-world testing", eventually narrowing the distance between theory, experience and practice.[12] Such a methodological turn enables international law and the context-based sociology of law to converge in fundamental orientation, which prompts us to examine specific legal theories and institutional settings in the Chinese context of time and space. It is necessary indeed to keep eyes on the written norms, but merely making up for the shortage of norms and matching the written expressions are far from enough to ensure a true domestication of international conventions. We need to be aware that a specific system rooted in a certain time and space is the product of that cultural context. Therefore, the domestic legalization of the Convention in China will inevitably involve a mediation model adapted to the Chinese context. This chapter is established on the normative differences in the definition of mediation in different legal systems, and then analyzes the contextual embedding of the dispute resolution mechanism, as well as the actual impact of the contextual characteristics of contemporary society and culture on Chinese dispute resolution practices. At last, from the position of China and referring to Singapore's legislative experience, the author attempts to design and construct the basic positioning and normative content of China's commercial mediation legislation in the balance and accommodation of the Chinese context and international standards.

2. MEDIATION MODES IN DIFFERENT LEGAL SYSTEMS

In 1996, according to the mediator's strategic characteristics and behavior in the mediation process, Professor Leonard L. Riskin proposed two modes of mediation: Evaluative Mediation and Facilitative Mediation. This classification has important typological significance and has a profound impact on mediation research. In evaluative mediation, the mediator proactively intervenes as an expert in dispute resolution, using his own knowledge and experience to substantially influence the dispute resolution process and results. In facilitative mediation, the mediator's role is to establish procedures and facilitate communication, and he will not intervene or exert substantial influence on the parties' judgment and decision-making, which features a "Negatively Effective" behavior. Professor Leonard L. Riskin pointed out that in an extreme evaluative mediation, the mediator will instruct and manipulate some or all of the

12 Ibid., 1.

conclusions and effects of mediation, while in an extreme assisting mediation, the mediator will simply request the parties to negotiate and understand each other.[13] It is thus easy to draw the conclusion that classifying mediation as evaluative and facilitative does not truly reflect the real mediation process, but construct theoretically a set of "ideal mediation types" that are mutually dialectical. In real mediation practice, the process of mediation is an intertwined evaluation and assistance to varying degrees; that is, evaluation and assistance are integrated in practice rather than opposed to each other.

Although in legal practice evaluative mediation and facilitative mediation are differentiated by the mediator's intervention, different legal systems do have different emphases on these two mediation modes. For example, in a rather long history, facilitative mediation has been the mainstream paradigm of mediation in the Anglo-American world, and its basic concepts have had a profound impact on the construction of Western mediation rules and ethical norms.[14] Under the facilitative mediation model in these legal systems, mediators are required not to provide their own opinions to the parties. There are two reasons for this requirement. First, from the perspective of the parties, the core of mediation is the autonomy of the parties, which is unlike the authoritative judgment of the court. The mediator's evaluative intervention will conflict with such a requirement of autonomy. Second, from the mediator's perspective, mediators need to abide by strict neutrality, which mediators will deviate from when making suggestions for the parties based on their own experience and knowledge.[15] Although the paradigm dominance of facilitative mediation encountered dual challenges from mediation practice and academic research in the 1980s and 1990s,[16] and there was a tendency towards harmonicity, its

[13] See Leonard L. Riskin, 'Understanding Mediators' Orientations, Strategies, and Techniques: A Grid for the Perplexed' (1997) 1 (7) *Harvard Negotiation Law Review* 23–24.

[14] See Roger Seaman, *Explorative Mediation at Work: The Importance of Dialogue for Mediation Practice* (Palgrave Macmillan, 2016) 4; Heather Conway et al., *The Emotional Dynamics of Law and Legal Discourse* (Hart Publishing, 2016) 215; Katina Foster, 'A Study in Mediation Styles: A Comparative Analysis of Evaluative and Transformative Styles', https://www.mediate.com/articles/fosterk1.cfm, accessed 10 November 2021.

[15] See Ellen A. Waldman, 'The Evaluative-Facilitative Debate in Mediation: Applying the Lens of Therapeutic Jurisprudence' (1998) 82 (1) *Marquette Law Review* 156–157.

[16] The critique of facilitated mediation is multidimensional. For example, in practice, since mediation is a complex process of interpersonal interaction, there is a transition spectrum from narrow evaluative mediation to narrow facilitative mediation, so it is impossible to just "assist" in practice. After all, the boundary between "suggestion" and "control" is very blurred in legal practices. Second, the

basic value still affects the rhetorical description and behavioral regulation of mediation in the legislation of Western countries. For example, in the model law, the Uniform Mediation Act of the US issued in 2001, mediation is defined as "a process in which a mediator facilitates communication and negotiation between parties to assist them in reaching a voluntary agreement regarding their dispute."[17] In the Australian National Mediation Standard, the restrictions on the conduct of mediators are more clearly expressed. The standard stipulates that "mediators do not advise upon, evaluate or determine disputes. They assist in managing the process of dispute and conflict resolution whereby the participants agree upon the outcomes, when appropriate. Mediation is essentially a process that maximizes the self determination of the participants. The principle of self-determination requires that mediation processes be non-directive as to content."[18] In Hong Kong, China, the legislation on mediation strictly follows the path of facilitative mediation. Article 4 of the Mediation Ordinance in Hong Kong, China clearly stipulates the boundaries and specific content of the mediator's behavior: mediation is a structured process comprising one or more sessions in which one or more impartial individuals, without adjudicating a dispute or any aspect of it, assist the parties to the dispute to do any or all of the following: (a) identify the issues in dispute; (b) explore and generate options; (c) communicate with one another; (d) reach an agreement

---

setting of facilitative mediation constitutes a standard framework for mediation, while the insistence on a specific mediation model actually ignores the diversity of mediation practices in different jurisdictions. See Dorcas Quek Anderson, 'Facilitative Versus Evaluative Mediation: Is There Necessarily a Dichotomy?' (2013) 66 *Asian Journal on Mediation* 69.

[17] It is worth mentioning that the "assistance" and "facilitation" were further explained in the legislative description of the U.S. Uniform Mediation Act drafted by the National Uniform State Law Committee. By "assistance", as distinguished from an arbitration process, it means the mediator shall not forcibly make a decision. For "facilitation", the legislator stated that this is not a preference for a specific mediation style, and that the legislator recognizes the diversity of mediation methods. See https://www.uniformlaws.org/HigherLogic/System/Download-DocumentFile.ashx?DocumentFileKey=9b244b42-269c-769e-9f89-590ce048d0dd&forceDialog=0, accessed 11 November 2021. It should be noted that this interpretation makes the U.S. Uniform Mediation Act reflect the conciliation theory of the mediation model, but the typical behavior and legislative wording of "evaluative mediation" have not been adopted in the definition of mediation in the legislative text.

[18] Quoted from Zhao Yun, *Mediation Practice and Skills* (Tsinghua University Press, 2011) 101.

regarding the resolution of the whole, or part, of the dispute.[19] To complement it, the Mediation Code in Hong Kong, China clearly stipulates the scope of the mediator's responsibilities and provides two-way guidance for the mediator's behavior by making a "positive list" and a "negative list":

> The Mediator will be neutral and impartial. The Mediator will assist the Parties to attempt to resolve the Dispute by helping them to: (a) systematically isolate the issues in dispute; (b) develop options for the resolution of these issues; and (c) explore the usefulness of these options to meet their interests and needs. The Mediator will not: (a) give legal or other professional advice to any Party; or (b) impose a result on any Party; or (c) make decisions for any Party.[20]

In contrast to the above-mentioned mediation legislation, the People's Mediation Law of the People's Republic of China defines mediation as: The people's mediation stated in this law refers to the activities of the people's mediation committee that *resolve* civil disputes by *promoting* the parties to voluntarily reach an agreement on the basis of equal consultation through methods such as *persuasion* and *counseling*. (Emphasis added by the author.) Even though people's mediation is considered to have the attribute of citizen autonomy and is participated in by citizens out of their own will, in terms of the definition of "mediation", the laws of the Chinese mainland still use wording that has overt intervening connotation. In other words, the normative texts of Chinese mainland laws use more intrusive and proactive expressions, which enable mediators to obtain a substantive power to intervene in the dispute resolution process. Such a basic setting of "assessment-based mediation" is also very obvious in the more recent local legislation in the Chinese mainland. For example, Article 24 of the Shanghai Municipal Regulations on Promoting Diversified Resolution of Conflicts and Disputes, which took effect in 2021, stipulates: "People's mediation organizations shall, on the basis of equal consultation, mutual understanding and mutual accommodation, *propose* conflict resolution solutions to *help* parties voluntarily reach an agreement." (Emphasis added by the author.) In other words, the legislation in the Chinese mainland allows mediators, as an active subject, to substantively intervene in the process of dispute resolution by "proposing a solution to conflicts and disputes".

The mediation in the Chinese mainland is more inclined to the "evaluative mediation" mode, which widely affects various mediation forms such as people's mediation, administrative mediation, lawyer mediation, and judicial

---

[19] Mediation Ordinance in Hong Kong, China, https://www.elegislation.gov.hk/hk/cap620!sc?xpid=ID_1438403538324_001, accessed 20 June 2021. The emphasis is added by the author.

[20] Hong Kong Mediation Code, http://www.hkmaal.org.hk/sc/HongKongMediationCode.php, accessed 20 June 2021.

mediation. Even if we only look at the relatively high-end and professional commercial mediation, it is easy to find that the relatively leading commercial mediation institutions in the Chinese mainland adopt a model that is nothing like the facilitative mediation in the West. When defining "mediation", commercial mediation institutions in the Chinese mainland hope to retain the power of mediators to substantively intervene in the dispute resolution on the premise of respecting the autonomy of the parties, rather than restricting such power to the utmost. For example, the Mediator's Code by Beijing International Arbitration Center stipulates: "The mediator should fully respect the autonomy of the parties in the mediation procedures and mediation results, and *use their creativity and experience to actively guide the mediation procedure, best meeting the parties' needs according to the specific dispute*."[21] Similarly, the Mediator's Code by the Shanghai Economic, Trade and Commercial Mediation Center stipulates that "mediators shall not force the parties to reach a settlement agreement", but the Code also rules that mediators should not only be satisfied with a "Negatively Effective" role; instead, they "should *guide* the parties to gradually reduce differences and reach a settlement agreement on the basis of mutual understanding and accommodation, *by insisting 'business is business and harmony is priceless in business'*."[22] In the above-mentioned two codes of mediator's conduct, there are no prohibitive provisions similar to those in other legal systems that prohibit mediators from substantively intervening in the dispute process.

3. THE CONTEXTUAL EMBEDDING OF NON-LITIGATION DISPUTE RESOLUTION PRACTICE IN CHINA

3.1 The Contextual Embedding of Non-Litigation Dispute Resolution Mechanism

We need to be aware that the aforementioned normative differences are generated because of different mediation contexts. Context was originally a literary definition, referring to the linguistic and semantic environment of discourse, and later developed more broader concepts – "It not only refers to the above

---

21 Rules for Mediators, Beijing International Arbitration Center, https://www.bjac.org.cn/#/mediation/1907621161514704897/1910512879302078466?categoryId=1910512879302078466, accessed 19 June 2021. The emphasis is added by the author.

22 Rules for Mediators, Shanghai Economic, Trade and Commercial Mediation Center, http://www.scmc.org.cn/page67?article_id=209&_l=en&menu_id=98, accessed 19 June 2021. The emphasis is added by the author.

and following sentences, paragraphs, and a specific text in an article, but also refers to an explanatory theory paradigm, a specific historical period and background, or the factors of all social, historical, cultural, scientific, political, psychological and many other areas and the entire facts of their interrelationships and interactions."[23] In jurisprudence, contextually examining a norm or institution is both a method and a value proposition. Context-based research requires researchers to understand the legitimacy and rationality of a long-standing system and norms in a historical context, emphasizing the interactions between the system and the social environment in which it is embedded. Also, researchers need to build their analysis on the relatively stable factors such as the natural endowment, natural environment, social productivity, technological development, and resources, and then provide specific suggestions on institutions and rules, finally explaining the legitimacy of such institutions and rules based on the social condition changes that have happened or are expected to happen soon.[24]

Social and cultural contexts have an impact on both litigation and non-litigation mechanisms, but the impact on non-litigation mechanisms is more obvious, and the contextual perspective is especially important when we examine non-litigation dispute resolution mechanisms. This is because although the judiciary is deeply rooted in culture in terms of institutional structure, litigation is expected to "not directly adjust the interests and behaviors of those individual existences, but use rational reasoning to form various formalized legal concepts and categories, and then apply these formalized concepts and categories to those social relations that need to be adjusted by law through judicial activities."[25] In practice, the judicial operation is relatively separated from social life, with highly specialized institutional settings, and legal professionals make independent, professional, and technically standardized decisions in accordance with unified logical norms.[26] The rational, logical, and conceptual institutional structure will produce the objective consequences of "dehumanization", which to a certain extent inhibits the initiation of a vivid, concrete, and dynamic social and cultural context in the litigation process. Compared with litigation, the contextual meaning in non-litigation dispute resolution will be

23 Guo Guichun and Liu Junxiang, 'Gadamer's Viewpoint on Context of Understanding' (2000) 7 *Research on Dialectics of Nature* 2.

24 See Su Li, 'Contextualism – An Approach and Method for the Study of Legal System' (2000) 1 *Chinese and Foreign Law* 41.

25 He Bosheng, *Mathematical Interpretation of Legal Culture* (The Commercial Press, 2015) 206.

26 See Simon Roberts and Michael Parmer Peng, *The Process of Dispute Resolution: ADR and the Primary Forms of Decision-Making* (2nd Edition), translated by Liu Zhewei (Peking University Press, 2011) 14.

more direct and obvious because the procedural structure, interpersonal interaction, and the formation of the final agreement are more comprehensively and deeply influenced by individual "humans". If the right of voluntary participation of the parties is guaranteed and more intervention of the parties' free will is allowed in the non-litigation process, then the participants' cognitive and cultural preferences and social values will not be screened or blocked by the rational, logical, and conceptual standard structure, and thus the participants will exert a more realistic impact on the dispute resolution. Because of this, Professor Sally Engle Merry clearly pointed out that non-litigation disputes cannot be regarded as "disembodied events separated from the social world", and disputes are endowed by the cultural and social context. Dimensions of meaning (including the meaning of procedure, the meaning of fairness, the involvement and ranking of certain values and morality, the recognition of disputes going from private to public, the preference for the meaning of interpersonal relationships among conflicting parties, and the understanding and cognition of rights) will make disputes and the process of dispute resolution necessarily have contextual characteristics, and make dispute resolution a cultural behavior that is highly related to the issue of meaning.[27] Therefore, in the real non-litigation dispute resolution process, it is a typical mistake to expect using a set of standardized toolboxes to provide a simplified text specification while losing the sensitivity and understanding of the delicate nature of dispute nature and the social environment in which the dispute is embedded.[28] It is in this sense that mediation is a local practice, a specific cultural behavior, and the selection and establishment of mediation models requires the intervention of a "local perspective" such as contextualism. Only in this way can the conceptual framework and order structure existing in the text be properly settled in the practical process of non-litigation dispute resolution.

3.2 Induction of Context in Contemporary China and Embedding of Non-Litigation Dispute Resolution Mechanism

As mentioned above, non-litigation dispute resolution is not a logical application of text norms, but a process of generating contextual meanings. The preference of ancient Chinese people to deal with disputes in a non-confrontational way has been contextually explained by modern scholars from multiple perspectives. According to these explanations, in the economic dimension, it is due to the rigid demand of the peasant economy for continuous interpersonal

---

27 See Sally Engle Merry, 'Book Review: *Dispute without Culture*' (1987) 100 (8) *Harvard Law Review* 2063.

28 Ibid., 2060.

coordination within the community;[29] in the political dimension, it is due to the need for social control arising from the maintenance of unified imperial power in a centralized society,[30] and the need to reach grassroots for the realization of ruling power;[31] in the cultural dimension, it is due to the great emphasis on values of collectivism and order such as "harmony" and "ethics and rituals" in traditional Chinese culture.[32] It is the combined influence of the above-mentioned facts that eventually led to a cultural character of the Chinese people who "like mediation but disgust disputes" when resolving disputes in traditional society.[33] But we need to be aware that society is constantly developing and changing. Compared with ancient China, the social structure and cultural appearance of contemporary China have undergone tremendous changes. When analyzing the social and cultural context in which China's dispute resolution mechanism is embedded, it is necessary to go beyond the a priori and speculative analytical framework of peasant economy, imperial power politics, and Confucian ethics, and then to provide a more contemporary interpretation of the context theory for the institutional structure of non-litigation dispute resolution based on the social and cultural reality of contemporary China.

When describing, comparing, and measuring the cultures of different countries, the famous Dutch psychologist Geert Hofstede has made important contributions by presenting his cultural dimensions theory. According to Hofstede, culture refers to "the common mental process of people in an environment. Culture is not an individual characteristic, but includes the characteristics of a group of people created by the same education and life experience."[34] Hofstede and his collaborators divided six dimensions to quantitatively analyze the cultures of different countries, endowing cultural studies

---

29 See You Chenjun, 'The Influence of Confucian Moral Views on Traditional Chinese Litigation Culture' (2018) 3 *Law Science* 144.

30 See Phillip M. Chen, *Law and Justice: The Legal System in China 2400 B.C. To 1960 A.D.* (Dunellen Publishing Co., 1973) 7.

31 See Qiang Shigong, 'Culture, Function and Governance – Three Paradigms for the Study of China's Mediation System' (2003) 2 *Tsinghua Law* 154–155.

32 See Albert H.Y. Chen, 'Mediation, Litigation and Justice: Confucian Reflections in Modern Liberal Society', in Daniel A. Bell and Hahm Chaibong, eds., *Confucianism for the Modern World* (Cambridge University Press, 2003) 260.

33 See Xu Xin ed., *Mediation: China and the World* (China University of Political Science and Law Press, 2013) 45; Yu Yuhe, 'On the historical roots and negative effects of the 'no-litigation' legal tradition' (2000) 1 *The Jurist* 113–116.

34 Geert Hofstede, 'Motivation, Leadership, and Organization: Do American Theories Apply Abroad?', in Steve Mortensen ed., *Cross-cultural Communication: An Eastern Perspective*, translated by Guan Shijie and Hu Xing, (China Social Sciences Press, 1999) 2.

a contemporary dimension and scientific significance. These six dimensions are: a) Power distance (refers to the degree of acceptance of hierarchy; lower scores represent higher acceptance of hierarchy and stronger recognition of the role of social hierarchy playing in social management and power operation); b) individualism and collectivism; c) masculinity and femininity (not referring to the biological sex. Masculinity represents tenacity, self-confidence, and the pursuit of achievement, while femininity represents humility, gentleness, care for life, and pursuit of happiness); d) attitude towards uncertainty; e) long-term orientation; f) indulgence.[35] Through these six important dimensions, Hofstede turned the abstract and intangible culture into human mental models and behavioral preferences, making "human" the realistic carrier of culture. Based on the Chinese data dynamically accumulated by Hofstede Insights, in the dimension of power distance, Chinese people accept the hierarchical order of bureaucracy and individuals are more easily influenced by authority; in the dimension of individualism and collectivism, China is a country with a very strong collectivism, and Chinese people are more willing to establish a sense of belonging and a cognitive framework from the perspective of "us", that is, the perspective of group; in the dimension of masculinity, Chinese people pursue the sense of accomplishment more than happiness and comfort, working relentlessly in exchange for more income rather than more leisure; in the dimension of avoiding uncertainty, Chinese people believe that rules can be flexible and believe in pragmatism in life; in the dimension of long-term orientation, Chinese people believe that the truth depends on the certain historical background and needs to be discussed accordingly, and they are willing to make plans and even sacrifice for the future, in order to better achieve the goal; in the dimension of indulgence, China's society restrains desires, and individual behavior is subject to evident social discipline.[36] If we look at the above dimensions at an international scale, then the contextual characteristics of Chinese culture will be more evident. From the data in Figure 8.1, it is easy to find that compared with Brazil, Germany, and the United States, China has obvious differences in five dimensions, which means Chinese people have the highest acceptance of authority, the strongest collectivism, flexibility, and inclination to long-term value, and Chinese people are most easily influenced by social discipline and thus get self-restrained. As culture is divided into six dimensions in a more detailed manner under Hofstede's theoretical framework, one single definition is not able to encompass the full contextual characteristics of contemporary Chinese culture. However, based on the above analysis, we can

[35] See Jean-Pierre Cohen and Marc Jacobs, *Negotiate Like a Local*, translated by Wang Kaihua (Fudan University Press, 2019) 122.

[36] See "China, Hofstede Insights", https://geerthofstede.com/country-comparison-bar-charts/, accessed 8 November 2021.

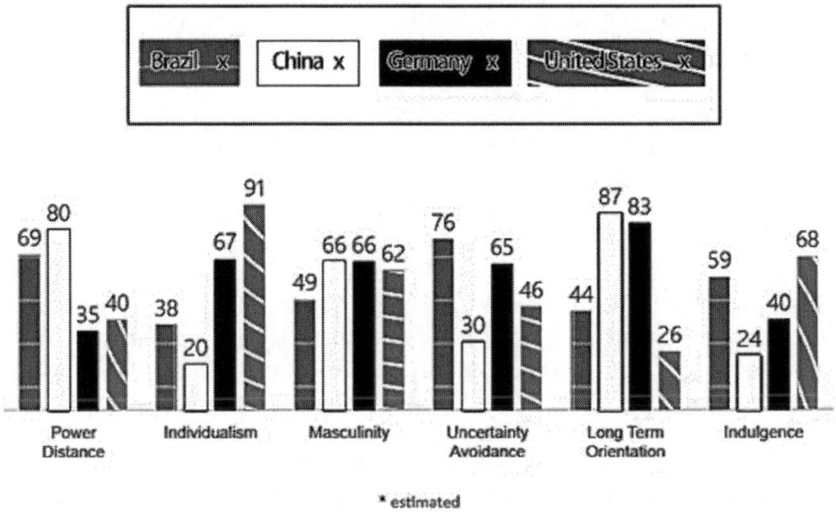

Note: The original picture is a color version.
Source: "Country Comparison, Hofstede Insights", https://www.hofstede-insights.com/country-comparison/brazil, China, Germany, the USA/, accessed 21 June 2021.

Figure 8.1 *A comparison of Hofstede's cultural dimensions in Brazil, China, Germany and the US*

draw the conclusion that the social and cultural context of contemporary China has a clear preference for "trust in authority" and "dependence on society".

Admittedly, there might be one critical question on the above conclusion: as human independent value and individualism grow significantly in China since the reform and opening-up, will the "trust in authority" and "dependence on society" be undermined? The author believes that it does not mean China's fundamental cultural structure has undergone an essential change towards individualism despite that China has seen a growing individual value and dependence, which in turn enriches Chinese culture. On one side, based on Hofstede's data analysis, culture, as an ultra-stable structure, evolves and changes very slowly, and will maintain a high stability for quite a long period of time. On the other side, the social surveys in China over the recent years have further confirmed the judgment on cultural stability. For example, in the "Interpersonal Values" section of the Survey on Contemporary Chinese Social Values launched by the Chinese Academy of Social Sciences in 2013, 42% of interviewees believed that "the relationship between people is interdependent, and other people are essential to my own success", which is the largest proportion when answering the question "how is the relationship between people in society".[37] Even if we focus on the younger generation in contemporary China, the interviewees born in the 1980s or 1990s recognize the overall, long-term, and community-based core values (such as social stability and national prosperity) significantly more than those core values of individualism and independence (such as participation in decision-making and freedom of speech). Thus, there is an argument that the Chinese younger generations hold a very different view on their world value compared to their counterparts in Western countries. The group value does not disappear against the backdrop of a growing individualism, and China hasn't seen a large-scale postmodern contempt or denial of tradition and authority that once appeared in the West.[38]

Based on the contextual characteristics of "trust in authority" and "dependence on society", the Chinese dispute resolution mechanism also reveals corresponding embedded features in both micro and macro aspects.

In the micro dimension of mediation, the parties to disputes in China are often regarded as embedded in a network of social relations rather than highly isolated and atomized individuals. From this perspective, resolving disputes is not only simply negotiating at the table but also involving a broader community that connects with the parties.[39] Therefore, there is close attention to and control of externalities in China's mediation model, so as to prevent disputes from impacting collective relations and social order. Based on such philosophy, as Fei Xiaotong observed in the first half of the 20th century, the Chinese mediation model expected mediators to actually intervene in the substantive process of dispute resolution with their own comments and criticism, rather than a simple resolution with the passive assistance of the mediator. The dispute resolution model is essentially a process of "reasoning".[40] In contemporary China, such a "criticizing-and-educating" mediation model remains and continues to affect the practice of dispute resolution. Even after the founding of the People's Republic of China in 1949 to today, China's mediation still relies on local authority figures such as officials of the CPC or the Communist Youth League, police, bureaucrats, and labor union activists, rather than profes-

37 See Sun Weiping ed., *Research Report on Social Values in Contemporary China* (China Social Sciences Press, 2013) 190–191.

38 See Bao Leiping, Cheng Fucai, et al., *Deep Modernization: Value Conflict and Identity of "Post-80s" and "Post-90s" Groups* (Shanghai Academy of Social Sciences Press, 2020) 9.

39 See Catherine H. Tinsley, 'Culture and Conflict: Enlarging Our Dispute Resolution Framework', in Michele J. Gelfand and Jeanne M. Brett, eds., *The Handbook of Negotiation and Culture* (Stanford University Press, 2004) 199–200.

40 See Feixiaotong, *From the Soil – The Foundations of Chinese Society* (People's Publishing House, 2015) 69.

sionals.[41] These authority figures' engagement in the mediation embodies the "trust in authority" in China's dispute resolution and also consequently brings the "criticizing-and-educating" nature into the mediation process. Some more detailed empirical studies on the mediation process have further confirmed the stability and persistence of this social and cultural influence. According to James A. Wall, Jr. and Michael Blum, in contemporary China, "educating" is the most common strategy adopted by people's mediators, with a usage rate of 0.55 times average per case. In contrast, "mediator assist" is used only 0.21 times per case.[42] The mediators will teach the parties what to do and what they should do, and their work has the meaning of social education in spite of the personal settlement of disputes. The mediator's authoritative intervention in the dispute resolution preserves the "trust in authority", a contextual feature of contemporary China's dispute resolution, in each specific and individual dispute resolution. As for commercial mediation, though there are few in-depth descriptions and analyses in the Chinese mainland, we can still find that mediators' active intervention is commonly seen in the hands-on experience of some commercial mediation practitioners. For example, mediators will guide parties to clarify their responsibilities, seek common ground while reserving differences, and eventually reach a consensus.[43] "The mediator verified on the spot the authenticity of the goods delivered by the respondent through the internet, and contacted the freight forwarding company to confirm the authenticity of the ocean bill of lading";[44] "The mediation center listened carefully to the introductions of both parties, conducted on-the-spot investigations on the leased site, and consulted the local government. It believed that: the subject of the contract signed by the two parties and the agreed rental price violated the law and the rental market at that time ... So, the mediation center pointed out to both parties that the respondent has broken the law by cutting off the applicant's water and electricity supply, and restricting the applicant to purchasing raw materials from other companies. In the meantime, the center also argued that the main body of applicant is not qualified when leasing the respondent's land and building.'[45] There are plenty of such cases. From the above description of the commercial mediation in China's mainland, we can easily find the active and positive intervention of mediators. When lawyers summarize the

---

41 *Supra* note 33, 4–5.

42 See James A. Wall, Jr. & Michael Blum, "Community Mediation in the People's Republic of China", *Journal of Conflict Resolution*, Vol. 35, No. 1 (1991), p. 14.

43 See He Guicai, *Comments on Foreign-related Commercial Mediation Cases*, (Guangming Daily Publishing House, 2013) p. 34.

44 *Supra* note 43, 56.

45 *Supra* note 43, 66.

practical methods they use in commercial mediation, such as "comprehensive understanding and field study", "leveraging authority, and introducing the third party", "signing contract and then following up implementation", it vividly shows their intervening role as the third party in commercial mediation in China's mainland.[46] Therefore, in the micro dimension of China's mediation, due to the social and cultural context, mediation is not a personal choice of behavior or an assistance to the formation of consensus, but a process that requires the mediator's intervention and education to maintain interpersonal relationships and clarify behavioral meaning. This endows dispute resolution in contemporary China with a social position beyond its function to "smooth differences between individuals".

In the macro dimension of mediation policy, due to the contextual feature of "dependence on society", Chinese people expect to minimize the social interference of disputes and prevent disputes from affecting social order and community harmony. For this purpose, Social Power is allowed to intervene in the private dispute resolution.[47] Reviewing the policy design of non-litigation dispute resolution in China in recent years, we can easily find that the understanding of dispute resolution from the institutional perspective at the national level has gone beyond the pure "private resolution of conflicts". Dispute resolution is playing the role of maintaining social stability and sustainable harmony by broadening and extending the state's intervention and empowerment in dispute resolution. The so-called "systematic governance", "overall governance", and "source governance", in spite of resolving disputes from the parties' perspective, also expect to mine the structural factors and contextual influences that lead to conflicts and disputes through effective governance, thus analyzing disputes in the long-term sequence of "anticipation, prevention, mediation, negotiation, resolution, and settlement" and the large social system. Therefore, in the relevant work requirements of the Supreme People's Court and the All-China Federation of Industry and Commerce to promote the mediation development of chambers of commerce, the more proactive and interventional mediation model is also placed in a prominent position – "Proactively investigate and monitor enterprise and industry disputes and give early warning, and strengthen the source governance of conflicts and disputes."[48] Furthermore, the above-mentioned policy evolution of China's dispute resolution institution

---

46 See Shenzhen Lawyers Association ADR Legal Professional Committee, *The Reshaping of Commercial Mediation by Lawyer Mediation* (Law Press, 2019) 199, 212, 213.

47 *Supra* note 39, 199–200.

48 "Notice of the Supreme People's Court and China Federation of Industry and Commerce on Issuing Opinions on Using the Advantages of Chambers of Commerce in Mediation to Promote a Diversified Dispute Resolution Mechanism

is mainly driven by the authority of the state. China's non-litigation dispute resolution institution is more or less semi-official. Its responsibility is to help the parties resolve interpersonal conflicts and, at the same time, eliminate disharmonious factors in society for the state through different dispute resolution mechanisms, so as to ultimately realize social governance.[49] It is also in this sense that the main driver behind the evolution of China's mediation institution after the reform and opening-up comes from top-down official (political) forces. For example, during Hu Jintao's term of office as China's president, "harmonious society" became the dominant ideological discourse. Under such political requirements, the Supreme People's Court began to promote the judicial policy that prefers closing cases by mediation and encouraged transformation towards mediation in dispute resolution. In the new era of socialism with Chinese characteristics, the emphasis on "Fengqiao Experience" (枫桥经验) has made the comprehensive and people-oriented grassroots social governance model an important driving force for a new round of mediation development. Therefore, the transition of China's mediation institution has a fundamental difference in the logic of occurrence and the source of motivation with the bottom-up ADR social movement that "attempts to empower the parties to disputes through various non-insitutional mechanisms and methods to strengthen their self-control, autonomy and self-determination over social life"[50] in the United States.

To sum up, whether in the micro or macro dimension, it is not difficult to find there is an obvious trust in authority and dependence on society in China's dispute resolution; that is, from the perspective of community survival and sustainability, order stability, environmental stability, and overall development to understand and perceive disputes and dispute resolution. In this perspective, the externalities of real disputes and conflicts are bound to co-exist, and the process of resolving conflicts and disputes opens up possibilities to impact social stability, social harmony, and even doubt the governance capacity of public power. These externalities need to be effectively managed in the Chinese social context. It is precisely because of this that the externalities of disputes and conflicts will be magnified and valued in the Chinese context,

in the Private Economy" (January 28, 2019), http://gongbao.court.gov.cn/Details/478131c77e3544a3104a7dd2d19d6c.html, accessed 9 November 2021.

49 See Ching Kwan Lee & Yonghong Zhang, 'Unraveling the Microfoundations of Bargained Authoritarianism in China' (2013) 188 (6) *American Journal of Sociology* 1480, 1496.

50 Xiong Hao, 'American ADR Movement from the Perspective of Sociology of Knowledge – Based on the Dual Perspective of Institutional History and Intellectual History' (2016) 1 *Global Law Review* 28.

and are even endowed with political attributes in the name of collectivism.[51] Although what most disputes mainly involve are still internal dimensions remaining within the parties, such as interest concerns, rights and obligations, emotional states, and realistic claims, Chinese culture is sensitive to the externalities of disputes and conflicts, giving disputes and conflicts integrated features that go beyond the parties. This makes the community, society, and even the country a stakeholder in a private dispute. Therefore, if representatives of authority and communities (whether they are judges, grassroots officials, social authorities, or any other power that can represent social interests to a certain extent) are completely absent in the mediation structure, or are not able to exert external force to intervene in dispute resolution, and they only serve as a passive and restrained procedural facilitator and communicator, then how can we guide and control the externalities of these disputes that may have an impact on social order and harmonious values? It is in the cultural and social context of "trust in authority" and "dependence on society" that we can understand why China is inclined to adopt an "evaluative mediation" model for a long time, understand the deep-down reason for an administration-and-judici alization-oriented mediation model in legal practices,[52] understand why the mediation system in China is not carried out in the form of individual mediation as expected in the Singapore Mediation Convention, but in the form of an organization, and understand that the judgment that "the limited application of mediator-led mediation is determined by the fact that China is still in a transition period, and the author believes this is only a temporary phenomenon"[53] may underestimate the great inertia of culture and the realistic characteristics of the social and cultural context in contemporary China.

4. "SINGAPORE EXPERIENCE" AND THE INSTITUTIONAL STRUCTURE OF COMMERCIAL MEDIATION IN CHINA FROM THE PERSPECTIVE OF CONTEXTUALISM

As mentioned above, on the issue of recognizing and implementing the Singapore Convention on Mediation and the institutional issue of Chinese commercial mediation arising therefrom, no matter what measures are adopted by China's laws, there are questions that can never be bypassed: what is mediation

51 See Su Li, 'Legalism, Public Opinion, and Difficult Cases' (2009) 1 *Chinese and Foreign Law* 105.

52 See Fan Yu, 'Comment on the People's Mediation Law of the People's Republic of China' (2011) 2 *The Jurist* 8.

53 Liao Yong'an et al., *Concept Innovation and Mechanism Reshaping of Chinese Mediation* (Renmin University of China Press, 2019) 82.

in the Chinese context, and what is the meaning and function of mediation in the Chinese context? This is the ontological issue of mediation laws, and the specific norms are designed on this basis. Therefore, the various tensions between the specific institutional settings for commercial mediation in China and abroad, as well as the paths for the domestication of the Convention, are actually based on different perceptions of this fundamental issue. Even if we adopt a dual legislative model that separates China's domestic mediation and international mediation, that is, to set independent regulations on international commercial mediation involved in the Convention, the fundamental issue of mediation still needs an answer. This is because, on the one hand, the regulations on mediation in China's mainland are scattered in different departmental laws, and none of them have clearly defined commercial mediation, which creates uncertainties on the fundamental issue of commercial mediation.[54] So, the issue cannot be avoided and must be answered. On the other hand, even in the dual legislative model, the specific design of norms and regulations such as the definition of mediation, basic principles, procedures, styles, and personnel qualifications are built on the response to this fundamental issue. We should be aware that people in different cultural contexts are inclined to different approaches to dispute resolution when they encounter conflicts.[55] This is not only the contextual feature of the system, but also the cultural preference and cultural rights of the parties in resolving disputes. This preference should not be erased in the Western-centric cognitive framework and legal-centric settings. Therefore, as to the suggestions for China's domestic legalization of the Convention, such as referring to the practices of mediator qualification and certification in Hong Kong, China for an institutional supplement,[56] or adjusting and reforming the inconsistent part between China's traditional culture and the mediation concept of the Convention,[57] whether these suggestions are appropriate, realistic, and what the specific implementation path is, all need to be responded to on the ground of figuring out "what exactly is Chinese mediation embedded in its cultural and social context".

---

54 See Feng Zihan, 'The Conflict and Response between the Singapore Convention on Mediation and the Chinese Legal System' (2022) 2 *Huxiang Law Review* 111.

55 See Sandra V. Sandy, Susan K. Boardman and Morton Deutsch, 'Personality and Conflict', in Morton Deutsch and Peter T. Coleman, eds., *The Handbook of Conflict Resolution: Theory and Practice* (Jossey-Bass Publishers, 2000) 344.

56 See Zhang Yan, Fang Xin, 'Research on the Execution of China's Commercial Mediation Agreements under the Singapore Convention on Mediation' (2021) 5 *Law Forum* 45.

57 *Supra* note 7, Yang Anqi and Yang Shudong, 78.

In the realistic context of contemporary China, "trust in authority and dependence on society" is widely accepted as a mental value and lifestyle, which makes "order" a much-expected existence and natural demand. To create and maintain order, the dispute resolution institution will accept the intervention of authority and take the society or community as an implicit stakeholder (an indirect dispute resolution participant), which makes the dispute resolution obtain more attributes beyond the single dimension of atomized individual. It is precisely because of this contextual embedding that we can see that the occurrence and development of China's non-litigation dispute resolution institution is obviously different from that in the West. Therefore, on the premise of recognizing the social and cultural contextual characteristics of China's non-litigation dispute resolution institution, we need to create a legislative structure that balances the Chinese context and the Singapore Convention on Mediation in the legislative design.

One general and integrated legislative strategy on the basis of the above ideas is: on the premise of fully guaranteeing the autonomy of the parties, not setting strict "facilitative" restrictions on mediators' behavior. In particular, there is no need to follow the legislation models of some Western countries or China's Hong Kong, and exclude the behavior of mediators' evaluative mediation. In order to protect the autonomy of the parties, based on the idea of facilitative mediation, external legal systems will strictly prohibit mediators from evaluating intervention in the dispute resolution while taking party autonomy as a principle. Such an institutional setting will establish a "two-layer structure" in the mediation legislation that protects the autonomy and restricts mediators' intervention. However, we have to realize that such institutional setting is embedded in its specific cultural context and is built on the value basis of individualism and liberalism in Western society. If China adopts regulations in its statutory law similar to that in the West, it will lead to a significant deviation between the mediation norms and the mediator's routines, and the effectiveness of the mediation agreement will be easily affected by the mediator's behavior. What's worse, the inherent conflict between this legislative orientation and the Chinese cultural context will have a negative impact on the effectiveness of dispute resolution.

It should be noted that the legislative design of the Singapore Convention on Mediation attempts to relieve the tension between different mediation models. During the legislative process, the working group of the Convention did realize that "the concept of 'mediation' in the Convention should be broadly inclusive."[58] Therefore, in terms of legislative technique, the definition of medi-

[58] *The Legislative Background and Interpretation of the United Nations Convention on International Settlement Agreements Resulting from Mediation*, edited by Sun Wei (Law Press, 2018) 26.

ation in the Convention is general and descriptive.[59] According to Paragraph 3, Article 2 in the Convention, "'Mediation' means a process, irrespective of the expression used or the basis upon which the process is carried out, whereby parties attempt to reach an amicable settlement of their dispute with the assistance of a third person or persons ('the mediator') lacking the authority to impose a solution upon the parties to the dispute."[60] Such a relatively open legislative orientation enables different mediation models (whether facilitative mediation or evaluative mediation) to be included.[61] Based on the open definition of mediation in the Convention, we can conclude what it restricts most is that the mediator has no right to "impose a solution". In other words, the final solution should be willingly accepted by both parties. For the complex and diverse mediation process, the Convention does not expressly exclude the necessary evaluative intervention of the mediator in the dispute resolution process, nor does it set prohibitive clauses to limit mediators' intervention. Therefore, from a literal perspective, the definition of mediation in the Convention should not be interpreted as a "facilitative" model, but rather as a simple definition of mediation that respects and accommodates the diversity of mediation in the Convention. For the vast institutional space released by this Convention, we should make the most of it during the domestication of the Convention. All in all, what commercial mediation needs to guarantee is the autonomy of the parties, and there may be various methods to maintain the autonomy of the parties. The mediators' intervention and evaluation are not necessarily a hindrance, but may also be a process of empowering the parties. The mediator's intervention allows the parties to know relevant information, understand the advantages and disadvantages of options, predict legal risks, and refer to past experience, so as to better make independent decisions. After all, knowing sufficient information and obtaining professional help are prerequisites for the parties to exercise real autonomy. Without sufficient information and professional reference, the so-called "autonomy" is actually a castle in the air.[62]

In fact, the preference for "evaluative mediation" does not only exist in China; it is also an important content of "Asian values". In Singapore, where

59 See Cai Wei, 'The Dilemma and Responses of the "Singapore Convention on Mediation"' (2022) 2 *Tsinghua Law* 202.

60 United Nations Convention on International Settlement Agreements Resulting from Mediation, https://uncitral.un.org/sites/default/files/media-documents/EN/Texts/UNCITRAL/Arbitration/mediation_convention_v1900316_eng.pdf, accessed 18 June 2021.

61 See Yun Zhao, 'The Singapore Mediation Convention: A Version of the New York Convention for Mediation?' (2021) 17 (3) *Journal of Private International Law* 543.

62 *Supra* note 16, 70.

the Convention was signed, there is also the problem of how to fit the Western mediation culture with the local social context. Therefore, how Singapore balances the local context with the requirements of the Convention is worthy of our reference. In Singapore, whether it is the Chinese community or the Malay community, resolving disputes through conversation can find its cultural legitimacy and practice in the cultural context of each ethnic group.[63] Therefore, Singapore's mediation is a hybrid style, which combines the multiple elements of facilitative mediation and evaluative mediation, but does not absolutely follow one of them and exclude the other.[64] According to Andrew Phang, Justice of the Supreme Court of Singapore, as East Asian countries are generally influenced by Confucianism, in terms of dispute resolution procedures, they will choose a relatively formal strategy that focuses on building friendly and sustainable relations for all parties. It is in this sense that Asian mediation is different from its Western counterpart. Unlike the Western mediation model, which puts the free will of the parties at the center, the Asian mediation model will place more emphasis on the central role of the mediator in the dispute resolution process. In such a cultural context, pure facilitative mediation, that is, a highly individualistic mediation model that allows more of the parties' participation and control and does not seek help from authority figures, cannot be effective. Taking the parties as the center will lead to direct confrontation and disputes between the parties in the dialogue, making the dispute resolution process out of control, thereby weakening the effectiveness of dispute resolution.[65] Therefore, under the guidance of "Asian values", mediators are expected to have more authority in the process of dispute resolution, and they need to play a greater cohesion and control function when handling disputes. They also need to provide more guidance for the parties and express their views and opinions.[66]

From above, it is not difficult to find that there is an inherent tension between the "Asian Values" and cultural premise of "facilitative mediation" which places individual autonomy in a lofty position.[67] Therefore, Singapore did not

---

[63] See Joel Lee and Teh Hwee Hwee, *An Asian Perspective on Mediation* (Academy Publication, 2009) 10–11.

[64] See Andrew Phang, 'Mediation and the Courts – The Singapore Experience, Keynote Speech on the 4th Asian Mediation Association Conference', 20th October 2016, https://www.judiciary.gov.sg/docs/default-source/news-docs/keynote-speech---4th-asian-mediation-conference.pdf, accessed 9 July 2021.

[65] Ibid.

[66] See Dorcas Quek Anderson, 'The Evolving Concept of Access to Justice in Singapore's Mediation Movement' (2020) 16 (2) *International Journal of Law in Context* 134.

[67] Ibid.

simply copy the Western "facilitative mediation" when formulating its mediation rules, but made corresponding adjustments according to local conditions. The purpose is not to exclude "facilitative mediation" from the legal practice, but to give sufficient legitimacy to the intervention of "evaluative mediation", so that mediation practice could be more diversified and more compatible with local cultural preferences. To be specific, Singapore did not integrate domestic mediation and international mediation into one, but constructed a dual legislative model. In its domestic mediation, the Community Mediation Centers Act gives a broad definition of mediation. In Article 2 of the Act, "mediation" includes "the undertaking of any activity for the purpose of promoting the discussion and settlement of disputes";[68] in Article 10, it stipulates that "the rules of evidence do not apply to mediation sessions, and a dispute may not be adjudicated or arbitrated upon at a mediation session";[69] in Article 12, it rules the voluntariness of participation: "(1) Attendance at and participation in a mediation session is voluntary. (2) A party to a mediation session may withdraw from the mediation session at any time. (3) Attendance at, participation in or withdrawal from, a mediation session conducted under this Act does not affect any rights or remedies that a party to a dispute has apart from this Act."[70] In other words, Singapore did not follow the Western definition of "facilitative mediation", nor evidently restrict the mediator's intervention. Instead, Singapore gave the mediation process more openness, inclusiveness and flexibility on the basis of ensuring the voluntary participation of the parties. In 2020, Singapore issued the Singapore Convention on Mediation Act. The Act adopts the same definition of mediation as in the Convention. Article 7 of the Act provides for restrictions on the conduct of the mediator as ruled in the Convention, which include material violations of international mediation standards to the extent that make the parties have legitimate doubts about the mediator's neutrality and independence, as well as mediators exerting substantial or undue influence (without which the parties will not form a consensus). In addition, Singapore's laws do not exclude the mediator's evaluative intervention in the actual mediation practice.[71] Moreover, the Singapore government suggested in its legislative proposals to the Working Group of the Singapore Convention on Mediation that the term of "neutral" should not be used in the definition of mediation, because this description would have a negative impact on mediators' substantial intervention in the dispute resolution. If it is expected

---

68 Community Mediation Centres Act, https://sso.agc.gov.sg/Act/CMCA1997#pr12-, accessed 9 July 2021.

69 Ibid.

70 Ibid.

71 See Singapore Convention on Mediation Act, https://sso.agc.gov.sg/Act/SCMA2020#pr7-, accessed 10 July 2021.

to protect the autonomy of the parties, terms such as "impartial" or "independent" can be used instead, thereby releasing the mediators' greater power to resolve disputes.[72]

From the perspective of mediation institutions, according to the Singapore International Mediation Association (SIMI) Code of Professional Conduct, "mediation is defined as a process where two or more parties appoint a third-party neutral (the SIMI Mediator) to assist them in a dialogue oriented toward managing conflict or resolving a dispute or issue, which can also include negotiating agreements."[73] Instead of mentioning words like "facilitate" or "evaluate", the definition uses words like "manage" and "resolve" which endow more flexibility in dispute resolution. In the section on mediator's behavior, the Code stipulates that "with the consent of all parties, SIMI Mediators should draw on their expertise and experience to assist the parties in developing sustainable settlements during the mediation. However, SIMI Mediators should rigorously guard against prescribing solutions or offering any statement, suggestion, or value judgment which may create an undue influence on any one party towards accepting a specific outcome."[74] Therefore, we can draw the conclusion that the key criterion is to protect the free will of the parties, rather than to impose various restrictions on the behavior of the mediator. The SIMI Code of Professional Conduct does not rule out in the abstract the influence of mediators on mediation, but regulates mediators' behavior in specific situations. With the consent of all parties, mediators can substantively intervene in dispute resolution. Regarding the limit of intervention, it is specifically stipulated that the intervention of the mediator will only be regarded as a violation of the rules when it coercively points to a specific result of a dispute resolution. We can learn from such legislative ideas in the design of China's commercial mediation institution. Specifically, the voluntary participation and independent decision need to be respected and guaranteed in China's commercial mediation, and there is no need to restrict or exclude the procedural intervention of the mediator. When defining "mediation", we can learn from Singapore's experience and use more open terms such as "resolute" and "manage" to describe the mediation process. For example, mediation can be defined as "the process in which the mediator, on the basis of fully respecting the wishes of the parties, comprehensively uses dispute resolution methods to manage the disputes

72 See Dispute settlement: Draft UNCITRAL mediation rules and notes on mediation/Compilation of comments from Governments-Singapore, https://undocs.org/en/A/CN.9/1031/Add.2, accessed 18 August 2021.

73 Singapore International Mediation Institute (SIMI) Code of Professional Conduct for SIMI Mediators, https://imimediation.org/wp-content/uploads/2022/02/IMI-Code-of-Conduct-EN.pdf, accessed 20 June 2021.

74 Ibid.

between the parties and reach a consensus." In order to protect the parties' will, we can learn from Singapore and set three provisions in the legislation to strengthen the subject status of the parties. First, mediators shall inform the parties of relevant information of mediation, such as the nature and procedures of mediation, the mediator's role and charge. Second, the mediator shall not impose a specific dispute resolution result on the parties. Third, the parties may withdraw from the mediation process at any stage of the mediation. Such legislative thinking styles and rule designs could guarantee the parties' will and autonomy while giving mediators great freedom to intervene.

5. CONCLUSION

Implementing the Singapore Convention on Mediation in China and establishing the supporting commercial mediation legislation are more than a matter of adapting rules and matching institutions. It is more of a problem to distinguish and integrate the mediation model in a certain cultural context. To this end, in the legislation design, the parties' autonomy of will has to be guaranteed, and there should not be any restriction on the mediator's intervention, comments, and guidance. This is not only because mediation is a comprehensive process and complex technicality, but also because there is a deep cultural root. In contemporary Chinese culture, there is still a strong respect for authority, an evident dependence and preference on community value, an emphasis on face and international relationships, and priority on order and harmony. These cultural traits related to dispute resolution preferences are the realistic context on which the mediation institution can effectively operate. Therefore, we need to understand the ontological differences between Western mediation and Chinese mediation and avoid blindly following Western paradigms. Based on China's perspective, we need to study and judge the value proposition of the Singapore Convention on Mediation and conclude the preferences on different mediation models. It is in an overall balance that we can design and construct the contents that both satisfy China's context and meet the requirement on commercial mediation legislation in the Singapore Convention on Mediation. Only in this way can we truly guarantee a smooth landing and effective implementation of the Convention in China and truly promote the continuous development of China's commercial mediation institution.

9. The rights and wrongs of the disadvantaged: the theories and principles of tax burden distribution in tax law

Zhang Mujun

Since the Third Plenary Session of the 18th Central Committee of the Communist Party of China (CPC) proposed "implementing the principle of statutory taxation", 12 of 18 of China's existing taxes have completed the legislation process. The main task of China's tax legislation is now gradually shifting from "providing legal basis" to "achieving good governance through sound laws". In particular, after the 19th National Congress of the CPC, narrowing the wealth gap and responding to the concept of social justice have become the most important goals in formulating and reforming tax laws in China. Accordingly, the research focus of Chinese tax law cannot only stay simple "statutory taxation", but on bridging specific tax rules to the attainment of justice, which clearly brings a higher requirement for improving the tax system. Hence the Chinese tax law community has embarked on the formulation of general principles of tax law and the compilation of a tax code, aiming to construct a unified and coherent tax law system. However, now we have to face an obvious challenge in this progress: Although Chinese scholars generally take "tax equity" as the fundamental principle for tax burden distribution,[1] there are actually some different interpretations of the concept of "tax equity" itself. Some scholars believe that tax equity should be understood as "based

[1] See Zhang Shouwen, *Theories of Taxation Law* (10th edition, Peking University Press 2021) 36; Xu Mengzhou, 'On the Basic Principles of Tax Law' (2000) 1 *Economic Law Review* 207; Liu Jianwen, 'The Basic Principles of Western Tax Law and Their Referential Significances for China', (1996) 3 *Law Review* 20, 22; Zhang Yurun, 'On the Positioning of the Basic Principles of Tax Law', (1998) 4 *Peking University Law Journal* 103, 105.

on individual's capacity",[2] while others advocate that the tax should be determined by "benefit received".[3] Among those who believe tax equity is based on "capacity", there are divisions on whether "capacity" should be understood as "economic capacity",[4] or as "sacrifice capacity".[5] Based on different understandings of tax equity, specific rules for tax burden distribution and statutory tax obligations could be formed completely differently. So, how should Chinese tax law deal with these different principles of tax burden allocation? If tax law recognizes multiple principles of tax burden allocation, can "tax" still constitute a definite legal concept? To answer these questions, we must look back to the social ideal of justice and examine the various principles of tax burden distribution and the theories behind them that have emerged under the name of tax equity.

1. "JUSTICE FOR THE DISADVANTAGED" IS THE CLAIM OF SOCIAL JUSTICE IN THE MARKET ECONOMY

The underlying assumption of modern political civilization regarding individuals is "equal", which can be traced back to Hobbes' discourse in Leviathan: "Nature hath made men so equal, in the faculties of body, and mind; as that though there be found one man sometimes manifestly stronger in body, or of quicker mind than another; yet when all is reckoned together, the difference between man and man is not so considerable, as that one man can thereupon

---

2 See Xu Duoqi, 'On the Ability-To-Pay Principle of Taxation', (2013) 5 *China Legal Science* 65, 69; Shi Zhengwen, 'Distributive Justice and Individual Income Tax Law Reform', (2011) 5 *China Legal Science* 32; Cao Mingxing, 'A New Theory of the Ability-to-Pay Principle', (2012) 7 *Taxation Research* 66; Li Gang, 'On the Relations between Tax Law with a Micro-Controlling Purpose and the Fundamental Principles of Tax Law', (2008) 3 *Journal of Xiamen University (Arts & Social Science)* 82, 85.

3 See Liu Jianwen and Xiong Wei, *Basic Theory of Tax Law* (Peking University Press 2004) 136–138; Liu Shuilin, 'Theory on Universal Presentation of Tax Equity Principle', (2021) 2 *Studies in Law and Business* 173, 174.

4 See Zhu Daqi, 'On the Basic Principles of Tax Law', (1999) 4 *Journal of Hunan Financial and Economic College* 32; Weng Wuyao, 'Principles of Taxation According to Ability to Pay and the New Round of Tax Legal System Reform in China', 2017 (5) *Journal of CUPL* 89, 91.

5 See Yang Xiaoqiang, 'Real Estate Tax Reform in Persistence and Ability to Pay', (2015) 2 *Journal of Political Science and Law* 57, 59; Ye Jinyu, *Research on A Holistic Tax Law: A Perspective of Inter Legal System Integration* (Peking University Press 2016) 17.

claim to himself any benefit, to which another may not pretend, as well as he."[6] Based on the equal status of every individual, citizens enjoy equal rights and bear equal obligations under the constitution. The assumption of "individual's faculty is roughly equal" not only is the origin idea of modern legal systems but also serves as a fundamental premise of the market economy. According to this premise, every person is a "rational economic agent", characterized by being "equally self-centred, prudent, active and free",[7] capable of recognizing and consistently pursuing their self-interests, and engaging in rational planning of personal life. When suppliers and consumers, who are both rational economic agents, independently make their economic plans and compete with each other within the legal framework, theoretically everyone will maximize their self-interests while satisfying the interests of others; then it could lead to a state of perfect competition through price adjustment in the economic process, achieving the most efficient allocation of resources. However, competition inherently leads to "survival of the fittest", where some individuals become winners and gain more wealth from the market, while others become losers and may even face bankruptcy. In other words, "equality before the law and material equality are therefore not only different but are in conflict with each other".[8]

There is a high tension between political equality and economic inequality. We can see a conversion of economic resources and political resources in the real world, and no one can deny that economic inequality sometimes leads to political inequality. Money can be used to purchase rights; besides illegal bribery, the rich can support favorable opinions and information through lawful financial contributions, influencing others' preferences in the collective decision-making process. "Whenever bargaining opportunity presents itself, the individual will find it profitable to invest resources in decision-making, in bargaining."[9] Individuals without resources can hardly bargain in collective decision-making; thus, their asserted rights may not be recognized by their community, and even their legitimate rights could be deprived. On the other hand, when individuals take their wealth as capital and put it into production, other individuals who are hired by them and are dependent on their wealth often

---

6 Thomas Hobbes, *Leviathan* (first published 1651, J. M. Dent & Sons Ltd. 1953) 63.

7 Gustav Radbruch, 'Legal's Image of Human' (2020) 40(4) *Oxford Journal of Legal Studies* 676.

8 Friedrich A. Von Hayek, *The Constitution of Liberty* (China Social Sciences Publishing House 1999) 87.

9 James M. Buchanan and Gordon Tullock, *The Calculus of Consent: Logical Foundations of Constitutional Democracy* (The University of Michigan Press 1974) 110.

become attached to them too. The reason behind this is that the high degree of division of labor and monetary exchange in the modern market economy makes workers able to obtain necessities only through monetary purchases, and they can also make money only by selling their labor. Therefore, "the laborer, whose only source of earning is the sale of his labor, cannot leave the whole class of its purchasers, that is, the capitalist class, without renouncing his own existence".[10] This attachment not only allows employers to control their employees to a certain extent, but also grants bigger employers who employ more workers a greater social impact.

The economic success and failure of individuals raise differences between citizens not only in economic power but also in political status. If we do not want to undermine the fundamental political assumption of "all men are created equal", we have to consider under what conditions we can accept the economic inequality caused by the market. This brings us to the issue of distributive justice in the market. Sociological research has found that the reason people accept unequal allocation of the market is that they believe what they possess is a reward for their past work and their willingness to go on working.[11] Markets are where people exchange existing wealth, in which initial resources can only be acquired through "work" – freewill labor guided by reasons and following principles,[12] and the existing wealth itself is also the result of past work, so people generally consider acquiring and possessing wealth through work in the market to be morally justified. Max Weber noted that this notion of "work legitimizing wealth" reflects a "rational economic ethic", where people believe that when a person does "restless, continuous, systematic work in a worldly calling",[13] the market, as a mechanism organized through economic rationality, will provide a reasonable evaluation and equivalent return based on the importance of their contribution to "the commonwealth". Therefore, the differences in various jobs constitute legitimate reasons for income distribu-

10 Karl Marx, Wage-Labor and Capital (J. L. Joynes tr, Twentieth Century Press 1893) 4.

11 Zygmunt Bauman, *Work, Consumerism, and the New Poor* (McGraw-Hill Education 2004) 5.

12 It might seem that the concepts of "work" and "labor" are the same in daily use, but according to Hannah Arendt, the fundamental difference between these two concepts lies in the fact that "work" is not aimed at satisfying one's own needs but rather at exchanging with others in the market. Therefore, "work" can be simply defined as "labor in the market," while the market is characterized as within the legal framework and organized through rationality. See Hannah Arendt, *The Human Condition* (2nd ed, The University of Chicago Press 1998) 136.

13 Max Weber, *The Protestant Ethic and the Spirit of Capitalism* (Taylor & Francis Group 2001) 116.

tion disparities in the market. People believe when they choose a proper job and put in more effort than others, or they are more frugal than others who made equivalent effort, then the additional wealth they acquire is just. Based on this belief, the anticipated and accepted consequence is that only lazy or wasteful people would fall into an economically disadvantaged position and experience political inequality. However, this perspective of distributive justice and expectations based on it are undoubtedly idealistic, and it is not difficult to see the hidden risk in it – a wealthy life and equal political status seem to be merely a matter of individual will and personal choice. This is clearly an excessive exaggeration of individual subjective agency because, based on general experience, at least three important factors in the process of acquiring and accumulating wealth are beyond individual control:

Firstly, individuals cannot choose their birth and gifts. It is undeniable that one can win the genetic lottery. At any time, having a sharp mind, a strong physique, or a beautiful appearance always endows individuals with competitive advantages. Further, if parents have already achieved economic success, they can invest in children's upbringing, reinforcing children's competitive advantage or compensating for their disadvantages. The distinction caused by birth and upbringing is actually a form of "unequal starting points", also known as "inequality of opportunity".[14] Individuals with weaker innate abilities or lower socio-economic backgrounds are already at a disadvantage from the moment they are born; they often face greater difficulty in obtaining job opportunities compared to those who are better off. Nevertheless, without job opportunities, it is impossible to accumulate wealth in the market, or even to be hardworking, thus with no chance to change the disadvantaged status.

Secondly, individuals cannot determine the needs of others. Participating in the market means that people work hard to prioritize meeting the needs of others through exchange, and then to satisfy their own needs.[15] Therefore, individual talents are evaluated more in terms of exchange value rather than absolute value, demonstrating stronger sociality and relativity. The hypothesis about the market assumes "the invisible hand" will encourage the physically stronger to engage in manual labor and the intellectually smarter to engage in mental labor, believing this will lead to efficiency. However, if there are more needs for intellectual products in a society, the utility of physical strength will be lower than that of intelligence, and the value that can be exchanged for

---

[14] John Rawls, *Justice as Fairness: A Restatement* (Harvard University Press 2001) 44.

[15] As Marx repeatedly stated, individuals in the market do not recognize each other as "human," but rather as "commodities" and "owners of commodities." See Karl Marx, *Capital: A Critical Analysis of Capitalist Production* (Samuel Moore and Edward Aveling tr, Appleton & co. 1889) 57, 82.

physical work will be lower than that of intellectual work. Thus some individuals, even if they possess certain talents and abilities, are "born at the wrong time" and seen as "useless" by others.[16]

Thirdly, humans cannot control the course of life. Although the developments in medicine have largely improved human health in general, there still appear to be some limits. No one can skip their childhood and old age, and we may get sick or encounter some other physical problems that make us unable to work at working age. Besides, unforeseen accidents can suddenly destroy one's ability to work. However, humans inevitably engage in continuous consumption in order to stay alive. Since personal wealth is the remainder after life-sustaining expenses, individuals who were originally similar in competitiveness and income may face economic failure due to unexpected accidents, illnesses, or simply because they have to incur more expenses for a long life. If a person dies before losing the ability to work, then it is obvious that less wealth will be accumulated and fewer utilities can be achieved than others. Once encountering these situations, one can easily become less advantaged among their peers and may pass their disadvantages on to the next generation, causing their children to experience unequal opportunities.

When people compete with each other in the market, any change of aforementioned factors can enhance or weaken their competitiveness. Therefore, even if two individuals work equally hard under completely equal working conditions, the wealth they can acquire and possess through work may still be different. While effort will indeed affect the acquisition and accumulation of wealth, the impact will not be extreme. However, luck and misfortune can greatly influence the outcomes of market distribution.[17] Especially those who suffer from misfortune of life can easily experience the slashing of living

---

[16] In fact, this is a major division between Rawls and Nozick on distributive justice: Rawls argues that if the value of an individual's talents is priced and protected by society rather than the individual, then it is morally arbitrary for individuals, and the benefits individuals derive from their talent should not be considered as "deserved," but rather allow society to make redistribution. In contrast, Nozick argues that regardless of whether the value of natural abilities is affected by social need or whether the benefits derived are morally "deserved," the justice of having natural assets (i.e., "justice in holdings") and the justice of the acquisition process (i.e., "justice in acquisition") gives the individual the right to claim the benefits, and this right is sufficient to resist the redistributive claims of society. See John Rawls, *A Theory of Justice* (China Social Sciences Publishing House 1999) 103; Robert Nozick, *Anarchy, State, and Utopia* (Basic Books Inc. 1974) 230.

[17] The word "fortune" can be used to refer both to "wealth" and "luck." The Latin root of this word is "Fortuna," the Roman goddess of chance or lot. It clearly indicates the recognition of the relationship between wealth and fate in the western world.

standards and social status, feeling the “downgrading”. This means that while the distributive justice of the market is rooted in the ethical view of “God rewards the diligent”, the outcomes of market allocation often fail to truly fulfill the promise of rewarding individual efforts.

In a modern society with a highly specified social division of labor and profession, showcasing individual talents through academic diligence (educational qualifications) and achievements (degrees) has become a prerequisite for participating in work. This leads to people being more willing than ever before to believe that the existing economic results truly reflect the fruits of their individual efforts. Therefore, “in market-driven societies, interpreting material success as a sign of moral desert is a persisting temptation”.[18] However, once people believe that success is solely derived from individual efforts, they tend to judge one’s worth and dignity based on economic achievements. We can see an absurd conclusion from this trend: “economic vulnerability” itself implies moral criticism of individuals, where failure in market competition constitutes a moral wrongdoing, and poverty is deemed a justifiable outcome of that wrongdoing. According to this logic, extreme wealth inequality is given a justifiable reason,[19] then we would no longer seek to equal rights for the poor, and political equality would become impossible.

It should be recognized that there may be some slackers among the losers in market competition, but hardworking people can also experience economic failure and become disadvantaged because of bad luck. While it is often said that “luck is part of one’s strength”, it is completely random, unpredictable, and beyond human control. If we still consider that what we get from the market is the result of our rational planning rather than speculative windfalls, irrational luck should not be seen as a determining factor in the legitimacy of personal wealth. Since everyone is susceptible to unforeseen misfortunes, if we are unwilling for ourselves and our descendants to be blamed for the random occurrence of misfortune, then behind “the veil of ignorance” we cannot consider the economic failures caused by misfortune as something that people “deserve”. If the social background, innate abilities, and accidents are morally neutral, then the resulting economic disadvantage should not attract societal discrimination. As long as individuals work equally hard, they “deserve” roughly equal social arrangements; that is, there should not be extreme disparities. This implies that the justice of the disadvantaged – the identity of the

---

18 Michael Sandel, *The Tyranny of Merit: What’s Become of the Common Good?* (Farrar, Straus and Giroux 2020) 213–214.

19 For example, Hayek states that extreme wealth inequality is inevitable, and any form of the concept of “social justice” is an infringement on individual freedom. See F. A. Hayek, *Law, Legislation and Liberty* (Taylor & Francis Group 1982) 97–99.

disadvantaged should not be solidified – requires social attention, and efforts should be made to enable unfortunate individuals to lead economically self-sufficient lives and attain political freedom equal to others. In fact, this constitutes a crucial aspect of social justice. When a society embraces the concept of justice for the disadvantaged, it demands that those who are fortunate enough to be "advantaged" utilize their strength to assist the disadvantaged, creating an environment where everyone can lead the life they desire through diligent work and effective social cooperation, thereby achieving the distributive justice of "to each according to their abilities, and to each according to their needs".

2. EXAMINATION ON THREE THEORIES OF TAX EQUITY

Achieving social justice requires joint efforts from every aspect of society; taxation is one of the most vital parts. The reason behind this is not that taxation could significantly reduce the income gap, but that taxes, as the main source of government revenue, materially determine the level of supply of public goods and therefore ensure the minimum income for the most vulnerable members of society.[20] Public goods refer to "goods and services that meet the needs and demands through the political system".[21] When a certain good or service is considered essential for individuals to exercise their rights while private entities are unwilling or unable to provide it, citizens often seek collective action at the national level, urging the government to step in and provide such goods or services.[22] However, all the inputs and consumption involved in the provision of public goods require products that have already been produced, since the

[20] In an economic sense, the personal use of public goods constitutes personal income. However, paying taxes and enjoying public goods generally does not significantly or directly reduce inequalities or raise income levels. See James A. Mirrlees, *Welfare, Incentives, and Taxation* (Oxford University Press 2006) 173.

[21] James M. Buchanan, *The Demand and Supply of Public Goods* (Liberty Fund, Inc. 1999) 1.

[22] Professor Huang Maorong suggests that public goods funded by tax should include "services that cannot, should not, or are unwilling to be provided by the private sector." However, since the 1980s, by claiming the public cost has become too high, the United States and European countries have undergone privatization reforms in traditional basic sectors such as energy, water supply, transportation, telecommunications, education, and healthcare. This indicates that there may be no initial "services that cannot be provided by private" behind the "veil of ignorance." See Huang Maorong, *Method of Jurisprudence and Modern Tax Law* (Peking University Press 2011) 190.

government itself does not possess the initial production capacity. This arouses public needs for tax to obtain material security for providing public goods.[23]

Providing goods and services to the whole society through political collective action has clear benefits for the disadvantaged. When goods or services are provided by private entities, consumers must pay competitive prices for exclusive access to those goods or services. In contrast, public goods are inherently indivisible and nonexclusive for all members of a country. Unless the law itself designates privileges, every member of society can benefit from public goods, and the consumption of public goods does not diminish the enjoyment of those goods for other members, without the need for competition. Although private entities can also be entrusted to provide public goods, based on existing experience, privatizing the provision of public goods often leads to a worsening situation for the disadvantaged.[24] Therefore, the optimal approach for achieving social justice in China at present is still to continue improving the level and capacity of providing public goods by government.

It should be noted that public goods come with a cost. The cost of public goods is primarily borne by taxation, which means that whenever the government supplies public goods, it needs to take a portion from private wealth. Since "all taxes are ultimately paid by persons",[25] there are two essential

---

[23] In China, public capital – including state-owned and communally owned property – accounts for a certain proportion of national capital, and the financing of public goods and repayment of public debt do not need to rely entirely on tax funding. However, according to data released by the Ministry of Finance, 85% of China's general public budget revenue in 2021 came from tax revenue, so we consider this condition applicable to China. See '2021 Chinese Fiscal Revenue and Expenditure' <http://www.gov.cn/shuju/2022-01/29/content_5671104.htm> accessed 20 August 2022.

[24] Research has found that in the process of privatization of public service providing, the cut of public service prices in the United States and European countries is mainly achieved by reducing employment and worsening working conditions to lower costs. This makes it difficult for the disadvantaged to enjoy public services even with lower prices, and the industrial sector benefits significantly more than the household sector. Meanwhile, some non-profitable public services cannot be privatized at all, thus the financial burden on the government actually does not decrease with the privatization of public services. Chinese scholars have also found that marketization has led to a decline in the quality of public services in areas such as education. See Barbara Dichhaus and Kristina Dietz, 'Private Gain – Public Loss? Consequences of the Privatization of Public Services in Europe', (2004) 7 *Policy Paper* 1; Li Rui, 'On the Public Service Supply Rights and Liabilities Allocation', (2019) 4 *China Legal Science* 128.

[25] G. W. J. Bruins et al., *Report on Double Taxation: Submitted to the Financial Committee*, [1923] League of Nations Document (E.F.S. 73 F. 19) 18.

questions that together constitute the problem of tax burden distribution: first, from whom the government should take wealth; and second, how much wealth to be taken is reasonable. Adam Smith's maxim of tax equity is acknowledged as the most authoritative answer to how to distribute the tax burden: "The subjects of every State ought to contribute towards the support of the Government as nearly as possible, in proportion to their respective abilities, that is, in proportion to the revenue which they respectively enjoy under the protection of the State."[26] This rule provides a definite answer to the first question, which is that the tax burden should be borne universally, and no one should enjoy the privilege of tax-free status. However, the answer to the second question involves three elements: proportion, protection, and respective abilities. Each of these elements can lay the foundation for a tax distribution principle alone. Thus, based on different understandings of "tax equity" and the pursuit of "optimum distribution", economics has developed three of the most influential theories of tax burden distribution through emphasis and a combination of different elements.

2.1 Sacrifice Theory

Based on the standpoint of laissez-faire and the philosophical foundation of utilitarianism, classical economics believed that government and its services should be kept to a minimum, containing only "necessary protection" – military, policing, and justice – so-called "night-watchman state". In this way, the total amount of government spending is fixed and is pure consumption for individuals. If individuals do not pay taxes, they can consume more to increase their own happiness or accumulate their own wealth. Therefore, "there are no taxes which have not a tendency to lessen the power to accumulate".[27] The total amount of taxes equals the overall social disutility, and the tax burden individuals bear is a "sacrifice" of their own utility. Since "[t]he utilitarian morality … the only self-renunciation which it applauds, is devotion to the happiness, or to some of the means of happiness, of others",[28] every citizen should sacrifice their own good to bear tax as government is necessary. However, according to the principle of utility or the greatest happiness principle, the tax burden should be minimized in order to ensure that society can still increase wealth overall. "As a government ought to make no distinction of persons or classes in the strength of their claims on it, whatever sacrifices it requires from them

---

26 Adam Smith, *An Inquiry into the Nature and Causes of the Wealth of Nations* (Vol. 3, 4th ed., Printed for A. Strahan and T. Cadell 1786) 255–256.

27 David Ricardo, *On the Principles of Political Economy and Taxation* (first published 1817, Penguin Books 1971) 169.

28 John Stuart Mill, *Utilitarianism* (The Floating Press 2009) 31.

should be made to bear as nearly as possible with the same pressure upon all … Equality of taxation, therefore, as a maxim of politics, means equality of sacrifice."[29]

This statement of John Stuart Mill can be understood in two ways: firstly, it can be read as "equal sacrifice", which means each taxpayer should sacrifice an equal amount of utility; secondly, it can also be read as "proportional sacrifice", so each person just sacrifices an equal proportion of total utility. A poll tax can be easily deduced from the idea of "equal sacrifice", as assuming that each person derives equal happiness from wealth, then equal sacrifice of happiness implies an equal amount of tax. Obviously, "equal sacrifice" does not differentiate the taxpayers' "respective abilities", which is blatantly opposite to Adam Smith's maxim. On the contrary, differentiating the total wealth of each individual and levying proportional taxes according to a certain ratio is more in line with the requirements of tax equity. This approach also allows for a progressive tax system when applied to the entire population, making it a favorable choice for the economically disadvantaged. Therefore, the theory of proportional sacrifice became the dominant theory of tax equity in the 19th century.

However, with the development of marginal utility theory in the late 19th century, it has been noticed "the value of the same amount of money decreases as income increases … the same percentage entails not proportional, but less than proportional sacrifice of enjoyment when income increases."[30] In other words, levying a proportional tax results in a "degressive progression", where wealthier individuals make smaller sacrifices. To uphold the sacrifice theory, scholars proposed replacing "equal sacrifice" and "proportional sacrifice" with "equimarginal sacrifice",[31] taxing the wealth of lowest marginal utility, thereby every taxpayer making equal marginal sacrifice and achieving the minimum sacrifice for society. This theory was inherited by welfare economics; Pigou believed that "maximum aggregate welfare is everywhere accepted as the right goal of government … In the special field of taxation this general principle is identical with the principle of least sacrifice."[32] Therefore, the least aggregate sacrifice should be taken as the fundamental principle of

---

[29] John Stuart Mill, *Principles of Political Economy: With Some of Their Applications to Social Philosophy* Vol. II (D. Appleton 1864) 396.

[30] Arnold Jacob Cohen Stuart, 'On Progressive Taxation' in Richard A. Musgrave and Alan T. Peacock (eds), *Classics in the Theory of Public Finance* (Macmillan & Co. Ltd. 1962) 52–53.

[31] See Francis Ysidro Edgeworth, 'The Pure Theory of Taxation', in Richard A. Musgrave and Alan T. Peacock (eds), *Classics in the Theory of Public Finance* (Macmillan & Co. Ltd. 1962) 131.

[32] A. C. Pigou, *A Study in Public Finance* (Macmillan & Co. Ltd. 1929) 61–62.

taxation, the distribution of taxation required to conform to equimarginal sacrifice "which makes the marginal—not the total—sacrifices borne by all the members of the community equal."[33]

2.2 Cost Theory

Early European scholars also believed that the government and its services should be suppressed to a minimum, but they did not view taxes as personal sacrifices; rather, they saw them as give-and-take for government services or as insurance for personal security.[34] Under the influence of Hegel's organicist theory of the state, European scholars at the end of the nineteenth century criticized the old theories of give-and-take and insurance, as well as the British sacrifice theory, for failing to recognize the productivity role of government expenditure. According to them, public fiscal activities are very much like private economic activities. When legislators approve the budget, it is inevitable to take the utility generated by fiscal expenditures into account. "Total satisfaction must be worth at least total sacrifice to the mind of the legislator, or, in other words, in the opinion of the average intelligence of Parliament."[35] With the expansion of government functions, "we can say that taxes are good when their yield is devoted to productive expenditure, such as work that the State is better able to perform than individuals or associations; we can add that, on the contrary, taxes are bad when their yield is put to unproductive or futile uses".[36] The Sacrifice Theory did not answer whether taxation is a good or an evil; it acknowledged the legitimacy of existing expenditures of government, but also blocked the possibility of future increases in public spending. Therefore, some scholars urged taking tax as a "cost-of-service" for public goods and allocating the tax burden based on taxpayers' subjective utility.

The cost theory states the purpose of collective activities is the promotion of individuals' welfare, "those withdrawn from individual economic units are the cost to each individual; the sum of goods used in collective activity is the

---

33 Ibid., 78.

34 See Edwin R. A. Seligman, *Progressive Taxation in Theory and Practice* (American Economic Association 1908) 158–180.

35 Maffeo Pantaleoni, 'Contribution to the Theory of the Distribution of Public Expenditure', in Richard A. Musgrave and Alan T. Peacock (eds), *Classics in the Theory of Public Finance* (Macmillan & Co. Ltd. 1962) 17.

36 Paul Leroy-Beaulieu, 'Taxation in General' in Richard A. Musgrave and Alan T. Peacock (eds), *Classics in the Theory of Public Finance* (Macmillan & Co. Ltd. 1962) 157.

cost to the community, i.e. the sum of its members as an acting subject".[37] Therefore, in the process of government function expansion, to achieve the goal of collective activities with reasonable cost, it should let individuals do cost valuation on their benefit received from collective activities. In other words, the cost theory suggests that individuals should determine the extent of their tax burden based on their own valuation. Based on this suggestion, Wicksell proposed the famous "principle of unanimity": "rejecting any public expenditure, along with its companion tax levy, which failed to render each taxpayer a service corresponding to this payment", "no measure should be carried out unless it has the prior unanimous or at any rate overwhelming support of the whole people".[38] According to this principle, if a public expenditure can obtain the agreement of all members of a community, then the general agreement implies a value judgment: for each one of them, the use value of public goods exceeds cost value.[39] From the principle of unanimity, Lindahl proposed that the tax burden distribution "by and large tends to correspond to marginal utility for each interested party",[40] and he believed that this could reflect the rationality of graduation of taxation. The cost theory has been developed in the public choice school. By introducing the concept of "social rent", Buchanan incorporates the "non-unanimous consent tax burden distribution" into the cost theory. According to this modern cost theory, tax burden is the opportunity cost paid by individuals for collective activity under the circumstance of "without organized collective activity, no product at all is generated".[41]

2.3 Capacity Theory

Other scholars have taken a completely different approach to understand the organicist theory of the state, arguing that the cost theory views the state as a mere aggregation of individuals and a tool for pursuing individual interests, neglecting the agency of the state as an independent actor. Advocates of this

---

[37] Emil Sax, 'The Valuation Theory of Taxation', in Richard A. Musgrave and Alan T. Peacock (eds), *Classics in the Theory of Public Finance* (Macmillan & Co. Ltd. 1962) 177–178.

[38] Knut Wichsell, 'A New Principle of Just Taxation', in Richard A. Musgrave and Alan T. Peacock (eds), *Classics in the Theory of Public Finance* (Macmillan & Co. Ltd. 1962) 75, 109.

[39] See *Supra* note 37, 185.

[40] Erik Lindahl, 'Just Taxation-A Positive Solution', in Richard A. Musgrave and Alan T. Peacock (eds), *Classics in the Theory of Public Finance* (Macmillan & Co. Ltd. 1962) 173.

[41] James M. Buchanan, *Explorations into Constitutional Economics* (Texas A & M University Press 1989) 312.

theory disagree with basing tax burden distribution on individuals' subjective utility evaluations, instead calling for the evaluation of individuals' ability to pay taxes by the state organization (government). For example, Adolph Wagner views the state as "the highest form of compulsory collective economy",[42] and the expansion of fiscal requirement is caused by social progress and the development of the public and private economy, especially compulsory public economy. Therefore, the level of public services cannot be determined solely based on costs or value, but should be considered comprehensively. "Thanks to its sovereignty, the State is free to define its own tasks, the manner of their discharge and thus the amount and kind of services to be provided for the people, without reference to their demand for these services", thus "[e]quality is taken as meaning 'taxation as far as possible according to economic capacity'".[43]

Another proponent of this view is Friedrich von Wieser. He believes that the collective expenditure of a country includes not only the public expenditure that increases private income, but also the government administrative expenditure that improves the lot of the masses, as well as "state necessities" that maintain national power and glory. "Collective expenditure is collective in the sense that common means are employed by one joint authority to produce services of indiscriminate benefit to all … Their aim is the independence of citizens in their activities directed to the satisfaction of their physical and cultural needs."[44] Therefore, there is a significant difference in valuation between the state and individuals. While individuals can assess the exchange value of others' labor as zero, the state must respect human dignity and cannot evaluate the marginal utility of labor. The state must protect the rights of all citizens, both as individuals and as members of society, without discrimination. "The State does recognize its obligation to protect the threatened vital interests of the workers to the best of its ability and if necessary with the help of public funds."[45] When the state must tax one group of citizens to protect the rights of another group, it cannot be based solely on the utility of public services to taxpayers, but rather on the judgment of the fundamental interests of society. However, the tax cannot be increased unlimited; the limit is "the economic capacity of the individuals from whom compulsory contributions are levied."[46]

---

42 Adolph Wagner, 'Three Extracts on Public Finance', in Richard A. Musgrave and Alan T. Peacock (eds), *Classics in the Theory of Public Finance* (Macmillan & Co. Ltd. 1962) 2.

43 Ibid., 5, 14.

44 Friedrich von Wieser, 'The Theory of the Public Economy', in Richard A. Musgrave and Alan T. Peacock (eds), Classics in the Theory of Public Finance (Macmillan & Co. Ltd. 1962) 192.

45 Ibid., 196.

46 Ibid., 199.

The economic capacity "means not only powers of production or results of powers of production, but also the capacity to make use of these powers or these results … The elements of faculty, then, are two-fold, (i) those connected with acquisition or production, (2) those connected with outlay or consumption".[47] In other words, the capacity theory believes that any economic activity of an individual, whether it creates new value or consumes existing value, can reflect a certain ability to bear taxes. The latest development of this theory is that Amartya Sen proposed that an individual's economic capacity is fundamentally "a person's capability to do things he or she has reason to value", and he advocated evaluating the real standard of living based on information of individual functioning.[48]

3. THE CHOICE OF TAX BURDEN DISTRIBUTION PRINCIPLES IN CHINESE TAX LAW UNDER THE PERSPECTIVE OF "JUSTICE FOR THE DISADVANTAGED"

As three of the most influential theories in economics regarding tax burden distribution, the sacrifice theory requires a proportional sacrifice of each individual's total wealth, the cost theory demands that the government increases individual wealth by supplying public goods, and the capacity theory necessitates assessing an individual's economic capacity based on their economic activities. In other words, based on Adam Smith's maxim of tax equity, the sacrifice theory emphasizes "proportion", the cost theory emphasizes "the protection of the State", and the capacity theory emphasizes "respective abilities". Among them, the sacrifice theory and capacity theory require measuring an individual's sacrifice capacity or economic capacity, thereby prioritizing a person's "ability" as the primary principle of tax equity. On the other hand, the cost theory distinctly extends tax equity to "benefit", stating that "the principle of taxation according to benefit, and even equality of Value and Countervalue, is completely appropriate … cannot and need not be influenced by any other notion of justice."[49]

China's pursuit of social justice requires socially privileged members who hold dominant economic positions to assume moral obligations to assist the disadvantaged. However, "the moral propositions do not become authoritatively

---

47 Edwin R. A. Seligman, 'The Theory of Progressive Taxation', (1893) 8(2) Political Science Quarterly 220, 245.

48 See Amartya K. Sen, *The Idea of Justice* (Penguin Books 2010) 230; Amartya K. Sen, *Commodities and Capabilities* (North-Holland 1985).

49 *Supra* note 38, 79.

established legal precepts".[50] Tax laws need to codify the moral obligation as a legal duty first before distributing tax burdens. From this perspective, neither the ability principle based on the sacrifice theory nor the benefit principle based on the cost theory is suitable to be the fundamental principle for distributing tax burdens in Chinese tax laws. This is because when taxation is a universal legal obligation, both the sacrifice theory and the cost theory would lead to conclusions that are unfavorable to the justice of the disadvantaged, no matter in terms of legitimacy or reasonableness of tax burden distribution.

Firstly, both the sacrifice theory and the cost theory are fundamentally based on individual utility rather than social justice as the moral foundation for tax burden distribution. The sacrifice theory bases tax burden distribution on individual marginal sacrifice, while the cost theory bases it on individual marginal benefit. Both theories adopt a methodological individualism approach. No matter how "individual sacrifice" and "individual benefit" clearly establish the legitimacy of tax burden distribution based on individual self-interest, pursuing satisfaction of private interests. That is to say, both the sacrifice theory and the cost theory focus only on the welfare of individuals, while the welfare of the community is merely "the sum of the interests of the several members who compose it",[51] then tax burden distribution is not necessarily linked to specific notions of social justice. The sacrifice theory argues that tax burden is the individual's choice to sacrifice their own utility in order to satisfy the interests of other individuals. While it has a certain level of altruism, it emphasizes the relationship between individuals rather than the relationship between individuals and society as a whole or individuals and their nation. The cost theory goes a step further by viewing tax burden as a cost that individuals choose to bear in order to satisfy their self-interest. It completely individualizes the demand for public goods and treats the public needs as solely driven by self-interest. Accordingly, whether tax burden is reasonable is also evaluated by individuals based on their own judgment since they have the integral right to tell their own happiness and suffering. If they believe that the sacrifice of their self-interest outweighs the happiness gained by others, or if public goods cannot promote the realization of their self-interest, they can deny the reason for tax burden distribution and refuse to bear the tax burden. In this case, if an economically disadvantaged person is more willing to sacrifice for the public good than an economically advantaged person, or if they can benefit equally or even more from public goods, according to the ability principle based on the sacrifice theory, or the benefit principle based on the cost theory, the economically

---

50 Roscoe Pound, *Law and Morals* (University of North Carolina Press 1924) 40.

51 Jeremy Bentham, *An Introduction to the Principle of Morals and Legislation* (Blackwell Publishing Ltd. 2013) 18.

disadvantaged one should not ask that the economically advantaged pay more taxes than themselves.

Secondly, both the sacrifice theory and the cost theory use individuals' subjective feelings rather than objective conditions as the criteria for evaluating the reasonableness of tax burden. The sacrifice theory views the tax burden as pure pain, while the cost theory sees the tax burden as pain that can be exchanged for greater happiness. In both theories, the total tax of the state is the sum of the pain borne by citizens in order to enjoy public goods, so the core of tax burden distribution lies in the calculation of individual happiness and pain. The problem lies in the fact that happiness and pain are subjective experiences, and each person's happiness and pain are not consistent. They cannot be felt by others and are difficult to transform into deterministic objective standards for evaluation. While economics may assume everyone's moral intuitions and value orientations are highly consistent, and the state of mind can be accurately measured by "marginal utility" or "marginal sacrifice", it is clearly too idealized and simplified. Even between two individuals with identical income, savings, and consumption, if one is more easily satisfied while the other is less easily satisfied, there will be a significant disparity in their evaluations of their economic status and their demand for public goods. Neither legislators, law enforcement, nor judges can, or should, assess whether others' feelings are pleasurable or painful. Thus, when tax laws distribute tax burdens based on the ability principle rooted in the sacrifice theory, "feeling dissatisfied" can be a legitimate reason for the wealthiest in society to resist taxation. And when tax laws distribute tax burdens based on the benefit principle rooted in the cost theory, "feeling satisfied" can as well become a legitimate reason for the wealthiest to resist taxation. As those who actually bear the costs, as long as they perceive that public goods are "ineffective", they will require that the government cease providing public goods, thereby exempting themselves from taxes.

Third, both the sacrifice theory and the cost theory distributing tax burdens focus on one aspect of the economic activities rather than the whole process. Since individuals can only make sacrifices after satisfying their own consumption needs and having surplus, the sacrifice theory emphasizes that the distribution of tax burdens should take place during the disposal stage of existing wealth. On the other hand, "cost" can only arise from inputs in production; thus, the cost theory emphasizes that the distribution of tax burdens should take place during the acquisition stage of new wealth. Clearly, neither of these theories takes an overall and comprehensive consideration of the economic situation of individuals; the time lag between bearing tax burdens and enjoying public goods has also been ignored. However, the decision-making process of collective activity is easily influenced by the subjective feelings of society members. Since an individual's subjective utility is based on the happiness and pain they personally experience, it is difficult to balance immediate pain with distant happiness when the immediate pain is too intense. As a result, public goods that should be objectively valued and considered beneficial to individuals in theory may be perceived as having no utility by individuals. Once it becomes uncertain whether public goods are beneficial to society, individuals are more likely to prefer using their wealth entirely for personal consumption rather than "sacrifice" it. If there is no expectation of future benefits from public goods, individuals may also be inclined to refrain from investing any initial costs.

Although the sacrifice theory and the cost theory do not repulse the assistance from the advantaged to the disadvantaged, both theories view such assistance as acts of personal sentiments, thus regarding taxation as a personal virtue rather than a morally obligated behavior based on justice as members of society. Even though the advantaged may still voluntarily assume certain legal tax obligations out of sympathy for the disadvantaged, "beneficence is always free, it cannot be extorted by force".[52] If the advantaged abandon the provision of public goods through collective action, then the disadvantaged cannot require the advantaged to share the tax burden based on the ability principle of the sacrifice theory or the benefit principle of the cost theory.

In the conditions of the modern market economy and the expansion of specialized division of labor to every corner of society, everyone is in fact involved in public life. Whether in politics, the economy, or ordinary life, the majority with whom individuals need to interact have no blood relation and may even be complete strangers. As members of the same society, we need to trust strangers, share public resources with them, and take care of strangers. However, this also poses a great challenge to human nature. As Olsen pointed out, individuals in atomized societies are prone to losing their motivation to contribute due to a "free-rider" mentality.[53] It is exactly because relationships between individuals are no longer easily maintained through blood ties and close face-to-face contact that there is a need for mandatory laws to provide basic behavioral guidelines and protection. Therefore, tax laws cannot solely cater to individual self-interest but must also play a role in cultivating civic spirit.[54] However, if we fundamentally see the tax burden as voluntary contributions rather than a civic duty, it would be difficult to justify the advantaged bearing a greater tax burden on tax law. As a result, even if we can construct tax laws in a way that makes the advantaged bear a greater tax burden than the

52 Adam Smith, *The Theory of Moral Sentiments* (H. G. Bohn 1853) 112.

53 See Mancur Olson, *The Logic of Collective Action: Public Goods and the Theory of Groups* (Harvard University Press 1971) 11.

54 See Shi Jichun, 'Multiple Purposes of Tax Laws and Non-tax Limitation Factors', (2019) 1 *Economic Law Review* 185.

disadvantaged through technical rule design, the rules themselves would lack principled support and could be easily overturned.

By comparison, the capacity theory, which bases the distribution of tax burdens on individual behavior rather than subjective perceptions, can maximize the limitation of arbitrariness in tax burden distribution. Moreover, distributing tax burdens according to individuals' economic capacities aligns naturally with the concept of "justice for the disadvantaged". Usually, if individuals act rationally, they would not and should not engage in behaviors that exceed their own economic capacity. In the market, individuals often perceive their own interests and make economic decisions based on the fair market value, which is determined by the exchange value determined by ordinary standard businesses.[55] The fair market value has to be a social recognition, thus an objective value criteria.[56] So individuals can develop a subjective understanding of their own economic capabilities in economic activities, and this understanding corresponds to the external, objective, and socially recognized economic capacities. The fairer market value individuals obtain, possess, or consume in specific economic activities, the stronger economic capacity they will self-perceive and demonstrate to society. So there is a natural pursuit of imposing lower tax burdens on those with weaker economic capacity and higher tax burdens on those with stronger economic capacity when the government demands taxes based on economic activities. In each economic activity, the understanding of the economic capacity of individuals combines both individual and social perspectives. Therefore, as Seligman pointed out, using economic capacity as the basis for tax burden distribution, the progression of taxes will constitute a necessary factor in understanding tax equity; then the ability principle based on the capacity theory is essentially the "progressive principle".[57] It can be seen that the ability principle based on the capacity theory is a better option for Chinese tax laws to pursue "justice for the disadvantaged".

Taking the ability principle as the basic principle for tax burden distribution in Chinese tax law should not be understood as completely excluding the benefit principle. Tax laws often include a large number of provisions aimed at achieving some policy objectives, and certain taxpayers may enjoy tax reduction even if the tax burden is already in accordance with their economic

---

55 See J. A. Hobson, *The Science of Wealth* (Williams & Norgate 1919) 172.

56 See Axel Honneth, *The Struggle for Recognition: The Moral Grammar of Social Conflicts* (Joel Anderson tr, The MIT Press 1995) 51. It is worth mentioning that with the digitalization of economics, the effectiveness of fair market value as an objective value standard is facing challenges. The "functionings" proposed by A. K. Sen could be the next standard, but we cannot be sure whether it is practical.

57 See Edwin R. A. Seligman, *The Income Tax* (The Macmillan Company 1911) 29–34.

capacity. Stanley S. Surrey found that these tax law provisions are essentially "non-tax" in nature, but the same as direct government fiscal expenditures, i.e. "tax expenditures".[58] However, unlike direct government fiscal expenditures providing indivisible public goods for all members of society, tax expenditures only reduce the tax burden for certain taxpayers, meaning that only a few people could benefit from it. In cases where public goods still need to be provided, individuals who have not enjoyed tax benefits not only continue to bear their own tax burden but also have to bear the tax burden that individuals who have had their taxes reduced. It means that taxpayers who have not enjoyed tax benefits not only need to fund public goods within their statutory tax burden but also need to provide additional funding for individuals who have had their tax burden reduced. This not only lacks clear benefits for those bearing the tax burden but also potentially grants individuals with reduced tax burdens a special advantage in wealth accumulation. In other words, tax expenditures may cause tax laws to show preferences towards specific taxpayers, undermining the neutrality of the tax system and even constituting reverse discrimination against those bearing the tax burden.

When we design a tax system based on the ability principle, select basic elements of tax law, and distribute tax burdens towards the advantaged and the disadvantaged in accordance with their economic capacities, the tax law itself will achieve a certain degree of distributive justice. However, this also easily makes us forget that justice in law "emphasizes the maintenance or restoration of balance or equality".[59] The moral neutrality of the identity of the disadvantaged implies that while no one should be punished because they are disadvantaged, neither should they be rewarded because of this identity. If people pursue privileges in the name of the disadvantaged or of assisting the disadvantaged, they themselves deviate from the path of justice. Therefore, as emphasized by proponents of the cost theory, it should be allowed for taxpayers to reasonably constrain public expenditure based on the benefit principle. Although the distribution of tax burdens should not be directly restricted by individuals during the construction of the tax system, once tax laws substantively answer the question of "what is fair tax burden distribution" through the "standard tax law elements", any relief or increase in tax burdens by law provisions should be deemed as deviating from the standard tax structure and

---

[58] See, e.g., Stanley S. Surrey, 'Tax Incentives as a Device for Implementing Government Policy: A Comparison with Direct Government Expenditures' (1970) 83(4) *Harvard Law Review* 705.

[59] Ye Shan, 'Legal Construction of the Ability-to-pay of Individual Income Tax' (2019) 1 *Peking University Law Review* 236, 239.

be constrained.[60] In particular, in addition to the tax law incentives provisions, China has enacted a large number of regulations, rules, and policy documents that provide tax preferential treatment. These tax expenditures formed by the tax law system should be supervised within the scope of the budget based on the benefit principle, to ensure that they do not bring substantial changes to the original tax burden distribution or grant undue economic advantages to specific taxpayers.

4. CONCLUSION

"Justice for the disadvantaged" is an inevitable pursuit for China in the context of a market economy. Driven by the market economy, some Chinese have become affluent, not only escaping poverty but even entering the ranks of the world's top riches. However, some still face difficulties in realizing their legal rights. This makes the concept of social justice and the demand for "justice for the disadvantaged" legitimate and necessary. Nowadays, people enjoy their rights in a legal rather than moral sense; therefore, all rights are positive and require active responses from the government.[61] The aspiration of the people to live a better life must push the Chinese government to continuously improve the level and capacity of providing public goods, and correspondingly require distribution of the tax burden among all members of society. In this process, not only should the distribution of the tax burden be equitable, but the concept of "tax equity" itself should, in principle, align with "justice for the disadvantaged".

Since the benefit principle requires the state to distribute the tax burden to individuals only when they benefit from public goods, while the ability principle does not require a direct link between the provision of public goods and specific individuals, allowing the state to distribute the tax burden based on one's ability to pay, there is an inherent conflict between these two principles. It is impossible for both to serve as the fundamental principles for tax burden distribution simultaneously. From the perspective of justice for the disadvantaged, the benefit principle leaves room for the advantaged to arbitrarily avoid bearing the tax burden; therefore, it cannot serve as the fundamental principle for tax burden distribution but is more suitable to be considered as what

---

60 See Zhang Mujun, 'The Structural Analysis of Enterprise Income Tax Law of China from the Perspective of Tax Expenditure' (2017) 9 *Academic Journal of Zhongzhou* 74.

61 Stephen Holmes and Cass R. Sunstein, *The Cost of Rights: Why Liberty Depends on Taxes* (W.W. Norton 2000) 35.

Dworkin would call a "relatively less important principle",[62] applicable for examining tax rules that increase or relieve tax burden for taxpayers. In order to enable the state to provide public goods to help the disadvantaged overcome difficulties, optimize the tax regime, eliminate loopholes and conflicts in existing tax laws, make the tax criteria objective and workable, we should take the ability principle as the fundamental principle for tax burden distribution in the future formulation of the General Principles of Taxation and the Tax Code, and "ability" should also be clearly defined as "measuring the taxpayer's objective economic capacity."

---

[62] Ronald Dworkin, *Taking Rights Seriously* (Harvard University Press 1978) 26.

10. Reconstructing the criminal attribution of securities market manipulation: from the dilemma in evaluating the manipulative control over information

Geng Jianing

1. PROPOSAL OF RESEARCH PROBLEM

Before the promulgation of Amendment (XI),[1] Article 182 of the Criminal Law explicitly lists only three types of securities market manipulation. As to what 'other practices' are covered by the 'catch-all' provision, heated debates exist in practice. Article 1 of the *Interpretation of the Supreme People's Court and the Supreme People's Procuratorate on Several Issues Concerning the Application of Law in Handling Criminal Cases of Securities or Futures Market Manipulation* on 27 June 2019 (hereinafter referred to as *Interpretation*) attempts to clarify the 'catch-all' provision by citing a few examples, which stipulate that 'other practices' include pump-and-dump manipulation, scalping, fabricating major events, manipulative control over information, and spoofing. Among them, pump-and-dump manipulation, spoofing and scalping, according to Amendment (XI) to the Criminal Law, have been introduced into the list of manipulation in parallel with the existing practices, namely continuous trading, improper matched orders and wash sale.

The absence of manipulative control over information in the recent legislative process prompts us to reconsider its relationship with the amended provisions in Article 182. Is it subsumed under the narrative clauses or still covered by the catch-all clause? If the answer is the former, it is essential to see by which narrative clause and how it is subsumed. If the answer is the latter, as to its homogeneity with the existing types of manipulation provided by Article 182 of the Criminal Law, further reflection – aimed at confirming whether this

[1] https://www.pkulaw.com/en_law/1c36a17d9fa0d40cbdfb.html?way=textLawChange.

homogeneity could be fully connoted by Article 1, Text 4 of the *Interpretation*[2] – is needed. From the practical perspective, the response to these questions is connected with the definition of manipulative control over information and its conviction standard. From the doctrinal perspective, the response may shake the hermeneutic preconception based on the dichotomy between trading-based manipulation and information-based manipulation, as well as transform the basis of criminal attribution from ontologism to functionalism.

2. SUBSUMPTION DILEMMA OF THE EXISTING NARRATIVE CLAUSES

There are theories and judgments that hold a positive attitude towards whether manipulative control over information could be subsumed by the existing narrative clauses. However, no consensus has been reached on the details, namely whether it could be subsumed into Text 5 (pump-and-dump manipulation) or Text 1 (continuous trading by using information advantage) of Article 182 of the Criminal Law. In the view of this chapter, neither solution avoids the subsumption dilemma.

2.1 Insufficient Capacity of the Provision on the Pump-and-Dump Manipulation

Literally, manipulative control over information is not limited to the use of false information to induce transactions, but also includes intentionally controlling listed companies to disclose real information. Moreover, the latter situation, of which the *Xu Xiang* case[3] is a typical example, does occur in practice. From this perspective, only by defining the pump-and-dump manipulation in a broad sense, Text 5 of Article 182 of the Criminal Law can fully subsume the manipulative control over information. However, the definition in a broad sense, according to which the pump-and-dump manipulation includes not only releasing materially false, inaccurate, incomplete, or uncertain information,

---

2 The provision on the manipulative control over information in Article 1, Text 4 of the *Interpretation* remains consistent with that stipulated by the *Provisions (II) of the Supreme People's Procuratorate and the Ministry of Public Security on the Standards for Filing Criminal Cases under the Jurisdiction of the Public Security Organs for Investigation and Prosecution* (2022 revision, hereinafter referred to as the *New Prosecution Standard II*).

3 See the Criminal Judgment No. 148 (2016) of Qingdao Intermediate People's Court of Shandong Province. When the judgment is made, neither law nor judicial interpretation has made express provision outlawing the pump-and-dump manipulation.

but also deliberately controlling the timing and pace of information disclosure to induce investment decisions,[4] should not be adopted, since it goes obviously beyond the semantic boundary of the law and does not meet the requirements of system interpretation. There is even a risk of making the relevant regulations on administrative offenses into a mere 'figurehead'.

Firstly, from the perspective of interpretation limited to the semantic boundary of the law, Article 182, Text 5 of the Criminal Law only regulates the conduct of 'inducing investors to engage in securities and futures trading by using false or uncertain material information'. Induced transactions based on real, incomplete, or inaccurate information are not included. Secondly, from the perspective of system interpretation, the *case of Teng A Xiong and other persons* who fabricated and spread false information on securities trading, No. VI of the model cases on securities crimes jointly published by the Supreme People's Procuratorate and the Securities Regulatory Commission on 6 November 2020, clearly stated the reason why the punishment of the crime of manipulating the securities market (which includes the pump-and-dump manipulation) is heavier than the punishment of the crime of fabricating and spreading false information on securities trading. In order to establish the former crime, one must take advantage of stock price fluctuations to make relevant transactions or to seek related profits, which is not required for the latter crime. In terms of the offensive consequence of abnormal fluctuations in the securities market caused by using information, the two crimes cannot be distinguished from each other. That is to say, there should be no significant difference between them in the defects of information involved. Since the object of the crime of fabricating and spreading false information on securities trading is limited to 'false information', the induced transactions based on non-false information should not be regulated by the provision on the pump-and-dump manipulation. Some scholars even take the discussion above as a basis for their different opinions on the Amendment (XI) to the Criminal Law which has provided 'uncertain information' as one of the objects of the pump-and-dump manipulation.[5] Finally, from the perspective of cooperation between criminal law and administrative law, once the induced transactions based on non-false information are fully subsumed into Article 182, Text 5 of the Criminal Law, the application of administrative sanctions will be greatly reduced, since according to Texts 3 and 7 of Article 2 of the *Interpretation*, unless the trading

---

4 See Li Zhen and Xia Zhongbao, 'The Gains and Losses of the Amendment of Market Manipulation Clauses in the New Securities Law' (2020)7 *Financial Theory & Practice* 84.

5 See Xie Jie and Ma Hongwei, *Road to Regulation: Criminal Law's Logic of Capital Market* (Law Press, 2021) 99.

volume is less than 10 million yuan and the amount of illegal income is less than 1 million yuan, the actor should be subject to criminal liability.

In short, the concept of pump-and-dump manipulation should be limited to induced transactions based on false information. As for the 'uncertain information' stipulated in Article 182, Text 5 of the Criminal Law, it can be seen as a procedural provision to indicate that the burden of proof for the falsity of information has been reversed. When the authenticity of information is doubtful (that is to say, it cannot be determined to be true), unless there is an effective defense, the information is presumed to be false, which means the lack of necessity for the prosecution to give incontestable proof.

2.2 The Provision on the Continuous Trading by Using Information Advantage is Unsound to Subsume

With regard to manipulative control over information which lies beyond the scope of the pump-and-dump manipulation, some scholars turn their focus to the clause of continuous trading in Article 182, Text 1 of the Criminal Law.[6] This point of view is also reflected in both cases *Zhu Dehong* and *Xu Xiang*. The characteristics that the two cases have in common can be found in the following aspects: the complexity of manipulation methods – in addition to controlling information disclosure, there are also associated transactions in the secondary market – and the non-falsity of the information involved. The court hearing the *Zhu Dehong* case holds that according to Article 182, Text 1 of the Criminal Law, Zhu Dehong and Yan Shaodong should bear criminal liability for the securities market manipulation, given the fact that Zhu Dehong, as the actual controller of Hongda New Material Company, guided the company to disseminate bullish information and informed Yang Shaodong at the same time; Yang Shaodong, who conspired with Zhu Dehong and thus was informed of the company's acquisition process and development strategies, drove up the stock price by continuous trading in the secondary market.[7] In the *Xu Xiang* case, the court also resorts to Text 1 of Article 182 of the Criminal Law as the basis for conviction and follows a similar subsumption approach by emphasizing that 'since Xu Xiang and his accomplices were aware of the timing and main content of the information released by listed companies, taking information advantage proved to be an important way for them to interfere with the stock price and the trading volume, while continuous trading was only one of the methods to drive up the price by using their information advantage'.

---

6 See Miu Yinzhi, 'The Enforcement Standards of the Informational Manipulation of Market' (2019)6 *Tsinghua University Law Journal* 176.

7 See the Criminal Judgment No. 86 (2017) of Shanghai First Intermediate People's Court.

Both the manipulative control over information and Article 182, Text 1 of the Criminal Law are characterized by information factors, which make it seem reasonable to subsume the former within the facts indicated by the latter. However, such a general approach will face a number of problems. On the one hand, Article 182, Text 1 of the Criminal Law, which actually refers to continuous trading by using information advantage, cannot cover the behaviors of manipulation realized exclusively by controlling information. On the other hand, even if the actor controls the generation or disclosure of information and carries out relevant transactions in the secondary market, taking this clause as the major premise to judge whether his behaviors conform to the constitutive elements of crime will give an open invitation to difficulties in identifying the 'serious circumstances'. One option is to maintain the subsumption of the manipulative control over information within trading-based manipulation, which means the volume of artificial transactions must reach a certain percentage in the market, while the other is to give up the above subsumption and turn to the conviction standard for information-based manipulation. The former option might lead to loopholes in punishment, while the latter option proves at risk of violating the hermeneutic rules of the 'catch-all' provision.

With regard to the manipulation coupled with hybrid model, transactions in the secondary market, usually complementary to the information speculation, are logically of lower intensity. Taking the *Xu Xiang* case and the *Zhu Dehong* case as examples, the cumulative trading volume generated over twenty consecutive trading days represents only 6% of the total turnover of the shares involved. In the *Zhu Dehong* case, even if there is a growing proportion of the trading volume, it still falls short of the 30% threshold under Article 39, Text 1 of the *Provisions (II) of the Supreme People's Procuratorate and the Ministry of Public Security on the Standards for Filing Criminal Cases under the Jurisdiction of the Public Security Organs for Investigation and Prosecution* on May 7, 2010 (expired, hereinafter the *Prosecution Standard II*). Therefore, if we take trading-based manipulation as the major premise to judge whether their behaviors conform to the constitutive elements of crime, ultimately, the perpetrators will not be held criminally responsible since they fail to meet the conviction standard mentioned above. The artificial transactions which should have been complementary to the information speculation in such a way become a safe harbor for them to get rid of punishment.

The reason why *Prosecution Standard II* requires the proportion of the trading volume in a determined period lies in its decisive influence on the stock price. When continuous trading reaches a certain strength, 'one deserves punishment because his behaviors have left a serious unwarranted interference in the free market's price-forming mechanism as well as its normal operation'.[8] The absence of requirement for the amount of funds used in the artificial transactions is mainly due to the fact that 'it is difficult to draw a line of conviction since in practice to achieve a trading-based manipulation, funds are repeatedly used of which the amount could reach hundreds of millions yuan or even hundreds of billions yuan'.[9] In the context where the conviction standard for trading-based manipulation (both relative and absolute values are required) is higher than that for information-based manipulation (only absolute value is required), in order to facilitate criminal prosecution and to avoid the above loopholes in punishment, the judicial organs tend to 'do one thing under the cover of another'. They refer to the provisions of trading-based manipulation to judge whether the manipulative control over information meets the constitutive elements of crime, while turning to the 'catch-all' provision to determine whether the circumstances are serious in aiming to apply the conviction standard for information-based manipulation.

Return to the *Xu Xiang* case. In terms of the constitutive elements of crime, the court resorts to Article 182, Text 1 of the Criminal Law, holding that 'Xu Xiang, Wang Wei and Zhu Yong who conspired with each other to obtain illegal interests, manipulated the price and volume of securities transactions by continuous trading with information advantage'. However, when determining whether the circumstances are serious, the same court turns to Article 39, Text 6 of the *Prosecution Standard II* which stipulates that 'if a listed company, any of its directors, supervisors or senior managers, its actual controllers or controlling shareholders or any other affiliates of it manipulate the securities price, separately or in concert with others, by using information advantage, shall be filed for investigation and prosecution', in such a way to emphasize that 'different from the securities market manipulation with capital or shareholding advantage, for the manipulation with information advantage neither the behaviors of continuous trading nor the proportion of the trading volume is necessary'. In other words, if the facts of the case can be subsumed within Article 182, Text 1 of the Criminal Law, and thus cannot be criminalized under that explicit clause, the court, instead of acquittal, moves towards the 'catch-all' provision as the basis for criminal liability, which violates the hermeneutic

---

[8] Xian Jie and Wu Qiaobin, 'Key and Difficult Issues of the Interpretation on Several Issues Concerning the Application of Law in Handling Criminal Cases of Securities or Futures Market Manipulation' *Procuratorate Daily* (August 18, 2019).

[9] Jiang Yongyi, Chen Xueyong and Zhu Hongwei, 'Understanding and Application of the Interpretation on Several Issues Concerning the Application of Law in Handling Criminal Cases of Securities or Futures Market Manipulation' *People's Court Daily* (March 12, 2020).

rules derived from the principle of legality – a 'catch-all' provision could be invoked only if each typical fact indicated by the narrative provisions fails to subsume the fact committed.[10]

2.3 Tip: Abandon the Formalized Subsumption Approach

As for a single-type manipulation, neither the subsumption nor the conviction causes great problems, but in the case of manipulation coupled with hybrid model which occurs more frequently in practice,[11] the same work proves more difficult. It seems that we have taken a wrong approach from the beginning which leads us to the dilemmatic alternative between the principle of proportionality in a narrow sense and the principle of legality. The existing approach is characterized by its formalism. Firstly, the narrative provision on the continuous trading with information advantage has been simplified to a combination of information advantage and continuous trading, which has been even further dwarfed as a collection of information factors and trading factors. In addition, what makes things worse is the attempt to syllogize the conformity of the fact committed to the constitutive elements of crime; once from a fact both information factors and trading factors can be decomposed, the syllogistic subsumption is complete.

In terms of methodology, this formalized subsumption approach conflicts with the existing judicial interpretation. In the *New Prosecution Standards II* and *Interpretation*, the categorization of manipulation is glued to the conviction standard, that is to say, for the trading-based manipulation they apply a relative criterion according to which the volume of artificial transactions must reach a certain percentage in the market, while for the information-based manipulation they move toward an absolute criterion that only requires the trading volume. At this point, the dichotomy between trading-based manipulation and information-based manipulation not only plays the role of cutting behaviors from their external side, but also represents an essential difference in the way in which offenses are realized. As a matter of methodology – in consideration of the judicial interpretation noted above – instead of the syllogistic subsumption which follows formal logic, we might attempt to take a

---

10 Ruan Qilin, 'Criminal Justice Shall Persist in the Substantial Evaluation of Responsibility' (2017) 4 *China Legal Science* 61.

11 Given the semi-strong efficient market in China, the dissemination and feedback of information seem inefficient. Due to the numerous market noises, it is difficult to achieve the manipulation only by information disclosure. In practice, the cooperation between information disclosure and artificial transactions in the secondary market proves more common.

more substantial approach which focuses on the offense against legal interests protected by the crime of securities market manipulation.

3. ANALOGY IS THE ESSENCE OF THE SUBSTANTIAL SUBSUMPTION APPROACH

In view of the difficulties brought by the formalized approach mentioned above, some scholars, in favor of a dynamic subsumption for the manipulation coupled with hybrid model, hope to measure substantially the influence of behaviors in order to determine whether the information disclosure or the continuous trading plays a bigger role in the fluctuations of stock price and trading volume. If the information disclosure plays a bigger role, the manipulation coupled with hybrid model is part of the information-based manipulation regulated by the 'catch-all' provision; otherwise, it falls under the trading-based manipulation and thus Article 182, Text 1 of the Criminal Law should be applied.[12]

3.1 Quantitative Comparison on Dominance is of 'Self-Deception' and the Concept of Information-Based Manipulation is at Risk of 'Pocketization' (Catch-All Offense)

Substantializing the subsumption process seems to provide us a solution to address the dilemma noted above, but a closer look reveals that the so-called substantial measurement on dominance appears to be self-deception.

According to the theoretical model of information-based manipulation, the dissemination of information could have a direct impact on investors in the secondary market, inducing their decisions on capital allocation in such a way as to bring fluctuations of stock price and trading volume. In the first causal process, it is impossible in practice to verify whether the decision-making of investors has been affected by the information disseminated, which means a great difficulty in proving the causation between the artificial information dissemination and the decision-making of investors. In the second causal process, it remains difficult to directly prove the causation between the trading behaviors of investors affected by the information and the abnormal fluctuations of stock price and trading volume, since the securities market is operated under

12 See Shang Haowen, 'On the Judicial Approach for Identifying the Crime of Information-based Manipulation of the Securities Market: from the Perspective of the Latest Judicial Interpretation by the Supreme People's Court and the Supreme People's Procuratorate in 2019' (2020) 5 *Law Science* 54–55.

complex economic rules, affected by a combination of inevitable factors and occasional factors.[13]

It can be seen that whether the artificially controlled disclosure of information dominates the price-forming in the securities market is already 'a deduction formed after a double presumption on conditional causality'.[14] A quantitative comparison on this basis is nothing more than another presumption of degree (giving a presumption on what factor plays a major role), which has lost its independent significance in judgment. Focusing on the question of whether the information disclosure or continuous trading plays a major role of which the response proves predetermined, the so-called substantial approach results in a formal self-justification. What's even more worrying is that the self-justification is more inclined to information-based manipulation for which a lower conviction standard is provided. Given the lack of ontological criteria in the quantitative comparison on dominance, the concept of information-based manipulation is at a higher risk of 'pocketization'.

As mentioned above, the main consideration of judicial interpretation in setting the conviction standard for trading-based manipulation consists of the influence of continuous trading and other behaviors on the market. The secondary role played by artificial transactions in the manipulation coupled with hybrid model means its failure to reach the conviction standard for trading-based manipulation. In other words, if a fact concerning the manipulation coupled with hybrid model is subsumed into trading-based manipulation, no one could be held criminally responsible. In the substantial approach, however, the same fact is more likely to be subsumed into information-based manipulation, which refers to a virtually lower conviction standard. Given the predetermined result of the quantitative comparison, the concept of information-based manipulation – as a tool to whitewash the conviction – is gradually moving away from the principle of legality. The substantial approach carries a clear preference for conviction. Taking this approach to its extreme, the aftermath is the exclusive subsumption of 'continuous trading by using information advantage' stipulated by Article 182, Text 1 of the Criminal Law within the information-based manipulation.[15] The concept of information-based manipulation, which is moving away from the principle of legality, triggers the 'pocketization' process of Text 1 of Article 182 of the Criminal Law. The buyers and the sellers

---

[13] See Wang Chongqing, *Research on the Security Crime under Circulation Time* (People's Public Security University of China Press, 2014) 142–143.

[14] Xie Jie, *Criminal Law in the Capital Market: the Regulation of Market Abuse* (Law Press, 2016) 223.

[15] See Zhang Zechen, 'On the Behavior Model of Information-based Manipulation of Securities Market and the Risk Prevention and Control' (2020) 2 *Research on Rule of Law* 24.

who take advantage of information, regardless of the authenticity of information and the identity of the person who disseminates it, are subject to criminal liability. As a result, the conviction of induced transactions concerning the generation and disclosure of information proves to be an analogy *in malam partem*, since neither the requirement of homogeneous interpretation nor the limitation on the falsity of information can be found.

3.2 Abandon the Dichotomy between Trading-Based Manipulation and Information-Based Manipulation

As to the manipulation coupled with hybrid model, the substantial subsumption approach, regardless of the ontological factors, breaks the static matching not only between 'information factors and the use of information advantage', but also between 'transaction factors and continuous trading'. What's more, the substantial judgment which takes the offense-forming process into consideration represents certain normative characteristics. However, this view has not yet abandoned the empirical dichotomy between trading-based manipulation and information-based manipulation, and seeks to simplify the concept of information-based manipulation to information-related manipulation. The analogy implicit therein may lead to an expansion of the scope of penalties for the offense of securities market manipulation.

So far in the discussion we have found that taking the subsumption formalized approach means a dilemmatic alternative between the principle of proportionality in a narrow sense and the principle of legality; however, turning to the substantial approach proves ineffective since the above dilemma is not fundamentally eliminated. Perhaps the root of the problem lies not in the subsumption criteria but in the *a priori* classification itself. Both approaches, formalized and substantial, follow a common logical premise, namely the dichotomy between trading-based manipulation and information-based manipulation. Under such a dichotomy structure, the first question to answer is in which type of manipulation the fact should be subsumed, so as to determine whether the fact conforms to the constitutive elements of crime and which standard of conviction should be applied.

In fact, hermeneutic activities, instead of being a grasp of legal texts without premise, are inevitably conditioned by preconception.[16] The dichotomy between trading-based manipulation and information-based manipulation occurs in the law in both the United States, where the securities industry is extremely developed, and other countries (such as Italy and Germany) under

[16] See Gao Hongjun, 'Gadamer's Hermeneutics and the Legal Interpretation in China' (2015) 2 *Tribune of Political Science and Law* 6.

the framework of EU law. Although this categorization has not been recognized by Chinese law, due to the 'preemption' of foreign legislation and justice, this dichotomy structure, inevitably absorbed in the experience of Chinese interpreters, becomes a hermeneutic preconception. However, the hermeneutic preconception based on foreign experience is different from propositions that no one can break through. In terms of the relation and demarcation between administrative offense and crime, there are significant differences between China and foreign countries. Therefore, the Chinese law, the meaning of which cannot be completely replaced by the preconception – namely the dichotomy between trading-based manipulation and information-based manipulation – must be the primary consideration of our hermeneutic activities. Different from the United States, Italy, and Germany, there is a 'double track' of unlawfulness in the Chinese legal system, consisting of crime and administrative offense, which is only punishable by administrative sanctions. Given the factors that indicate the demarcation between them – such as 'circumstance' and 'amount' – the dichotomy in terms of conviction standard for trading-based manipulation and information-based manipulation can be imagined. The judicial interpretation, seeking to solve the qualitative problem and the quantitative problem, provides different circumstances for different types of manipulation. A dual role has been attributed to the subsumption activities, which are thus bound to both the principle of proportionality in a narrow sense and the principle of legality. In consideration of the single role assumed by the subsumption activities in foreign countries, it is not appropriate for us to completely copy their experience. Our own solution is to accommodate the classification logic of market manipulation to the functional orientation of subsumption activities.

Given the least importance of the dichotomy between trading-based manipulation and information-based manipulation, could we radically change the approach, giving up the hermeneutic preconception and the classification logic behind it which is oriented by both ontological and functionalist considerations, and analyzing the market manipulation from a purely functionalist perspective?

4. A PROPER APPROACH: ESTABLISH THE FUNCTIONALIST PERSPECTIVE IN THE CRIMINAL ATTRIBUTION OF MANIPULATION

Analyzing the market manipulation from a purely functionalist perspective means not only completely abandoning the empirical approach based on the material-oriented logic and paying more attention to the equivalence of unlawfulness between the manipulative control over information (except pump-and-dump manipulation) and the existing types of manipulation provided in Article

182 of the Criminal Law, but also a simultaneous transformation of the classification logic and the attribution basis.

The concept of market manipulation is inherently related to consequence, of which the unlawfulness does not arise solely from behaviors.[17] With regard to the *actus reus* of market manipulation, besides the behaviors of continuous trading, improper matched orders, wash sale, pump-and-dump manipulation, spoofing and scalping, it is also required that there be an abnormal fluctuation in the securities market that can be attributed to them. For this purpose, it deserves an independent review on whether the behaviors noted above bring an unwarranted interference in the market's normal price-forming mechanism.[18] The attribution of abnormal fluctuations to the behaviors involved becomes the key to clarifying the *actus reus* of market manipulation. In this sense, the term 'attribution' in this chapter refers to the attribution of the objective typical facts[19] (*Die Zurechnung zum objektiven Tatbestand*)[20] or the attribution of unlawfulness realized by the principal offender (*Täter*), aimed at defining from a normative perspective the *actus reus* of the crime of securities market manipulation.

4.1 Functionalization of the Unlawfulness Attribution: The Dichotomy between Organizational Jurisdiction and Institutional Jurisdiction

Jakobs, in favor of pure functionalism, regards 'jurisdiction' as the key to demonstrating the unlawfulness realized by the principal offender.[21] In his view,

---

17 See Liu Xianquan and Xie Jie, 'Deconstruction of the Essence of Criminal Market Manipulation: A Legal and Economic Analysis' (2014) 6 *Modern Law Science* 80.

18 This chapter agrees that price is the core element of the securities market and that the market's price-forming mechanism should be the focus of criminal protection. However, in view of Amendment VI to the Criminal Law, the normal formation of trading volume has not been excluded from the legal interests of this crime. In fact, in defining the legal interests protected by the crime of market manipulation, besides the 'correct price-forming of financial instruments', in Italy both jurisprudence and general doctrine take the 'correct and effective operation of the market' into account.

19 See Li Shiyang, 'New Study on the Behavior Theory in the Criminal Law' (2018) 2 *China Legal Science* 157.

20 Compare Roxin, *Strafrecht Allgemeiner Teil* (Band I, 4th edition, C.H. Beck, 2006) §11 para. 1.

21 See Geng Jianing, 'Evaluation of Participation in the Crime by Inaction and Change of the Foundation of Criminal Theory' (2015) 2 *Contemporary Law Review* 41.

'people can organize the world, but they also always live in a world with various institutions that has been organized'.[22] We are free to organize the world in such a way that is not harmful to others; otherwise, the harmful results will be attributed to our behaviors of organization. This kind of attribution follows the logic of organizational jurisdiction, which is based on the negative obligation not to harm others. When we step out of our own world into the field of others, people gathered in the same field give mutual recognition to each other in terms of differences in social achievements and abilities,[23] which leads to the delamination of roles. In this process, some people are given an obligation by the institution to promote the welfare of others. Within the range of the institution, once the interests of other members are infringed, the infringement should be attributed to those who deviate from their institutional roles, even if the occurrence of infringement is not under their control. This kind of attribution follows the logic of institutional jurisdiction, which is based on the positive obligation to 'build a common world with others'.

In this sense, it is the type of jurisdiction, rather than the type of empirical subsumption, that determines the attribution of unlawfulness realized by the principal offender. Besides the causality related to the violation of negative obligation, there is another basis for attribution, purely normative, related to the violation of positive obligation (deviating from the institutional role). For Jakobs, positive obligation is just the obligation of solidarity.[24] In order to justify social solidarity, rather than resorting to the philosophy of subjectivity oriented by economic rationality and utilitarianism in the period of 'contractual solidarity', the modern solution consists of 'the guarantee of dignity' and 'the recognition of differences in personal achievements and abilities'.[25] From the perspective of functionalism, the positive obligation is different from the guarantor's duty, which is based on empirical factors (such as the possibility of dominating the realization of facts outlawed), and the institutional jurisdiction does not refer to a universal criterion of principal offender abstracted from personal identity.[26] Only when a person is embedded in a specific institution,

22 He Qingren, *Studien zum Pflichtdelikt* (China Renmin University Press, 2010) 25.

23 Axel Honneth, *Kampf um Anerkennung* (translated by Hu Jihua, proofread by Cao Weidong, Shanghai People's Publishing House, 2005) 134.

24 See *supra* note 21, 27.

25 See Wang Hui, 'Concept of Solidarity and Fundamental Obligations in Law' (2015) 3 *Tsinghua University Law Journal* 15–16.

26 Zhou Xiaotian 'packages' Jakobs's theory with Roxin's theory, arguing that the universal criterion for principal offender abstracted from the identity is one of the common features of the two theories. See Zhou Xiaotian, 'Consideration and Critique on Theory of Duty Crime' (2016) 1 *The Jurist* 152.

could he acquire an identity in the sense of institutional jurisdiction and therefore assume the positive obligation.[27]

4.2 Differences in the Attribution Basis of Unlawfulness within the Subsumption of Trading-Based Manipulation

Chinese scholars usually regard the manipulation that has a direct effect on the financial products in the secondary market, namely continuous trading, improper matched orders and wash sales, as trading-based manipulation.[28] Although the three types of manipulation share the same superior concept, only for market manipulation by continuous trading, Article 182 of the Criminal Law requires the use of market power consisting of capital, shareholding or information advantage. Why is there no similar requirement for improperly matched orders and wash sales? To answer this question, we are forced to clarify the special role played by the relative advantage position of the principal offender in shaping the outlawed facts of manipulation.

As we all know, continuous trading is based on 'genuine' transactions, while improper matched orders and wash sales, even with the appearance of active trading, do not actually transfer the ownership of securities and funds. According to classical theory in economics, the market's price-forming mechanism depends on the unimpeded operation of ordinary market forces of supply and demand, which makes the price up and down. With regard to improper matched orders and wash sales, both of which convey false information as to the supply of and demand for investments, the fraud theory derived from the judicial precedent of the common law system is able to explain how the market is manipulated. Since the price should be set by the unimpeded collective judgment of buyers and sellers, artificial transactions that disrupt the market's normal price-forming mechanism are held to be a fraud on investors.[29] However, in the case of continuous trading, the application of fraud theory implies the tendency to reinforce the objective interference of behaviors with the actor's intention to manipulate the market. This theory attempts to explain the deceptiveness of information conveyed by continuous trading by demonstrating that 'the artificially controlled supply of and demand for investments removes securities transactions from the competitive environment of the real market'. However, the demand–supply signals released by continuous trading are based on the actual transfer of property rights; the information that has been concealed is limited to the plan of reverse transactions in the future.

---

27 See *supra* note 21, 289.

28 See *supra* note 16, 89.

29 See *United States v. Brown et al.*, 5 F. Supp. 81, 85 (District Court for the Southern District of New York 1933).

Given the speculative nature of capital allocation decisions, which are based on investors' judgment about the future value of particular stocks, it remains normal for investors to take various transactions that objectively occur as material for judgment. The trend-pursued transactions should be regarded as commercially motivated when investors who are able to predict risks decide to buy or sell stocks only because they believe that they themselves will benefit from market fluctuations before the reverse change. Therefore, the information concealed by general subjects who are engaged in continuous trading is not beyond the investors' reasonable expectations on the securities market.

In foreign countries, it seems inevitable to reinforce the objective interference of behaviors with the actor's intention to manipulate the market, since the trading-based manipulation, regardless of its specific form, is regulated in general terms of law. However, given the express requirement in Article 182, Text 1 of the Criminal Law, in the view of the Chinese legislator, rather than behaviors of continuous trading based on actual transactions which prove insufficient to reveal the unlawfulness of manipulation, the key point consists of the relative advantage position of the principal offender in capital, shareholding or information. The principal offender, due to his advantage in capital, shareholding or static information,[30] assumes a positive obligation based on institutional jurisdiction to ensure free competition in the operation of the price-forming mechanism. In addition, for utilitarian reasons, if the speculative fluctuations of stock price and trading volume caused by continuous trading (such as short selling subsequent to securities lending) contribute to discovering or revealing the stocks' real value and to improving the pricing efficiency,[31] the criminal attribution might be excluded since the risks involved are permissible.

The express requirement of the relative advantage position in capital, shareholding or information which is set by Article 182, Text 1 of the Criminal Law, should be regarded not only as an external restriction of punishment for the principal offender but as a confirmation—beyond utilitarianism—of

---

30 Referring to Article 19 of the *Guidelines for Identifying Securities Market Manipulation (Trial) of the Securities Regulatory Commission*, the term 'information advantage' in Article 182, Paragraph 1, Text 1 of the Criminal Law refers to the static information advantage that the actor has of 'obtaining or understanding material information about specific securities and related matters more easily, earlier, more accurately, and more completely compared with general investors in the market'.

31 See Shi Yanan, Chen Ran and Ao Bo, *Commentary and Cases of the Amendment (XI) to the Criminal Law* (China Legal Publishing House, 2021) 183; Li Zhisheng, Chen Chen and Lin Bingxuan, 'Does Short Selling Improve Price Efficiency in the Chinese Stock Market? Evidence from Natural Experiments' (2015) 4 *Economic Research Journal* 76.

the special role played by subjects in relative advantage position in the price-forming mechanism for free competition. For these subjects, the deviation from institutional roles and the violation of positive obligations become the attribution basis of the crime of securities market manipulation. Continuous trading is only one of the behaviors that indicate an obligation violation. The manipulative interference of behaviors is not an empirical fact to be discovered but a kind of risk distribution designed in advance by the normative system in terms of the abnormal fluctuations in the securities market. The dichotomy between organizational jurisdiction and institutional jurisdiction can find its normative comparison in the different requirements pursuant to Texts 1, 2, and 3 of Article 182 of the Criminal Law. The unlawfulness of securities market manipulation, on the one hand, consists of the fraud that creates false signals of trading price and trading volume; on the other hand, it derives from the abuse of the relative advantage position and the subsequent failure to carry out positive obligations aimed at maintaining free competition in the market's price-forming process.

4.3 Implementation: The New Dichotomy Based on 'Jurisdiction' in the Crime of Securities Market Manipulation

From the perspective of functionalism, each participant of the securities market is free to allocate capital or to disseminate information, comments and forecasts. However, they are not allowed to create false signals of trading price and trading volume which deceive investors' reasonable expectations for the market, since Articles 4 and 5 of the Securities Law draw an obligation pursuant to the principle of good faith. There may be various violations of this negative obligation, namely disseminating false information (pump-and-dump manipulation), concealing major conflicts of interest (scalping), undertaking false transactions that do not actually transfer the ownership of stocks and funds (improper matched orders and wash sales) and spoofing. Once someone occupies the relative advantage position in the securities market, they are no longer a simple participant, thus expected to improve institutional welfare for the ordinary investors by creating a free-competition environment. 'In an unimpeded securities market, it is the free competition among different market participants that makes the price up and down'.[32] In economics, free competition which contributes to pricing efficiency requires the appearance of full participation, that is, each variable plays its role as market forces of supply and

---

[32] Tian Hongjie, 'Crime of Manipulating the Securities Market: the Essence of Behavior and Its Judicial Determination' in Liu Renwen (ed.) *Securities and Futures Crimes: Criminal Regulation and Its Improvement* (Social Sciences Academic Press, 2018) 85.

demand. In addition, rational participation should not be forgotten, since irrational participation with severe informational asymmetry fails to activate the market to independently discover the stock price. What's worse, it may bring a greater divergence in the judgment of buyers and sellers, which increases the risk of market volatility. Correspondingly, in terms of institutional jurisdiction, the positive obligation to maintain free competition in the price-forming process includes two basic requirements. One is to ensure that other variables are fully involved in this process, generally referred to as the obligation not to exclude other factors. The other is to ensure the rational participation of other variables, generally referred to as the obligation to maintain the symmetry of market information. Given the requirements of both full and rational participation, the concept of positive obligation is able to unify the duty not to act within the context of prohibition norms and the duty to act within the context of command norms.

With regard to the unlawfulness in common of the behaviors listed in Article 182 of the Criminal Law, rather than an empirical evaluation, the key point is to identify the logic of attribution. We are given two alternative models – organizational jurisdiction and institutional jurisdiction. Among the practices stipulated in Texts 2 to 6 of Article 182 of the Criminal Law, there are both trading-based manipulation and information-based manipulation, of which, however, the common basis of unlawful attribution lies in the violation of negative obligation derived from the organizational jurisdiction by creating false signals concerning trading price and trading volume which deceive investors' reasonable expectations for the market. On the contrary, although the empirical subsumption of the practices stipulated in Text 1 of the same article within the trading-based manipulation, the unlawfulness is attached to the positive obligation derived from the institutional jurisdiction. The violation of this obligation becomes the exclusive reason for which the abnormal fluctuations of stock price can be attributed to the activities that seem to be commercially motivated, such as continuous trading, improper matched orders and wash sales.[33] However, the positive obligation should be limited within the specific institutional role.[34] For example, since the institution does not require those who have capital advantage to maintain the symmetry of market information, in the case of spoofing (bidding or offering with the intention to cancel the bid or offer before execution) it remains necessary to examine whether their behaviors have created false signals concerning trading price and trading volume which deceive investors' reasonable expectations for the market – in

[33] In this case, how to evaluate the violation of positive obligation in the sense of domination has lost its independent significance. See *supra* note 21, 309.

[34] See He Qingren, 'Criminal Imputation of Special Cognition' (2015) 4 *Peking University Law Journal* 1039.

other words, the attribution should still follow the logic of organizational jurisdiction (rather than the logic of institutional jurisdiction).

In short, the way in which the market is manipulated loses its significance for criminal evaluation. It is the 'jurisdiction' that draws a line between fraud manipulation consisting of the creation of false signals concerning trading price and trading volume which deceive investors' reasonable expectations for the market, and advantage abuse that leads to an improper exclusion of other variables from the price-forming process and a more asymmetric distribution of market information. In order to clarify the essential differences between the new dichotomy and the traditional dichotomy, we return to the empirical criterion engaged in the traditional dichotomy, as shown in Figure 10.1, where both fraud manipulation and advantage abuse can be further divided into trading-based manipulation and information-based manipulation.

At this point, the new dichotomy between 'fraud manipulation based on organizational jurisdiction' and 'advantage abuse based on institutional jurisdiction' has completely replaced the traditional dichotomy between trading-based manipulation and information-based manipulation. The empirical criterion engaged in the traditional dichotomy that can only serve as a 'comparison table' loses its significance for the objective attribution of unlawfulness. The transition from ontologism to functionalism is correspondingly

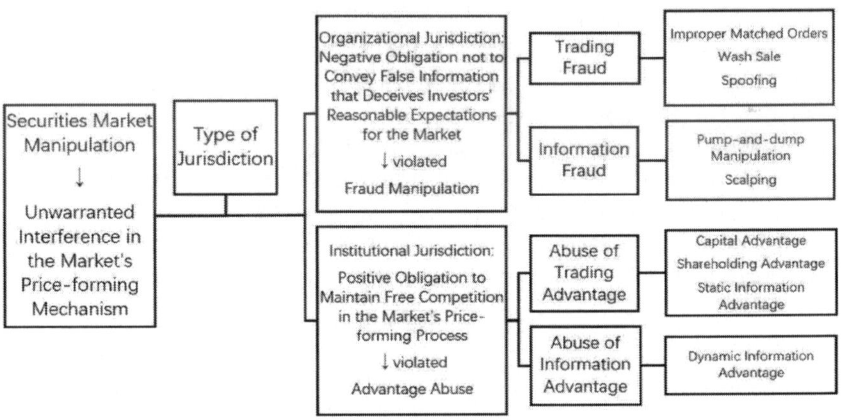

Source: Author's own.

Figure 10.1 *Relationship between 'fraud manipulation and advantage abuse' and 'trading-based manipulation and information-based manipulation'*

taking place in terms of both the homogeneous interpretation of the 'catch-all' provision and the attribution basis of unlawful manipulation.

5. MANIPULATIVE CONTROL OVER INFORMATION IN TERMS OF BOTH ORGANIZATIONAL JURISDICTION AND INSTITUTIONAL JURISDICTION

Article 1, Text 4 of the *Interpretation* describes the manipulative control over information as 'controlling the generation of information related to issuers and listed companies, or controlling the content as well as the timing and pace of information disclosure, to induce investors whose collective judgment can bring impact on the trading price or trading volume of securities'. Since both false information and real information can be involved in the *Interpretation*, the first step to define the manipulative control over information is to distinguish the pump-and-dump manipulation stipulated in Article 182, Text 5 of the Criminal Law, of which the attribution relies on the violation of negative obligation derived from the organizational jurisdiction, from the advantage abuse of which the attribution relies on the violation of positive obligation derived from the institutional jurisdiction. When the information generated or disclosed is false, the market may be manipulated by creating false signals of trading price and trading volume which deceive investors' reasonable expectations for the market. When the information involved is not false, manipulation may occur only if the market power has been improperly used, homogeneous with the advantage abuse regulated by Article 182, Text 1 of the Criminal Law consisting of artificial dissemination of information. Specifically, the criminal attribution should follow the principle of institutional jurisdiction that presupposes actors having relative advantage position in the securities market and hence having the positive obligation of maintaining free competition in the price-forming process. The provision on the manipulative control over information in Article 1, Text 4 of the *Interpretation* proves not sufficient to reflect this homogeneity.

Given the rules of homogeneity interpretation, the 'catch-all' provision remains inapplicable unless the principal offender has a dynamic information advantage comparable to the express advantage provided by Article 182 of the Criminal Law in terms of capital, shareholding or static information. Due to the full implementation of the stock issuance registration system promoted by the revised Securities Law (2019), both the listed company and its internal personnel are playing an increasingly prominent role in maintaining the symmetry of market information.[35] In the view of this chapter, the listed companies and their directors, supervisors, senior managers, actual controllers as well as the shareholders who own more than 5% of the total shares have a dynamic information advantage in controlling the creation or disclosure of information and thus are in a specific position in terms of institutional jurisdiction. For the same reason, they are subject to the positive obligation to ensure the symmetry of market information, which proves homogeneous with the obligation not to improperly exclude other variables from the price-forming process.

It is necessary to reiterate that the positive obligation is different from the guarantor's obligation based on the possibility of dominating the realization of facts outlawed. In order to distinguish the positive obligation from the guarantor's obligation, we have to identify whether the obligation is exclusive to the principal offender. Take the crime of breach of trust to the detriment of a listed company's benefits, for example; the duty of fidelity that the company's directors, supervisors, and senior managers assume is not a positive obligation. According to Article 169 (a), Paragraph 2 of the Criminal Law, the controlling shareholders and the actual controllers also have the same duty of loyalty. Therefore, the key to the assumption of the duty of loyalty is that the actor has the actual possibility of controlling the business activities of the listed company, regardless of whether he or she is a trusted party in a special relationship of reliance or whether he or she carries the positive expectations of a property owner for a professional manager under the separation of property and management in the post-industrial era. In contrast, in the case of small capitalization stocks, the cumulative volume of continuous trading by investors without advantage for ten consecutive trading days can also reach 20% of the total turnover of the stocks involved, which proves sufficient to interfere with the participation of other variables in the price-forming process. According to Article 182 of the Criminal Law, continuous trading by investors who do not have any advantage remains insufficient to constitute the crime. Therefore, the positive obligation of maintaining free competition in the price-forming process is exclusive to those who occupy a relative advantage position. Different from the guarantor's obligation, the establishment of the positive obligation has institutional reason – advantage recognized in social solidarity – beyond the empirical possibility of dominating the unlawful facts. For the same reason, the violation of the positive obligation represents the authentic figure of the crime of securities market manipulation in objective terms and connotes the unlawfulness of typical facts indicated in Article 182 of the Criminal Law,

35 See Article 63, Paragraph 3, Article 82, Paragraph 3, Article 84, Paragraph 1 and Article 84, Paragraph 2 of the Securities Law.

while the failure to meet the guarantor's obligation does not have a similar effect.

The creation of asymmetric information by those who have a dynamic information advantage – homogeneous with the abuse of advantage in capital or shareholding expressly provided by Article 182 of the Criminal Law – may weaken effective competition in the market and impair pricing efficiency, so as to be regarded as a violation of the institutional obligation. Take the *Xian Yan* case[36] for example; the violation of positive obligations justifies the attribution of unlawfulness to the principal offender. On the contrary, for those who do not have a dynamic information advantage and thus are not positively bound to maintain the symmetry of market information, a violation of the negative obligation remains essential. It is the creation of false signals concerning trading price and trading volume that determines the attribution of unlawfulness – homogeneous with the fraud manipulation. In other words, it is not allowed to attribute abnormal fluctuations in the securities market to a single person without special identities who uses non-false information to induce investments.

In practice, the cases of manipulative control over information are mostly manifested as internal and external collusion. In the case of manipulative control over information[37] without transactions in the secondary market, such as the administrative case of securities market manipulation by Butterfly Assets (Shanghai) Limited Liability Company and others,[38] the actual controller of the company, referring to the recommendations given by outsiders, creates, processes, and splits the information and determines the timing of information disclosure. As for the outsiders, an independent attribution of unlawfulness does not occur, since they do not have dynamic information advantage and thus are not positively bound to maintain the symmetry of market information. The outsiders, in consideration of their collusion in terms of advantage-abuse manipulation with those who assume the positive obligation, can only be punished as an accomplice.[39] In particular, it should be noted that generalization of the identity of participants cannot justify the requirement of control over the general subject of information manipulation stipulated in Article 1, Text

---

36 See the Criminal Judgment No. 110 (2019) of Shanghai High People's Court.

37 The term of 'manipulative control over information' specifically refers to the manipulative control over information other than pump-and-dump manipulation.

38 See the Decision of Administrative Sanctions No. 80 (2017) of the Securities Regulatory Commission.

39 The exclusivity of positive obligation emphasizes that only those who bear this obligation could directly destabilize the system. It does not mean that outsiders who are not bound to positive obligation cannot be punished as an accomplice.

4 of the *Interpretation*.[40] Rather than removing restrictions on the identity of the principal offender, it would be more reasonable to punish those who do not assume a positive obligation with the help of provisions relating to 'joint crime'.

In the case of manipulation coupled with hybrid model, such as the *Zhu Dehong* case and the *Xu Xiang* case, in cooperation with the dissemination of information, the outsiders may also undertake artificial transactions in the secondary market aimed at creating the appearance of active trading. As mentioned above, the unlawfulness of continuous trading based on actual transfer of property rights – pursuant to the logic of institutional jurisdiction – lies in the advantage that the principal offender has in capital, shareholding or static information. With regard to the outsiders, the static information advantage usually needs to be eliminated; otherwise, it might lead to a repeated evaluation of their behaviors of planning and suggesting. In this context, outsiders who have neither capital advantage nor shareholding advantage can only be punished as an accomplice of the advantage-abuse manipulation, due to their collusion in terms of creating asymmetric information with insiders who have dynamic information advantage. Outsiders who have capital advantage or shareholding advantage, on the one hand, can be punished as principal offenders of the advantage-abuse manipulation due to their own breach of positive obligations by continuous trading, which proves sufficient to exclude other variables from the price-forming process; on the other hand, they can be punished as an accomplice of the advantage-abuse manipulation, due to their collusion in terms of creating asymmetric information with insiders. According to the principle that behaviors of principal offenders absorb behaviors of accomplices, the outsiders mentioned above should finally be punished as principal offenders.

In short, the outsiders – regardless of their specific roles in securities market manipulation, giving advice to a listed company or its insiders about improper disclosure of information, or undertaking artificial transactions – can only be punished as an accomplice, unless they have capital advantage or shareholding advantage. When dealing with market manipulation cases in the form of internal and external collusion, judicial and administrative organs show a common preference for punishment – severe punishment for outsiders, light punishment

40 The reason for the *Interpretation* to remove the requirement that has been set by the *Prosecution Standard II* in terms of the manipulative control over information for the identity of subjects lies in the practical diversity of perpetrators' identities – 'outsiders not only conspire with insiders to manipulate the securities market, but also control the generation and dissemination of information by bribing insiders'.

for insiders and virtually no punishment for listed companies.[41] The conception noted above contributes to correcting such improper preference.

6. CONCLUSION

In order to criminally attribute abnormal fluctuations in the securities market to manipulative control over information, an alternative arises between ontological and functionalist criteria. From the perspective of ontologism, due to the dichotomy between trading-based manipulation and information-based manipulation, the formalized subsumption approach cannot meet the requirements of both the principle of legality and the principle of proportionality in a narrow sense, nor can the substantial subsumption approach completely solve this problem. To find a way out of the dilemma, we may break the hermeneutic preconception based on foreign experience and abandon the empirical dichotomy between trading-based manipulation and information-based manipulation.

Given the semantic connotation of consequence inherently related to the term 'manipulation' as well as the concept of 'jurisdiction' which focuses on the criminal attribution, it is the attribution basis that configures the crime of securities market manipulation in terms of objective constitutive elements. From the perspective of functionalism, besides the causality related to the violation of negative obligation, there is another basis for attribution, purely normative, related to the violation of positive obligation. The establishment of the positive obligation of maintaining free competition in the market's price-forming process has institutional reason – 'recognized advantage' that justifies the solidarity of the risk-taking community – beyond the empirical possibility of dominating the unlawful facts. The express requirement of the relative advantage position in capital, shareholding or information which is set by Article 182, Text 1 of the Criminal Law confirms that instead of quantitative comparison between interests, the deviation from institutional roles determines the unlawfulness of facts committed by the principal offender, while continuous trading is only one of the behaviors that indicate an obligation violation. 'Manipulation' is not an empirical fact to be discovered, but represents the reason why abnormal fluctuations should be attributed and the way designed in advance by the normative system in which the risk of market volatility should be distributed. The new dichotomy between fraud manipulation based on organizational jurisdiction and advantage abuse based on institutional jurisdiction contributes to revealing systemic risks contained in the

41 See *supra* note 5, 171.

financing reform of China's capital market and to deciding how to distribute these risks in a targeted manner.

ACKNOWLEDGMENT

This chapter is funded by the Ministry of Education's Humanities and Social Sciences Research Project, 'Study on the Application Mechanism of Special Confiscation in Cases of Evil Forces Crimes under the Threshold between Law and Law' (21YJC820011).

11. The interpretation of "the instigated person has not committed the instigated crime" – based on the indigenization of accomplice subordination principle

Xiao Peng

Crime participation has always been an important issue in China's criminal legal theory. There are considerable controversies about the interpretation of "the instigated person has not committed the instigated crime" in Article 29, Section 2 of China's Criminal Code. Almost all the global disputes in joint crime can be reflected in the interpretation of this clause, such as the limited concept of principal offender and the expanded concept of principal offender, the distinction system and unitary principal offender system, accomplice's subordination and independence, cause-based accomplice theory and liability-based accomplice theory, and even the theory of crime commonness and the theory of act commonness. The complexity of the problem has led to the diversity of theories. There are more than 10 different theories within the scope of the author's reading. If the differences in the detailed viewpoints are considered, the types of related theories may even be more. This chapter will first sort out and analyze the existing views, then combine the basic principle of accomplice's subordination with the specific provisions of China's Criminal Code, and demonstrate that "the instigated person has not committed the instigated crime" means the instigated person has prepared for the crime but has not perpetrated the crime.

1. ANALYSIS OF THE STANDPOINT OF CHINA'S CRIMINAL CODE

The reason why the interpretation of the "instigated person has not committed the instigated crime" attracts so much attention is that this issue determines whether to insist on the accomplice's subordination principle and how to insist on this principle. This issue not only affects the identification and punishment of instigators, but also has a general effect on the scope of punishment for joint crimes. For this problem, the traditional viewpoint is the "bi-nature solicitation theory".[1] However, after systematic criticism in the academic community, it has been recognized that the "bi-nature solicitation theory" not only misunderstands the meaning of the independence and subordination of accomplices, but also makes it difficult to achieve the necessary logical self-consistency, and also causes the imbalance of punishment in practice, which has obvious and significant defects.[2] However, the academic research on this issue seems to have fallen into a deadlock of "breaking without establishing". Although scholars have put forward "solicitation independence theory",[3] "solicitation exceptional independence theory",[4] "attempt indirect principal theory",[5] "the theory that the instigated crime has been attempted but not accomplished",[6] "the theory that treat solicitation according to preparatory crime",[7] "the theory of special distinction system",[8] "the theory that treat solicitation according to omission",[9] "the theory that treat solicitation as an independent accusation",[10]

---

1 See Wu Liucun, "On the Bi-nature of Solicitation", *Chinese Journal of Law*, No. 1 (1982), p. 17; Zhao Bingzhi, Wei Dong, "On the Attempt of Solicitation--Concurrently Discussing Article 29, Paragraph 2 of the New Criminal Code", *The Jurist*, No. 3 (1999), p. 30; Gao Mingxuan, Ma Kechang eds, "*Criminal Law*" (8th edition, Beijing University Press 2017) 179.

2 See Zhang Mingkai, "On the Nature of Solicitation", Chen Xingliang ed., *Criminal Law Review*, Vol. 21 (Beijing University Press, 2007) 77–82.

3 See Yu Gancai, "On the Criminal Liability of Solicitation", *Journal of Anhui University*, No. 2 (1983), p. 63; Li Fengmei, "Soliciting Act: Participating Act or Principal Act?", *Criminal Science*, No. 1 (2009), p. 28.

4 See Cai Guisheng, "A Jurisprudential Analysis of Article 29.2 of Criminal Law", *The Jurist*, No. 1 (2014), p. 72.

5 See He Qingren, "Two Meanings of Solicitation in China's Criminal Code", *Chinese Journal of Law*, No. 5 (2004), p. 47.

6 *Supra* note 2, 88–89.

7 See Qin Xuena, "The Plights and Outlets of the Theory of Subservience of Accomplice in China", *The Jurist*, No. 4 (2015), pp. 137–139.

8 See Tian Ran, "The Understanding and Application of 'Attempted Solicitation' Based on the Special Dividing System of the Principal and Accomplice", in Zhao Bingzhi ed., *Criminal Law Review*, Vol. 51 (Law Press, 2018) 52–58.

9 See Xia Hua, "New Exploration of Solicitation", *Political Science and Law*, No. 4 (1991), pp. 26–27.

10 See Lu Qinzhong, "On the Establishment of Solicitation", *Modern Law Science*, No. 6 (1996), pp. 91–93; Wu Qingshu, Yan Tieheng, "Rethinking and Positioning of Solicitation", *Journal of Political Science and Law*, No. 6 (1999), pp. 10–13.

"the theory based on formal unitary principal offender system"[11] and "the theory based on functional unitary principal offender system".[12] However, none of the above views has achieved a decisive victory, and only "the theory that the instigated crime has been attempted but not accomplished" and the view based on the (formal) unitary principal offender system have relatively larger influence. The author is unable to give a detailed analysis of more than ten theories in just one chapter and can only make a special comment on the two relatively influential theories.

Obviously, the debate between these two views is not a partial and detailed debate, but a general confrontation between the two basic positions of the accomplice theory of the distinction system and the unitary principal offender system. Therefore, in order to solve the problem of "instigated person has not committed the instigated crime", it is necessary to respond positively to the debate between the distinction system (mainly the accomplice subordination theory) and the (formal) unitary principal offender system. To resolve this debate, we must first clarify the basic position of China's Criminal Code and judge whether China's Criminal Code generally supports any of the above views.[13] We believe that if legislators generally support a certain criminal participation system, it will be stipulated in an uncontroversial way. However, the general provisions of China's Criminal Code neither clearly stipulate what is a principal offender and the principle of punishment for principal offenders, nor clearly stipulate that those who make contribution to a crime are principal offenders. Therefore, China's Criminal Code does not generally support the distinction system, nor does it generally support the unitary principal offender system. Therefore, neither of the two interpretation schemes violates the positive law. The core problem is which of the two interpretation schemes is more reasonable.

---

11 See Liu Mingxiang, "The Interpretation of 'the Instigated Person Has not Committed the Instigated Crime'", *Chinese Journal of Law*, No. 1 (2011), p. 149.

12 See Jiang Su, "Beyond Dispute of Independent Theory of Accomplice and Accessorial Theory of Accomplice – Reinterpretation of Para. 2, Article 29 of Chinese Criminal Code", *Journal of Soochow University* (Law Edition), No. 2 (2014), p. 31.

13 Under the framework of the dogmatics of criminal law, if one of the two views is in conformity with the positive law and the other violates the positive law, then the difference between the two is the question of right and wrong, and we can only choose the view that conforms to the positive law. If both views have a certain legal basis, then the difference between the two is not a question of right and wrong, but a question of what is more reasonable.

1.1 China's Criminal Code Does Not Generally Support the Distinction System

Professor Zhou Guangquan believes that the provisions of China's Criminal Code do not match the characteristics of the unitary system because the Criminal Code does not clearly stipulate that those who make contribution to a crime are principal offenders. The legislation emphasizes the difference between the forms of accomplice acts by separately stipulating the helper and the instigator. The penalty should be applied according to the types of the offender. For example, the accessory offender cannot be applied to the punishment of the principal offender but should be "lighter, mitigated or exempted from punishment".[14] However, two different classification methods of accomplices should not be confused. Perpetrator, helper, and instigator are the concepts under the classification of labor, while principal offender, accessory offender, and coerced accessory are the concepts under the classification of contribution. These two groups of concepts are based on different classification standards, and there is no strict one-to-one correspondence between them. According to Professor Zhou Guangquan, although the relevant provisions of China's Criminal Code do not explicitly use the concept of principal offender, the two types of accomplices in narrow sense – aiding and instigating – are clearly stipulated in Article 27 and Article 29, Paragraph 1. The concept of principal offender can be clearly defined from the distinction and comparison with accomplices in a narrow sense.[15] However, Article 27 of China's Criminal Code is clearly about the accessory offender. If one ignores the clear expression and takes it for granted that Article 27 of China's Criminal Code is about the helper, it may be difficult to be convincing. In fact, helping acts may play a major role in joint crime.[16] If someone believes that a helper must be an accessory offender, he or she will definitely encounter trouble in the subsequent sentencing issue.

Professor He Qingren advocates excluding the interpretation scheme of the unitary principal offender system through constitutional interpretation, thus limiting the provisions of China's Criminal Code to the framework of the accomplice subordination system. In this view, Article 29, paragraph 2 of the Criminal Code punishes preparatory offenders with the penalty of attempted

---

14 See Zhou Guangquan, "The Understanding of 'The Instigated Person Has Not Committed the Instigated Crime' – Also Discussing with Professor Liu Mingxiang", *Chinese Journal of Law*, No. 4 (2013), p. 184.

15 Ibid., 182.

16 See Qin Xuena, "On the Normative Reconstruction of the Standard of Core Offender: From 'Post-Effect' to 'Normative Ability'", *Journal of Comparative Law*, No. 3 (2020), p. 90.

crimes, which is suspected of violating the constitutional principles of equality and proportionality. Therefore, only by interpreting the clause in accordance with the accomplice subordination system can it be constitutional.[17]

However, the principle of equality does not exclude reasonable differences. Compared with ordinary preparatory acts, instigating acts reflect the higher personal danger of the actor and the higher necessity of prevention. As a result, it does not violate the principle of equality to impose a heavier penalty for solicitation. To a certain extent, Professor He Qingren also agrees with the rationality of this preventive purpose, but emphasizes that simply and recklessly increasing the penalties for such acts in order to achieve the purpose violates the principle of necessity, because the preventive purpose can be achieved just by raising the actual prosecution rate of instigating preparatory offenders.[18] However, compared with ordinary preparatory offenders, Article 29, Paragraph 2 of China's Criminal Code only deletes the exemption from punishment and just slightly increases the punishment. In addition, in the case of maintaining a low prosecution rate of preparatory offenders, it has little impact on the actual life of whether the penalty for attempted solicitation at the legislative level "can be lighter, mitigated or exempted from punishment" or "can be lighter or mitigated". If the actual prosecution rate is to be increased, as an alternative proposed by Professor He Qingren, it will inevitably have an impact on the actual life of citizens, and the degree of restriction on civil liberties is actually higher.

1.2 China's Criminal Code Does Not Generally Support Unitary Principal Offender System

In theory, it is generally agreed that the unitary principal offender system has the following five characteristics: first of all, in the unitary principal offender system, anyone who makes a contribution to the crime is a principal offender; secondly, this system does not pay much attention to the form of the act; thirdly, on the establishment of the crime, the act of each principal offender should be discussed separately; fourthly, the same statutory sentence should be applied to each principal offender; fifthly, the punishment should be determined by the contribution each offender makes to the crime.[19] If someone holds the position that China's Criminal Code adopts the unitary principal offender system, he or

---

[17] See He Qingren, "Interpretation of Paragraph 2 of Article 29 of Criminal Law of China from the Perspective of Constitutionality", *Political Science and Law*, No. 8 (2021), pp. 91–93.

[18] Ibid., 92.

[19] See Norio Takahashi, translated by Feng Jun and Mao Naichun, "*Accomplice System and Accomplice Theory*" (China Renmin University Press 2010) 6.

she will tend to think that "the instigated person has not committed the instigated crime" includes five situations: the instigating information has not been communicated, the instigated person has refused to instigate, the instigated person has accepted the instigation but has not implemented the preparatory act, the instigated person has accepted the instigation but later changes their intention, and the instigated person has implemented the preparatory act or perpetrating act after accepting the instigation.[20] In Professor Liu Mingxiang's view, the provisions of Article 25, Paragraph 1 of China's Criminal Code indicate that as long as two or more people commit joint acts that infringe the legal interests protected by the criminal law with joint intention, they constitute a joint crime. As a result, those who participate in the crime or create conditions for the crime are joint offenders.[21] However, this chapter believes that it cannot be deduced from this provision that China's legislation generally supports the unitary principal offender system.

On the one hand, there is still a big gap between China's legislation and that of the countries which are recognized to have adopted the unitary principal offender system. For example, there is no dispute that Italy has adopted the unitary principal offender system. Article 110 of the Italian Criminal Code stipulates: "When several people participate in the same crime, each of them should be sentenced to the penalty prescribed for the crime, unless it is otherwise provided by law."[22] When comparing China's Criminal Code with Italy's Criminal Code, it is not difficult to find that there is a clear and significant difference. That is, there is no requirement for joint intent according to Italy's Criminal Code. Correspondingly, Italian scholars clearly affirm in theory that negligent acts can constitute a joint crime. Even in intentional crimes, "a joint crime can be established as long as one of the actors has such intent".[23] In fact, if the internal logic of the unitary principal offender system is strictly followed and all the actors who have a conditional relationship with the results of the infringement of legal interests are regarded as principal offenders, it is indeed unnecessary to require the existence of common intent between each accomplice.[24] Therefore, if Article 25 of China's Criminal Code is considered

---

20 *Supra* note 11, 149.

21 See Liu Mingxiang, "On the Crime Participation System With Chinese Characteristics", *China Legal Science*, No. 6 (2013), p. 119.

22 Huang Feng translates, "*The Latest Italian Criminal Code*" (Law Press 2007) 42–43.

23 Tullio Padovani, translated by Chen Zhonglin, "*Italian Criminal Law Theories (Commentary Edition)*" (China Renmin University Press 2004) 289.

24 It can be seen from Professor Liu Mingxiang's treatment plan for "case of hunting and killing one's personal enemy" and "case of helping the person without

to generally support the unitary principal offender system, it is impossible to explain why legislators are so obsessed with the common intent in joint crimes.

On the other hand, from the perspective of interpretation technique, even though the Criminal Code has stipulated that "a joint crime is an intentional crime committed by two or more persons jointly", it does not necessarily mean that the necessary and sufficient condition for a joint crime is the joint act with joint intention. This is because in order to limit the state's penalty power and prevent overcriminalization, it does not violate the principle of legality to add unwritten constituent elements. If those who have a conditional relationship with the result of the infringement of legal interests are regarded as the principal offender, the scope of the joint crime will be too expanded. As a result, it is necessary to interpret this provision restrictively. That is, Article 25, Paragraph 1 of China's Criminal Code is just about the joint principal offender.

In a word, although it is true that Professor Liu Mingxiang argues: "China's Criminal Code is not a legislative system that distinguishes between principal offenders and accomplices as Germany and Japan",[25] China's Criminal Code also does not adopt the same unitary principal offender system as Italy. It should be admitted that neither does China's Criminal Code generally support the distinction system, nor does it generally support the unitary principal offender system. It leaves a certain space for both interpretation schemes. Therefore, these two interpretation schemes do not violate China's Criminal Code. It can be seen that in the context of China's legislation, the debate between the distinction system and the unitary principal offender system is not a question of legality, not a question of right or wrong, but a question of rationality, a question to achieve the appropriateness of punishment.

2. LIMITATIONS OF EXISTING INTERPRETATION SCHEMES

Under China's Criminal Code, there is room for both the unitary principal offender system and the distinction system. To compare the advantages and disadvantages of the two views, it is necessary to further analyze the substantive rationality of them. This chapter argues that the unitary principal offender system itself has many defects, and it is not suitable to be the theoretical basis of Article 29, Paragraph 2 of China's Criminal Code. Although the distinction system is relatively reasonable, it does not necessarily mean "the theory that the instigated crime has been attempted but not accomplished" is reasonable.

---

criminal responsibility to kill" in another article that it is not important for each actor to have a common intention in crime participation.

25 See Liu Mingxiang, "There Is No Provision about Co-perpetrator in China's Criminal Law", *The Jurist*, No. 1 (2022), p. 145.

The existing views under the distinction system still fail to give sufficient basis for their opinions.

2.1 Unitary Principal Offender System: Lack of Substantial Rationality

Supporters of the unitary principal offender system argue that not only has China's legislation adopted the unitary principal offender system, but also this accomplice participation system has obvious advantages compared with the distinction system, which is embodied in the following four aspects. First of all, it is difficult to distinguish between accomplices and principal offenders in the distinction system. The unitary principal offender system could overcome this disadvantage. Secondly, the unitary principal offender system is more scientific in crime conviction because it does not require accomplices to be subordinated principal offenders. Thirdly, the unitary principal offender system is more reasonable in sentencing because the punishment is determined by the contribution of each participant to the result of the infringement of legal interests. Fourthly, the unitary principal offender system is simpler for operation because it does not need to distinguish between the principal offender and the accessory offender, nor does it need to distinguish between indirect principal offender and accomplice.[26]

The above first and fourth points are essentially the same; that is, the distinction system must face the problems of various complex classifications of accomplices, and the unitary principal offender system can bypass these problems. However, criminal law is about people's property, freedom, and even life. In the ultimate sense, the purpose of any criminal law theory is to achieve the fairness and justice of punishment. Therefore, if a certain theory is more conducive to realizing the rationality and appropriateness of punishment in the entity, it is acceptable if the theory is a little more troublesome at the operational level. Moreover, the existence of the Criminal Code itself is a kind of trouble, but obviously we cannot abandon the Criminal Code and go back to the era of arbitrary punishment just because the very existence of the criminal code is a nuisance. In addition, the unitary system is not necessarily simpler than the distinction system in the whole judicial procedure because even if the act type of the accomplice participant is not considered at the conviction stage, it will eventually be considered at the sentencing stage.

This chapter can't agree with the above second point. When Professor Liu Mingxiang demonstrates that the unitary principal offender system is more scientific than the distinction system, he lists the following problems: the

---

[26] *Supra* note 21, 120–126.

theoretical basis of the distinction system is the limited concept of principal offender, and the theoretical basis of the unitary principal offender system is the concept of expanded principal offender. Compared with the latter, the former is less capable of protecting the legal interest; there is no essential difference between using others to commit crimes and using tools to commit crimes, so the internal logic of the unitary principal offender system is more reasonable; the unitary principal offender system can make the conviction of joint intentional crime and joint negligent crime consistent.

According to this chapter, it is true that the distinction system and the unitary principal offender system do correspond to the concept of restricted principal offender and the concept of expanded principal offender, respectively, but this is an advantage rather than a disadvantage of the distinction system. The concept of expanded principal offender holds that those who are causally related to the result of legal interest damage are principal offenders. This position undermines the clarity of constituent elements and improperly expands the scope of crimes. Although, according to the theory of accomplice subordination, in the case that the perpetrator buys the other party with heavy money to engage in terrorist activities of mass murder, the perpetrator cannot be treated as an instigator. The penalty loophole in this extreme case can be filled by the legislative provision of independent preparatory crime. China's legislation does do so. Although the above situation does not constitute a solicitation in China, it can be directly convicted and punished in accordance with the crime of preparing to commit terrorist activities, and then there will be no penalty loopholes for certain acts.

As for the problem that the unitary principal offender system can achieve the coordination of the punishment between joint intentional crime and joint negligent crime, this chapter holds that it is not inconsistent to adopt a distinction system for joint intentional crime while a unitary principal offender system for joint negligent crime. This difference is determined by the different characteristics of the two. Negligent crimes are always consequential crimes in a narrow sense, making it unnecessary to ask whether they are accomplished. In this case, even if the unitary principal offender system is adopted, it will not lead to excessive expansion of punishment. For example, the core issue of the debate between the distinction system and the unitary principal offender system is that "the instigated person has not committed the instigated crime". One important reason for the distinction system to criticize the unitary principal offender system is that the unitary principal offender system punishes the attempted solicitation as other attempted crimes, which will lead to the improper expansion of the punishment scope. However, a similar problem will not exist in negligent crimes because a negligent crime is a consequential crime in a narrow sense. In addition, the establishment of a negligent crime requires the violation of the caring obligation and the result avoidance obligation (if the modified old negligence theory is adopted, there is also a need for negligent conduct). These mechanisms have acted as a "firewall" in the identification of negligent crimes and prevented the improper expansion of negligent crimes. For joint negligent crime, even if the unitary principal offender is adopted, it does not necessarily mean "all the actors who have a causal relationship with the result of legal interest infringement are regarded as principal offenders" in the operation process.

This chapter partially agrees with the above third point. Although the principle that "the punishment of accessory offender is lighter than that of principal offender" is appropriate in most cases, it will harm the appropriateness of punishment on some special occasions if this principle is thoroughly implemented without any exemption. This is indeed a deficiency of the mainstream distinction system. However, it should be noted that the shortcomings of the distinction system are not necessarily the advantages of the unitary principal offender system. The standard of "considering the degree and nature of each offender's participation and giving different penalties" adopted by the unitary principal offender system is good, but it does not actually provide more content than the principle of suiting punishment to crime and responsibility, making it difficult to become the specific guidance of judicial practice. Of course, in order to completely solve the problem of sentencing, it is necessary to re-examine the function of the accomplice's subordination principle and make it clear that the most important function of this principle is to maintain the clarity of the constituent elements. Then we can "untie" the conviction function and sentencing function of the accomplice's subordination principle.[27] In this way, we can use the "objective formal theory" to identify the perpetrator and respond to the query of "perpetrator becoming principal offender".[28]

It can be seen that, although the distinction system is not perfect, the unitary principal offender system is not as perfect as its proponents claim it to be. In addition, there are some serious and even fatal flaws in the unitary principal offender system. In addition to the well-known defect of imbalance in penalties,[29] the flaws of the unitary principal system have been discussed by other scholars in detail, including the following aspects:

---

[27] See Yan Erpeng, "The Experience of Germany and Japan and the Reality of China of Joint Crime Dogmatic – Thinking from the Aspect to Clarify Perpetrators from Principal Offenders", *Science of Law*, No. 5 (2017), p. 181.

[28] *Supra* note 21, 124.

[29] According to the unitary principal offender system, when the instigated person commits a preparatory act, Article 22 of the Criminal Code can be applied to the instigator, who can be given a lesser punishment or a mitigated punishment or be exempted from punishment; whereas when the instigated person does not even commit a preparatory act, the instigator is subject to Article 29, Paragraph 2 of

First, the unitary principal offender system undermines the clarity of the constituent elements. The unitary principal offender system treats participatory acts with remote causal relationships as equivalent to the constituent elements, which undermines the boundary function of the constituent elements. Professor Liu Mingxiang also admits that the unitary principal offender system does undermine the clarity of the constituent elements. However, by using an analogy to the theory of modified constituent elements, he argues that since the theory of modified constituent elements does not violate the clarity of constituent elements, then the unitary principal offender system does not violate it either.[30] However, such a defense cannot be sustained. In the first place, the modified constituent elements doctrine itself has faced criticism, one of which is that it "deflates the meaning and scope of perpetrating act".[31] Therefore, the modified theory of constituent elements cannot provide a sound basis for the unitary principal offender system. Secondly, despite their superficial similarity, there is a substantial difference between the unitary principal offender system and the modified constituent elements theory. The theoretical basis of the unitary principal offender system is the expanded concept of principal offender; it does not regard the punishment of narrowly defined accomplices as the expansion of the cause of the penalty, even if there are no general provisions in Criminal Law on joint crime. Because the instigating and helping acts are also in line with the constituent elements stipulated in sub-paragraphs of Criminal Code, these relevant provisions can be used directly to punish the instigator and helper. In this sense, the provisions of joint crimes in the Criminal Code merely establish more specific rules for sentencing. However, the theory of modified constituent elements is a different line of analysis, in which the constituent elements stipulated in the sub-paragraphs of Criminal Code just describe the situation of attempting to commit a crime, which is called the basic constituent element. The combination of the basic constituent element and the provisions in Criminal Law to punish joint crimes and the unaccomplished crimes becomes the modified constituent element. Accordingly, although an act does not meet the basic constituent elements, it can be convicted and punished if it meets the modified constituent elements. Since the modified constituent elements are created by combining the basic constituent elements and the provisions in the General Provisions of the Criminal Code, if there were no provision in the General Provisions of the Criminal Code on joint crimes, there would be no modified constituent ele-

---

the Criminal Code, which can only mitigate the punishment at most but cannot exempt the punishment.

30 *Supra* note 21, 127.

31 See Chen Xuan, "The Negation of the Theory of Modified Constituent Element of Crimes", *Science in Law and Business*, No. 4 (2007), p. 142.

ments for helpers and instigators, and no possibility of punishing helpers and instigators. Thus, the modified constituent elements essentially imply the basic position of the limited concept of principal offender, which is inconsistent with the unitary principal offender system.

Secondly, the unitary principal offender system violates the theory of perpetrating. In the view of the unitary principal offender system, instigating acts, helping acts, and preparatory acts are all in line with the constitutive elements stipulated in the Criminal Code. This standpoint is bound to make the instigating act be interpreted as a perpetrating act, thus leading to the shaking of the concept of perpetrating. Professor Liu Mingxiang responds that there is no essential difference between using others to commit a crime and using animals or natural tools to commit a crime. This does not necessarily mean the using act itself is a perpetrating act. The establishment of perpetrating is determined by whether there is a realistic and urgent danger to the legal interests. In the case of instigating or helping others to hurt the victim, the starting point of the perpetrating act should also be the time point when the instigated person or the helped person commits the perpetrating act.[32] This response is actually to advocate the substantive objective theory and the unitary principal offender system at the same time. However, this view of "whether the accomplice in the narrow sense perpetrates depends on whether the principal offender perpetrates" has actually adopted the accomplice subordination theory, which is contrary to the position of the unitary principal offender system.

Thirdly, it is difficult for the unitary principal offender system to deal with pure identity crimes. According to the unitary principal offender system, each criminal participant is a principal offender and bears criminal responsibility for his own illegality and guilt. In some crimes, the establishment of a crime requires not only a causal relationship between the act and the result, but also some illegal elements with personal specificity, such as crimes against oneself and pure identity crimes. In this scene, the unitary principal offender system will get into trouble. For example, normal citizen A instigates public officer B to commit corruption. Although A does not have a special identity, it cannot constitute the principal offender of corruption, but it can constitute the instigator of corruption according to the distinction system, so the crime would not be indulged; however, according to the unitary principal offender system, all participants in the joint crime are principal offenders, and the crime of corruption is a pure identity crime. Therefore, normal citizen A can never constitute the crime of corruption without the status of public officer. Such a conclusion is obviously unreasonable.

---

32 *Supra* note 21, 128.

Professor Liu Mingxiang responded that the "principal offender" in the unitary principal offender system and the "principal offender" in the distinction system are not the same concept. The "principal offender" in the unitary principal offender system includes the principal offender and accomplice in the distinction system. Therefore, no matter a whether they are a direct perpetrator, helper, or instigator, they are all in the scope of the "principal offender" in the unitary principal offender system, so the person without identity can also become the perpetrator (the "principal offender" in the unitary principal offender system) of corruption and bribery by instigating and helping. As a result, there will not be a situation that the instigator and helper cannot be punished just because of the lack of a certain identity.[33] However, the key to the problem is not what is the "principal offender", but what is the "pure identity crime"? According to the general understanding, "pure identity crime refers to a crime that takes a special identity as the main element, and the crime cannot be established without this special identity".[34] It can be seen that in pure identity crime, the existence of special identity is the necessary condition for conviction. According to Professor Liu Mingxiang, the special identity in pure identity crime does not affect the conviction of the crime, because the person without a certain identity can also constitute the principal offender of pure identity crime through the instigating and helping act. It does not affect the distinction between principal offender and accomplice either, because the unitary principal offender system no longer distinguishes between principal offender and accomplice. In a nutshell, the special identity does not play any role in the process of conviction, which is obviously inconsistent with the meaning of "pure identity crime". From the above analysis, we can also see that the unitary principal offender system is not a subjective theory, as some scholars claim.[35] On the contrary, the main defect of the unitary principal offender system is (almost) completely ignoring the worthlessness of the act. The illegal elements with personal specificity, such as special identity, are not considered in the analysis framework of the unitary principal offender system.

Fourthly, the theoretical basis of the unitary principal offender system in the field of causal relationship is the conditional theory. But the conditional theory itself has many defects. In the view of the conditional theory, all the conditions that cannot be imagined to disappear are objectively equivalent. Because of the conditional relationship between the perpetrator, the helper, and the instigator, and the result of the infringement of legal interests, they should also be subject

[33] See Liu Mingxiang, "Consider the Difficulties of Joint Crime in Bribery from the Perspective of Unitary Principal Offender", The Jurists, No.2 (2017), p. 73.

[34] *Supra* note 1, Gao Mingxuan, Ma Kechang, 'Criminal Law' 95.

[35] *Supra* note 14, 187.

to the same normative evaluation. Thus, the supporters of the unitary principal offender system believe that there is "no essential difference" between accomplice illegality and principal offender illegality.[36] However, the problem of conditional theory is obvious and serious,[37] making it unsuitable to become the theoretical basis of other theories. Professor Liu Mingxiang argues that causality is only a necessary condition rather than a sufficient condition for the imputation of results. No matter the formal unitary principal offender system or the functional principal offender system, it has absorbed the theory of considerable causality or the idea of objective imputation. For example, Italy, which adopts a formal unitary principal offender system, has shifted from the theory of "equal cause" (conditional theory) to the theory of "sufficient cause" (equivalent cause theory).[38] However, the reason why the unitary principal offender system believes that it is not necessary to distinguish various forms of criminal participation is that the conditional theory holds that each condition is objectively equivalent. If it absorbs the substantial imputation theory, it will directly destroy its theoretical foundation. For example, if the theory of causality is changed from "equal cause theory" to "sufficient cause theory", it will be impossible to consider that perpetrating, helping, and instigating are equivalent, because only perpetrating is the "sufficient cause" of the result of infringement of legal interests. Thus, different forms of criminal participation have to be distinguished at the level of constituent elements. In this way, it will gradually reverse to the position of the distinction system.

To sum up, although China's legislation generally supports neither the distinction system nor the unitary principal offender system, the distinction system is more reasonable than the unitary principal offender system. Thus, it is not appropriate to use the unitary principal offender system to explain the relevant provisions of joint crime in China's Criminal Code.

2.2 The Existing Interpretation Scheme Under the Distinction System: Lack of Textual Basis in Form

Taking various defects of the unitary principal offender system into consideration, many scholars have adopted the accomplice subordination theory under the distinction system. However, Article 29, Paragraph 2 of the China's Criminal Code instantly becomes a significant obstacle to the accomplice subordination theory. Any scholar who wants to advocate the accomplice subordination theory under China's Criminal Code must give a convincing solution

---

36 *Supra* note 21, 127.

37 See Zhang Mingkai, *Criminal Law* (5th edition, Law Press 2016) 176.

38 See Jiang Su, "Several Clarifications for the Unitary Principal Offender System", *Contemporary Law Review*, No. 5 (2011), p. 80.

to this problem. To this end, scholars have put forward many views, among which the most influential view is the theory that the instigated crime has been attempted but not accomplished. According to this view, "the instigated person has not committed the instigated crime" refers to the situation that the instigated has not been accomplished by the instigated person. In other words, when the instigated crime is attempted but not accomplished, the instigated person commits an incomplete crime, and the instigator commits an attempted crime correspondingly. Thus the sentence rule of "may be lighter or mitigated" should be applied. Reasons supporting this theory include the following: Firstly, the term "committing … crime" has multiple meanings in criminal law, which can refer to the establishment of a crime or the completion of a crime. Therefore, the interpretation of the author does not violate the meaning of the text. Secondly, from the characteristics of the instigator, the instigator aims to make the instigated person commit a crime, so when the instigator does not commit a crime, it can be said that "the instigated person has not committed the instigated crime". Thirdly, from the perspective of substantial rationality, this approach can avoid the inconsistency between Article 29, Paragraph 2 and Article 22 of China's Criminal Code.[39]

The above reasons are true in themselves. However, at most they can only prove that "the instigated person has not committed the instigated crime" includes the situation that the instigated person has attempted but not accomplished the crime, but cannot prove that "the instigated person has not committed the instigated crime" is limited to such situation. For example, the term "commit … crime" does have multiple meanings, so "the instigated person has not committed the instigated crime" can be interpreted as "the instigated person has not accomplished the instigated crime". However, "the instigated person has not committed the instigated crime" clearly includes many situations, such as the instigated person refuses the instigation, accepts the instigation but does not carry out the preparatory act, has prepared but not perpetrated, has attempted, and so on. There is no reason to limit the "the instigated person has not committed the instigated crime" to the last situation. In the case where the instigated person has attempted but not accomplished, it is true that the instigator's will has not been realized, which can be described as "the instigated person has not committed the instigated crime". However, as long as the whole crime has not been accomplished, the instigator's will has not been realized, and why to exclude the failure of the instigation? Thus, the most important reason to support this view is still the ability to achieve the consistency of Article 29, Paragraph 2 and Article 22 of China's Criminal Code. This is certainly correct, but this alone is not enough. In the research of legal dogmatic,

---

39 *Supra* note 2, 88–89.

no matter how strong the substantive rationality of an interpretation scheme is, it must have a textual basis at a minimum level. However, the scholars can not prove their views at the level of textual interpretation, so the problem comes full circle back to the original point: if the Article 29, Paragraph 2 of China's Criminal Code is interpreted according to the accomplice subordination theory, does it violate the literal meaning of the phrase "the instigated person has not committed the instigated crime"?

3. THE THEORETICAL PROOF OF THE THEORY THAT THE "INSTIGATED PERSON HAS PREPARED FOR THE CRIME BUT HAS NOT PERPETRATED THE CRIME"

As mentioned above, this chapter is in favor of the accomplice subordination theory in principle, but we cannot introduce foreign theories without the consideration of positive law. The foreign theories should be combined with the specific situation of domestic legislation and modified correspondingly. To solve the tension between the accomplice subordination theory and China's Criminal Code, the key is to localize the accomplice subordination theory. In this regard, this chapter will first analyze the internal logic of the accomplice subordination theory and propose that the position of "preparatory subordination" should be adopted in the context of China and interpret "the instigated person has not committed the instigated crime" based on this position.

3.1 The Localization of Perpetrating Subordination Theory

There is an important difference between China's Criminal Code and that of the traditional civil law countries and regions. That is the existence of the general provision for the punishment for preparatory crimes in China's Criminal Code. This difference will also lead to different understandings of the accomplice subordination theory. The traditional view holds that: "the so-called accomplice subordination theory means the accomplice cannot commit a crime if the principal offender has not perpetrated the crime".[40] This principle is also known as perpetrating subordination theory. However, in the context of China's Criminal Code, we should make a modification to this theory.

How does the accomplice subordination theory come into being? The scholars have achieved a clear consensus. Based on the causal accomplice theory,

---

40 See Ma Kechang, "Several Controversial Issues in the Theory of Joint Crime", *Journal of Huazhong University of Science and Technology*, No. 1 (2004), p. 20.

since the punishment basis of the accomplice is the same as that of the principal offender, the same standard should be adopted for when the accomplice can be punished as an attempted offender.[41] Ultimately, the meaning of perpetrating subordination is not "the accomplice cannot be punished unless the principal offender is punished", but "the accomplice cannot commit an attempted crime without the perpetrating of the principal offender". In the case that the accomplice does not constitute the attempted crime, it still remains to be judged whether it can constitute other forms of criminal cessation. However, in traditional civil law countries and regions, preparatory acts are usually not punished by criminal law, unless there are special provisions in the sub-paragraphs of Criminal Code, or the legislation stipulates substantive preparatory crimes independently. From this basic position, there is a very important proposition: the beginning of the perpetrating is the basis of illegality of intentional crime, and also the starting point of its criminal punishability (hereinafter referred to as "proposition 1").[42] Under the limited concept of principal offender, in order to prevent the excessive expansion of punishment, it is necessary to ensure that the above proposition is fully implemented in both individual crime and joint crime. That is to say, in the structure of joint crime, the proposition that "the beginning of perpetrating is the starting point of criminal punishability" should still be abided by. As a result, the act of the accomplice in the narrow sense does not constitute a crime without the perpetrating act of the principal offender. This is the very internal logic of the accomplice subordination theory. In China, although Professor Lao Dongyan holds that "despite the fact that the provisions of China's Criminal Code on preparatory crime are different from those of Germany and Japan, there is no essential difference in the position of not punishing preparatory crime in principle",[43] this standpoint will not be adopted by this chapter because it directly ignores China's positive law, which violates the basic principle of criminal dogmatics. This chapter argues that although there is no doubt that the scope of preparatory crime should be limited at the level of law interpretation, it should be admitted that China's Criminal Code at least "formally punishes the preparatory crime as a principle".[44] Therefore, in the context of China's Criminal Code, proposition 1 no longer stands, but should be adjusted accordingly. In China, the starting point of the criminal punishability of intentional crime is no longer perpetrating, but the preparatory act (hereinafter referred to as "proposition 2"). In the countries and regions that adhere to Proposition 1, the accomplice

---

[41] *Supra* note 37, 411.

[42] See Lao Dongyan, "On the Commencement of Implementation and the Basis of Illegality", *Peking University Law Journal*, No. 6 (2011), p. 1238.

[43] Ibid., 1238.

[44] *Supra* note 14, 190.

subordination theory means that the accomplice in the narrow sense is not punished without the perpetrating of the principal offender. Then in China, which adheres to proposition 2, the meaning of the accomplice subordination theory should be that if the principal offender does not carry out preparatory acts, the accomplice is not punished. At the same time, if the principal offender does not perpetrate the crime, the accomplice in the narrow sense cannot be punished as having committed an attempted crime. If this position is applied to the situation of attempted solicitation, the instigator may establish a preparatory crime only when the instigated person commits a preparatory act.[45]

3.2 The Further Discussion of the Preparatory Subordination Theory

3.2.1 The preparatory subordination theory does not violate the positive law

The preparatory subordination theory does not violate the China's Criminal Code, which is embodied in two aspects. On the one hand, the preparatory subordination theory does not violate the provisions on the punishment of instigators. As mentioned above, neither does China's Criminal Code generally support the distinction system, nor does it generally support the unitary principal offender system. Therefore, neither of the two views violates China's Criminal Code. Therefore, the interpretation scheme of Article 29, Paragraph 2 based on the preparatory subordination theory is between the above two theories, which naturally does not violate the China's Criminal Code.

On the other hand, the preparatory subordination theory does not violate the provisions on the punishment of preparatory offenders. Despite the early view that treats instigating as perpetrating, today both the distinguishing system[46] and the principal offender system[47] acknowledge that an instigating act is not a perpetrating act but a preparatory act. The chapter also agrees with the above consensus, but it should be emphasized that this does not mean that "the instigation can be punished directly according to the theory of punishing the preparatory crime" as advocated by some scholars,[48] because Article 22, Paragraph 1 of China's Criminal Code only stipulates the preparatory act rather than the preparatory crime. As scholars have pointed out, at most we can draw the conclusion that "the preparatory crime is a criminal preparation that meets the constituent elements, illegality and responsibility" from Article 22, but it is unable to know the exact scope of preparatory crimes just from

---

45 *Supra* note 37, 411.

46 *Supra* note 4, 71.

47 *Supra* note 21, 128.

48 Zhu Daohua, "*Research on Solicitation*", (Law Press 201) 109.

Article 22.[49] Such a position not only has a legal basis, but also has substantive rationality. Because if China's criminal law were interpreted to punish all the acts of "preparing tools and manufacturing conditions for crime" without any limitation, it would inevitably face many questions such as the legitimacy of jurisprudence, and the necessity and operability of criminal policy.[50] Although it is not yet possible to comprehensively sort out the scope of preparatory crimes, we can limit the scope of preparatory crimes at least in the case of attempted solicitation. That is, an instigator constitutes a preparatory crime only after the instigated person commits the preparatory act.

3.2.2 The preparatory subordination theory does not violate the criminal law theories

Some scholars explicitly oppose the punishability of preparatory accomplice based on the accomplice subordination theory. The reasons are as follows. First of all, subordination is the nature of accomplices. The responsibility of accomplices is a secondary responsibility. Its punishability is originally lower than that of principal offender, and the preparatory offender is punished only in very exceptional situations, and the punishment is lighter, mitigated or exempted from punishment compared to the accomplished offender. Therefore, it is appropriate to exempt the accomplice from punishment. Secondly, there are cases in which failed instigation is not prosecuted in China's judicial practice.[51]

However, the punishability of accomplices is not always lower than that of perpetrators. In practice, it is possible that the role of instigator is equal to or even more important than that of perpetrators. It is also inappropriate to use the punishment provisions for preparatory offenders to demonstrate the exceptionality of the punishment of the instigator. According to China's Criminal Code, the sentencing rule of the preparatory offender is "can be given a lighter or mitigated punishment, or be exempted from punishment", which is even heavier than that of the accomplice, "should be given a lighter or mitigated punishment, or be exempted from punishment". Since only a few scholars argue to punish the accomplice only in exceptional circumstances, it is also

---

49 See Lei Yiming, "On the Standard of Delimitating Uncompleted Crimes Based on Criminal Law", *Journal of National Prosecutor College*, No. 5 (2018), p. 91.

50 See Liang Genlin, "The Dilemma and Breakthrough of the Principle of Universal Punishment for All Preparatory Crimes – Interpretation and Reconfiguration of Article 22 of China's Criminal Code", *China's Legal Science*, No.2 (2011), p. 156.

51 See Zhang Kaijun, "The Further Implementation of the Accomplice Subordination Principle", *Journal of Soochow University (Law Edition)*, No. 1 (2016), pp. 108–109.

difficult to use the instigator's sentencing rule to justify the exceptionality of punishment. In addition, even if there are cases in which failed instigation is not prosecuted in judicial practice, and we assume that the judiciary's handling is correct, it can only prove that not all failed instigation should be punished, rather than that no failed instigation should be punished.

Some scholars argue that although the instigator can be punished as a preparatory crime when the instigator has carried out the preparatory act but has not perpetrated the crime, this is only based on the jurisprudence of the preparatory crime and has nothing to do with the subordination of the accomplice. On the one hand, the reason why instigating preparatory crime is punished is that the instigator recognizes (other people's) preparatory crime, which is the application of the principle of preparatory crime, rather than the application of the accomplice subordination theory. On the other hand, excessively expanding the "range" of accomplice subordination theory in a context where objectivism has not been well implemented in criminal law will shake the concept of principal offender and the notion of the constituent elements of crimes, thus bringing negative effects.[52]

However, the above views are also unconvincing. On the one hand, the first reason is only the emphasis on the scholar's own position, and there is no substantive proof for that position; on the other hand, the concept of preparatory subordination will indeed expand the "range" of accomplice subordination jurisprudence, but why is this an "excessive expansion"? Why does the recognition of preparatory subordination shake the concept of principal offender and the concept of constitutive elements? For these key issues, the scholar gives no explanation. In fact, the subordination of accomplice is a theory that limits the scope of punishment of accomplice. The wider the scope of the theory of subordination of accomplice, the stricter the punishment of accomplice, and the less likely it is to shake the concept of principal offender and the concept of constitutive elements,[53] and vice versa. In some cases, it is precisely because the subordination of accomplices has not been fully implemented that the scope of punishment has been improperly expanded.

52 *Supra* note 16, 191.

53 Perhaps because of this, Article 115 of the 'Italian Penal Code', which adopts a single principal offender system as a whole, has specifically made a 'patch' in order to limit the scope of punishment, stipulating that unless the law provides otherwise, when abetting has been accepted but the crime has not been committed, all participants in the crime will not be punished. (*Supra* note 24, 44) However, for the 'German Criminal Code' which adopts the theory of accomplice subordination as a whole, it is not necessary to put a similar 'patch' specifically to limit the scope of punishment.

In June 2017, Liu Mingling found Xing and wanted to hire the latter to poison Zhang. Xing did not have the criminal intent to murder, but he used the medicinal liquor for the treatment of rheumatism to pretend to be a potent poison, and sold it to Liu Mingling at a price of 10,000 yuan, and instructed Liu Jun to pretend to be the person who would use the "poison". In the name of harming Zhang's "labor service fee", Liu Jun and Xing repeatedly defrauded Liu Mingling for a total of 150,000 yuan. Then, Xing approached Zhang, informed him that Liu Mingling wanted to harm Zhang, and extorted Zhang for a total of 60,000 yuan in two payments by means of verbal intimidation. The court found that Liu Mingling constituted the crime of intentional harm (solicitation), and because the instigated person did not commit the instigated crime, it applied Article 29, Paragraph 2 of China's Criminal Code. As a result, Liu Mingling was sentenced to a lighter punishment of 6 years' imprisonment.[54]

In this case, the court convicted and sentenced Liu Mingling for the crime of intentional harm, which is precisely the result of the "subordination of preparation" not receiving sufficient attention from the judicial authorities. Literally, Liu Mingling's act of instigating others to commit a crime can indeed be evaluated as a preparatory act, making Liu Mingling be punished as a preparatory offender. According to the preparatory subordination theory advocated by this chapter, the instigator can be punished as a preparatory offender only when the instigator carries out the preparatory act. Therefore, in this case, although Liu Mingling implemented an instigating act, the instigated person (Zhang) did not carry out the preparatory act for the instigated crime, so Liu Mingling's act has not yet reached the starting point of criminal punishability in China and should not be punished as the crime of intentional harm (solicitation). It can be seen that the preparatory subordination theory does help to narrow the scope of preparatory offenders.

3.2.3 The theoretical advantages of the theory that the instigated person has prepared for but not perpetrated the crime

From the above analysis, in the context of China's legislations, although the preparatory subordination is not the only right answer, at least it is a potential choice. Based on this position, Article 29, Paragraph 2 of the Criminal Code provides a special preparatory crime, which is the special provision of Article 22 of China's Criminal Code. When the situation of Article 29, Paragraph 2 occurs, this provision should be applied directly and Article 22 should be excluded. Therefore, "the instigated person has not committed the instigated crime" refers to the situation where the instigated person has carried out the

[54] No. 0105 First Instance Criminal Judgment of Tianjin Hebei District People's Court (津0105刑初259号) (2018).

preparatory act but has not yet perpetrated the instigated crime. In order to help the reader to comprehensively understand the position of this chapter, there will be a form of a list to compare the views of this chapter with the two mainstream interpretation schemes, as shown in Figure 11.1.

Compared to the mainstream interpretation schemes, the theory adopted by this chapter has the following advantages.

First, compared with the unitary principal offender system, the theory adopted by this chapter will not cause uncoordinated punishment. Since the theoretical basis adopted by this chapter is still the accomplice subordination theory, it can avoid the general problems existing in the unitary principal offender system. Thus, this theory can avoid the situation of uncoordinated punishment in the case of solicitation. As mentioned above, one of the most difficult problems of the unitary principal offender system at the operational level is that when the instigated person implements the preparatory act, the instigator can still be punished under Article 22 of China's Criminal Code. The sentencing rules are "lighter, mitigated punishment or exemption from punishment." When the instigated person does not even commit the preparatory act, the instigator can only apply the "lighter or mitigated punishment" of Article 29, Paragraph 2 of China's Criminal Code, and its sentencing is even heavier.

If the view of this article is adopted, the above problem will not occur. Based on the position of preparatory subordination, when the principal offender does not implement the preparatory act, the accomplice cannot be punished as a preparatory offender. Therefore, when the instigated person has prepared for but not perpetrated the crime, this belongs to "the instigated person has not committed the instigated crime", to which Article 29, Paragraph 2 of China's Criminal Code applies. When the instigated person has not even carried out the preparatory act, the instigator should not be punished as the instigated crime. In this way, it is ensured that when the instigated person implements the preparatory act, the punishment of the instigator must be heavier than the punishment of the instigator when the instigated person does not implement the preparatory act.

Secondly, compared with "the theory that the instigated crime has been attempted but not accomplished", the view adopted by this chapter will not make Article 29, Paragraph 2 of China's Criminal Code an attention provision. As Professor Zhang Mingkai said, the literal meaning of Article 29, Paragraph 2 of China's Criminal Code is a major obstacle to the accomplice subordination theory. In order to adopt the accomplice subordination theory, it is necessary to reinterpret this provision.[55] The so-called "reinterpretation" is actually

55 *Supra* note 42, 412.

Interpretation scheme / Specific situation	The theory that the instigated person has perpetrated but not accomplished the crime[a]	The theory based on the unitary principal offender system[b]	The theory that the instigated person has prepared for but not perpetrated the crime (the position of this paper)
The instigating information is not conveyed	Not guilty[c]	Article 29, Paragraph 2	Not guilty
The instigated person refuses the instigation	Not guilty	Article 29, Paragraph 2	Not guilty
The instigated person accepts the instigation but does not commit any preparatory act	Not guilty	Article 29, Paragraph 2	Not guilty
The instigated person has prepared for but not perpetrated the crime	Apply both Article 29, Paragraph 1 and Article 22 if there is a need to punish the instigator[d]	Apply both Article 29, Paragraph 1 and Article 22	Apply both Article 29, Paragraph 1 and Article 29, Paragraph 2
The instigated person has perpetrated but not accomplished the crime	Apply both the Article 29, Paragraph 1 and Article 29, Paragraph 2	Apply both Article 29, Paragraph 1 and Article 23	Apply both Article 29, Paragraph 1 and Article 23

Notes: [a] *Supra* note 42, 412–414; [b] *supra* note 11, 147–149; [c] The term "not guilty" in this form specifically refers to the instigator not committing the instigated crime. Whether the instigating act itself constitutes other crimes (such as the crime of infringing citizens' personal information) is another matter; [d] Professor Zhou Guangquan believes that the punishment of the instigator is only based on the legal principle of the preparatory crime, which seems to mean that he believes that only Article 22 can be applied in this case. *Supra* note 16, 191.

Figure 11.1 The comparison between the mainstream views and this chapter on the interpretation of "the instigated person does not commit the instigated crime"

to interpret the provision as if it does not exist, or to interpret it as a kind of notice provision. According to Professor Zhang Mingkai, "the instigated person has not committed the instigated crime" means that the instigated person perpetrated the crime but has not completed it. No matter whether the instigated crime is attempted or suspended, it constitutes an attempted crime for the instigator, so it is necessary to apply the sentencing rules of "can be lighter or mitigated". However, whether there is Article 29, Paragraph 2 or not, Article 23, Paragraph 2 should be applied to the instigator in this case without any doubt, and the punishment of the instigator can be lighter or mitigated. That is to say, according to the theory that the instigated crime has been attempted but not accomplished, Article 29, Paragraph 2 of China's Criminal Code is totally superfluous. In this regard, Professor Liu Mingxiang also accurately pointed out: "Interpreting Article 29, paragraph 2 of China's Criminal Code as something redundant (or meaningless) is the purpose of 'the theory that the instigated crime has been attempted but not accomplished'."[56] Although legislators do sometimes use the legislative technique of attention provision, the attention provision is a "provision that prompts the attention of the judiciary so as not to be confused or ignored by the judiciary".[57] In the case that the instigated person has perpetrated but not accomplished the crime, the instigator should be treated as an attempted offender, which is very simple and straightforward. It is difficult to imagine that confusion will occur on this issue in judicial practice. There is no need to set up special attention provisions. In this sense, "the theory that the instigated crime has been attempted but not accomplished" may lack a convincing explanation for why Article 29, Paragraph 2 of China's Criminal Code should be interpreted as an attention provision.

If view of this article is adopted, Article 29, Paragraph 2 of China's Criminal Code will not be interpreted as a notice provision. This chapter argues Article 29, Paragraph 2 is the special provision of Article 22, Paragraph 2. Specifically, in the case where the instigator has already committed a preparatory act and has not yet perpetrated, if there were no Article 29, Paragraph 2, Article 22, Paragraph 2 should be applied and a "lighter, mitigated or exempted from punishment" should be sentenced to the instigator. However, the existence of Article 29, Paragraph 2 indicates that a special provision has been made in this case, thus excluding the application of Article 22, Paragraph 2. That is to say, in the view of legislators, although solicitation is also a kind of preparatory crime, its social harmfulness is more serious than that of ordinary preparatory crime, so it cannot enjoy the treatment of "exemption from punishment"

56 *Supra* note 11, 145.

57 See Wu Xuebin, "The Attention Provisions and Statutory Fiction in China's Criminal Code", Studies in Law and Business, No. 5 (2004), p. 49.

like ordinary preparatory crime, but only "can be given a lighter or mitigated punishment", so it is specially stipulated in Article 29, Paragraph 2 of China's Criminal Code. This interpretation scheme also has substantive rationality because it is the consistent position of China and other countries in the world to crack down on instigators.[58]

4. RESPONSES AND EXPLANATIONS TO RELATED QUESTIONS

As a new view, it is not enough for this chapter to just make a positive argument. This chapter also needs to respond and explain in advance to the questions that may be raised by the readers or where confusion may occur. Specifically, it includes the following aspects:

4.1 Whether the "Punishment of Preparatory Crime in Principle" Conflicts with the Principle of Legality

The logical basis of the theory put forth by this chapter is that China's Criminal Code has adopted the position of "punishing preparatory offenders in principle", but this is not unquestioned. A quite strong point of view holds that only perpetrating acts have a clear figure, which provides a stable basis for criminal punishability and the state's penalty power. Therefore, in order to maintain the principle of legality, it is necessary to generally exclude the punishability of preparatory crime.[59]

This chapter acknowledges that there does exist a certain tension between the position of "punishing preparatory offenders in principle" and the principle of legality, but this is not a reason to completely deny this position. On the one hand, since Article 22 has clearly stipulated the punishment for preparatory offenders, we should not turn a blind eye to the explicit provisions of legislation; on the other hand, the aforementioned tensions can and should be resolved through efforts at the level of interpretation. The conflicts of legal principles are very common. This conflict usually does not end with one completely overwhelming the other, but must be resolved in a specific situation. This chapter is precisely a theoretical attempt to resolve this conflict. As mentioned above, as long as there is an instigation act, it can be literally evaluated as a preparatory act, but according to this chapter, the instigator can be punished only when the instigated person has carried out the preparatory act, which reduces

[58] See Xiong Hongwen, "The Identification of the Role of Instigators in Joint Crime – Also on the Rule that the Instigator is not the Principal offender", *People's Procuratorial Semimonthly*, No.4 (2011), p. 62.

[59] *Supra* note 50, 174.

the punishment scope for the special preparatory crime of solicitation, so as to realize the coordination between the position of "punishing preparatory offenders in principle" and the principle of legality to a certain extent.

4.2 The Criminal Cessation Form Stipulated in Article 29, Paragraph 2 of China's Criminal Code

The sentencing rule in Article 29, Paragraph 2 of China's Criminal Code is "may be lighter or mitigated", which is consistent with the attempted crime. This chapter interprets this provision as a preparatory crime. Is it reasonable? As long as the theory of attempt is not completely reversed, then the instigation can only be evaluated as a preparatory act rather than perpetration. As for the consistency between the sentencing rules in Article 29, Paragraph 2 of China's Criminal Code and the punishment rules for attempted crimes, this similarity is determined by the limitations of language and the objective reality that "the law is limited but situations in life are infinite". Specifically, when legislators set sentencing rules for various lenient punishments, they can only use a limited number of expressions to arrange and combine the terms "may" and "shall" with the terms "lighter punishment", "mitigated punishment", and "exempted punishment". Although the legislators use the same expression at the legislative level, it does not mean their effects in the judiciary are exactly the same. For example, the legal consequences of attempted crime and normal meritorious service are both "lighter or mitigated punishment", but according to the Supreme People's Court's "Notice on the Implementation of the Revised Sentencing Guidance" (Court Announcement [2017] No.7), the punishment of attempted crime can reduce the benchmark penalty by less than 50% considering the specific circumstance, while the normal meritorious service can only reduce the benchmark penalty by less than 20%. There is a clear gap between the two. Therefore, even if Article 29, Paragraph 2 of China's Criminal Code uses the expression "may be lighter or mitigated", it does not necessarily mean that this is the provision for attempted crime. In my opinion, it can be interpreted as a special and heavier preparatory crime. Since the sentencing rule of the preparatory crime is already "can be mitigated, mitigated or exempted from punishment," if we want to set up a slightly heavier preparatory crime, we have to use the expression "can be mitigated or mitigated" at least logically, so this expression has to "crash" with the punishment rule of attempted crime.

Although the punishment rules of preparatory crime and attempted crime both contain the part of "can be lighter or mitigated," the substantive meaning of the two is not the same, and the degree of "lighter or mitigated" in preparatory crime should obviously be greater than that of attempted crime. Therefore, although the principle of punishment stipulated in Article 29, Paragraph 2 of China's Criminal Code seems to be the same as that of attempted crime, in practical application, the degree of "lighter" and "mitigated" in this article should be consistent with preparatory crime. The only difference is that the perpetrator shall not be exempted from punishment when this provision is applied.

4.3 The Treatment of the Situation When the Instigated Person Has Perpetrated but Not Accomplished the Crime

Since Article 29, Paragraph 2 of China's Criminal Law applies to the situation where the instigated person has prepared for but not perpetrated the crime, how should we deal with the situation where the instigated person has perpetrated but not accomplished the crime? According to this chapter, the situation that the instigated person has perpetrated but not accomplished the crime can also be literally evaluated as "the instigated person has not committed the instigated crime". However, from the perspective of systematic interpretation, since this chapter defines Article 29, Paragraph 2 as a provision about a special kind of preparatory crime, the situation that the instigated person has perpetrated but not accomplished the crime should be excluded from this provision. In this situation, we can directly apply Article 29, Paragraph 1 and Article 23 of China's Criminal Code to the instigator, and there is no need to apply Article 29, Paragraph 2. As mentioned above, the degree of "lighter and mitigated" of preparatory crime and attempted crime is different. Therefore, even if we apply Article 29, Paragraph 2 to the situation that the instigated person has perpetrated but not accomplished the crime, it is still necessary to distinguish the two different situations of preparatory crime and attempted crime, and apply a higher lenient degree to the preparatory crime and a lower lenient degree to the attempted crime. Instead of going around in circles like this, it is better to simply hold that Article 29, Paragraph 2 of China's Criminal Code only includes the situation that the instigated person has perpetrated but not prepared for the crime, and does not include the situation that the instigated person has prepared for but not accomplished the crime.

4.4 Whether the Accomplice Subordination Theory and Strict Punishment of the Instigator Are Contradictory

This chapter insists on the accomplice subordination theory while advocating strict punishment of instigators. Is this contradictory? This chapter believes that the strict punishment of the instigator is reasonable in criminal policy because, from the perspective of social governance, source governance is indeed more effective than end governance.[60] However, we shouldn't pursue criminal policy at the expense of undermining the principle of legality. Interpreting the unitary perpetrator system instigating and helping as constitutive elements makes the boundary of constitutive elements blurred, which is really unacceptable. It should be pointed out that although scholars who support the accomplice subordination theory in China generally believe that the punishment of the instigator should be lighter than that of the perpetrator, because the instigator does not commit the act of constituent elements and does not substantially dominate the process of criminal facts.[61] But in my opinion, such a position cannot be pushed to an extreme degree. The core value of the accomplice subordination theory is to maintain the clarity of the constituent elements. When insisting on the accomplice subordination theory at the conviction level, the severity of sentencing actually has room for maneuver. Even in Germany, which generally supports the accomplice subordination in legislation, there is no lighter punishment for the instigator.[62] It is true that the perpetrator is the direct cause of the infringement of legal interests, while the accomplice is the indirect cause of the infringement of legal interests, but this can only show that under the same other conditions, the punishment of the perpetrator should be heavier than that of the accomplice, but it cannot show that the punishment of the perpetrator should always be heavier than that of the accomplice. As we all know, illegality is not the only factor that determines the sentencing. If we do not adopt the monism of result worthlessness, the infringement of legal interests is not the only factor that determines the illegality. The application of penalty in individual cases is affected by many factors including illegality, responsibility, and even criminal policy. It is difficult for a single factor to lead to the result of "heavier punishment in principle". Therefore, even if the difference in the structure between the perpetrator and the accomplice is recognized, it can only be considered that the punishment of the perpetrator is heavier than that of the accomplice under the same other conditions. However, if the complexity of the sentencing process and other factors are considered, it is possible that

[60] See Ma Kai, "Efforts to strengthen and innovate social management", *Journal of Chinese Academy of Governance*, No. 5 (2010), p. 7.

[61] See Qian Yeliu, "The Distinction between Perpetrators and Accomplices under the Two-tier Distinction system", *Chinese Journal of Law*, No. 1 (2012), p. 142.

[62] Article 26 of the German Criminal Code stipulates: "A person who intentionally instigates another person to intentionally commit an illegal act is an instigator. The punishment of instigator is the same as that of the principal offender." See Li Shengjie, Pan Yihong, translate, "*German Criminal Code*", (Yuanzhao Press 2017), p. 21.

the sentencing of the accomplice is equal to or even heavier than that of the perpetrator, as stipulated in Article 29, Paragraph 2 of China's Criminal Code.

5. CONCLUSION

The main views of this chapter include the following aspects.

Firstly, China's Criminal Code does not generally support the distinction system, nor does it generally support the unitary principal offender system. In terms of substantive rationality, the distinction system is better than the unitary principal offender system.

Secondly, in the countries and regions where the preparatory crime is exceptionally punished, there is a proposition that "the beginning of the perpetrating is the basis of illegality of intentional crime", and it is appropriate to understand the accomplice subordination theory as the implementation subordination. However, since China's criminal law clearly stipulates the punishment of preparatory crimes, it is not appropriate to stubbornly insist that "the beginning of the perpetrating is the basis of illegality of intentional crime" and simply equate the accomplice subordination theory with the implementation subordination, but should be adapted to local conditions. The subordination of accomplices in the context of China should be understood as preparatory subordination.

Thirdly, the position of preparatory subordination does not violate the provisions of the current criminal law, nor does it violate the theory of criminal law. According to this position, Article 29, Paragraph 2 of China's Criminal Code is a special kind of preparatory crime, and "the instigated person has not committed the instigated crime" refers to the situation where the instigator has carried out preparatory acts but has not yet perpetrated the crime.

Fourthly, compared with the unitary principal offender system, the theory adopted by this chapter will not lead to the inconsistency of punishment. Compared with the theory of "the instigator has been prepared to say", it will not make Article 29, Paragraph 2 of China's Criminal Code become a provision of notice, and can properly deal with the relevant theoretical issues, making this theory have a relative theoretical advantage to a certain extent.

12. From 'Yīnsī' to 'Yǐnsī': the evolution of privacy ideas in modern China

Lou Chanhou[1]

1. INTRODUCTION

The critique of ideas cannot replace the context of critique, but the critique of ideas can explain the context of critique. The Civil Code of the People's Republic of China (the PRC), promulgated in 2020, explicitly stipulates the right to privacy. However, unlike the digital age imprint of the concept of 'personal information', 'privacy' is not a newly emerging concept in contemporary times. Academia generally believes that 'privacy' as a legal concept originated from the famous paper 'The Right to Privacy' co-authored by American scholars Samuel D. Warren and Louis D. Brandeis.[2] This claim certainly reveals the legal concept transplantation from 'privacy' in English to 'Yǐnsī' (隐私) in Chinese, but it overlooks the spontaneous understanding of *Yǐnsī* in Chinese law.[3] When Warren and Brandeis published the aforementioned paper in the *Harvard Law Review* in 1890, it was the end of the 19th century, more than 130 years ago. In the past hundred years, how did the connotation of the concept of 'Yǐnsī' change in modern China?

---

1 Co-translator, Tang Shuchen, PhD candidate at Tsinghua University School of Law; co-translator, Chen Sihan, Juris Master candidate at Tsinghua University School of Law.

2 See Samuel D. Warren and Louis D. Brandeis, 'Right to Privacy' (1890) 5 *Harvard Law Review* 193–220.

3 For the study in the field of Chinese linguistics represented by Wang Zejian's monograph, which generally argues the formation of the right to Yǐnsī from the perspective of comparative law, involving the investigation of the impact caused by the transplantation of laws from the United States, the United Kingdom, Germany, France, etc., but without deeply investigating the endogeneity of privacy in China, see Wang Zejian, *The Law of Personality Rights: Legal Hermeneutics, Comparative Law, Case Study* (Peking University Press 2013) 177–204.

To answer the above question, it is thought best to meticulously comb through the endogenous logic of the 'Yǐnsī' (阴私) concept in China.[4] The intuitive answer from academia to this can be summarized as the Yīnsī theory, that is, it is believed that the concept of 'Yǐnsī' evolved from the concept of 'Yīnsī'. A specific example that can confirm this understanding is the explanation in the 'Legal Dictionary' column on page No. 4 of the newspaper named *Renmin Ribao* (《人民日报》) [the *People's Daily*] on 30 October 1988: 'Privacy cases: They are also known as "Yīnsī cases," involving affairs, violations of social norms, or other private affairs … To avoid causing adverse effects and protect the reputation of the persons involved, Chinese law stipulates those cases involving personal privacy are not publicly tried; but verdicts are always publicly announced.'[5] Therefore, Yīnsī is the object to be criticized, but the right to privacy that is positively evaluated in law can be used to criticize others for infringement in torts. Some scholars believe that this conceptual transformation from 'Yīnsī' to 'Yǐnsī' is due to the conceptual changes brought about by the reform and opening up of the PRC.[6] But the problem is that both 'Yīnsī' and 'Yǐnsī' were used as early as in the Republic of China (the ROC). Although Su Li does not specifically discuss the concept of 'Yīnsī', he believes that the idea of 'Yǐnsī' preceded the emergence of the concept of 'Yǐnsī'.[7] Some researchers in journalism discuss how the Yīnsī legislation in the field of modern Chinese journalism failed,[8] but do not carefully study the reasons for the elimination of Yīnsī and the rise of Yǐnsī.

From the above introduction of previous studies, the academic community's revelation of the conceptual transformation from 'Yīnsī' to 'Yǐnsī' is not clear. An important question that deserves further research is, how does the 'Yīnsī' concept that 'is criticized by others' (derogatory) evolve into the

---

4 See He Hancheng, 'Marriage Cases Are Not Yīnsī Cases' (1981) 8 *People's Judicature* 18; Yang Ziyuan, 'A Word of Advice – Suggest to Unify "Yīnsī" and "Yǐnsī"' (1982) 6 *Law Science* 23; Zheng Hongzhang, 'Investigation of Yīnsī Cases Should Not Entangle the Trivial Details of the Case' (1983) 3 *People's Judicature* 13; Xu Canweng, 'Yǐnsī and Yīnsī' (1986) 2 *Law Science Magazine* 26; Wang Liming, 'The Locality and Timeliness of the "General Provisions of Civil Law"' (2017) 3 SJTU Law Review 92.

5 'Legal Dictionary' *People's Daily* (Beijing, 30 October 1988) 4.

6 See Zhou Hanhua, 'Legal Positioning of Personal Information Protection' (2020) 3 *Studies in Law and Business* 71.

7 See Su Li, 'Legal Thought on Yǐnsī Tort – Starting from the Event of Li Hui Questioning Wen Huisha' (2019) 2 *Tsinghua University Law Journal* 125–128.

8 See Cao Ruiqing, 'Why is it Difficult for Concept to Become Institution – The Debate and Failure of 'Yīnsī' Legislation in Modern China's News Publishing Field' (2020) 5 *Journalism Review* 74–87.

'Yǐnsī' concept that 'criticizes others' (commendatory)? The discussion of this question requires distinguishing between two different contexts of criticism (criticizing official Yīnsī and criticizing civilian Yīnsī) and three different conceptual criticisms (political public morality, social public morality, and private morality).[9] The governance theory of political public morality and the individualism of private morality give birth to two 'Yǐnsī' that criticize others; the former serves national historical integration, and the latter serves the rights inheritance in the sense of English 'privacy'; however, social public morality leads to 'Yǐnsī' being criticized by others. This article will use the process of the formulation of *Qinding Bao Lü* (《钦定报律》) [Imperial Newspaper Law] in the Qing Dynasty, the judicial interpretation of *Dali Yuan* (大理院) [the Preparatory Supreme Court] during the early ROC, the narrative of the revision of the Publication Law during the ROC, the statutory clause of public morality in the PRC founding document named 'Common Program of the Chinese People's Political Consultative Conference', and the judicial interpretation of the 'General Principles of Civil Law' of the PRC as the 'source material', combined with the contexts shown in the news reported by the *Ta Kung Pao* (《大公报》) and the People's Daily in history, to show the transformation of the 'Yǐnsī' [privacy] ideas in China in the 20th century.[10] These pictures are the 'montage' selected by the author, showing the rhythm of transformation with a series of split screen pictures and cross editing, rather than sticking to the plain narrative of the stream of consciousness. 'The interpretation of legal texts and the application of legal rules … cannot provide us with de-contextualized, uninterrupted neutral reading.'[11] News contents can provide historical and local contexts for this, and can be used to avoid judging the past with today's standards and the Chinese with the Western standards when

---

[9] The distinction between concept and idea is like John Bordley Rawls' distinction between the concept of justice and the idea of justice; that is, multiple ideas of justice explain the concept of justice and seek consensus on the concept of justice in the communication of the ideas. See John Rawls, *A Theory of Justice* (He Huaihong, He Baogang, Liao Shenbai tr, China Social Sciences Press 1988) 3–4.

[10] The author chooses the press texts of *Ta Kung Pao* and *the People's Daily* as specific analysis samples and generally takes the year of 1949 as the time node, connecting the samples of the two before and after. This is the control variable of four sameness, that is, whether there are multiple semantics under the conditions of 'same era, same media, same publishing standard, same Yǐnsī symbol'. Especially considering that these two representative newspapers' strictness to the 'same publishing standard' is beneficial to the control of multiple variables.

[11] Feng Xiang, 'Law and Literature' in Feng Xiang, *Wooden-Legged Justice* (Peking University Press 2007) 25.

conducting research.[12] Similar to Wang Hui's conceptual context pondering of seeing 'big history' from 'small texts', and Michael Schudson's demystification of the right to know with culture,[13] this article is based on the Chinese context, summarizing the historical transformation of the connotation of the privacy ideas in modern China, and theoretically summarizing its endogenous logic proposition as 'the theory of two contexts and three ideas'.

2. DIFFERENT CONTEXTS OF CRITICIZING OFFICIALS VERSUS CRITICIZING CITIZENS

If an official solicits prostitutes in private, can the media report on it? Suppose the official as the plaintiff claims the right to privacy against the media as the defendant, can the plaintiff request the court to prohibit the media from reporting on this based on Article 997 of the Civil Code of the PRC? According to the inference from the sensational 'Shanghai judges' collective prostitution' incident in 2013,[14] the news can report on this, and it is difficult for officials to claim the right to privacy. Some people might say: 'Is this really a question in China? If officials and celebrities do bad things, they should of course be reported, so that the public will know.' However, the path of explanation that forcibly applies the 'public figure theory' from the foreign legal community has been criticized by Su Li as facing the predicament of 'post-referencing' and 'suppressing fame'.[15] The question that the author intends to pursue is, where is the native legal principle of 'varying from person to person' to protect privacy?

If Yīnsī is criticized by others and Yǐnsī is to criticize others, then soliciting prostitutes obviously belongs to the former and not the latter. Although the concept of Yīnsī is no longer adopted by Chinese current legislation, does Yīnsī continue to exist as the 'other' of Yǐnsī? According to this logic, the right to privacy shows a basic contradiction, that is, the contradiction between 'Yǐnsī does not want to be known and criticized by others' and 'Yīnsī is known and criticized by others'. In this regard, Yīnsī is the key to solving this contradiction. Combined with the native concept of 'Guan yu Min' (官与民) [Officials

---

12 See Wang Hui, *The Rise of Modern Chinese Thought (Vol. 1)* (SDX Joint Publishing Company 2004) 1.

13 See Michael Schudson, *The Rise of the Right to Know: Politics and the Culture of Transparency, 1945–1975* (Zheng Yihui tr, Peking University Press 2018) 17–19.

14 See Hao Hong, '4 Judges in Shanghai High Court Confirmed to be Involved in Prostitution' *People's Daily* (Beijing, 7 August 2013) 8.

15 See *supra* note 7, 119–121.

and Citizens],[16] this chapter distinguishes Yīnsī into *Piguan Yīnsī* (批官阴私) [criticizing official Yīnsī] and *Pimin Yīnsī* (批民阴私) [criticizing civilian Yīnsī], the former refers to the context where officials are criticized, and the latter refers to the context where citizens are criticized. For criticizing official Yīnsī, both ideas of Yīnsī and Yǐnsī tend to be derogatory and are criticized by others; for criticizing civilian Yīnsī, Yīnsī and Yǐnsī are separated, the idea of Yīnsī tends to be derogatory and is criticized, and the idea of Yǐnsī tends to be commendatory to criticize others. The chapter will argue the above points in the following text in conjunction with the *Qinding Bao Lü* and the judicial interpretation of the Dali Yuan during the early ROC.

2.1 *Qinding Bao Lü* and Criticizing Official Yīnsī

Evil deeds (Yīnsī) travel a thousand miles. The emergence of modern news media has changed the structure of information circulation in modern China. For example, the form of newspapers was no longer limited to *Dichao* (邸钞) [Government Gazettes].[17] Using market contracts and postal technology, the public obtained information about a society of strangers, thereby breaking through the barriers of geography and acquaintances to information. In the historical context of constitutionalism in the late Qing Dynasty, Article 11 of the *Qinding Bao Lü* promulgated in 1911 stipulates: 'Newspapers must not carry words that damage the reputation of others, but those that are exclusively for public interest and do not involve Yīnsī are not limited to this.'[18] Compared with the *Da Qing Yinshua Wu Zhuan Lü* (《大清印刷物专律》)

[16] The typification of the 'officials and citizens' scene can avoid the inconvenience of writing caused by the typification of 'public and private'. As some Sinologists have pointed out, the concept of 'private' in China – relative to the concept of 'public' – has a dual code of neutrality (quantity) and derogation (quality), different from the neutral (quantity) code of the concept of 'private' in Japan. See Mizoguchi Yuzo, *China's Public and Private* (Zheng Jing tr, Sun Ge ed, SDX Joint Publishing Company 2011) 86. Therefore, contextual typification needs to avoid prejudice that derogatory code is dominant. Moreover, the contextual typification of the 'officials and citizens' can avoid the presupposition of ideas such as public morality and private morality, thereby realizing the distinction between contexts and ideas in this article.

[17] See Fang Hanqi, 'Newspapers and Historical Research' (2004) 4 *Historical Archives* 31–35.

[18] 'Sunhai taren mingyu zhi yu, baozhi bu de dengzai, dan zhuan wei gongyi bu she yīnsi zhe, bu zai ci xian. (损害他人名誉之语，报纸不得登载，但专为公益不涉阴私者，不在此限)' Guo Wei ed, *Full Text of the Interpretation of the Grand Council* (Huiwen Tang New Record Bookstore 1931) 5; 'Imperial Decree on Newspaper Law' *Ta Kung Pao* (Tianjin, 21 February 1911) 6.

[Printing Law of Tsing Dynasty] introduced in 1906 and the old *Da Qing Bao Lü* (《大清报律》) [Newspaper Law of Tsing Dynasty] promulgated in 1908,[19] Article 11 of the 1911 *Qinding Bao Lü* was a new provision and explicitly adopted the concept of 'Yīnsī'.

From the perspective of semantic interpretation, Article 11 of the *Qinding Bao Lü* includes a prohibition clause on reputation reporting, as well as an exception clause that is 'exclusively for public interest and do not involve Yīnsī'. If the plaintiff claims that the defendant media's report has damaged their reputation and requests to prohibit the latter from reporting, then the defendant media can make a defense 'exclusively for public interest and do not involve Yīnsī', but they should bear the burden of proof. Among them, 'exclusively for public interest' and 'does not involve Yīnsī' are parallel conditions. The former is a positive condition, and the latter is a negative condition; only when both are satisfied can an exception be constituted. So, is it difficult for the defendant to provide evidence? The answer is affirmative, because Yīnsī is a legal concept with strong uncertainty. If the scope of Yīnsī (negative condition) is difficult to clarify, then how can we demand that the defendant media prove that its report 'does not involve Yīnsī'? This will lead to the difficulty of applying the exception, thereby restricting the space of news reporting.

This controversy was specifically reflected in the legislation of the *Qinding Bao Lü.* There was a significant dispute between the constitutionalists and conservatives over whether to retain the 'Yīnsī' in the exception clause of Article 11 of this law. During the third legislative reading of the draft bill of the *Qinding Bao Lü* held by *Zi Zheng Yuan* (资政院) [the Political Advisory Council] as the Preparatory Congress in 1910, the government special commissioner advocated for modifying the aforementioned Article 11 to 'Newspapers must not carry words that damage the reputation of others; except for public interest and not involving Yīnsī, it is not limited to not being able to post', but the Political Advisory Council ultimately passed the version 'Newspapers must not carry words that damage the reputation of others, but those that are exclusively for public interest are not limited to this'.[20] Among them,

---

19 See Huai Xiaofeng ed, *Historical Materials of Legal Reform in Late Qing Dynasty* (China University of Political Science and Law Press 2010) 332–334; 'Constitutional Compilation and Investigation Bureau Approved Forty-five Newspaper Laws' *Ta Kung Pao* (20 March 1908) 5.

20 'Consult the Grand Ministry of State to Review and Amend the Bill of Newspaper Law' *Ta Kung Pao* (Tianjin, 19 February 1911, 20 February 1911) 6. Also see Li Qicheng ed, *Proceedings of the Meeting of Zi Zheng Yuan – The Record of the Debate of the Late Qing Preparatory Congress* (Shanghai Sanlian Bookstore 2011) 227; Fang Chen, Wang Mingliang, 'From Autocratic Legislation to Parliamentary Legislation: The Preparatory Parliament and the Revision of the

constitutionalist representatives opposed the negative condition of 'Yīnsī' and advocated deleting this condition. For example, Representative Tao Jun (陶峻) believed that 'exposing Yīnsī has no boundary';[21] Representative Yi Zongkui (易宗夔) used the example of the corrupt official Cai Naihuang (蔡乃煌) in Shanghai to argue that corrupt officials may accuse newspapers of normal public opinion supervision on the grounds of involving Yīnsī.[22] However, when the legislative resolution of the Political Advisory Council was passed and was presented to Junji Dachen (军机大臣) [the Grand Ministers of State] for consultation and then submitted to the Emperor, Junji Chu (军机处) [the Grand Ministry of State] opposed deleting 'Yīnsī'. The Grand Ministry of State believed that the prohibition clause in Article 11 is virtually in name only, because no matter what things are directly or indirectly related to public interest, the definition of 'public interest' has no boundaries, so 'Yīnsī' as a negative condition should define the boundaries. 'As long as it does not offend, everyone has the joy of reading newspapers and will not turn against the newspaper'; Therefore, the Grand Ministry of State re-added 'Yīnsī' as a negative condition, limited the matter of exposing Yīnsī, and sent back the legislative resolution to the Political Advisory Council for reconsideration according to Article 17 of the Charter of the Political Advisory Council Charter.[23] Although the constitutionalist representatives opposed the actions of the Grand Ministry of State, they were unsuccessful. The proposal of the Grand Ministry of State was passed by the Political Advisory Council and became the promulgated version of the *Qinding Bao Lü*. The above case shows that the constitutionalists believed that Yīnsī as the negative condition of exception has no boundary, but the conservative Grand Ministry of State believed that public interest as the positive condition of exception has no boundary.

From the perspective of purpose interpretation, the condition of 'not involving Yīnsī' aims to limit the expansive interpretation of 'exclusively for public interest', thereby preventing the prohibition clause of Article 11 of *Qinding Bao Lü* from becoming a figurehead. However, if we think deeply about this

Late Qing Newspaper Law' (2016) 13 Press Circles 25–26; Wang Xuechen, 'The Making of the Late Qing Newspaper Law' (1994) 1 Sun Yatsen University Forum 235; 'Preparatory Congress Chronicle' *Ta Kung Pao* (Tianjin, 27 November 1910) 6; 'Preparatory Congress Chronicle', *Ta Kung Pao* (Tianjin, 3 December 1910) 5; 'Preparatory Congress Chronicle', *Ta Kung Pao* (Tianjin, 12 December 1910) 6.

21 Ibid., Li Qicheng's edited book, 227.

22 Ibid., Fang Chen and Wang Mingliang's paper, 25. For the incident of Cai Naihuang's corruption and Chen Qitai's death, see 'Wishful Thinking' *Ta Kung Pao* (Tianjin, 24 June 1909) 2.

23 See 'Consult the Grand Ministry of State to Review and Amend the Bill of Newspaper Law' *Ta Kung Pao* (Tianjin, 19 February 1911, 20 February 1911) 6.

clause, we will find that the expansive interpretation of 'not involving Yīnsī' will also nullify the exception clause. So, what was the legislator's understanding of 'Yīnsī'? The debate around the text of *Qinding Bao Lü* in the Political Advisory Council provides clues in this regard. The so-called 'everyone' of the Grand Ministry of State is indeed an official, and its so-called 'Yīnsī' refers to the Yīnsī of officials.[24] From the discourse of newspapers, criticizing officials' Yīnsī and Yǐnsī had similar meanings at that time. On the one hand, in 1902, the then newly established *Ta Kung Pao* published an article 'The problem of strict newspaper law', criticizing 'the enactment of the press law is actually afraid that *Qing Yi* (清议) [public discussions] will expose their (officials) Yǐnsī'.[25] In 1909, Ta Kung Pao reported that 'foreign ambassadors sent telegrams asking the Chinese government to correct the newspaper law that privileges *Yǐnsī* [privacy]'.[26] On the other hand, *Ta Kung Pao* published a news report in 1904, stating that 'a few days ago, *Yu Shi* (御史) [superintendent officials] had repeatedly disclosed *Yīnsī* of a certain local officials and governors of various provinces, and although there were officials who received great favors [from the Emperor], it was inevitable that they would delay and mislead political affairs',[27] and published an article in 1907 titled 'The relationship between the press and the preparatory constitutional era', commenting '[the government] is not allowed [by constitution] to suddenly ban [a newspaper] because of the news on *Yīnsī* of a senior official.'[28] This is the alternate use of the derogatory language of Yǐnsī and Yīnsī in the same newspaper. In the language used to criticize officials, Yīnsī and Yǐnsī were derogatory. The author calls it 'Piguan Yīnsī', which means 'criticizing official Yīnsī'.

There are two implications for this discourse. First, it reflects the contradiction of Article 11 of *Qinding Bao Lü* – the contradiction between being exclusively for public interest (to criticize officials) and not being involved in *Yīnsī*

24 In the debate of *Qin Din Bao Lü* in *Zhi Zheng Yuan*, Gu Ao (顾鳌), a special commissioner of *Xian Zheng Bian Cha Guan* (宪政编查馆) [the Constitutional Compilation and Inspection Office], defended that *Yīnsī* refers exclusively to personal private practice and has nothing to do with the officials' corruption. However, constitutionalist Representative Lei Fen (雷奋) opposed, holding that corruption cases reported in newspapers can be interpreted as *Yīnsī* if there are no facts, and then the scope of *Yīnsī* is undoubtedly too broad. See *supra* note 20, Li Qicheng's edited book, 683.

25 'Discussing the Issue of Strictly Setting Newspaper Law' *Ta Kung Pao* (Tianjin, 25 November 1902) 1.

26 'Important News' *Ta Kung Pao* (Tianjin, 20 August 1909) 2.

27 'Important News' *Ta Kung Pao* (Tianjin, 16 December 1904) 2.

28 'The Relationship between Newspapers and the Preparatory Constitutional Era' *Ta Kung Pao* (Tianjin, 9 October 1907) 1.

(not to criticize officials). The above-mentioned discourse of the newspaper shows that *Yīnsī* refers to officials' corruptions, which means *Piguan Yīnsī*.[29] This reveals that the Grand Ministry of State, which proposed the condition of *Yīnsī* in the 1911 *Qinding Bao Lü*, attempted to 'privilege' this law, which means officials represented by the Grand Ministers of State did not want their corruptions to be reported in a newspaper.[30] Second, it aligns with the historical background of that era. Although the media audience had expanded to ordinary citizens, the media theme has not expanded accordingly, because ordinary citizens have not yet consciously become interested in themselves, so there is no market demand and media supply. As Mao Zedong observed, 'History is created by the people, but on the stage of old dramas (in all the old literatures and old arts that are divorced from the people) the people became scum, and the lords, the lords' wives and their children (young lords and young ladies) ruled the stage … .'[31] In other words, at that time, those whose *Yīnsī* could be disclosed by the media were usually dominant groups who were Manchu aristocracy, *Shi Da Fu* (士大夫) [scholar officials], *Beiyang* (北洋) military factions, and business tycoons,[32] so the threat to *Yīnsī* of 'everyone'

---

29 Some people may advocate legal doctrines of interpretation to equalize the scope of interpretation of *Yīnsī* with public interest, so as not to expand *Yīnsī* to *Piguan Yīnsī*, so corruptions would fall into public interests rather than *Yīnsī*. However, the author disagrees with it because: first, it is difficult to use legal doctrine to explain legal texts in late Qing where the Constitution and the rule of law had not been well developed; otherwise, legal doctrines may be too naïve to explain the historic narratives. Second, from the perspective of legal doctrines alone, this interpretation also places a heavy burden of proof on the defendant's media, because the plaintiff's official only needs to prove that the news involves *Yīnsī*, and the defendant needs to complete the proof 'exclusively for common interest' (excluding Yīnsī); otherwise, if the truth is not clear, then the defendant might fail to carry the burden of proof and lose the case.

30 Article 11 implied *Piguan Yīnsī* was different from other articles that *Qin Din Bao Lü* prohibited reporting on '*Mao Du Chen Yu*' (冒渎乘舆) [Offending the Emperor] and '*Hun Xiao Zheng Ti*' (淆乱政体) [Offending the Sovereign Regime] under Article 10, and 'Diplomatic, Army and Navy Incidents, and Other Government Affairs' under Article 12. Because Article 10 pointed to the whole political system of late Qing dynasty, and Article 12 pointed to the official act of duty, they differed from Article 11, which prohibited reporting on political corruptions that are not recognized by the formal political system of late Qing dynasty.

31 Mao Zedong, 'Letter to Yan'an Ping Opera House After Watching "Forced to Liangshan"' *People's Daily* (Beijing, 25 May 1967) 2.

32 After the abolition of the imperial examination in the late Qing Dynasty, due to the lack of a 'career bureaucrat nurturing system', many military personnel and industrial and commercial workers were able to enter the bureaucratic system.

was not the danger of individualism. In another word, this privileged *Yīnsī* has little to do with ordinary citizens.[33] 'Everyone' essentially refers to the dangers of officials and their corruptions with other elites, that is, officials are worried about the news media reporting their bad deeds.

Therefore, the discourse of 'Yīnsī' in Article 11 of *Qinding Bao Lü* was *Yīnsī* to be criticized, that is, mainly pointing to the criticism of official *Yīnsī*. This Yīnsī neither has a normative effect of criticizing others, nor does it have a right nature applicable to general individuals. In essence, Article 11 of *Qinding Bao Lü* was to hide official corruptions in the pretext of the rule of law. The reason is the same as the criticism of 'fake constitutionalism and true corruption'.

2.2 Judicial Interpretation of Dali Yuan and Criticizing Civilian Yīnsī

Not long after the implementation of *Qinding Bao Lü*, the Grand Ministry of State was replaced by the Royal Cabinet, which was soon eliminated by history after the abdication of the Qing Emperor.[34] *Qinding Bao Lü*, the Newspaper Law of the former Qing Dynasty continued to be applied in the ROC, so how to interpret the 'not involving Yīnsī' mentioned in the aforementioned Article 11 with the new ideas of the ROC? *Dali Yuan*, the Preparatory Supreme Court as the highest judicial branch during the Beiyang (北洋) Government period of the ROC, took on this responsibility and issued a 'Uniform No. 10' judicial interpretation on March 26, 1913.[35]

See Luo Zhitian, 'The Social Impact of the Reform of the Imperial Examination System in the Late Qing Dynasty' (1998) 4 *Social Sciences in China* 191.

33 Opponents may start with the case of 'Yang Naiwu and Xiao Baicai' (杨乃武与小白菜) that *Shun Pao* (申报) reported in the 1870s as a counterexample, but that case is not sufficient to oppose the author's argument. This is because Yang Naiwu was Ju Ren (举人) [a senior candidate in the process of the imperial examination] and was eligible to be a scholar official, which is different from the common people who lack this eligibility. Furthermore, the case was not Yang Naiwu's unwillingness to be picked up by the newspaper, but a grievance that he was willing to let the news report his unjust situation. See Lu Yongdi, 'The Setting Sun: The Historical, Social and Institutional Factors of the Reversal of Yang Naiwu's Case in the Late Qing Dynasty' (2007) 4 *Peking University Law Journal* 411, 428–433.

34 In May 1911, the Grand Ministry of State was replaced by the Cabinet (Royal Cabinet). See 'Imperial Edict' *Ta Kung Pao* (Tianjin, 9 May 1911) 1; 'The Insight of the Governor in Shandong against the Royal Cabinet' *Ta Kung Pao* (Tianjin, 23–24 June 1911) 2.

35 See *supra* note 18, 5.

First of all, this judicial interpretation was made upon the request of the Beijing Fourth Primary Prosecution Office, which believed that the concept of 'Yīnsī' mentioned in Article 11 of *Qinding Bao Lü* of the former Qing Dynasty is not certain in its concept range, which makes it difficult to apply the law. The Prosecution Office explained and requested to *Dali Yuan* that: 'The meaning of it [Yīnsī] varies widely and narrowly, so the range of interpretation cannot be the same. For example, it is reported that a certain representatives spent a certain amount of money to run for election; a certain official used a certain amount of money to run for a job vacancy. Furthermore, it says that someone has always liked smoking and gambling, and some have always liked to visit prostitution. In such cases, can it be considered as involving Yīnsī? Our prosecutors have different opinions. If we don't ask for interpretation [from *Dali Yuan*] and determine the scope, the interpretation of the law will inevitably misunderstand each other; and the litigation process will inevitably have difficulties. For this, please explain in detail and determine the scope, reply as soon as possible, so as to follow.'[36]

The above four situations listed by the Beijing Fourth Primary Prosecution Office involved the difference between criticizing official Yīnsī and criticizing civilian Yīnsī. Among them, bribery and buying officials belonged to the former, and smoking, gambling, and prostitution belonged to the latter.

Furthermore, this judicial interpretation did not directly define what 'Yīnsī' is to respond to the request by the Prosecution Office, but provided an overall interpretation of Article 11 of *Qinding Bao Lü*, that is, advocating 'there are two prerequisites for 'exclusively serving public interest and not involving Yīnsī': first, it must be able to prove its facts; second, the facts must be related to public interest, not be exclusive to *Si De* (私德) [Private Morality]. The various examples raised in the original request, according to this standard, can naturally be interpreted.'[37] The author believes that the judicial interpretation of the Preparatory Supreme Court is different from the statutory interpretation of Article 11 of *Qinding Bao Lü*, because the former reduces the burden of proof for the defendant media on the exception clause, thus expanding the liberty space for media news reporting.

What does it mean? Suppose that there are two circle sets named the set of public interest and the set of private morality, and the two sets partially overlap, then this intersection refers to 'ambiguous' news, that is, news that is difficult to be clearly classified into the category of public interest or private morality. If according to the textual interpretation of Article 11 of *Qinding Bao Lü*, the exception of 'exclusively serving public interest and not involving

---

36 Ibid., 5.
37 Ibid., 5.

Yīnsī' is limited to the part left after the public interest set is deducted from the intersection. However, if according to the 'related to public interest, not be exclusive to private morality' explained by the Preparatory Supreme Court, then the range of exceptions not only includes the part left after the public interest set is deducted from the intersection, but also includes the intersection. It can be seen that since the reporting of ambiguous news is not prohibited, the scope of the exception is expanded.

Moreover, this expansion of the scope of exceptions also has procedural support. Based on the burden of proof, it is easier for the defendant press to prove that it is 'related to public interest' than to prove that it is 'exclusively serving public interest' because it does not need to reach the exclusive standard. In other words, as long as the defendant press can prove that its reporting behavior is related to public interest, then its behavior can constitute a statutory exception. In comparison, it is more difficult for the plaintiff to prove 'not exclusive to private morality' to exclude the application of exceptions because no one is not in society nor related to public interest. For this purpose, the Preparatory Supreme Court of the early ROC turned 'not involving Yīnsī' into 'not exclusive to private morality'. Why is it said to be a makeover? Because this interpretation has gone beyond the range of legal intention – the derogatory concept of Yīnsī is replaced by the commendatory concept of private morality. Private morality is not Yīnsī, and damage to private morality is equivalent to Yīnsī. Based on the purpose of this judicial interpretation, the Preparatory Supreme Court in the early ROC eliminated the effect of restricting news reporting caused by the 'not involving Yīnsī' provision left over from the Qing Dynasty.

It is worth noting that this interpretation had externalities. First, the concept of Yīnsī being criticized by others has changed to the concept of criticizing others' private morality. As a result, the commendatory concept of private morality may inherit the commendatory idea of privacy, and the idea of 'privacy rights' from foreign legal discourse may have the opportunity to be accepted. Second, the criticism of civilian Yīnsī is different from the criticism of official Yīnsī, reflecting the conscious public subjectivity (civilians are interested in themselves, and the media responds to market demand and reports on civilians). Thirdly, combined with the two points above, the criticism of civilian Yīnsī has a derogatory nature, which is different from the commendatory privacy that developed from the concept of private morality, thus initially forming the difference between 'Yīnsī criticized by others' and 'privacy criticizing others'. Moreover, this civilian Yīnsī is different from official Yīnsī, as the meanings of Yīnsī and privacy are both toward the derogatory tendency in the context of official Yīnsī.

In a word, the above change was confirmed in the newspaper discourses of that time. On the one hand, the derogatory discourse of Yīnsī (阴私) and

Yǐnsī (隐私) [privacy] in the criticism of official Yīnsī continued into the period of the ROC. In 1915, *Ta Kung Pao* republished a comment titled 'On the Moral Heart of Official Service,' analogizing that '[everyone] has a candle [the right to know] to enlighten far away, so as to disclose the Yǐnsī [privacy] of officials.'[38] In 1922, the representatives in Jiangsu province like Hua Yanquan (华彦铨) denounced the crime of Wu Peifu (吴佩孚) as '*Mie Kou* (灭口) [dispose of a witness] so as to conceal [Wu's] Yǐnsī [privacy].'[39] On the other hand, the derogatory concept of Yīnsī and the commendatory idea of Yǐnsī [privacy] were separated in the criticism of civilian Yīnsī. The functions of *Qinding Bao Lü* at the end of the Qing Dynasty and the Publication Law in the early ROC are similar. In 1925, the Minister of Justice Zhang Shizhao (章士钊) discussed the question of whether the 1914 Publication Law should be abolished, and explained the reason why he supported abolishing the law from the beginning but in fact the law was not easy to be abolished. Zhang stated: 'That [the reason] is because the press industry seldom criticizes the policy of the public sector, or it does not dare to attack the public sector; But it prefers to attack private behavior, or expose people's privacy.'[40] From this, the author concludes that, first, the 'Yǐnsī' referred to by Zhang Shizhao is consistent with the criticism of civilian Yīnsī, and different from the criticism of official Yīnsī. Second, Zhang Shizhao deliberately chose the term 'Yǐnsī' instead of the term 'Yīnsī' in Article 11 of the 1914 Publication Law, which stated that 'Documents and pictures that have one of the following situations shall not be published … Situation Eight, attacking others' Yīnsī, damaging their reputation.'[41] This shows that he consciously distinguished between the commendatory concept of Yǐnsī [privacy] and the derogatory concept of Yīnsī. In addition, in the 'Notice of Our Newspaper' published by *Ta Kung Pao* in 1928, it stated, 'Our newspaper's comments and facts have always been righteous and bright, and all words related to attacking individual Yǐnsī [privacy]

38 'On the Moral Heart of Official Service' *Ta Kung Pao* (Tianjin, 20 August 1915) 2. Moreover, there was a news report stating that 'the insight into *Yǐnsī* is so that the greedy can do nothing.' See 'The Fundamental Talk on Rectifying the Official' *Ta Kung Pao* (Tianjin, 25 September 1915) 2.

39 'Legislative Delegates in Su Zhou denounce Wu Peifu's Ten Major Crimes' *Ta Kung Pao* (Tianjin, 12 March 1922) 3. Also, a news item praised that a local Governor Wang disposed of 'the *Yǐnsī* of the official for many years.' See 'Governor Wang's Determination to Ban Tobacco' *Ta Kung Pao* (Tianjin, 14 September) 10.

40 'Minister of Justice Talks about the Abolition of the Publishing Law: Offending Yǐnsī should be Prohibited' *Ta Kung Pao* (Tianjin, 31 March 1925) 4.

41 See 'Publishing Law' *Ta Kung Pao* (Tianjin, 29 November 1914) 6.

will not be published.'[42] The term 'Yǐnsī' here refers to commendatory privacy, not derogatory Yīnsī.

In summary, in the scenario of criticizing civilian Yīnsī, the connotation of the idea of privacy gradually changed from derogatory to commendatory. This analysis is based on the distinction between the two contexts, criticizing official Yīnsī and criticizing civilian Yīnsī, and then depends on the interpretation of the ideas of public interest and private morality in these two contexts. So, what was the relationship between public interest and private morality? How did private morality cultivate a commendatory idea of privacy? The following section will continue to analyze these questions.

3. THE IDEAS OF PUBLIC MORALITY AND PRIVATE MORALITY

In *Xinminshuo* (《新民说》) [*On the New Citizens*], Liang Qichao (梁启超) discussed both public morality and private morality, reflecting the idea of political public morality. Meanwhile, the debate between Cai Yuanpei (蔡元培) and Hu Shi (胡适) over the reporting of prostitution demonstrated their respective ideas of social public morality and private morality. The competition of these three ideas gave birth to two potential evolution directions of the connotation of privacy: governance-oriented and individual-oriented.

3.1 Governance-Oriented View under Political Morality

Liang Qichao's book *Xinminshuo*, serialized and published from 1902 to 1906, discussed public morality in Chapter 5 of the book and private morality in Chapter 18 of the book.[43] This popular work had influence on the aforementioned judicial interpretation of the Preparatory Supreme Court in 1913. *Xinminshuo* began with a clear thesis: 'If we expect our nation to be secure, wealthy, respected, and glorious, the path of the new citizens cannot be ignored.'[44] The author generalized this idea, proposed for national prosperity and strength, as 'political public morality'.

In Chapter 5, 'On Public Morality', of *Xinminshuo*, Liang Qichao distinguished between 'private morality' and 'public morality' in terms of their definitions. He believed that private morality meant 'everyone individually perfects themselves … without private morality, one cannot stand', while

---

[42] See 'Special Notice of This Newspaper' *Ta Kung Pao* (Tianjin, 8 August 1928) 3.

[43] See Liang Qichao, *Xinminshuo* (The Commercial Press in Shanghai 1916) 19–26, 200–244.

[44] Ibid., 2.

public morality meant 'everyone collectively unites their group … without public morality, they cannot form a nation'.[45] Both served politics; otherwise, 'a nation cannot form'. However, Liang Qichao believed that Chinese valued private morality over public morality, i.e., 'the Chinese people emphasize private morality, while public morality is almost completely lacking.'[46] Therefore, Liang Qichao distinguished between the old and new ethics. The old Chinese ethics referred to 'the morality of one private individual interacting with another', while the new Western ethics referred to 'a private individual's affairs within a group'.[47] Liang Qichao believed that the old ethics were steeped in Confucian rites, hence the emphasis on private morality, but they lacked the 'benefit to group' characteristic of the new ethics. Liang Qichao advocated incorporating 'benefit to the group' into public morality in order to 'invent a new morality'. The phrase 'the spirit of morality always arises from the interest of a group' proved the aforementioned assumption that public interest and public morality were synonymous.[48] Therefore, public morality was compatible with new ethics, while old ethics were categorized under private morality.

However, Liang Qichao's view changed in Chapter 18 of *Xinminshuo*, namely *On Private Morality*. At that point, he no longer viewed private and public morality as parallel. Instead, he believed that private morality was a necessary precondition for public morality. In other words, without private morality, there could be no public morality. He admitted, 'I had been writing *Xinminshuo* since last year. … When discussing morality, I singled out public morality, not because I thought private morality could be neglected. Instead, I thought that private morality had long been understood and practiced by everyone.'[49] He noticed a decline in private morality and therefore no longer distinguished between public and private morality, but combined both to construct a broad view of public morality with the standard of 'benefiting the group'.[50] Liang Qichao's change in viewpoint still served political purposes, as he attributed the decline in private morality to the 'molding of autocracy' and the 'destruction of contemporary despots'.[51]

45 Ibid., 19–20.
46 Ibid., 20.
47 Ibid., 20–21.
48 Ibid., 24–25.
49 Ibid., 200–201.
50 'Although communication with a minority or a majority, with a private person or a public entity, differs in objects, the subject is the same. Therefore, no matter East or West, morality benefits public order and welfare is the best', Ibid., 202.
51 Ibid., 203–205.

The author believes that the change in Liang Qichao's view reflected the 'governance power' of political morality over private morality; hence, the author generalizes this idea of political morality as a 'governance-oriented' view. Firstly, the governance-oriented view maintained the derogatory nature of criticizing officials' privacy, as criticizing political corruption was a self-referential mechanism of political morality.[52] Secondly, with higher fault tolerance, the governance-oriented view allowed a shift from criticizing the privacy of people to an affirmative attitude of privacy protection, which was reflected in the following two aspects.

On the one hand, the distinction between 'new ethics–public morality' and 'old ethics–private morality' provided an autonomous space for private morality, where the old ethics could continue to operate in private morality, without challenging the dominant position of 'new ethics–public morality'. What lay behind this? It's because the idea of political morality required a 'fault tolerance mechanism'.[53] Especially during times of regime change or when many things were awaiting improvement, the political system needed a higher fault tolerance to remain robust (stability). In other words, public morality granted private morality a greater autonomous space to accommodate old ethics, thereby achieving a reconciliation between the old and new ethics and integrating the nation's historical narrative.[54] For example, the *Qingdi Xunwei Zhaoshu* (《清帝逊位诏书》) [*Imperial Rescript of Emperor Xuantong's Abdication*] in 1912 announced the 'elimination of bias (new ethics against old ethics), mutual protection of public order (between public and private morality)' under the

---

52 'There are many factors in Chinese culture that make it (cultural morality) aim at corruption, which is particularly visible. If a society is very sensitive to corruption, it means that whether it can contain and eliminate corruption is decisive to the stability and long-term stability of the political system.' See Wang Huning, *Anti-Corruption: A Chinese Experiment* (Sanhuan Press 1990) 21.

53 The term 'fault-tolerant mechanism' was originally a term in engineering design and has been extended to administrative management in the Reform and Opening Up. This article uses it to explain political public morality. See Ma Yide, 'Construct Fault-tolerant Mechanism with the Rule of Law' *Guangming Daily* (Beijing, 13 June 2016) 11. The fault-tolerant mechanism is similar to the buffer mechanism of the economic transition process, which allows people to gradually adapt to environmental changes with governmental regulation over the rate of change. See Lan Xiaohuang, *Stand Inside: Chinese Government and Economic Development* (Shanghai People's Press 2021) 305.

54 Robustness refers to the ability of the system to exist in exceptional states (abnormally dangerous situations). See Hiroaki Kitano, 'Biological robustness' (2004) 5 *Nature Reviews Genetics*, 826–837. In this chapter, the biological term is used to explain the robustness of political systems by analogy.

new republican government of the ROC.[55] If we try to compare, it is not hard to see that the right to privacy was based on the logic of 'individual autonomy', while the aforementioned idea of 'privacy' was based on the logic of 'private morality autonomy'. This was the autonomous space of private morality that political morality could tolerate. It's worth noting that this normative privacy within the autonomous space of private morality was built on the integration of national history, rather than upon the old ethics that were criticized by others.

On the other hand, the governance-oriented view determined the centralization or decentralization of political morality, that is, to expand or shrink the autonomous space of private morality. The autonomy of private morality was not inherent, which was completely different from the innate human rights myth of 'privacy', namely the fundamental right in the individualistic sense. The reason Liang Qichao changed his mind was because he realized later that the 'decline of private morality' had led to a situation where 'the entire nation is in disarray, and the so-called improvement cause of the nation and group are hardly visible'.[56] Under such circumstances, private morality autonomy affected the dominant position of political morality. In this case, political morality intervened in private morality autonomy and eliminated the normative effect of privacy ideas. Ultimately, it still depended on the fault tolerance. On the one hand, if the political system could not maintain robustness even with a high fault tolerance, it would be better to sweep away the old ethics in private morality and create a pure new ethics of public morality. As Liang Qichao said, 'China has been destroyed by them, and we can only hope that the young people with the new education will fight for its resurrection to death'.[57] On the other hand, if peace and prosperity prevailed throughout the nation, the political system would no longer rely on a high fault tolerance to maintain robustness. Therefore, political morality in a dominant position would inevitably govern and restrict private morality autonomy and replace old ethics with its own new ethics, as few political systems lacked confidence in the advancement of their own ethics. Therefore, a 'deviation' in the fault tolerance rate would eliminate the normative effect of this idea of privacy.

In summary, the governance-oriented view of political morality maintains the same derogatory nature of the concept of privacy as in the context of criticizing official Yīnsī. The scene of criticizing the civilian Yīnsī gave birth to a

---

55 'Qingdi Xunwei Zhaoshu' *Shun Pao* (Shanghai, 21 February 1912) 1. 'All those who died in the battle of Autumn and Winter of 1911 Revolution should be saluted by our compatriots, no matter the imperial and the rebelling army … .' See 'Martyr of Qing Dynasty should not be overdiscriminated' *Ta Kung Pao* (26 June 1912) 6.

56 See *supra* note 49, 201.

57 Ibid., 231.

positive, normative concept of privacy, which served the integration of nation history. However, this concept of privacy was not inherent, but depended on the governance of political morality over the autonomy of private morality. More specifically, it depended on the need for fault tolerance in the political system. Therefore, the autonomy of private morality in the scene of criticizing the civilian Yīnsī led to the separation of the derogatory sense from the positive sense of privacy. Various opinions over this issue will be presented as follows.

3.2 Debate between Public Morality and Private Morality

During the ROC period, a professor was rumored to visit prostitutes. Should the media report this? Cai Yuanpei and Hu Shi had different opinions on this issue, representing the debate between public morality and private morality. The former believed it could be reported, which the latter denied.

Cai Yuanpei believed that media reports could force the parties to have self-reflection and change their behavior, and thus should not be glossed over. In 1918, Cai Yuanpei wrote in *Beida Jindehui Zhiqushu* (The Purpose of Peking University's Advancement of Morality Association) [《北大进德会旨趣书》], 'since I returned back to China, I first went to Jiangsu and Zhejiang and saw that in the fields of education and industry, almost everyone who stood out was using prostitution and gambling for social networking, which greatly saddened me. When I arrived in Beijing, this trend was even worse.' He also mentioned, 'Peking University has long been slandered. *Canyi Yuan* (参议院) [The Senate House], Zhongyi Yuan (众议院) [The Representative House] and *Jingshi Daxuetang* (京师大学堂) [Imperial University of Peking, the former name of Peking University] are repeat customers of prostitutes … If these are not the facts, then the etiquette is not violated, why worry about what others say? However, please ask the members of our university one by one, are all these slanders groundless?'[58] As a response, Cai Yuanpei initiated the *Beida Jindehui* (北大进德会) [Peking University Advancement of Morality Association], calling on its members to 'not visit prostitutes, not gamble, and not take concubines'. He believed, 'since there is this cause, then it is precisely because of this slander that our people are awakened, otherwise they will be overwhelmed by criticism! To seek to suppress slander without removing its cause, is trying to avoid one's shadow while running hastily, what good will it

[58] Cai Yuanpei, 'Beida Jindehui Zhiqushu' *Peking University Daily* (18 January 1918), in Gao Shuping, *Book Series of Modern Chinese Figures: The Complete Works of Cai Yuanpei (Volume 3)* (Zhonghua Book Company 1984) 126, 128.

do?' Therefore, in Cai Yuanpei's view, reporting was 'to wake up our people', while privacy was to 'hastily avoiding the shadow'.[59]

The author describes Cai Yuanpei's idea above as 'social public morality'. First of all, Cai Yuanpei subtly criticized Liang Qichao's 'On Public Morality', arguing that 'today's people often say that the Western people value public morality, while the Easterns value private morality; and they believe that if one can fulfill public morality, then the details of private morality are not worth paying attention to, which is a misunderstanding. Since we are all members of society, the corruption of a member cannot have no impact on the whole.'[60] Unlike the political public morality view which allowed private morality autonomy, the social public morality view opposed private morality autonomy, believing that private morality and public morality were the same; when one flourished, all would flourish, and when one corrupted, all would follow. Therefore, the norm of privacy built on the basis of private morality autonomy could not exist in the view of social public morality. Secondly, Cai Yuanpei also criticized Liang Qichao's viewpoint change in 'On Private Morality'. Although they both agreed that a sound private morality was a necessary precondition for a sound public morality, Liang Qichao's private morality was limited to serving political public morality. So, in considering the fault tolerance, it was difficult to thoroughly criticize behaviors like visiting prostitutes or taking concubines, unless these behaviors might undermine or subvert political public morality.[61] In contrast, Cai Yuanpei's private morality served social public morality, so he criticized social customs like visiting prostitutes and taking concubines, but he was reluctant to use political coercion. For example, Cai Yuanpei's proposal for Beida Jindehui was a voluntary association, without means of political coercion. In the aforementioned incident, Cai Yuanpei first considered whether the professor who visited prostitutes was a member of the Association. If he was, then the professor was considered to have violated the 'gentleman's promise', and the media should expose his privacy.

Hu Shi, on the other hand, disagreed with Cai Yuanpei's view. He believed that visiting prostitutes privately was a 'private act' of the professor and should not be reported. In 1935, Hu Shi mentioned in *Zhi Tangerhe Han* (《致汤尔和函》) [*Letter to Tang Erhe*] that 'what the tabloid reported (the professor visiting prostitutes) and what was spread in the street were all baseless

59 Ibid., 128.

60 Ibid., 124.

61 Liang Qichao mentioned the 'deprave of private morality' in *On Private Morality*, but did not criticize the custom of soliciting prostitutes and concubines. Chen Lai demonstrated that Liang Qichao's so-called public morality was political public morality. See Chen Lai, 'The Deviation of Putting Social Morality over Private Virtue in China since Modern Times' (2020) 1 *Wen Shi Zhe* 7.

rumors, yet the scholar leaders took them as facts. Isn't that strange … And you gentlemen can't differentiate between private acts and public acts, and thus fall into the traps of wicked people.'[62] It can be seen that Hu Shi advocated differentiating between private and public acts. This was transplanted from the public–private dichotomy in Western law, trying to distinguish between private rights and public power, emphasizing that the former private rights should not be interfered with by the latter public power within the scope of individual freedom.

The author calls Hu Shi's above concept an 'individualistic view of private morality'. Firstly, private morality held a dominant position. Unlike Liang Qichao and Cai Yuanpei's view that public morality took a dominant position, Hu Shi's private morality focused on the individual. This required the separation of two kinds of individual behaviors, namely public behavior related to the public interest and private behavior unrelated to the public interest. Therefore, whether it was the private behavior of officials or professors, it should not be reported. This was like the 'no lying speech' in the ten bans of Buddhist monks, where the 'no' stimulated the normative effect of the positive concept of privacy. Individualism introduced the right to privacy from Western ideas, thus generating the individualistic view of privacy. Secondly, the individualistic view of privacy differed from the governance-oriented view of privacy. As mentioned above, the idea of governance-oriented privacy was not inherent, which relied on the autonomy of private morality permitted by the governance of political public morality and reflected the need for fault tolerance in political public morality. In stark contrast, the idea of individualistic privacy was inherent, depending on individual autonomy and influenced by the myth of innate human rights. At that time, due to the internal troubles and foreign aggression, along with the self-reference mechanism of criticizing officials' private affairs, political public morality often enjoyed the priority position of concept competition. However, the idea of private morality would adopt the narrative technique of 'sacrifice' and hide the normative effect of the idea of individualistic privacy. This concurrence of ideas is left for further analysis.

In summary, the governance-oriented view of political public morality and the individualistic view of private morality led to two commendatory ideas of Yǐnsī [privacy], with the former serving the integration of nation history and the latter serving the inheritance of the right to privacy. The view of social public morality had a certain restrictive effect on the development of these two privacy views, but such effect was limited. Both of these conceptual changes from the derogatory Yīnsī to the commendatory Yǐnsī [privacy] were achieved

62 Hu Shi, 'Zhi Tangerhe Han', in Gengyunzhi and Ouyang Zhesheng eds, *Letters Collection of Hushi* (Peking University Press 1999) 675, 677.

through the scenario path of 'criticizing civilian Yīnsī – private morality – Yǐnsī as privacy'. In contrast, the context of criticizing official Yīnsī involved the criticism that political public morality was self-referential, the criticism that social public morality was unwilling to involve, and the criticism that private morality was criticizing in terms of public behaviors. Therefore, in such a criticism of political corruption, the two concepts of 'Yīnsī' and 'Yǐnsī' tended to converge in derogation and remained, without being changed by the above views.

4. THE INTERPRETATION OF IDEAS TO CONTEXTS

Ideas interpret contexts. The similarities and differences of ideas influence the understanding of contexts. So, how did the three ideas mentioned above influence the transformation of the idea of privacy? To figure this out, three distinct historical scenarios from the 1930s, 1950s, and 1980s will be analyzed to gain a comprehension of the subject.

4.1 On the Eve of the Anti-Japanese War: Individualistic Mutation and Sacrifice

In July 1935, when the Nanjing Nationalist Government was in power, the Legislative Yuan passed a revised version of the Publication Law. Article 21 of this law stipulated that 'Yīnsī concerning individuals or families shall not be published.'[63] However, this particular article encountered substantial controversy, leading to its non-promulgation at that time. Subsequently, the Publication Law underwent further revisions before being ultimately enacted in 1937.

In examining the controversy surrounding the revision process of the aforementioned Publication Law, a comparison was made between the draft text of the Publication Law in 1935 and subsequent revisions. Initially, the draft text proposed by the Central Political Conference of Kuomintang (国民党) [Chinese Nationalist Party, KMT] contained a provision stating that 'Yīnsī concerning individuals or families shall not be published in any form, such as news, essays, advertisements, or representative notices, without the permission of the police authorities. The text of the publication shall follow what is issued by the police authorities and shall not be tampered with.'[64] During the review by the Legislative Yuan's Legal Committee, this provision underwent

63 'Full Text of the Publishing Law (continued)' *Ta Kung Pao* (Tianjin, 15 July 1935) 3.

64 'The Discussion of the New Publishing Law in the Legislative Yuan' *Ta Kung Pao* (Tianjin, 16 July 1935) 3.

modification to read as follows: 'Yīnsī concerning individuals or families that are irrelevant to the public interest shall not be published.'[65] Notably, this version resembled a judicial interpretation previously issued by *Dali Yuan*, which asserted that matters connected to public interest shall not be prohibited from publication, implying that the prohibited were those unrelated to public interest. However, the restrictive clause 'irrelevant to public interest' was ultimately omitted from the final version of the Publication Law of 1935.[66]

Article 21 of the Publication Law of 1935 exemplified the influence of the individualistic perspective on private morality, thereby acknowledging the right to 'privacy'. Firstly, Article 21 of the 'Publication Law' of 1935 not only emphasized the protection of 'individual' privacy but also extended this safeguard to encompass 'family' matters. The prohibitive language of 'shall not be published' within the article served to establish a normative effect, reinforcing the notion of privacy protection. Secondly, the significance of Article 21 lay in its abolition of the 'public interest – new ethics' restriction, illustrating the contrast between the individualistic view of privacy and the governance-oriented view of privacy. By avoiding any mention of public interest, the article effectively restricted political public morality from intervening directly in private morality autonomy through legal means. The legislative intent appeared to be aimed at relinquishing the influence of political public morality and advocating for an individual-centric perspective on privacy.

Amidst the prevailing dominance of the political public morality view, why did Article 21 of the 1935 Publication Law undergo a sudden shift towards individualism,[67] only to be subsequently abandoned? Scholars have attributed this phenomenon to the 'collective protest' from the publishing industry, which sought to safeguard freedom of publication.[68] This interpretation highlights the inherent contradiction within individualism, specifically the tension between privacy and freedom of publication. However, it may overlook the prevailing influence of the concept of political public morality during

---

65 Ibid., 3.

66 The draft of the 'Publishing Law' proposed by the Central Political Conference of the KMT included a restriction clause akin to 'not related to public interest'. This condition stemmed from the provision stating that the police agency (administrative agency) would possess the authority to exercise discretionary judgment on matters deemed 'not allowed'. Consequently, this discretionary power effectively granted the police agency the ability to determine whether a publication was relevant to public interest.

67 This shift is also reflected in Article 21 of the Publishing Law. The provision uses the derogatory concept of Yīnsī, but shows the pragmatic use of the laudatory concept of privacy.

68 See *supra* note 8, 80.

that period. The author argues that the primary reason for the failure lies not merely in opposition from the industry but rather in the interference of political public morality in Article 21 of the 1935 Publication Law, which subverted the essence of individualism. In August 1935, the Central Political Conference of KMT submitted the draft of the Publication Law for reevaluation to the Legal Committee of the Legislative Yuan, while simultaneously the Executive Yuan suspended the review of the 'Executive Rules for the Implementation of the Publication Law'.[69]

Why did the Publication Law undergo a shift towards individualism, particularly in relation to the draft proposed by the Central Political Conference of KMT, which opted for the restriction of 'irrelevant to public interest'? This transformation is intricately tied to the historical context of legislators. On 8 March 1935, Ruan Lingyu (阮玲玉), a film star, was widely reported by the media due to emotional entanglements and legal disputes with Zhang Damin (张达民) and Tang Jishan (唐季珊). Ruan Lingyu, unable to bear the pressure of public opinion, committed suicide.[70] Ruan Lingyu's death aroused public concern and had an impact on the revision of the Publication Law in July of the same year. Legislator Fu Bingchang (傅秉常) expressed his support for strictly restricting publication under Article 21 of the Publication Law, because as he knew, 'newspapers in Guangzhou often specifically attack personal or family Yīnsī, delving into intimate details of individuals' lives, the more they are described in this way, the more they can sell newspapers.'[71]

The phenomenon described above exemplifies the manifestation of individualism from three distinct perspectives. Firstly, it highlights individual awareness. The public began to show interest in topics concerning ordinary civilians, signifying a self-awakening of individualism. A poignant commentary by Lu Xun (鲁迅) on Ruan Lingyu's death, 'People's words can be fearsome,' sharply criticized the gossipy perspective stemming from this growing individual awareness.[72] Newspapers, catering to the market demand for such

---

69 See 'The Central Political Conference Decides to Re-examine the Amendment of the Publishing Law in Principle' *Ta Kung Pao* (Tianjin, 14 September 1935) 3.

70 See 'Ruan Lingyu's Suicide Note Clears Resentment and Says She Has Never Wronged Zhang Damin in Her Life. Tang Jishan Received the Coffin Yesterday' *Ta Kung Pao* (Tianjin, 10 March 1935) 4.

71 See *supra* note 64, 3.

72 'The petty bourgeoisie always takes delight in hearing about people's scandals, especially those involving acquaintances. The old devout women in the streets and lanes of Shanghai become captivated once they learn of the sex affairs occurring in their neighbor's A-er sister's house. However, if you were to share news about someone in Gansu stealing another person's partner or someone in

'gossip', delved into the 'personal or family Yīnsī' to enhance circulation. Secondly, the critique of Yīnsī undergoes civilian differentiation due to the modernization of capitalism. Ruan Lingyu, hailing from an ordinary background, achieved celebrity status through the film industry. Consequently, the concept of celebrities expanded beyond traditional figures like emperors, generals, talented literati, and beauties, now encompassing ordinary individuals. These non-politicized celebrities disrupted the legitimacy of governance based on political morality. Thirdly, individual empathy emerges as a crucial aspect of individualism. It challenged feudal hierarchies, with individuals aspiring to challenge the supremacy of the top, leading the public to relate empathetically through newspapers and other media. As Lu Xun eloquently expressed, when readers saw this, some might think that although they were not as beautiful as Ruan Lingyu, they were more virtuous than her.'[73] The tragic demise of Ruan Lingyu stirred empathy as individuals contemplated the possibility of encountering the fearsome power of public opinion.

Under the influence of individualism, the death of Ruan Lingyu served as a catalyst that, to some extent, triggered a sudden shift in Article 21 of the Publication Law. However, the prevailing political morality of that time presented formidable obstacles to the advancement of individualism, resulting in the suppression of its development. On 10 July 1935, the *Ta Kung Pao* published a comment on the 'Publication Law Storm', pointing out the situation of individualism in the era, 'Today is an era where collectivism prevails over individualism, and when it comes to the interests of the whole, individuals must sacrifice … Therefore, the libertarians of the past, what they considered to be righteous and heavenly, the modern state, all use the needs of collectivism to control.'[74] Such an esoteric writing technique subtly implied that in the face of political morality's dominance, private morality (represented by individualism) must be willing to make sacrifices. Consequently, private morality may be momentarily subdued but remains poised to restore its normative influence when the opportunity arises.[75]

Xinjiang remarrying, they would show no interest in hearing such gossip.' (Lu Xun, *The Complete Works of Lu Xun (Vol. 6)* (People's Literature Publishing House 2005) 344.

[73] Ibid., 344.

[74] 'The Re-Examination of the New Publishing Law' *Ta Kung Pao* (Tianjin, 30 July 1935) 2.

[75] Each (event of) 'Death of Ruan Lingyu' can be incorporated into the narrative of voluntary sacrifice while preserving the notion of individualism as an imagined narrative necessary for the unity of the nation.

The revised Publication Law finally passed on 27 November 1936, with Article 21 completely deleted from the previous legal text, thus declaring the temporary failure of the individualistic view of privacy.

4.2 During the Early PRC: The Integration of Two Moral Perspectives

After the establishment of the PRC, political public morality and social public morality were integrated to construct a socialist moral perspective. The Common Program of the Chinese People's Political Consultative Conference (hereinafter referred to as the 'Common Program'), adopted on 29 September 1949, included Article 42, which stipulates 'Advocating love for the motherland, love for the people, love for labor, love for science, and care for public property as the public morals of all citizens of the PRC'. Xu Teli (徐特立), Mao Zedong's teacher, further expounded on this concept in his article *On National Morality*, stating that the Common Program determines the public morality of all citizens but does not dictate the private morality of individuals. He emphasized the social nature of humans and how individual goodness or badness is determined by society.[76] From this perspective, it becomes evident that socialist morality integrates political moral discourse, such as 'love the motherland', with social moral discourse, such as 'social transformation'. Additionally, socialist morality plays a crucial role in determining private morality. This stance contrasted with the views of Liang Qichao and Cai Yuanpei, who argued that private morality determines public morality and that private morality serves as a prerequisite for public morality. In contrast, socialist morality does not depend on the political system's tolerance for traditional ethical values in private morality. Instead, it emphasizes the need to 'purge feudal, comprador, fascist thoughts' (Article 41 of the Common Program). Consequently, the socialist moral view offers a critical examination of the legitimacy of private morality autonomy.

This ideology was intricately linked to the formidable external circumstances faced by the political system at that time. Expressions like 'making a fresh start' and 'cleaning the room for guests' indicated the challenges the political system encountered in implementing a high tolerance strategy to ensure resilience. Consequently, the call to establish PRC and propose new ideas became imperative. Louis Pierre Althusser's insightful critique, drawing from Antonio Gramsci's perspective on the public–private dichotomy, sheds light on this matter. Althusser emphasized that the distinction between public

76 See Xu Teli, 'On National Public Morality (I)', (1950) 3 *People's Education* 17–18.

and private lies within the confines of bourgeois legal rights, operating effectively within the domain where these rights exercise power as subordinates.[77] However, the state transcends this distinction, as it stands above the law: a state belonging to the ruling class, neither public nor private. On the contrary, the state serves as the foundation for all distinctions between the public and the private. Likewise, the socialist state's legal power (the ideological state apparatus) dismantled the traditional binary opposition between public and private morality. Instead, it amalgamated these two concepts, giving rise to a socialist moral perspective (ideology). Consequently, private morality was determined and eventually annulled, for 'there is no need to conceal one's actions if selfishness is absent'.

Therefore, the originally positive idea of Yǐnsī transformed into a negative usage, converging with the notion of Yīnsī. Firstly, the idea of Yǐnsī was employed to describe exceptional circumstances during public trials. Article 76 of the 1954 Constitution specifies: 'People's courts shall conduct trials in public, except in special circumstances provided by law.' This provision is particularly evident in the implementation of the public trial system by the People's Courts. In 1956, the Standing Committee of China's National People's Congress issued a decision stating that People's courts may conduct trials in private for cases involving state secrets, cases involving the personal Yīnsī of the parties, and crimes committed by minors under the age of eighteen.[78] Although the term 'Yīnsī' was used here, the commentary in the *Renmin Ribao* continued to use the concept of 'Yǐnsī'. It advocated that those cases involving private matters with adverse effects on society should not be made public, considering the perspectives of safeguarding the interests of the state and the people, respecting democratic rights, and promoting social welfare.[79] In both quotations above, the terms Yīnsī and Yǐnsī carry negative connotations in pragmatics, indicating the potential for 'adverse effects'. Additionally, it abstracts the notion of 'reproduction of family production relations', which initially belonged to private moral autonomy, as part of the ideological state apparatus. It posits that because privacy can influence social production,

---

[77] See Louis Althusser, *On Reproduction*, Wu Zifeng tr (Northwestern University Press 2019) 455–6.

[78] Decision of the Standing Committee of the National People's Congress on Cases Not to Be Tried in Public (Passed on 8 May 1956). See 'Three Decisions of the Standing Committee of the National People's Congress' *People's Daily* (Beijing, 9 May 1956) 1.

[79] Si Xuan, 'The Significance of Public Trial in People's Courts' *People's Daily* (Beijing, 19 February 1955) 3.

efforts should be made to avoid its detrimental effects.[80] Secondly, the concept of Yǐnsī was utilized to describe the objects of criticism. Specific examples include references to the 'Yǐnsī of two-party politicians' and the 'Yǐnsī of spies' in the realm of international politics.[81] In the field of culture and art, expressions such as 'hoping that Hu Feng will reveal all his Yǐnsī', '(writers) seemingly having some unspeakable Yǐnsī,' and 'exposing the Yǐnsī of Zhou Yang and others' illustrated this trend.[82] The cultural critique mentioned here reflects the normative position of public morality as stated in Article 42 of the Common Program, which is located within the fifth chapter, Cultural and Educational Policies, of the same program. In relation to this, Article 49 at the end of the fifth chapter of the Common Program stipulates the protection of 'the freedom to report true news'. This emphasis on reporting true news highlights the disappearance of Yǐnsī norms.

Therefore, the privacy perspective of political moral governance and private moral individualism faced challenges in sustaining relevance at that time. The anti-privacy position of social morality converged with the critical approach of political morality within the same normative framework, leading to constraints on the development of the positive concept of Yǐnsī.

4.3 Reform and Opening-Up Period: The Revival of Yǐnsī and the Transformation of Yīnsī

Drawing from a profound reevaluation of the *Wenhua Dageming* (文化大革命) [Cultural Revolution in China from 1966 to 1976], Article 38 of the 1982 Constitution established the principle of personal dignity. This pivotal objective value found further expression in Article 101 of the 1986 *Minfa Tongze* (《民法通则》) [*General Principles of Civil Law*], which underscores that 'both citizens and legal entities hold the right of reputation; the personal dignity of citizens is safeguarded by legal measures, and it is proscribed to tarnish the reputation of citizens and legal entities through means such as insult

80 This reflects that socialist public morality determines private morality, not the other way around.

81 See 'The Democratic and Republican Parties in the United States Continue to Scold Each Other and the Scandals of the Two Parties Are Increasing' *People's Daily* (Beijing, 29 September 1952) 4; 'International News' *People's Daily* (Beijing, 6 January 1953) 4.

82 Wu Boxiao, 'The Dark Soul' *People's Daily* (Beijing, 21 May 1955) 3; Wu Boxiao, 'Peer Publications' *People's Daily* (Beijing, 22 November 1957) 8; Tan Jun, Li Ding, 'This Old Account Must Be Thoroughly Settled – A Critique of the Reactionary Films "Lin's Shop" and "Never Night City"' *People's Daily* (Beijing, 4 June 1967) 3.

and defamation.' Although this clause does not overtly invoke the notion of Yǐnsī, the Supreme People's Court articulated in its 1988 judicial interpretation that 'publicizing another's Yǐnsī through written or oral forms, or fabricating facts to openly degrade an individual's character, and impairing another's reputation through methods like insult and slander, if causing a discernible impact, should be deemed an infringement of citizens' reputation right.'[83] Hence, it's evident that the positive understanding of Yǐnsī has been reinstated in its regulatory capacity and is formally embedded in legal discourse. Why then has the concept of Yǐnsī, previously confined, undergone a resurgence during the era of reform and opening up, acquiring a laudable normativity? This inquiry can be approached through a threefold analysis.

4.3.1 Political morality restores private moral autonomy

Firstly, political morality achieves national unity through the strategy of tolerance. 'The Resolution on Several Historical Issues of the Party Since the Founding of the People's Republic of China' passed during the Sixth Plenary Session of the 11th Central Committee of the Communist Party of China on 27 June 1981, 'provides a fundamental summary of past events, favoring brevity over excessive detail,' and 'guides everyone to unite and look ahead'.[84] This indicates that after the conclusion of the *Wenhua Dageming,* China needed to employ a strategy of tolerance to foster the Chinese nation's progression towards reform and opening up. Tolerance signifies that political morality permits autonomous private morals, thus reinstating the governance-oriented perspective on privacy.

Secondly, the emerging individualistic perspective on Yǐnsī and the governance-oriented perspective on Yǐnsī have found common ground. In his work *The Transformation of Private Life*, based on field surveys, Yan Yunxiang (阎云翔), conducted in the early stages of China's Reform and Opening-up, asserts: 'The rise of individuality and individualism is the outcome of a dual interaction – the socialist transformation of local moral norms by the state during the era of collectivization and the impact of commodity-driven production and consumerism following decollectivization.'[85] This underscores that political morality, interlinked with social morality (owing to the assimilation

[83] Opinions of the Supreme People's Court on Several Issues Concerning the Implementation of the *Minfa Tongze* of the People's Republic of China' (Trial Implementation) ([1988] No. 6), Article 140.

[84] Deng Xiaoping, *Selected Works of Deng Xiaoping (Vol. 2)* (People's Publishing House 1994) 292.

[85] Yan Yunxiang, T*he Transformation of Private Life – Love, Family and Intimate Relationships in a Chinese Village (1949–1999)* Gong Xiaoxia tr (Shanghai People's Publishing House 2017) 266.

of the socialist moral standpoint), relinquishes its influence over the realm of private moral autonomy. This vacuum, created by the departure of these concepts (attributable to the extended critique and erosion of archaic ethical norms by social morality), was being filled by the ascending individualism driven by the tide of reform and opening-up. Private moral autonomy no longer harbored the traditional ethics but rather nurtured individualism. This blossoming individualism of the 1980s has rekindled the dormant individualistic perspective on Yǐnsī that was eclipsed during the sacrifices of the 1930s. Furthermore, the production relations of *Ge Ti* Hu (个体户) [individual households] and *Jiating Lianchan Chengbao* (家庭联产承包) [Family Contract Responsibility System] within the ideological state apparatus transform the abstract individual and family back into tangible entities, thus embodying the essence of individualism.

Furthermore, this individualism has sparked an awareness of Yǐnsī rights. For instance, a reader named Wang from Hebei, who worked as a statistician in a farm machinery company, wrote a letter to the People's Daily in 1987. She accused a female writer Liu of distorting and revealing her Yǐnsī. Wang believed that Liu's action of exposing her Yǐnsī was a retaliatory strike against her report on the 'Bu Zheng Zhi Feng (不正之风) [some unhealthy practice or malpractices]' within the farm machinery bureau and company.[86] In this case, the two perspectives on Yǐnsī came into a paradoxical unity. The discourse of individualistic Yǐnsī was employed by an individual to shield herself from retaliatory actions that stemmed from critiquing officials' Yǐnsī. Simultaneously, the act of scrutinizing officials' Yǐnsī was endorsed by political morality, and retaliation was countered by political morality. Consequently, the *People's Daily* supported the publication of the reader's letter, facilitating a reconciliation between the governance view of Yǐnsī and the individualistic view of Yǐnsī. Imperfections are inherent to humanity; this means that if personal Yǐnsī can be arbitrarily exposed, it could potentially provide an avenue for retaliation, inducing a chilling effect and rendering it challenging for political morality to incentivize individuals to scrutinize officials' Yǐnsī.

Once again, the ideological reproduction gives rise to the economic developmental function of Yǐnsī. Several articles appearing in the *People's Daily* during that time partially substantiated the economic significance of Yǐnsī. For instance, the phrase 'advocating self-management and respecting others' Yǐnsī rights' was seen as the 'key to high efficiency.'[87] Conversely, the absence of Yǐnsī could lead colleagues within a unit to 'speculate about one another

86 See Wang Fayin, 'Letter from Wang Fayin, a Reader in Hebei' *People's Daily* (Beijing, December 16, 1987) 5.

87 Jiang Hanzhen, 'The Secret of High Efficiency' *People's Daily* (Beijing, 7 March 1987) 3.

and engage in intrigue.'[88] Naturally, within the interplay of the two Yǐnsī perspectives, the governance-oriented view of Yǐnsī remained superior to the individualistic perspective. For instance, an article published in the *People's Daily* in 1986 remarked, 'Love letters are largely Yǐnsī matters, not suitable for public display, presumably this has been the case throughout history … they offer not only solace and inspiration to the recipient themselves, but also to others … love letters on the battlefield were open for all to see.'[89] This discourse revisited the wartime during peacetime, thereby advocating the flexible governance of political morality according to the prevailing circumstances.

4.3.2 The change of view of social morality on Yǐnsī

Firstly, the perspective of social morality no longer imposes restrictions on Yǐnsī but rather supports it, as it reshapes the pragmatic use of the Yǐnsī concept. In the previous context, Yǐnsī sheltered old ethics, thus safeguarding it against criticism from social morality. However, in the new context, Yǐnsī safeguards individualism, which doesn't obstruct and may even facilitate the production relations of reform and opening up. Consequently, social morality no longer needs to criticize Yǐnsī. Expressions in this regard include statements like 'it (referring to Yǐnsī – author's note) doesn't hinder the interests of others and society,'[90] and 'it doesn't pose a threat to society and others; hence, no individual should be subject to unwarranted accusations and unreasonable interference.'[91]

Secondly, the perspective of social morality aids Yǐnsī in critiquing new targets. The kind of neighborhood gossip criticized by Lu Xun in his commentary on Ruan Lingyu's death is now condemned by the social moral view as a manifestation of feudal backwardness – publicly removing the tattered hat from the head of 'A Q' (阿Q) [a tragic character in Lu Xun's novel], exposing his scars, and eliciting laughter from the crowd; this kind of harmful practice is an expression of feudal thinking's belittling of the value of human beings and disrespect for human dignity.[92] Additionally, the 'popular literature' and 'underground novels' that reveal the Yǐnsī between men and women are now

---

88 Nan Fan, 'Briefly Discuss Liu Zhenyun's *Unit*' *People's Daily* (Beijing, 9 May 1989) 6.

89 Zhang Yusheng, 'Reading Open Love Letters' *People's Daily* (Beijing, 13 May 1986) 8.

90 Zeng Xianbin, Zheng Hui, 'Respect for Citizens' Right to Privacy' *People's Daily* (24 May 1987) 1.

91 Cao Ping, 'Respect for Privacy' *People's Daily* (16 May 1988) 4.

92 See *supra* note 90, 1.

denounced as manifestations of bourgeois liberalization.[93] As a result, notions that impede Yǐnsī become subjects of criticism from the perspective of social morality.

4.3.3 The concealment of criticizing civilian Yīnsī and the transfer of criticizing official Yīnsī

Firstly, the *People's Daily* gradually ceased using the Yīnsī concept starting from the late 1980s. When analyzing the shifts in the pragmatics of the Yīnsī concept, it's important to distinguish between two distinct scenarios and avoid making blanket statements. In the context of criticizing private matters within the community, the concept of Yīnsī is obscured due to the establishment of privacy rights. As previously mentioned, there are pragmatic differences between the derogatory Yīnsī and the commendatory Yǐnsī. Drawing from jurisprudence, the construction of privacy rights necessitates the development of a self-referential and internally consistent rights discourse system. This involves substantiating the legitimacy of privacy rights through a cycle of positive feedback. Consequently, the concept of Yīnsī, functioning as a reverse pragmatics, is intentionally left behind in order to preserve the internal consistency of jurisprudential thought.

Secondly, the aforementioned logic doesn't apply to the context of criticizing official privacy. This is because the act of self-referential criticism of official privacy as a component of political morality persists, exhibiting conceptual inertia and enjoying support from the socialist moral perspective. Therefore, the criticism of official privacy necessitates adopting a strategy of conceptual transfer in order to avoid the negative connotations of the derogatory Yīnsī concept interfering with the positive framework of privacy rights. In accordance with Article 41 of the 1982 Constitution of the PRC, the criticism of official privacy is transformed into legal concepts such as the right to criticize, the right to accuse, and the right to report. Behaviors that expose the illegal or negligent actions of officials without fabrication or distortion are endorsed by the Constitution.

5. CONCLUSION

Back to the key question of this article: How does the derogatory idea of Yīnsī, which means being criticized by others, morph into the commendatory idea of

---

[93] See Zhou Denggao, 'Strengthening the Criticism of Popular Literature' *People's Daily* (Beijing, 5 July 1988) 5; Sun Li, 'On Mirrors and Moonlight' *People's Daily* (Beijing, 26 July 1988) 8; Gao Ning, 'Wang Meng Stresses at the Chinese Writers' Association that Literature and Art Should Pay Attention to Reform to Prevent Vulgarization' *People's Daily* (Beijing, 21 November 1988) 3.

Yǐnsī, a term used to criticize others? The author's answer is: this transformation was not linear, and it involved a sudden change in individualistic privacy, a temporary disappearance of the two ideas of privacy, or as a recovery and development of the two ideas of privacy, and even the establishment of the right to privacy.

This explains why 'it is acceptable to report on an official's private prostitution' seems to be common sense rather than a problem. In the scene of criticizing official Yīnsī, Yīnsī has always been the 'Other' of Yǐnsī, deconstructing the commendatory discourse of the right to privacy (Yǐnsī) through the derogatory discourse of Yīnsī, which makes officials find it hard to defend with privacy rights. By this logic, Su Li's criticism of the myth after the 'public figure theory' can be easily resolved.[94] Without understanding the transformation of the privacy ideas, it would be difficult to accurately grasp the meaning of the right to privacy within modern contexts.

Admittedly, due to the focus and the limited length of this article, the research could continue from the following two aspects. Firstly, tracing back to the past legal history further. From spontaneous to self-conscious, there might be 'spontaneous privacy' in ancient Chinese thoughts. But did 'self-conscious privacy' really exist? This is a question worth exploring.[95] Secondly, the translation of foreign ideas in China. Researchers can shift the paradigm from the history of ideas to the history of concepts, focusing on the succession and localization of the 'privacy' concept from foreign jurisdictions. The emphasis of this article on the indigenous logic of the privacy concept in China does not exclude communication with Western scholars at that time. It is not difficult to see that the transformation of the ideas of privacy in modern China causes tension in media, literature, and art, such as newspapers and films.[96] Warren and Brandeis also observed something similar in their article 'The Right to Privacy': 'instant photography and the news industry have invaded the sacred realm of private and family life.'[97] This shows that research on the

---

94 See *supra* note 7, 128.

95 For example, the Special Commissioner of the Constitutional Compilation Bureau, Gu Ao, thought that 'Yīnsī' originated from traditional criminal law. 'In short, since the Tang Dynasty in China, the criminal law has been restricted the behavior of attacking people's Yīnsī, so as to preserve one's reputation. It has become a common practice ...' See *supra* note 20, the book revised by Li Qicheng, 683.

96 On the relationship between governance-oriented privacy, political morality and the literature and art, see Mao Zedong, 'Speech at The Forum of Art and Literature In Yan'an', in *Selected Works of Mao Zedong Volume 3* (Renmin Press 1991) 847–879.

97 See *supra* note 2, 195.

right to privacy under the Chinese contexts can communicate reasonably with the Western academic community.

Furthermore, the aforementioned approaches can provide disenchanting insights into the contemporary protection of the right to privacy. Firstly, the discourse of personal information protection may make privacy a puppet. Nowadays, Chinese courts prefer the discourse of instrumental rationality of personal information interests, rather than the discourse of privacy within moralities (even fundamental rights). Therefore, the research of the aforementioned approaches, which are detached from moralities, may serve for the reproduction of 'human-machine-human' in the production relations of the digital age as well as the commodification of information.[98] Secondly, the fair use of private information may be justified. Article 999 of the Civil Code of the PRC stipulates that private information 'may be reasonably used by those engaged in news reporting, supervision of public opinions, or the like, for public interests'. In a sense, this can be seen as a historically contemporary counterpart of the legislative context of the aforementioned Newspaper Law in Qing Dynasty and Publishing Law in the ROC. Thirdly, the two ideas of privacy may be harmonized. The governance-oriented view of privacy is mainly for national integration, not for defending against public power. However, when the 'private power' of platform business in the digital economy poses a risk to national integration,[99] political morality should remind the self-awareness of private morality, so as to awaken the individualistic privacy and jointly with the governance-oriented privacy regulate the 'uncontrolled expansion of capital'.

[98] For example, judges have upheld plaintiffs' personal information protection claims in some cases but rejected privacy claims. See Ling v. Beijing Micro-Broadcast Video Technology Company ('TikTok Case'), Beijing Internet Court (2019); Huang v. Tencent Technology Company ('WeChat Reading Application Case'), Beijing Internet Court (2019).

[99] See Liu Han, 'Logic of Platform Power – The Recentralization Mechanism of Online Society' (2021) 1 *Beijing Cultural Review* 31, 34.

Index